QATARI STYLE

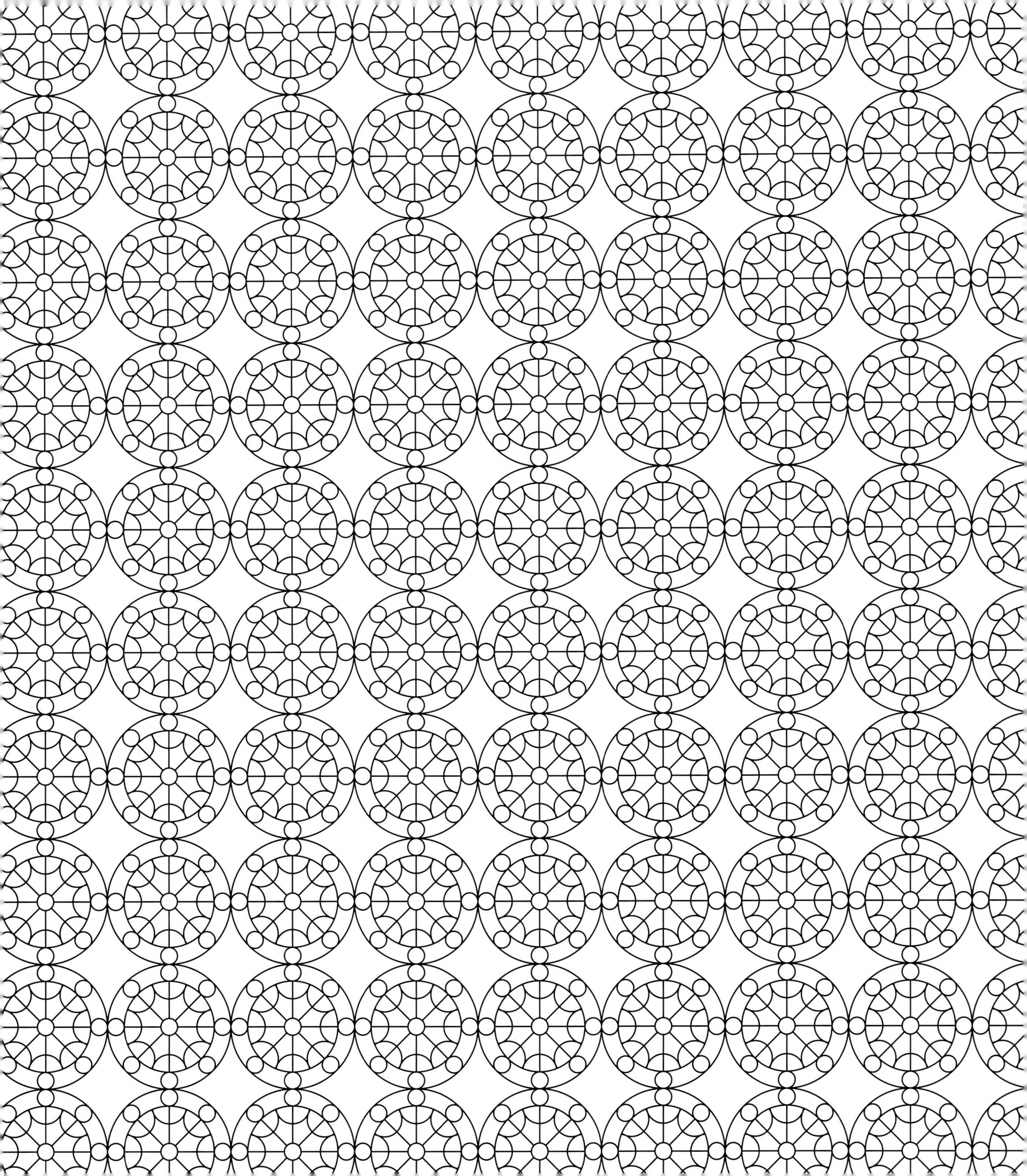

IBRAHIM MOHAMED JAIDAH

QATARI STYLE

HIRMER

DEDICATION

To all young and emerging Qatari interior designers.
I hope that this book will serve them as a reference
to further develop a contemporary Qatari interior style.

To our ancestors who travelled the world
and brought back from their trips the elements of
foreign styles that have been embedded in our culture
and have become an integrated part of it.

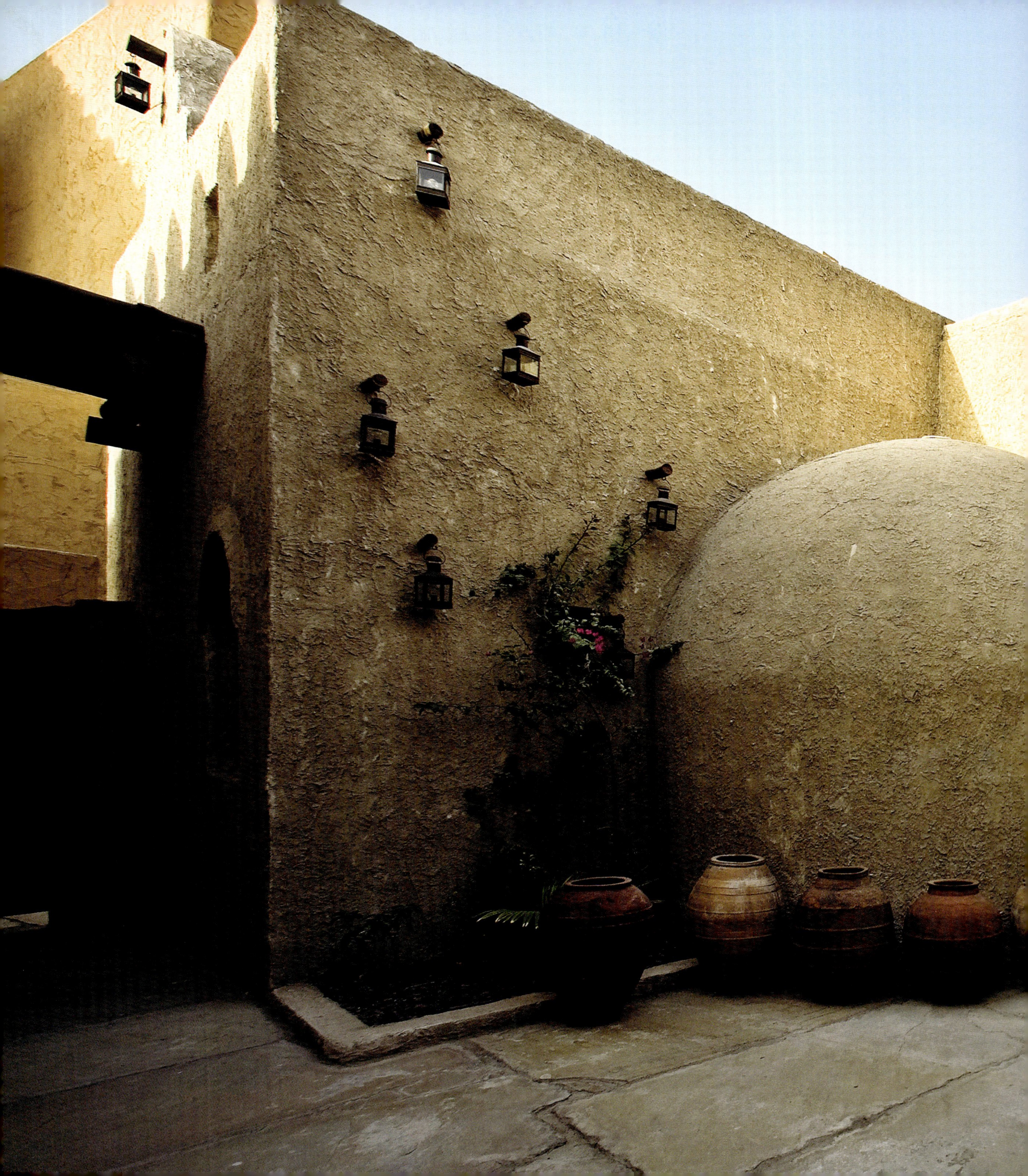

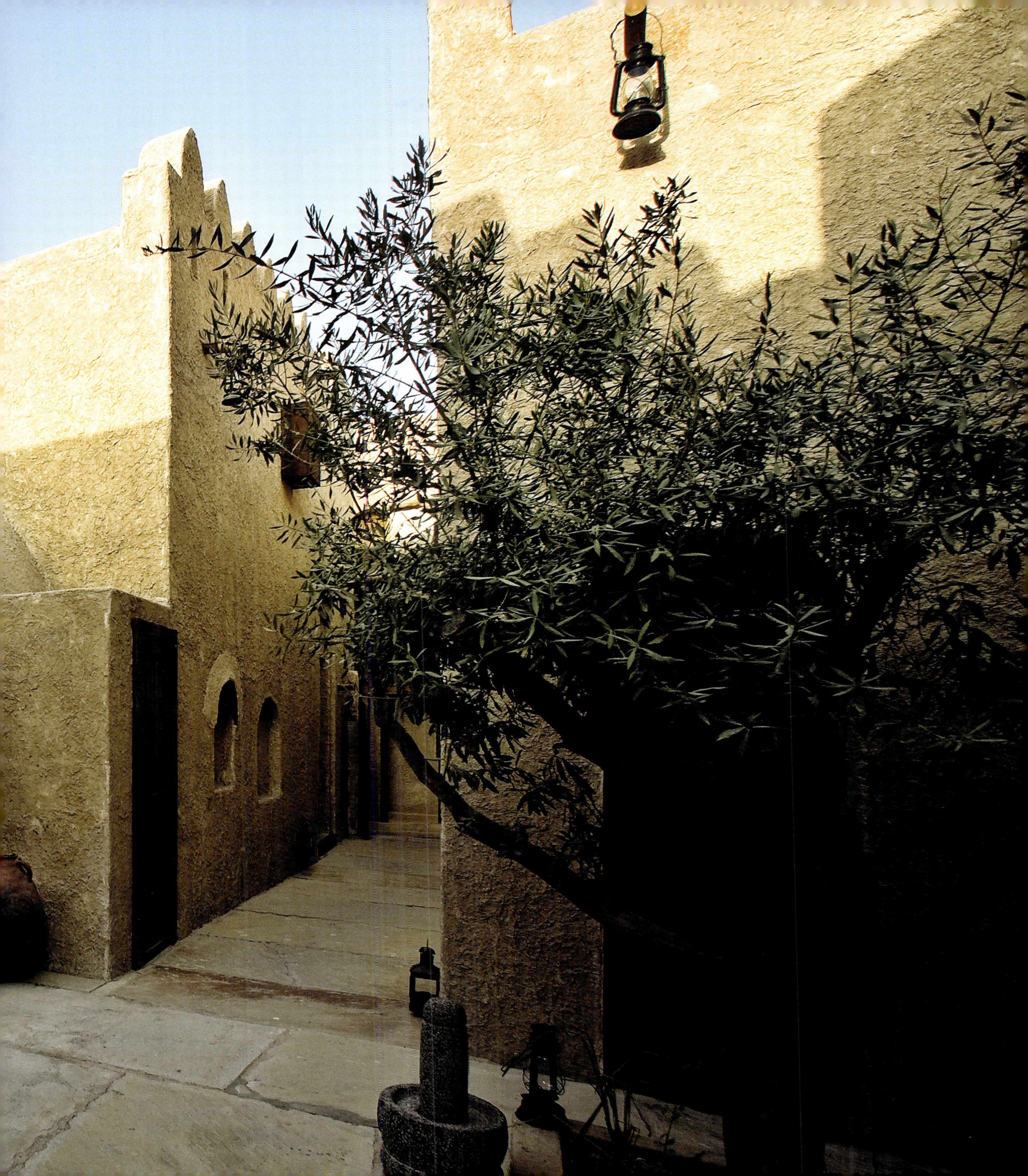

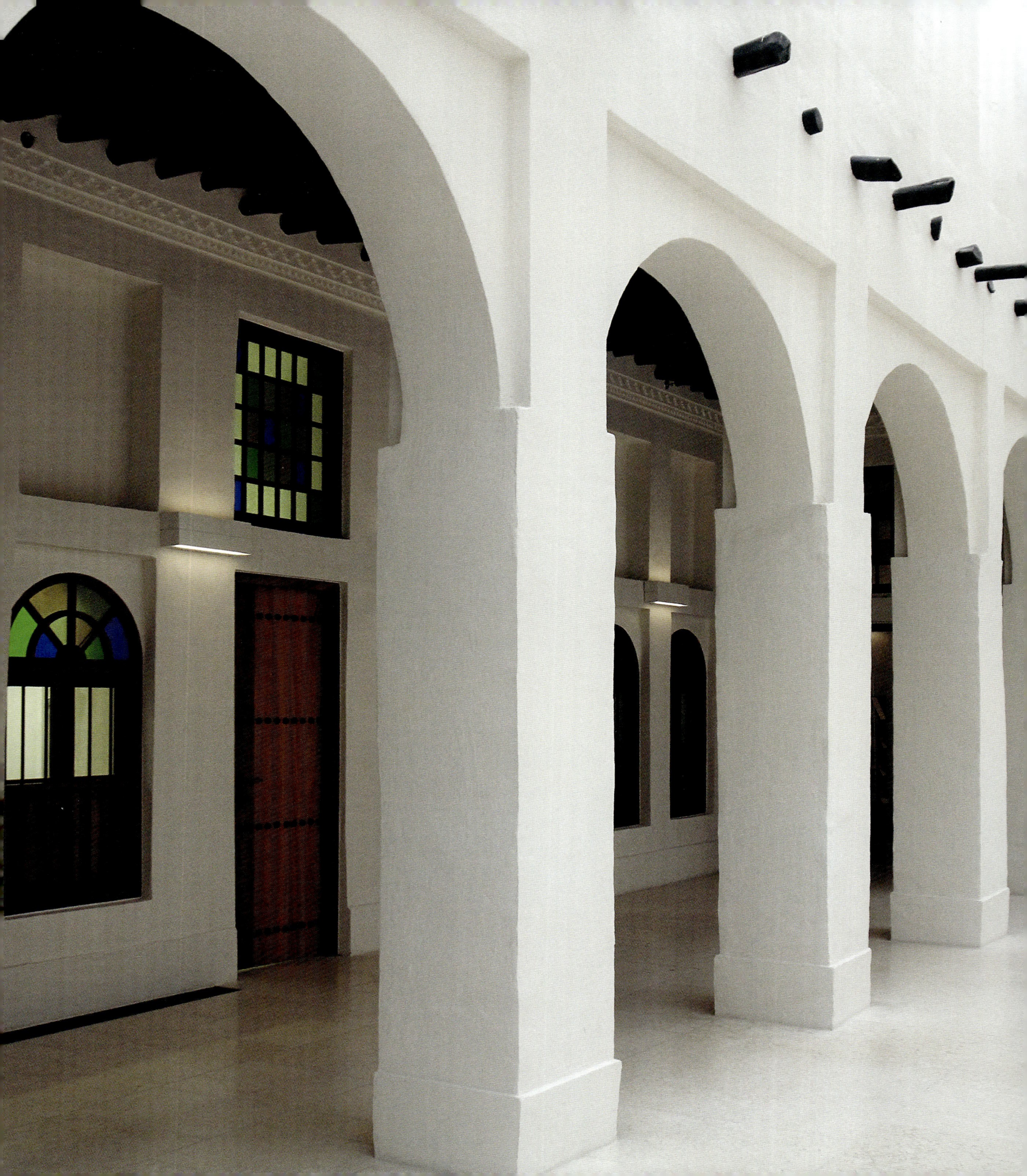

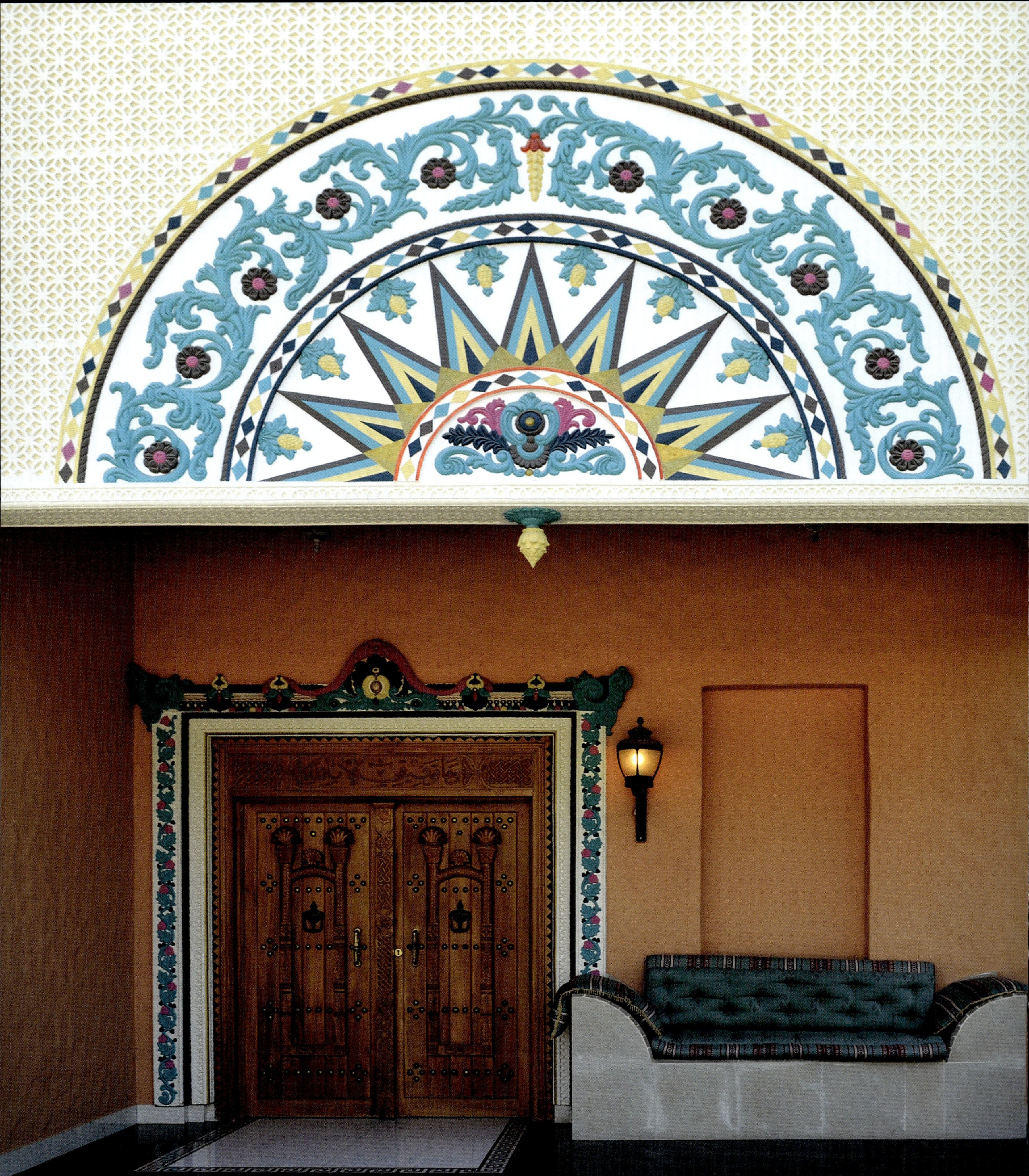

ACKNOWLEDGEMENTS

To my mother: I am forever indebted.
Thank you for teaching me how to dream.

To my wife and my children: I am very grateful for
your continuous and unconditional love and support.

This book would not have been possible without
the support and input of the Qatari community.

While researching for this book many new
friendships and relationships have been forged,
and I take this opportunity to thank individuals who have
so graciously granted me access to their private space
and agreed to have it featured in this book.

I am appreciative of the support from institutions
such as Sh. Faisal Bin Qassim Museum and Msheireb
Museums, that have supported our process.

I am thankful to my team from AEB
who supported me with their dedicated work.
No sections of the book were neglected,
and they paid attention to every detail with a keen eye
to make the publishing of this manuscript possible.

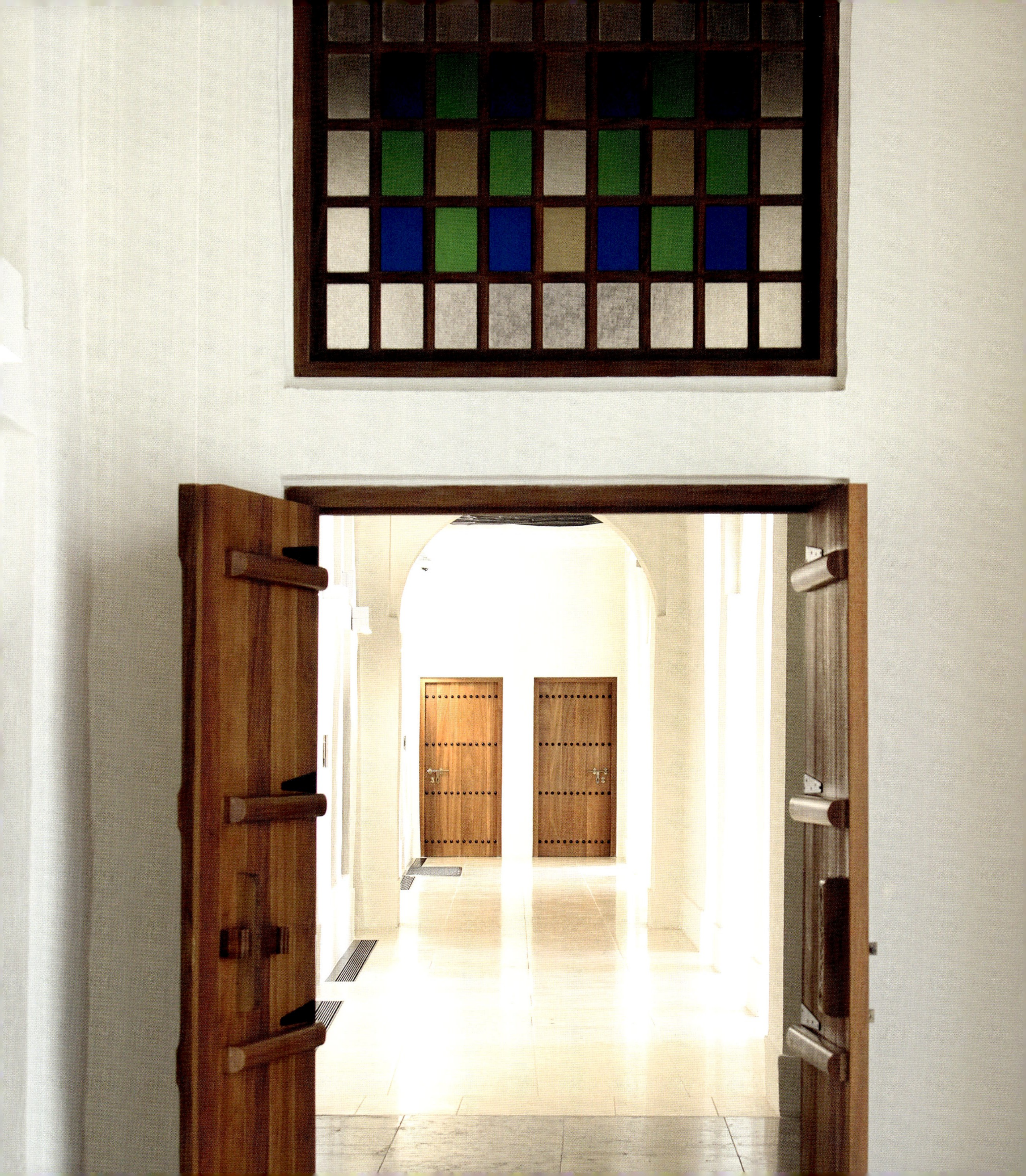

INTRODUCTION

This book stems from my personal interest in the Qatari architecture, interiors, and design that are rooted in our local traditions and culture.

After graduating abroad and returning home to start my career as an architect, I was surprised to find that the architecture of Qatar was seldom documented. Consequently, I started recording old buildings. Twelve years of research resulted in my first published manuscript titled "History of Qatari Architecture 1800–1950", which introduces a collection of buildings from Qatar dating from the period before the discovery of oil. It became an academic reference for vernacular Qatari architecture.

In this book, my intention is to create another reference to our traditions, but this time to the interior design tendencies in Qatar. Unlike my first publication, this volume takes the reader on a journey of style. The first section of the book reveals the traditional style derived from the social, economic, and geographical influences in the region. It does not take us to the very beginning of the history of Qatar, but rather to a particular point in time in the early twentieth century, before the discovery of oil. It features the style of the interiors of our grandparents' generation and showcases a design that reflects and evokes our true vernacular culture and identity. The first section focuses on the typical traditional houses that have disappeared over time and are now mostly preserved in museums, in addition to *mayālis* that are functional until this day.

The second section of the book takes us on a journey through the style that evolved in Qatar after the discovery of oil until the turn of the new century. As the local economy changed, the local style adapted to new variables, while retaining reminiscences of the pearl diving and commodity trading of the past. This new style, born in the transition between traditional and modern, borrows from the traditional Qatari style and way of living and translates into the modern era. I found that it is best portrayed in a private house that is kept for the owner's guests and visitors to the family farm, and in some public spaces such as restaurants and museums.

The third section features the contemporary style that was further influenced by the new, more globalized, realities of Qatar. It showcases hotels that reinterpret the vernacular Qatari everyday elements to create a contemporary style with a vibrant local identity. We learn from this section that the contemporary style of Qatar is strongly influenced by the traditional style but is reinterpreted in a way that suits the needs of a modern lifestyle.

The purpose of this book is to document the Qatari interior style, one that was born out of, transformed by, and exists within the fast-changing socio-economic context. I hope that I have succeeded in recording some of the fast-disappearing trends of interior design in Qatar that will remain for future generations at least in manuscript form, and that this will enable them to refer back to their roots. We aim to provide the new generation with a seed to research the character of Qatari interior design and to create their own contemporary Qatari style that is based on their revived identity.

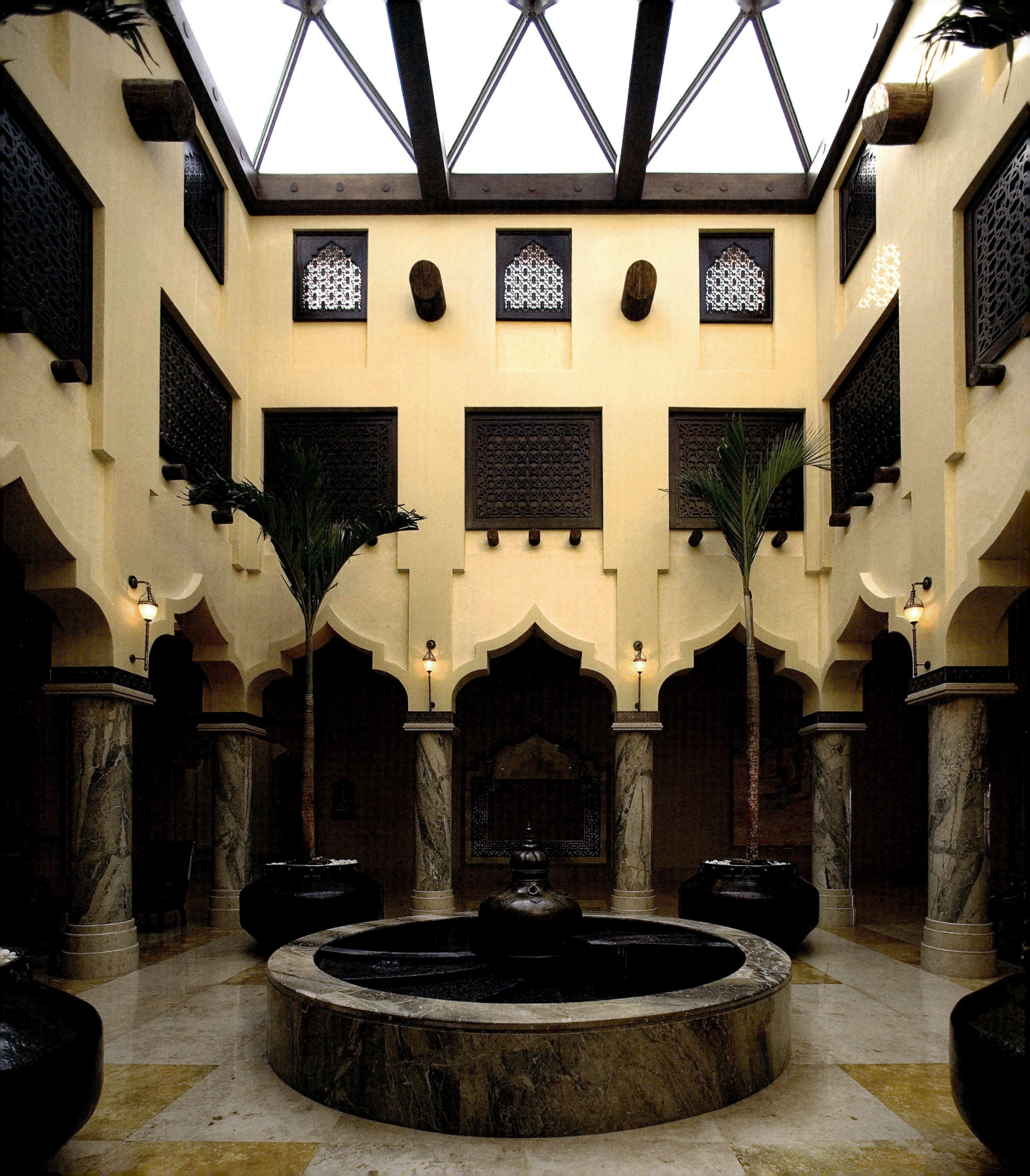

INFLUENCES AND ELEMENTS OF STYLE

Qatar's history as a state is brief in a much larger regional context, but its name, Katara, is over 1800 years old and is one of the oldest names in the region. Qatar's significantly longer history before its statehood shaped much of its local cultural heritage. In its more recent history, and especially during the twentieth century, Qatar witnessed unprecedented economic development as a result of the discovery of oil which influenced all spheres of the socio-cultural life of the local population. Although this book attempts to explain the style that evolved just before, around and after that event, it is evident that Qatari style is constantly adapting to the currents of change. Various migrations, Qatar's unique geographic location, past trading history, the spread of Islam, and sea travels have had an impact on Qatari style which became an interesting combination of the local elements and those that were imported based on the population's perceptions of different places in the world.

Before the discovery of oil, Qatari style was humble in its decorations, color, and even forms. More intricate façade carvings, decorative ceilings, and decorative wooden features were limited to the style of those of a higher social status: members of the royal family and pearl and commodities merchants. During this period, culture was shaped by the effect of the geography of the place: its unique climate, resources, and proximity to ancient civilizations. For a long time before the discovery of oil, the inhabitants of Qatar inhabited both the deserts and seashores and would very often move with the changing seasons. The sea and desert environment influenced the vernacular design in numerous ways. The temporary tent settlements of the desert nomads were made from materials readily available to them. Women would spin camel, sheep, and goat hair on spindles and would weave black and white textiles for the *bayt al shaar*, or would color the wool with dyes they could gather from various plants in their immediate surroundings to weave *sadw* fabric. This was used for furnishings and allowed women to weave their own visual language, represented in a series of geometric pictograms that when put together tell a story. By comparison, those who lived near the seashore did so in the areas where the sea was rich in pearls, since pearling was the most valuable commodity available to the people of Qatar. They lived in structures that were made of the limestone and dolomite which were available resources for building. These settlements, pale in color, blended into the desert environment, and created the basis for the traditional Qatari architecture. Trading and access to the sea influenced Qatari style with numerous imported construction materials, such as *danāshil*, and a variety of everyday objects that were brought from abroad.

Due to its geographical position, Qatar was located on a number of sea and land trade routes, which further influenced the availability of construction materials. After the spread of Islam, the Arabian Gulf region established trade relations by the sea with the coasts of East Africa, Zanzibar, India, and Southeast Asia. For sea travelers, the Qatari coast had certain advantages: the deeper water areas around it, which allowed the ships to set sail when the tide was high; and the availability of fresh water and dates. Accordingly, many sea travelers who moored their ships for repairs here came ashore in Qatar bringing along some of their cargo for trading.[1] In addition to the sea routes, the prominent land trade routes through Qatar were those between Oman, Yemen, and Iraq. The mostly commonly traded materials on both routes were spices, wood, cotton, silk, paper, and musk; and as a result, the inhabitants of Qatar had access to the materials passing through their lands.[2] Wood, which was essential for construction, was scarce and much valued, so that it had to be imported. It is said that when a family chose to resettle, they would dismantle the *danāshil* and reuse them for building their new houses as they were too valuable to be left behind. Although traditional Qatari houses were simple and inherently minimalist, the trade-route location resulted in imported functional and decorative items such as *ṣanādyq imbaīyt* and *kūrāfi* being quickly adapted and becoming an integral part of the local culture.

In addition to tradesmen who were temporary settlers in those lands, Qatari style was directly influenced by more permanent migrations, economic or other, that affected Qatar's socio-cultural mix. The eighteenth-century migration within the Middle Eastern region and Persia saw many skilled sailors and merchants settle in Qatar from the Arabian Peninsula,[3] bringing with them the Najdi style (prominent in the Najd region). During the same time the entire Arabian Gulf witnessed movements of people in all directions throughout the Arab and Persian sides of the Gulf as a result of the religious, political, and economic changes in the area.[2] Many Arabs settled along the coast of Persia and later returned to their homelands, bringing with them new building techniques and decorative items. Traces of the Persian influence, such as the colorful pastoral imagery of open green fields and colorful peacocks, are still seen today in Qatar. Additionally, for many decades, Qatar lay on the Indian Ocean slave-trading route and the majority of enslaved people were brought from Africa and Southeast Asia. When the slave trade was abolished by the British authority in the region in the twentieth century, some of the former slaves became integrated into Qatari society. As a result, they taught the locals some of their traditions, songs, and crafts that became part of the local culture.

The discovery of oil in the mid-twentieth century has had not only an economic impact on Qatar, but also made a significant socio-cultural impression. During this period the Qatari style was influenced by a fascination with the other worlds with which the oil revenues brought the local community into contact, since the local population was not only able to travel, but workers and experts from all over the world also arrived to help in the development process. This phase witnessed cross-border influences with the Levant, North Africa, India, and the West. The Qatari style became an interesting combination of elements that the local community had seen in different places in the world. The transitional era still maintained the aesthetics of the local vernacular but with the introduction of luxury materials and everyday and decorative objects. As stated above, some of these luxury items were present in the pre-oil period in houses of more affluent families, but in a simpler manner. During the transitional period the luxury objects became omnipresent and reflected collections brought back by travelers. Vibrant colors and images of lush greenery and animals that we see depicted on the walls and some items of furniture were valued as they were lacking in the Qatari harsh desert environment. This continued one of the most important dynamics of local design, which is the contrast between the vibrant and pale colors in the interiors. Even though Qatar was rapidly moving forward with influences from a much larger global context, a strong presence of Indian style was evident. The definition of style and memories of the generation that shaped the style of the transitional period were reminiscent of the pearl trade with maharajas from the Indian subcontinent from the pre-oil period.

At the turn of the twenty-first century, when Qatar witnessed true developmental prosperity, we see the shift to a revival of the traditional vernacular style. Taking elements from the local traditional style and implementing them into the current socio-cultural mix using state-of-the-art technologies resulted in an interesting contemporary Qatari style. Here, we see the fusion of both worlds, local and global, creating a new style direction. It is a style that is defined by the simplicity of traditional form and color that is coupled with global design trends.This is the style that has emerged since the Qatari nation learnt to quickly adapt and accommodate the global influence, but at the same time appreciate their own heritage. This is the ancestors' legacy to the current generation, and this generation's legacy to their children.

1 دراسات في التاريخ الاقتصادي لمنطقة الخليج في العصور الوسطى، سيف بن شاهين بن خلف المريخي، 2011
2 الزخرفة الجبسية في الخليج ، محمد على عبد الله، 1985
3 Qatar Enchantment of the World, Terri Willis, 2004

TRADITIONAL

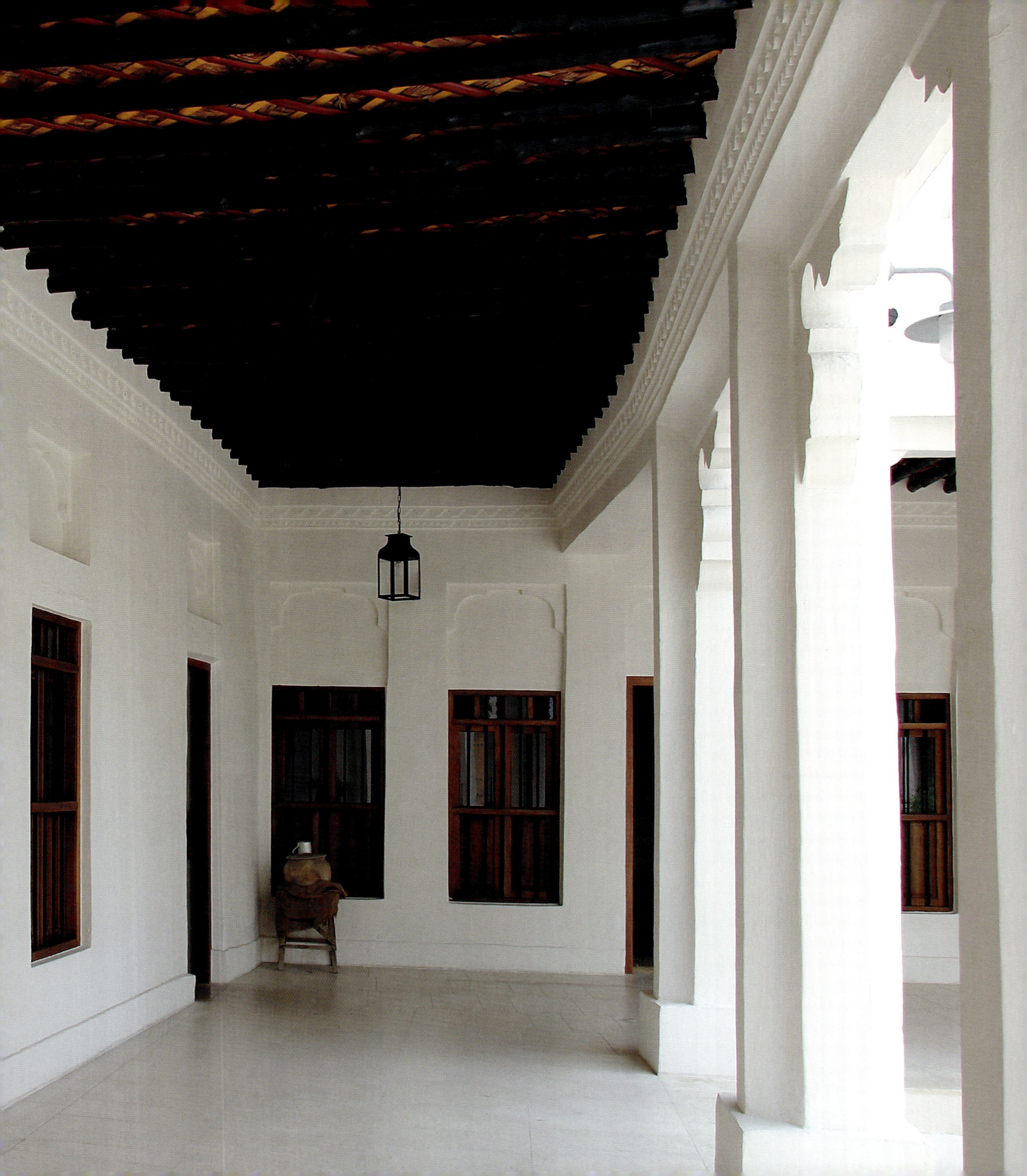

THE QATARI Saharan environment is not a colorful one. The dominant colors of the environment are the yellow of the desert sand, the teal of the sea, the brown of the cattle and the short-lived green of the few trees. However, the interiors of Qatari traditional houses contrast with the external environment. Bright colors dominate the textiles. The *sadw,* traditionally woven by women from goat, sheep and camel hair, is in vivid colors. Women would draw inspiration from folklore stories and their immediate surroundings and would create geometric pictograms, weaving their own stories into the *sadw* fabric. Furthermore, the traditional dresses worn by women under their black *abāāt* were also equally colorful, mostly in floral patterns and for those from more affluent backgrounds embroidered in silver or golden threads. The brightly-colored interiors and garments compensated for the paucity of colors in the environment. Other items in the house were left in their natural colors like *ḥaṣīr,* made of dried palm reeds and *basjīl,* made of imported bamboo.

The courtyards of Qatari houses were not always enhanced with decorative items. It was said that you were lucky if there was a single tree in your courtyard. Thus, the builders of that time, *asātidhah,* decorated the courtyards using wall carvings. These carvings were their version of landscaping in the harsh environment of the desert.

The changing seasons played a considerable role in the daily lives of Qataris in the pre-oil period. Each space within the house was designated for a season. In the winter, the ground floor rooms were ideal; during the warmer months, the *līwān* was preferred as it offered enough shade and breeze while daily household chores were carried out. While the *līwān* was used for daily activities, the roofs of the houses were used for sleeping when darkness would offer sufficient privacy.

In general, most rooms in a traditional Qatari house would be used for multiple purposes. We are told that the *maylis* was a place for adults to use for socializing during the day, and by night was a place for the younger generation of the family to sleep.

The *asātidhah* would organize open and closed spaces of the house to allow maximum protection from the intense sun and to take full advantage of prevailing winds. While traditional houses expanded organically as the family grew, the familiarity with the seasonal changes and the environment was fundamental and this knowledge was passed from one generation of *asātidhah* to the next.

In principle, the traditional Qatari house is organized around a central open courtyard, the *ḥawsh*. There would be one main entrance to the courtyard, from where all other spaces were accessible. Living spaces were multi-purpose single or double-storey blocks where all openings faced the courtyard. The courtyard offered an outdoor space for family members to go about their lives with complete privacy. The *maylis* was the only part of the house that had windows overlooking the street. It was also the only part of the house accessible directly from the street so that visiting men would not disturb the privacy of other family members.

Although the traditional Qatari house is planned in a specific manner, certain architectural elements of the house were also influenced by the habits of its residents. For example, people traditionally sat and slept on *dawāshig* on the floor. Therefore, in most seating areas, including the *mayālis,* windows are positioned very close to the floor, allowing for the maximum breeze to get in. The traditional way of building also allowed for certain fixed elements, such as *rūshanāt,* which were both practical and decorative. They were used as shelves for various everyday objects, while from an architectural perspective, these recesses were necessary to lighten the weight of the walls as structures went up without any structural beams.

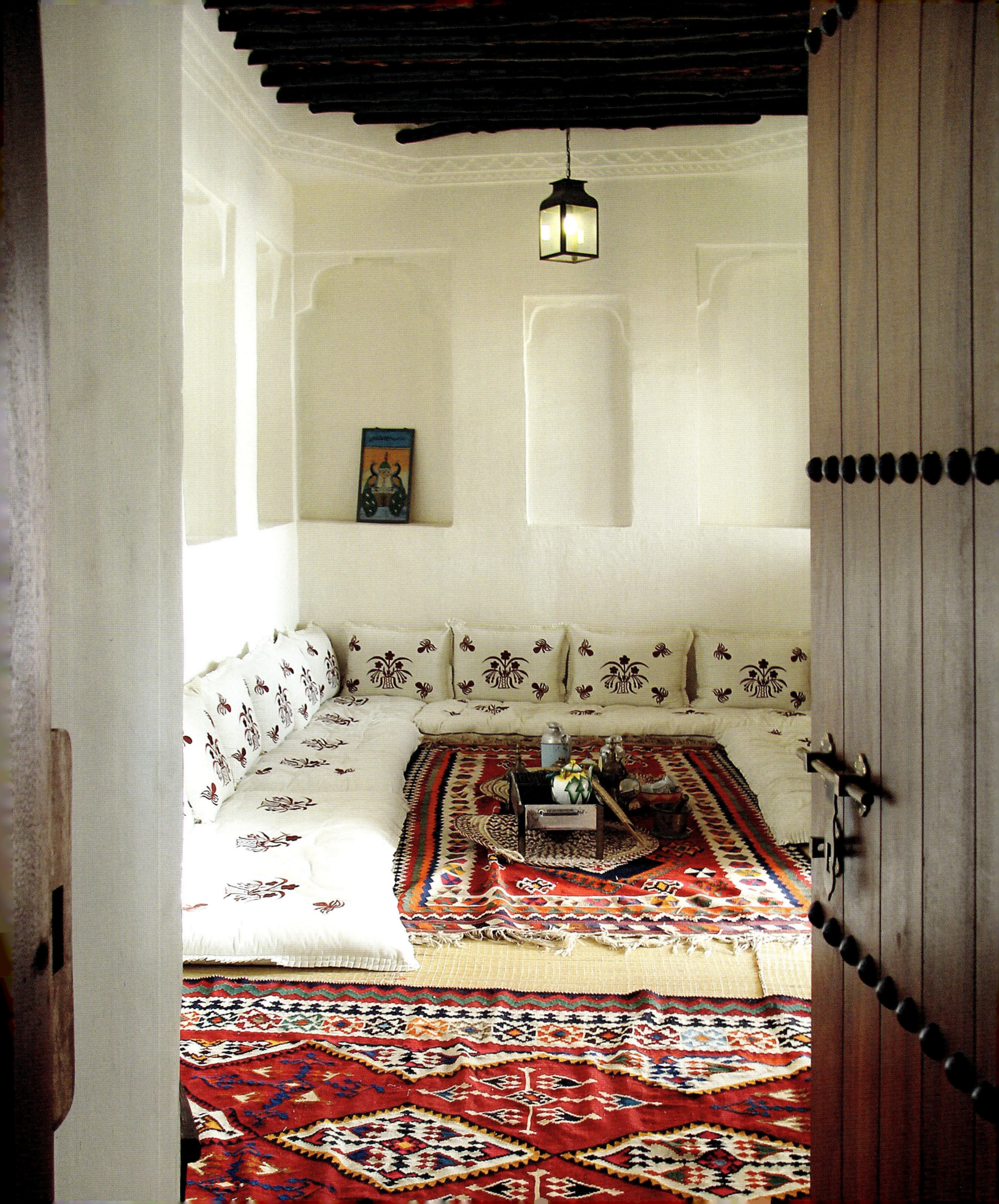

RADWANI HOUSE

Radwani House is the one of the very few surviving examples of an original traditional Qatari house. The house was renovated as a part of the Msheireb Downtown Doha urban regeneration project, and is now part of the Msheireb Museums. These comprise four historic houses located in the old commercial center of Doha, Msheireb; they honor Qatar's unique socio-cultural development and tell the story of and about the people of Qatar. Radwani House is a living museum and it recreates a traditional setting for Qatari everyday family life in the early to mid-twentieth century.

The house was first built in the 1920s and has undergone a number of renovations since then. The living quarters are arranged around the *ḥawsh* with *lawāwīn* wrapping around. During the latest renovation, a much older structure was uncovered under a part of the house and now forms a part of the museum's exhibition. The remainder of the space displays the family room, kitchen and bedrooms, all exhibiting a collection of everyday objects and furniture from that period. The *ḥawsh* at the Radwani House contains a single tree and is covered in seashells, as most of the courtyards were back in the day to minimize the dust.

Here we see typical floor seating made up of floor mattresses, *dawāshig,* with pillows as the back rests, *masānid.* In the center of the seating area is an arrangement for serving coffee displayed on two round *sufar.* It is tradition to serve Arabic coffee when greeting people during formal and informal events. It is a way of acknowledging that someone is your guest and is considered a means of opening a conversation. Adjacent to the main living room is a small kitchen that displays *raḥá*, *ḥaṣīr, jafīr,* burlap sacks containing various grains, and a selection of cooking pots. The cooking pots were generally very large because the extended family used to live in the same house. Traditionally, rice was the basis for most meals. Fish and meat would be added according to availability.

In evidence here are also traditional roofing comprising of *danāshil* and *bāsjīl*, and wall recesses *rūshanāt. Rūshanāt* are used as shelving and to hold everyday items such as perfume bottles, especially the metal elongated rose water bottles, *mirāshīh*. In Qatar, perfuming clothes is traditionally carried out by absorbing the smoke of the *bukhūr* from the *mibkharah.* Clothes were placed on the wooden structure, *midkhan*, and *bukhūr* would be burned in the *mibkharah* underneath.

One other element to note in Radwani House is the *yīḥlah.* This is the clay pot usually placed on the *līwān* that would contain drinking water. The porous material of the pot allows droplets of water to penetrate, so when the wind blows it cools down the whole jar. Therefore, the temperature of the water inside is cooler than outside. The older generation still tells stories about how the pots had to be tapped a few times to scare any worms or insects away before opening it for drinking.

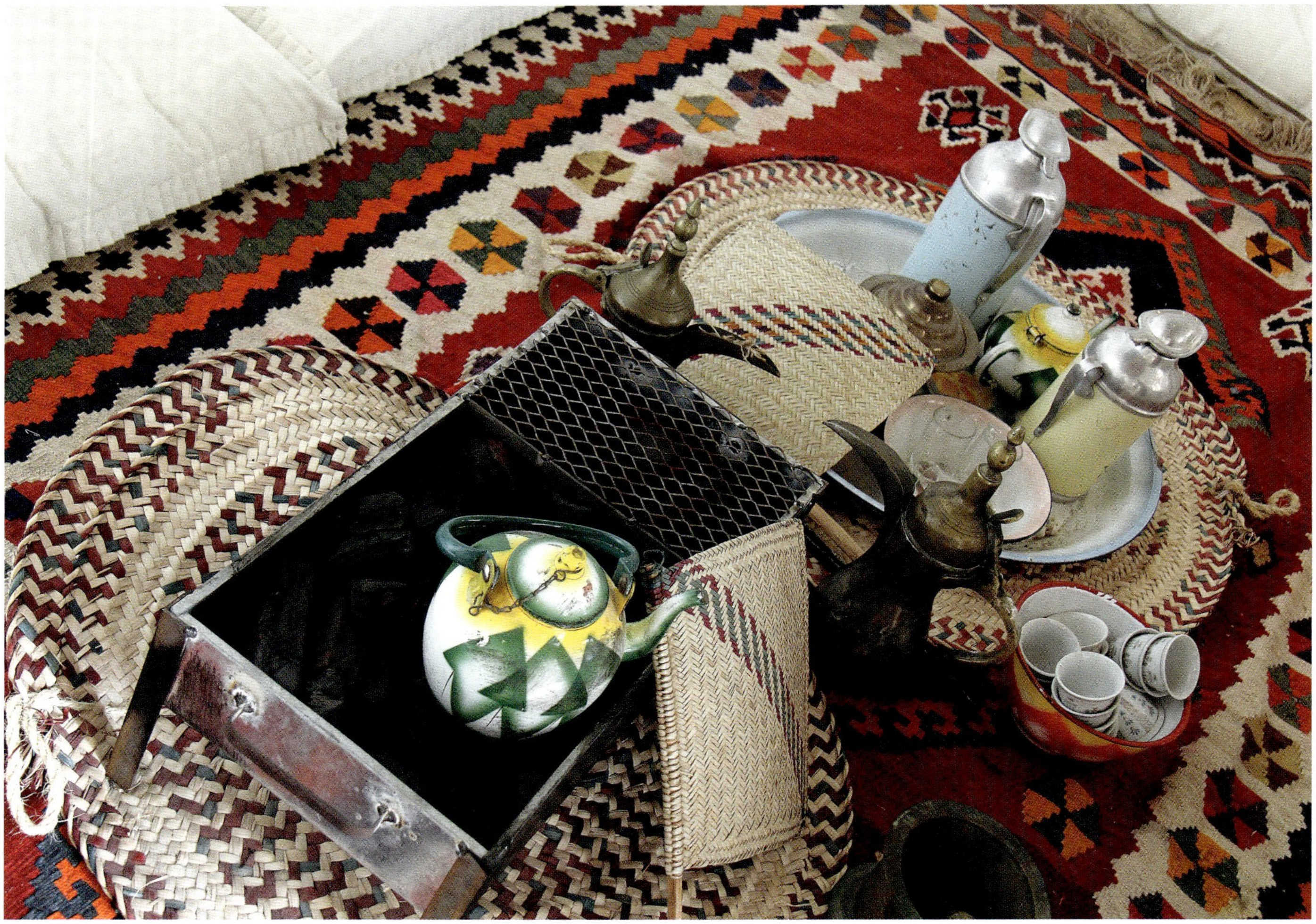

Above: A typical Arabic coffee and tea setting.

Right-hand page: A traditional family living room in a house featuring numerous wall recesses—*rūshanāt*—which are not only decorative, but also provide a creative way of permitting the construction of taller walls by using recesses to make them lighter.

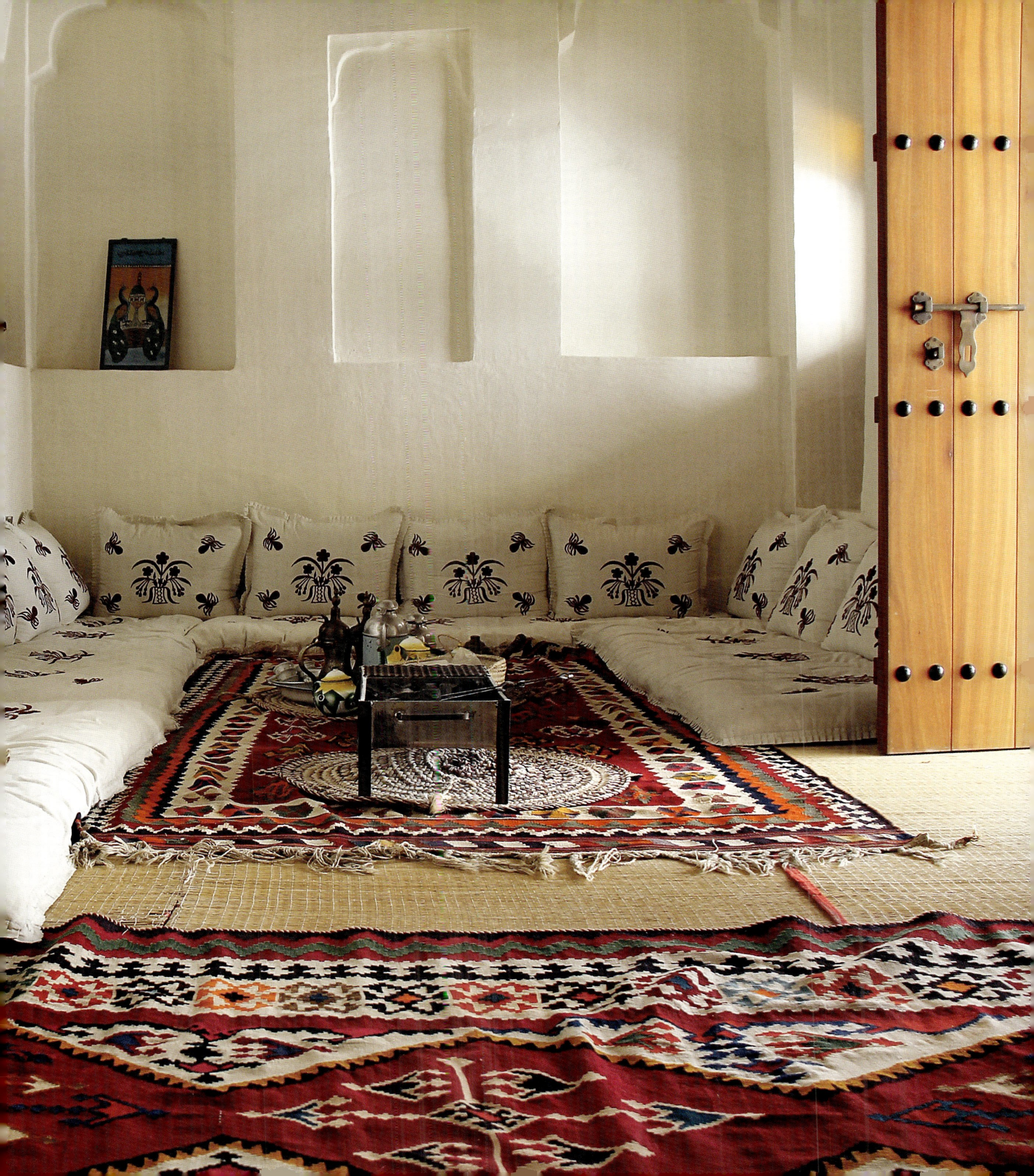

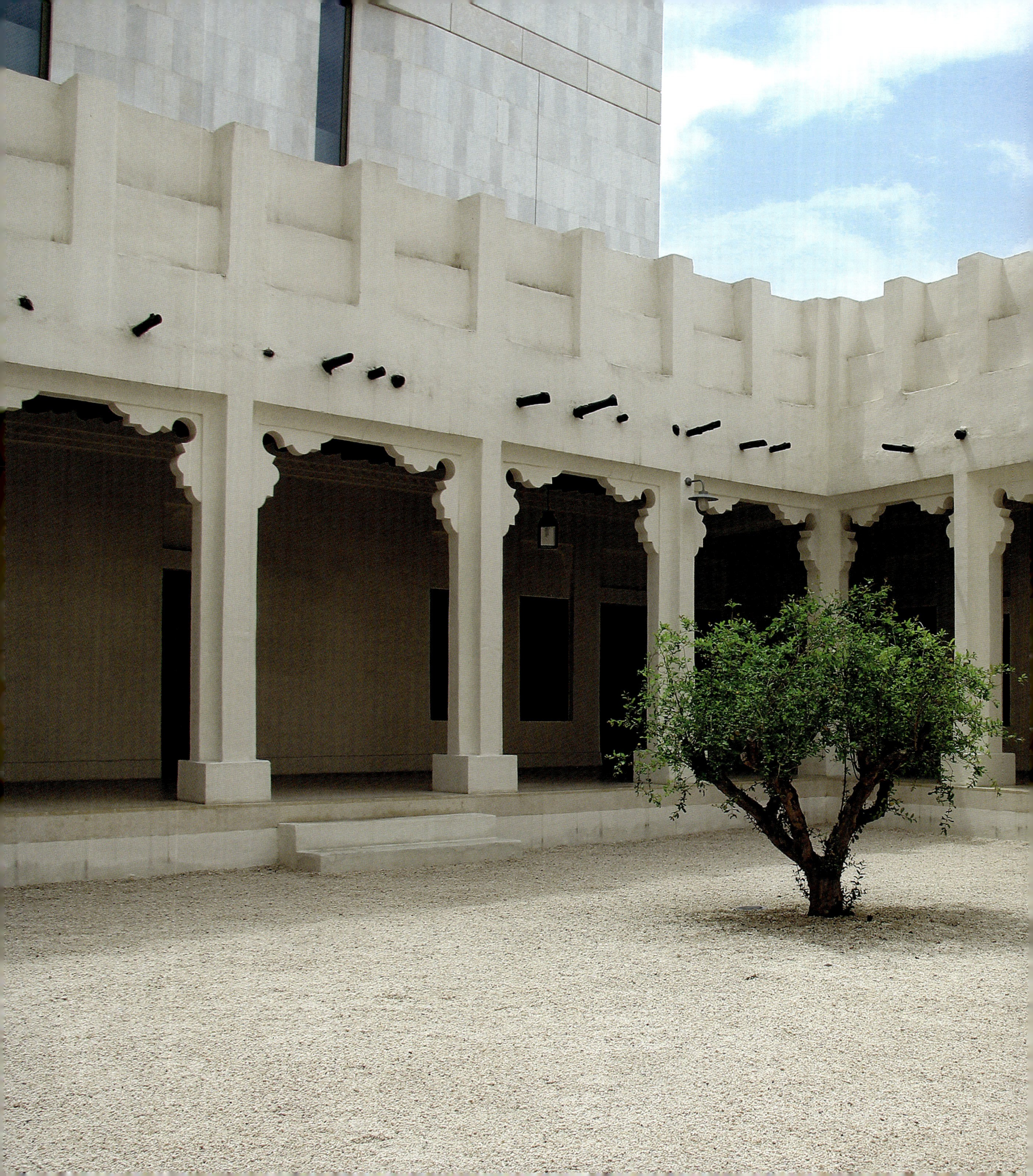

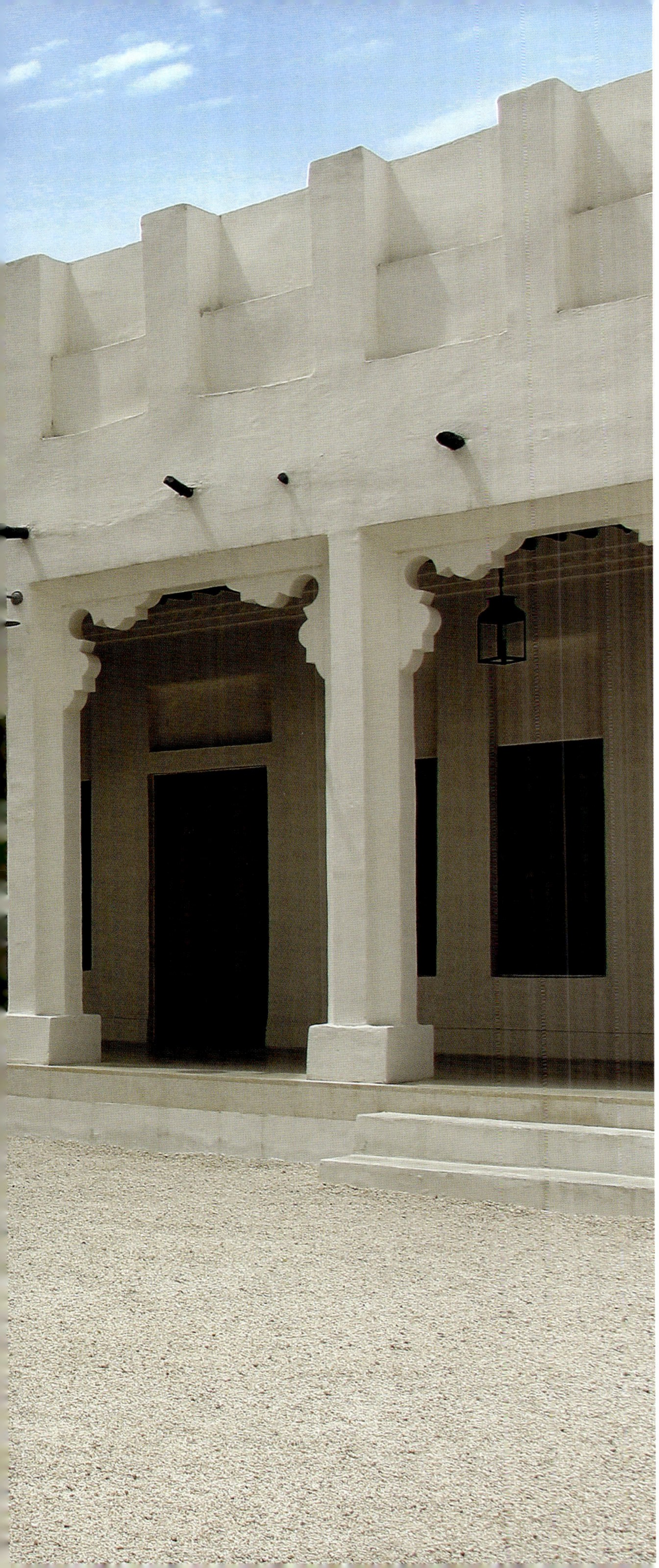

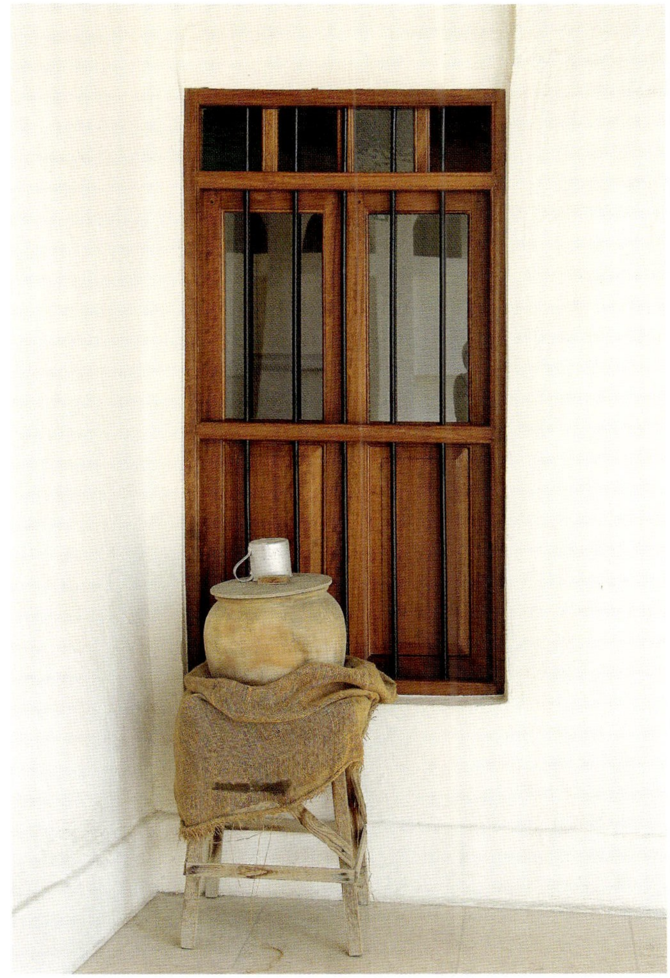

Above: A clay *yīḥlah* exhibited in the shade of the *līwān*.

Left: A typical courtyard of an affluent family home, surrounded by *lawāwīn* and featuring a sidr tree in the center. The *līwān* is not only a practical architectural feature to shade the walls and windows; it also has an important social aspect as it provides a shaded area for residents to carry out different activities.

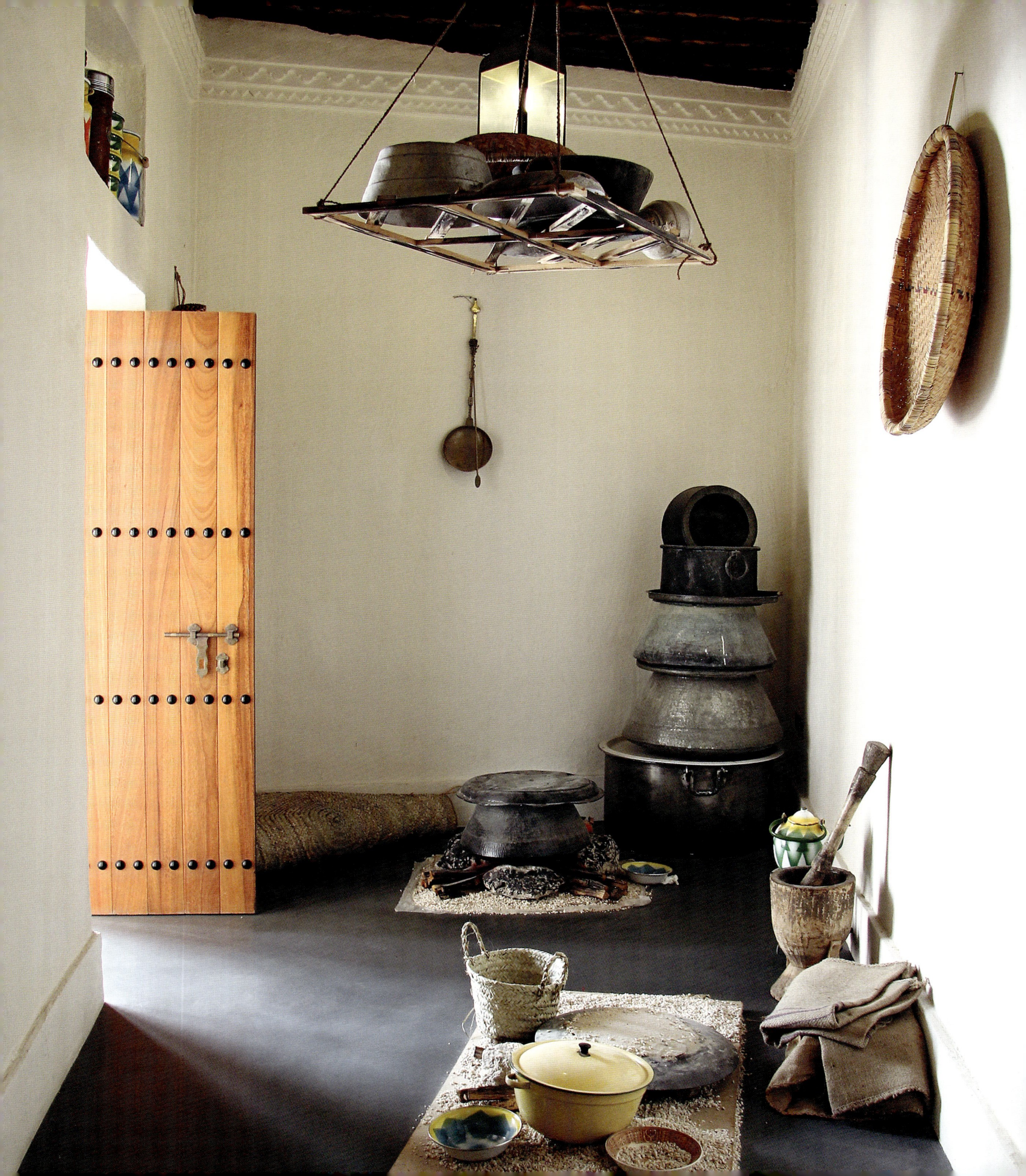

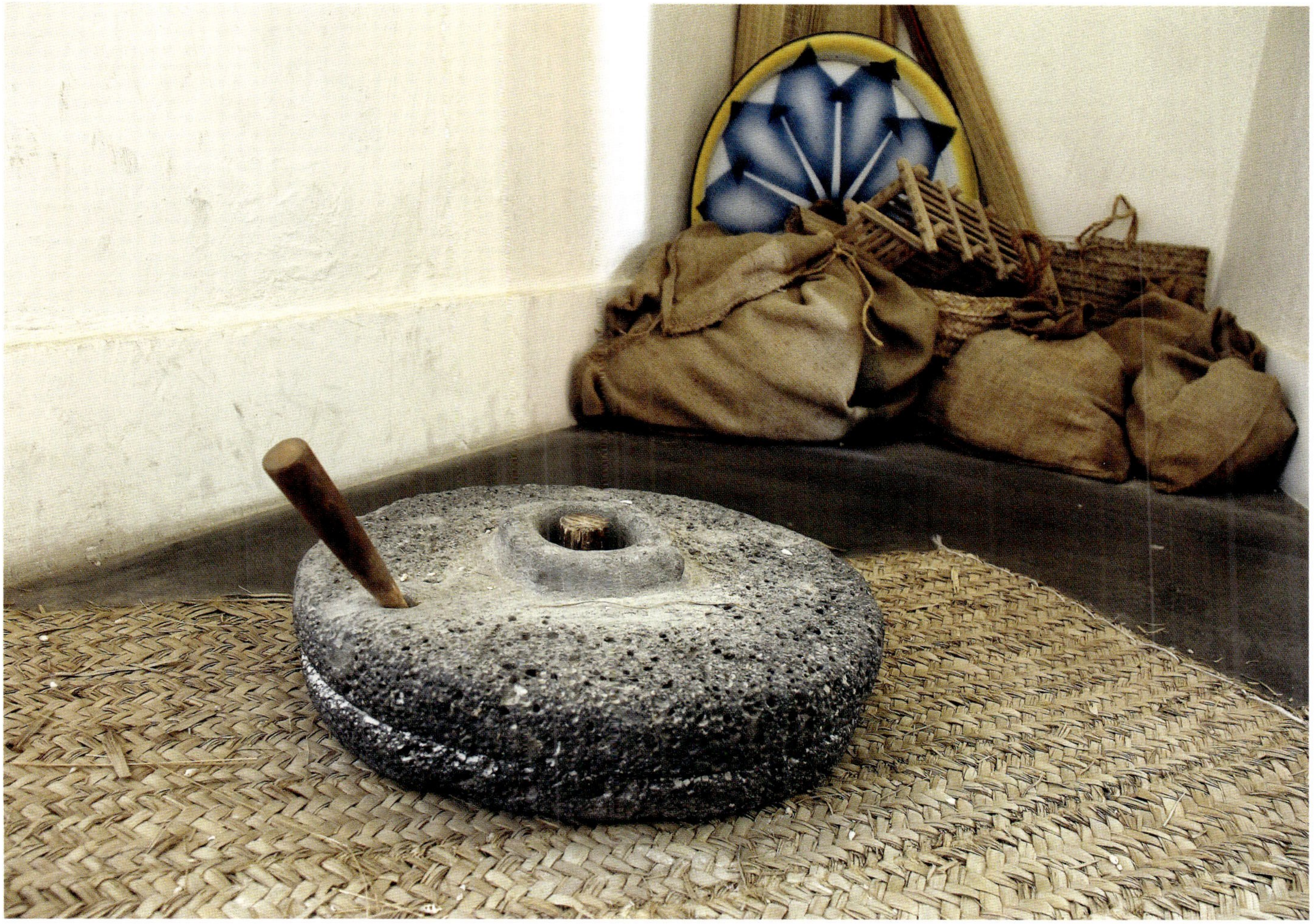

Above: A manually operated grinder made out of stone.

Left-hand page: Traditional cookware exhibited in Radwani House.

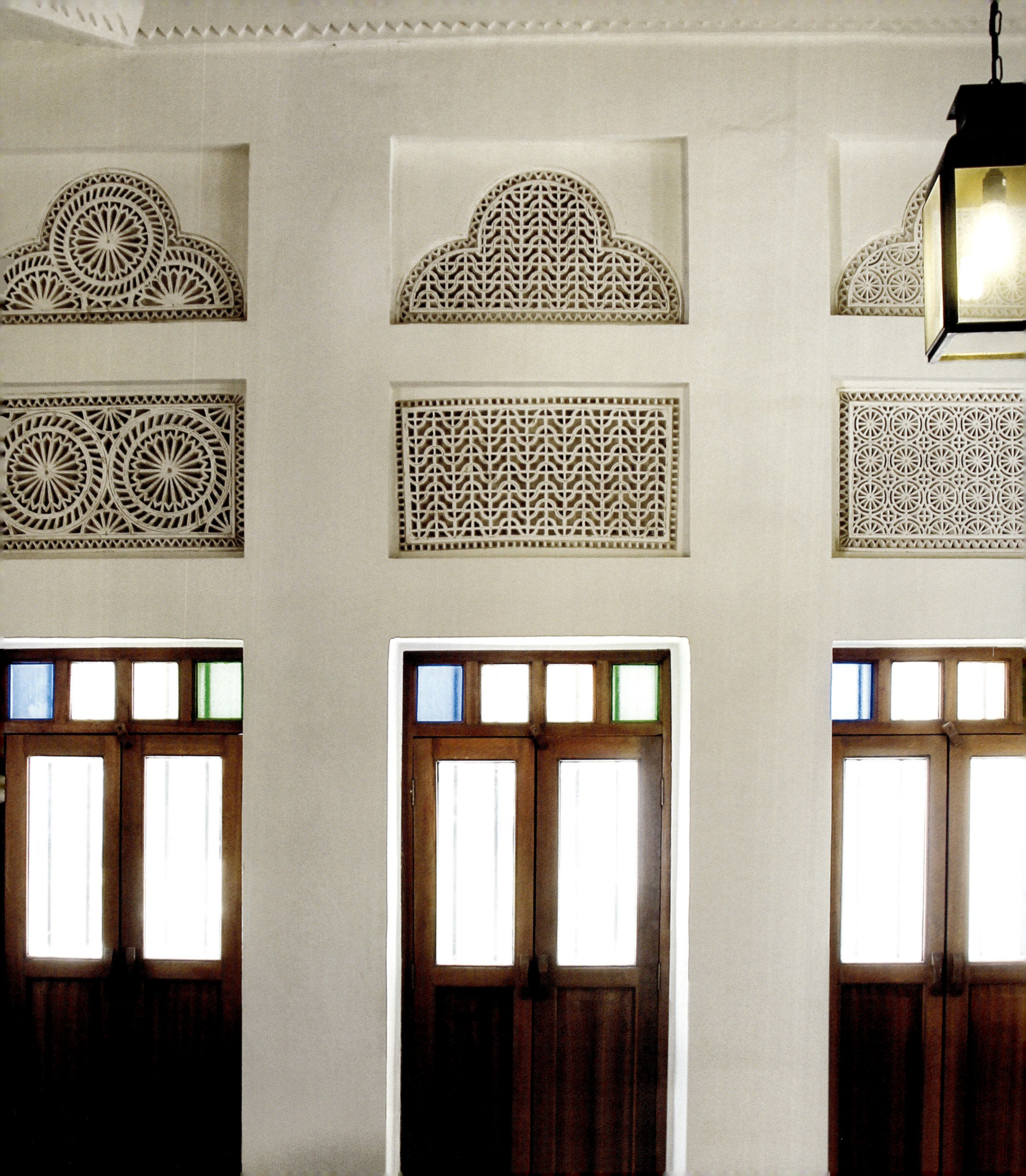

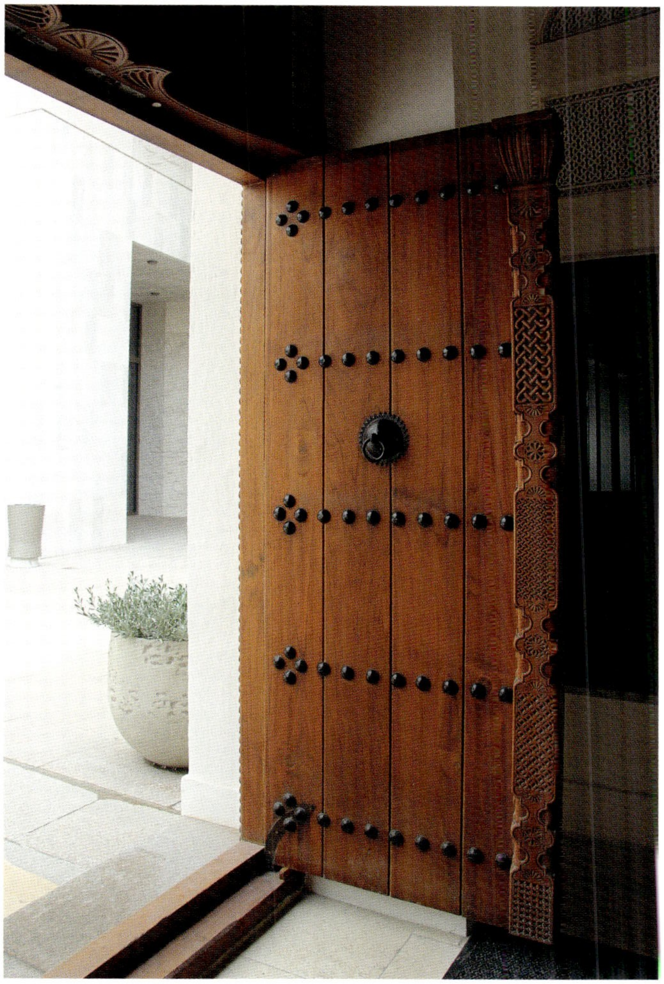

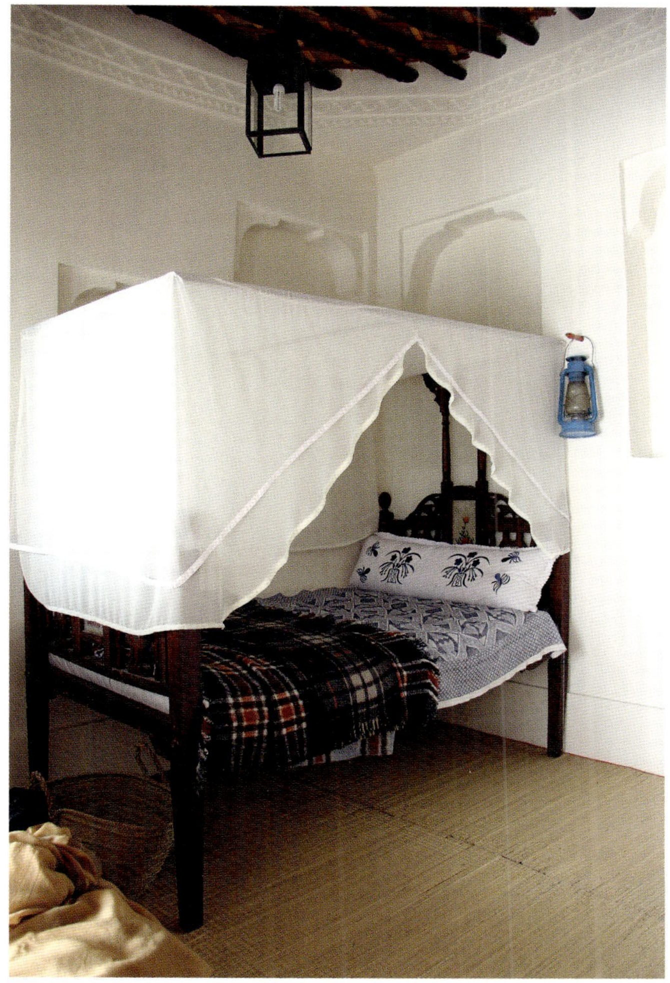

Above left: Wooden doors framed in intricate geometric patterns are decorated with large brass rivets.

Above right: A traditional *kurfāyah* elevated to provide more storage below.

Left-hand page: Typical Qatari decorative gypsum patterns.

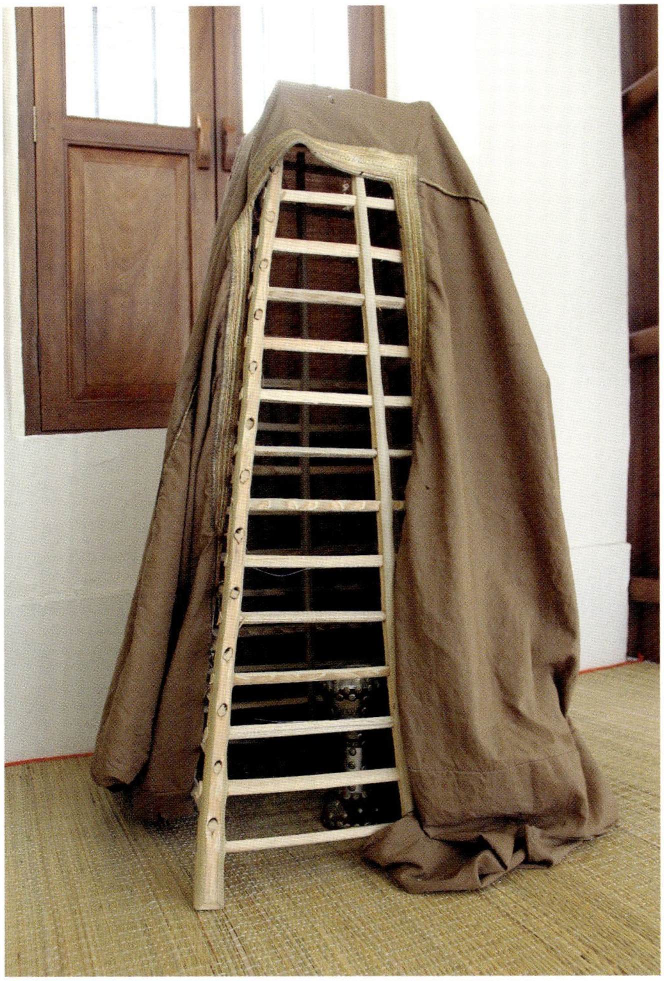

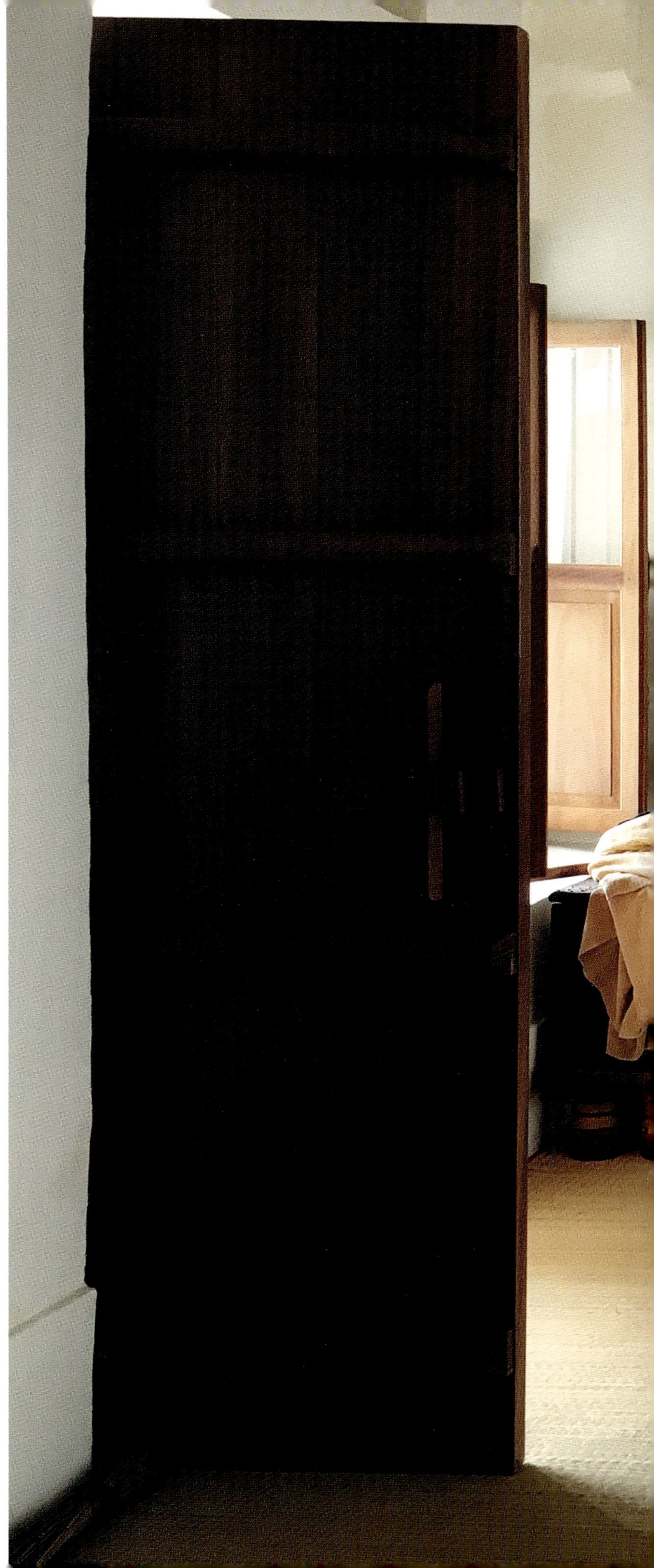

Above: A ceremonial men's garment lying on the *midkhan*.

Right: A traditional bedroom arrangement; the room has multiple functions with a seating area formed by *dawāshig*.

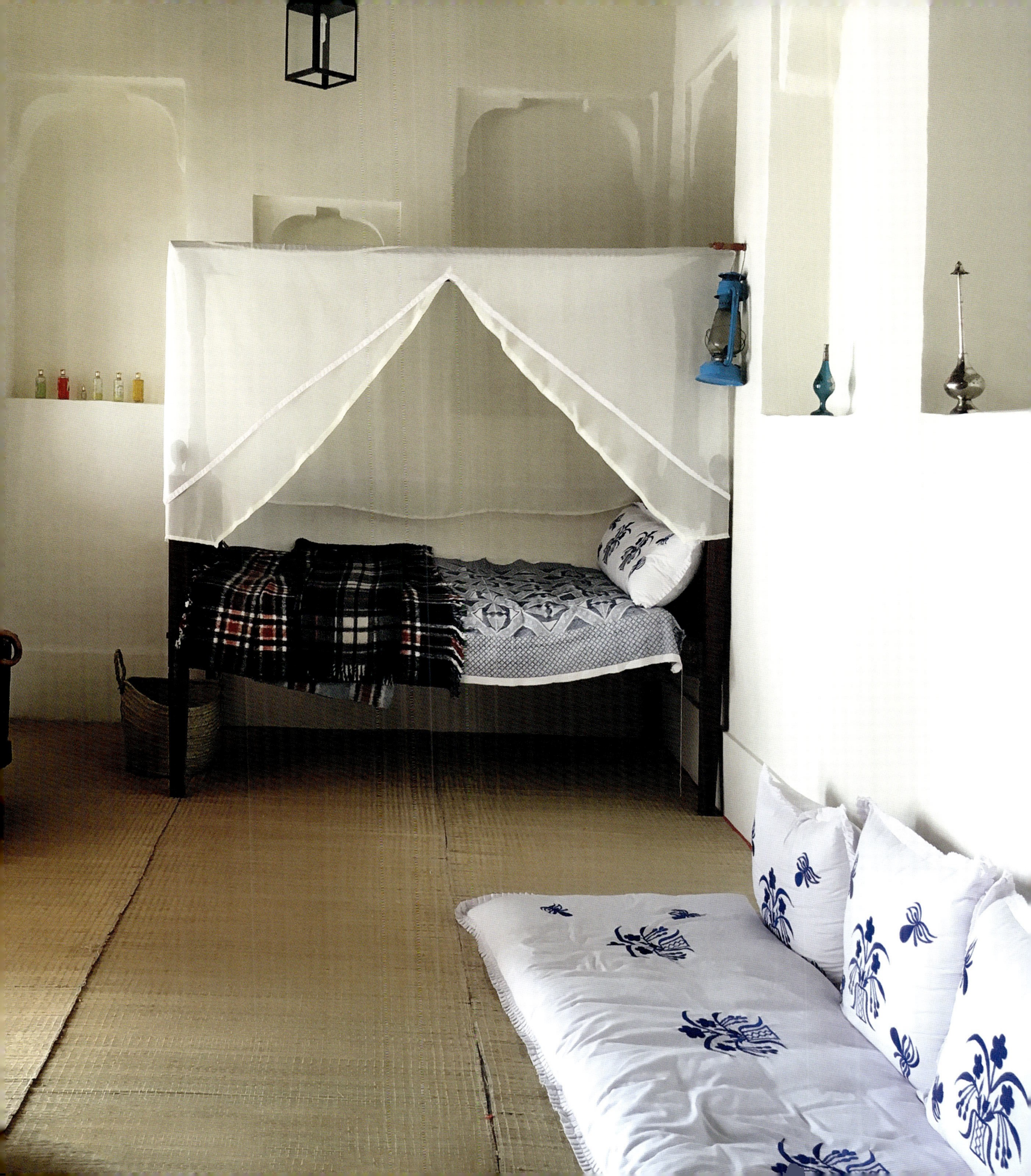

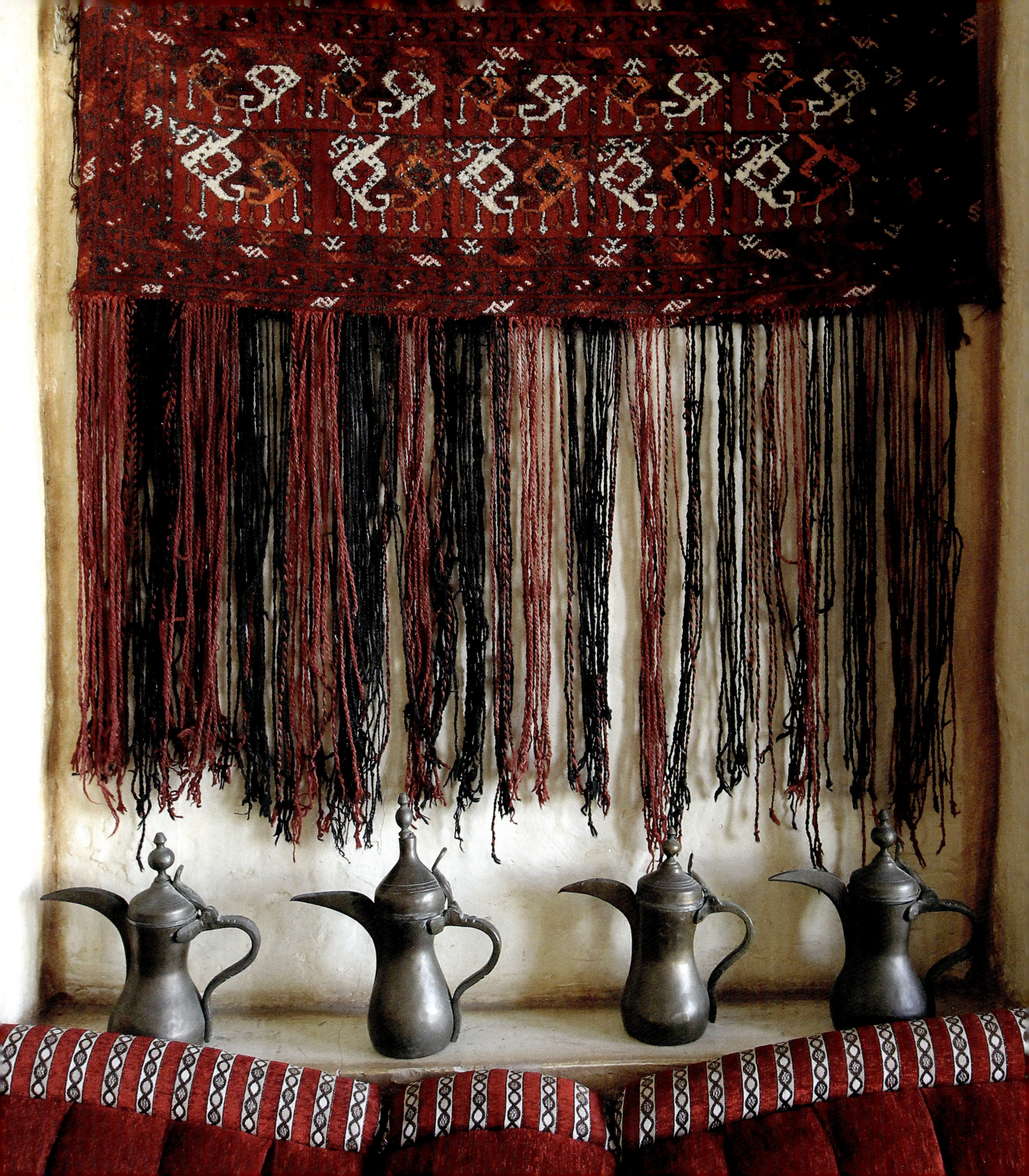

AL MANA MAJLIS

Al Mana Majlis is a traditional family *maylis* of the kind well known in Qatari society. It echoes a heritage dating back to the early twentieth century. The *Al Mana*ᶜ family owned an older *maylis* than the one depicted here. It was in the heart of old Souq Waqif and was frequented by family members, friends, and *sūq* visitors.

In more recent years, the *Al Mana*ᶜ family has built a new *maylis* in a different location. Alongside the new modern *maylis,* it added a small but very traditional structure. The thick walls are treated to give a traditional unpolished effect and the corners are hand-painted in a darker color, giving an impression of age. There are numerous *rūshanāt*, in which various antique items such as old arrows, *dilal,* and *ghūārī* are displayed. A continuous seating area reminiscent of a typical traditional *maylis* setting runs along the three walls. Many of the functional elements of the past have been reintroduced, including the *yīḥal* and *sadw*.

The interior of this *maylis* is somewhat untypical in the sense that external features have been brought indoors. The *dūwah*, which is an open fire pit used mostly for keeping *gahwa, tchāi* and *karak* warm for serving throughout the day, was brought inside even though it is originally an outdoor feature. Another unusual feature of this *maylis* is the decorative cornices around the ceiling, which became quite popular after the discovery of oil, and became an integral feature in the traditional Qatari style.

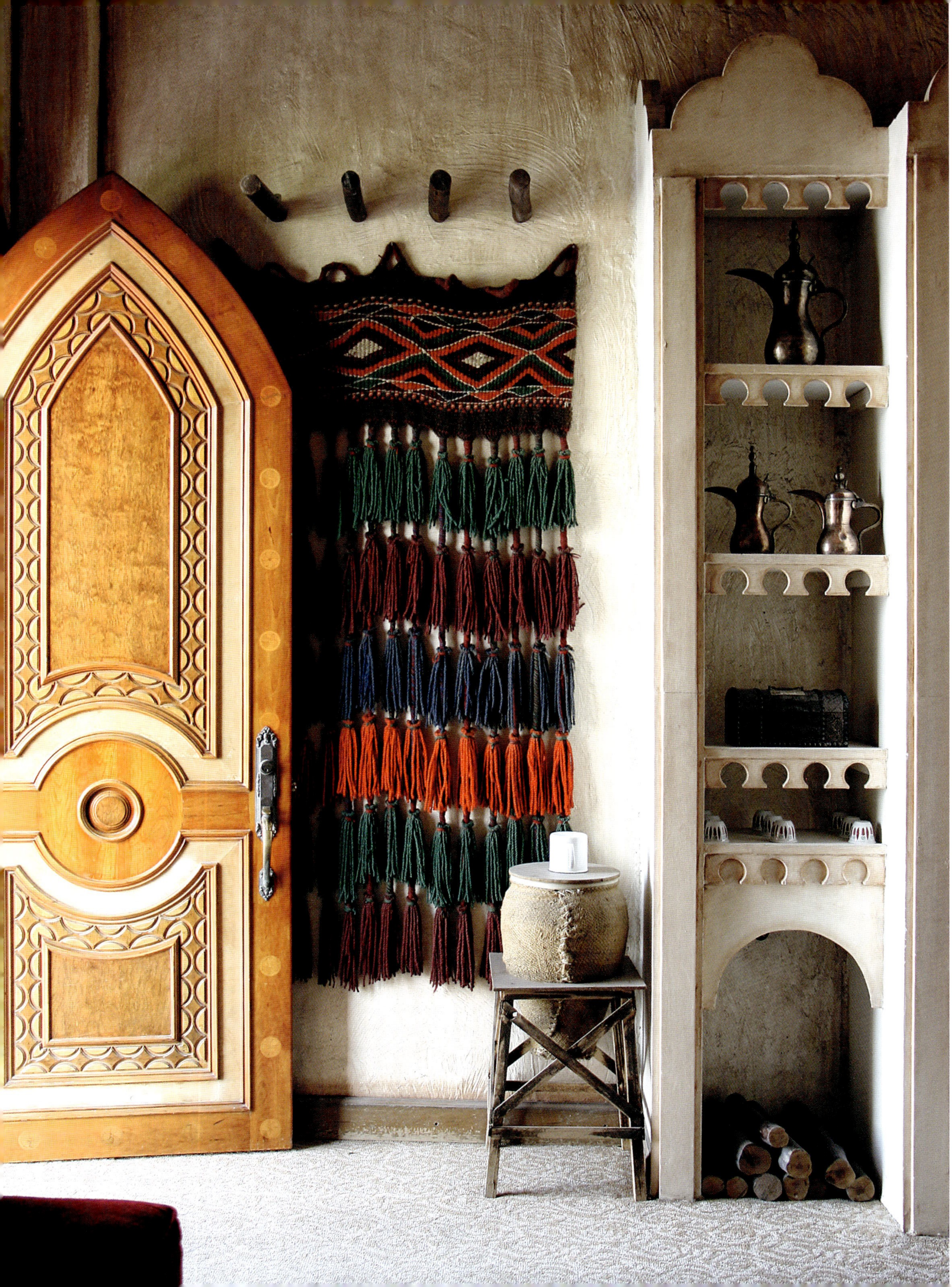

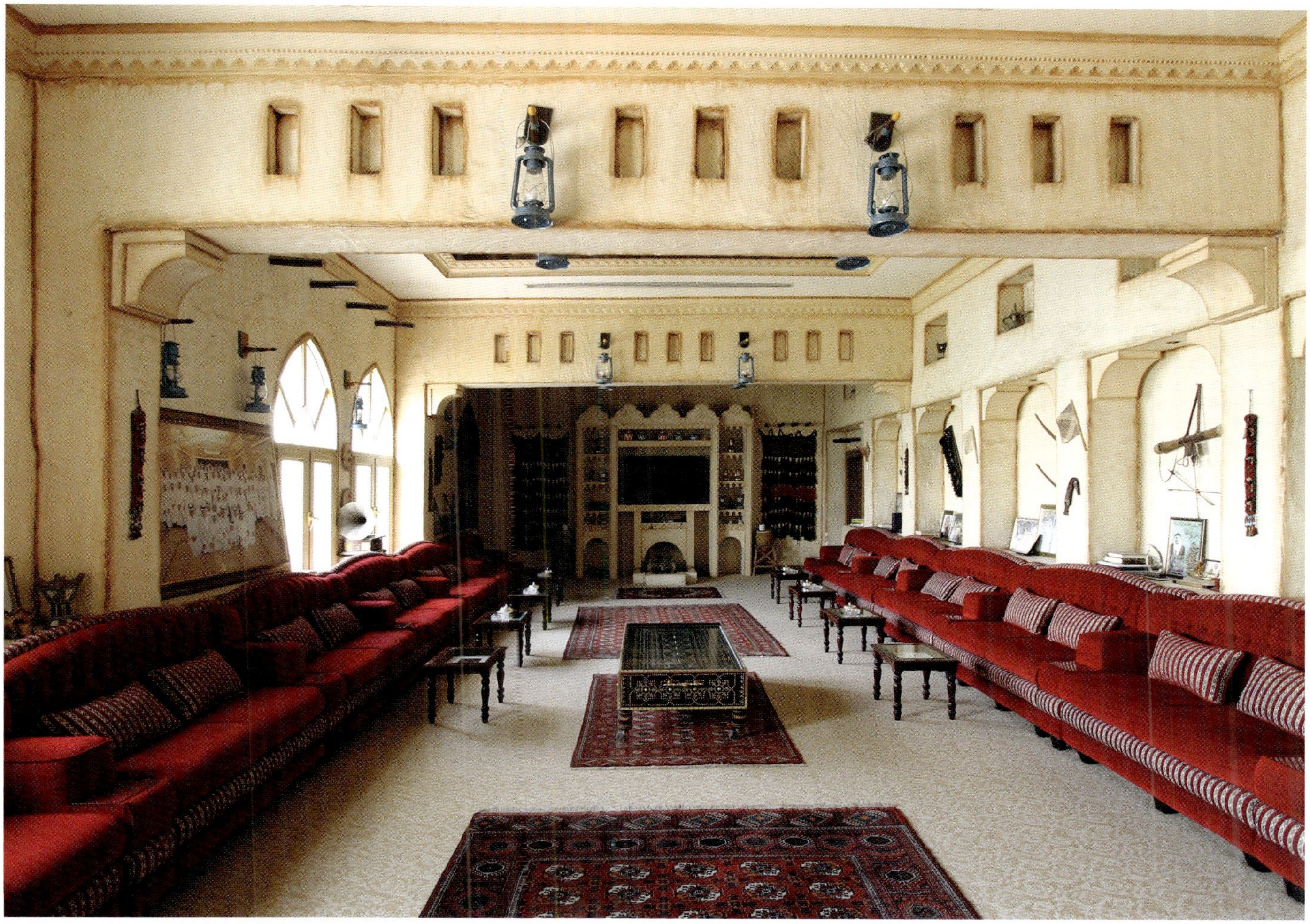

Above: The traditional *maylis* seating is reinterpreted as sofas lined against the walls.

Left-hand page: A wooden arched entrance door to Al Mana Majlis.

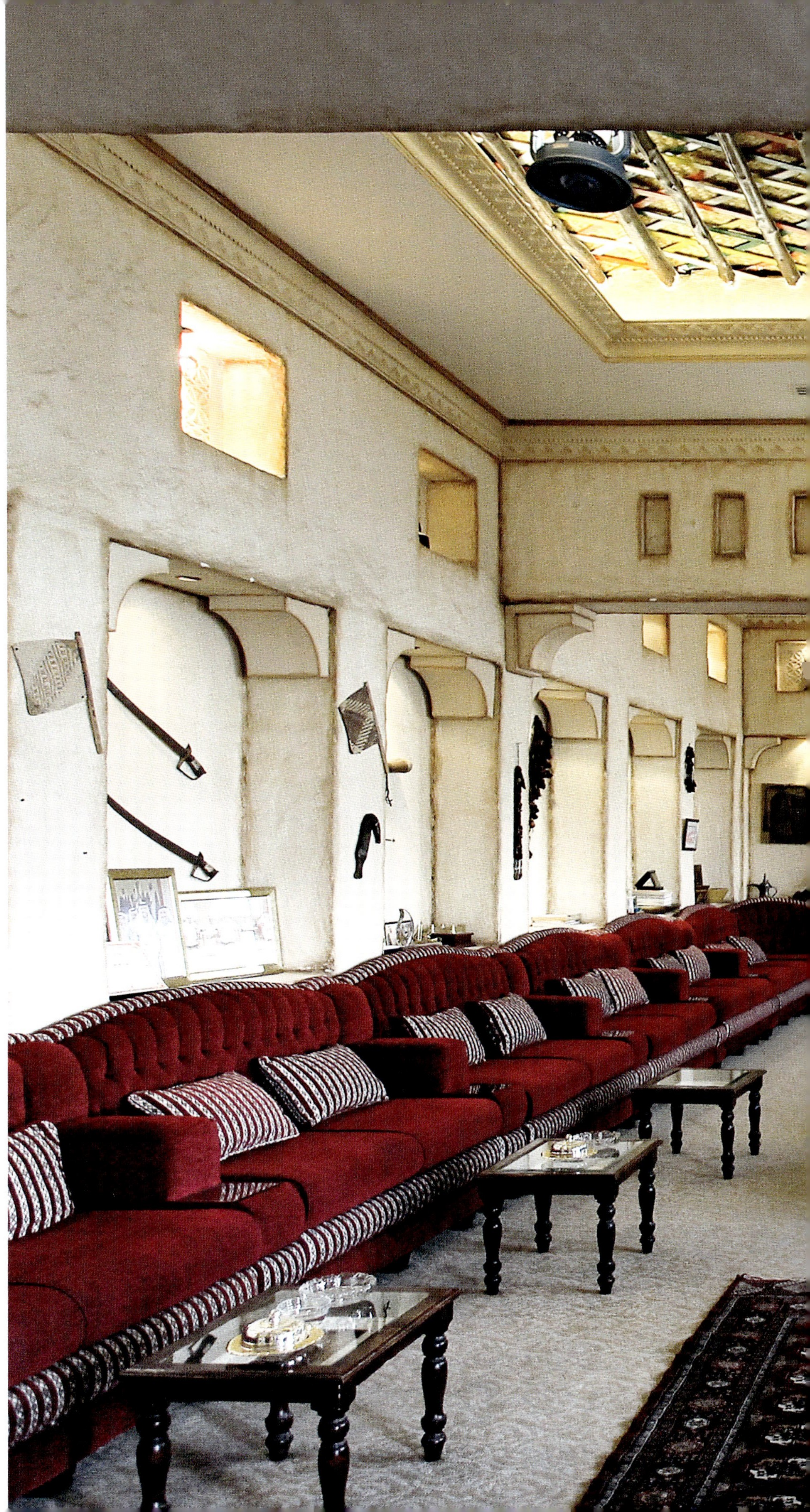

Evident here is the adaptation of exterior architectural elements in the *maylis*. Numerous items such as photographs, kitchenware, and weapons are exhibited inside the wall recesses.

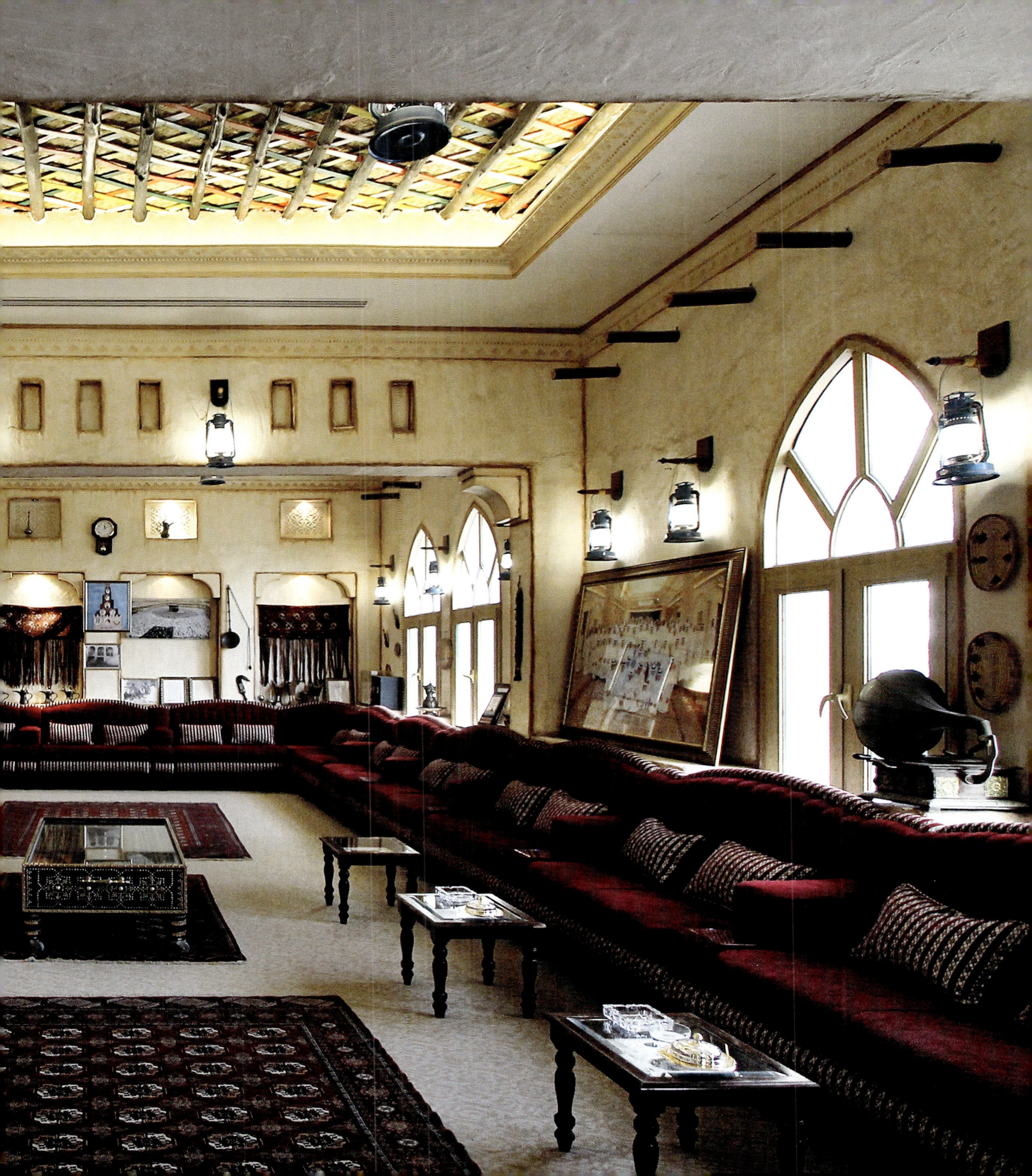

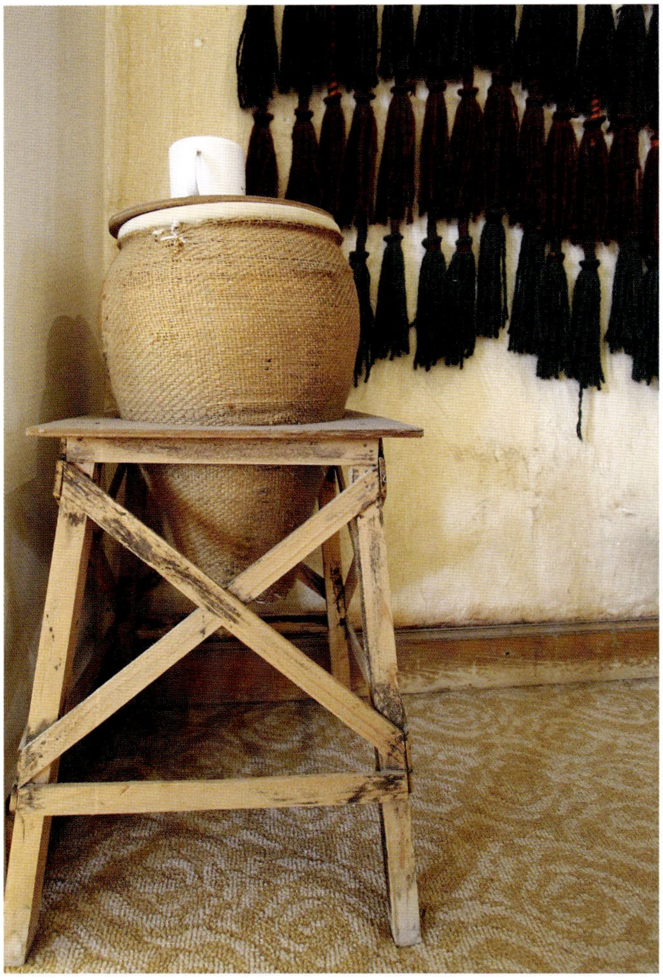 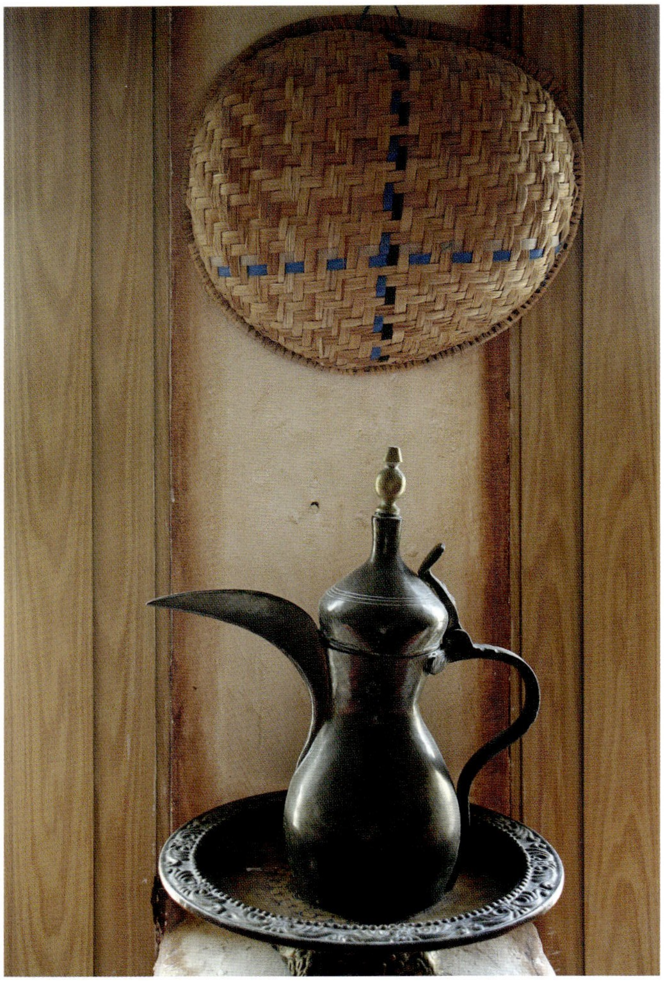

Above left: A clay *yīḥlah* elevated on a wooden stand.

Above right: Various everyday items can be found in Al Mana Majlis.

Right-hand page: A *dūwah* is more commonly an outdoor item.
Here it has been brought inside the Al Mana Majlis.

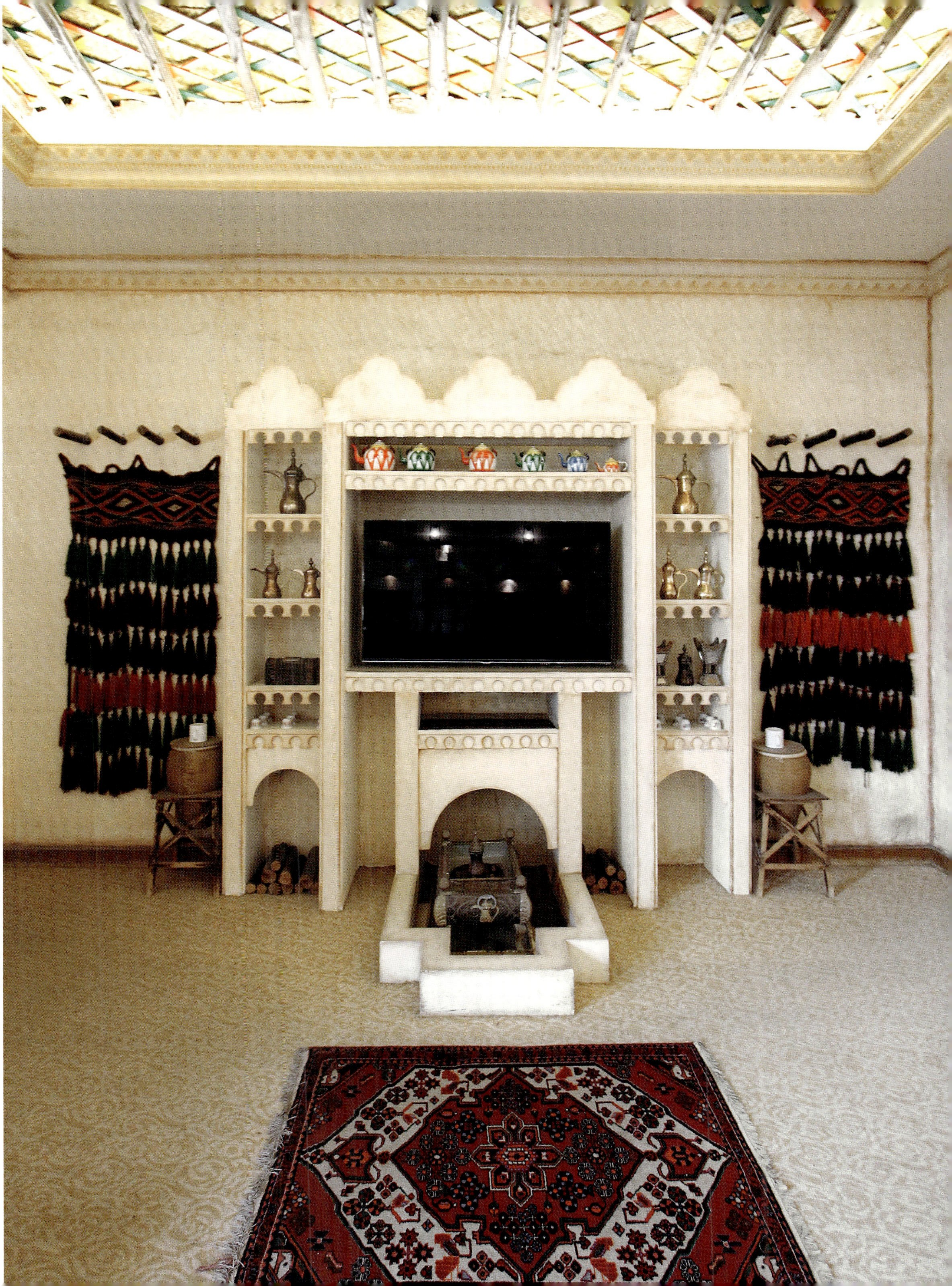

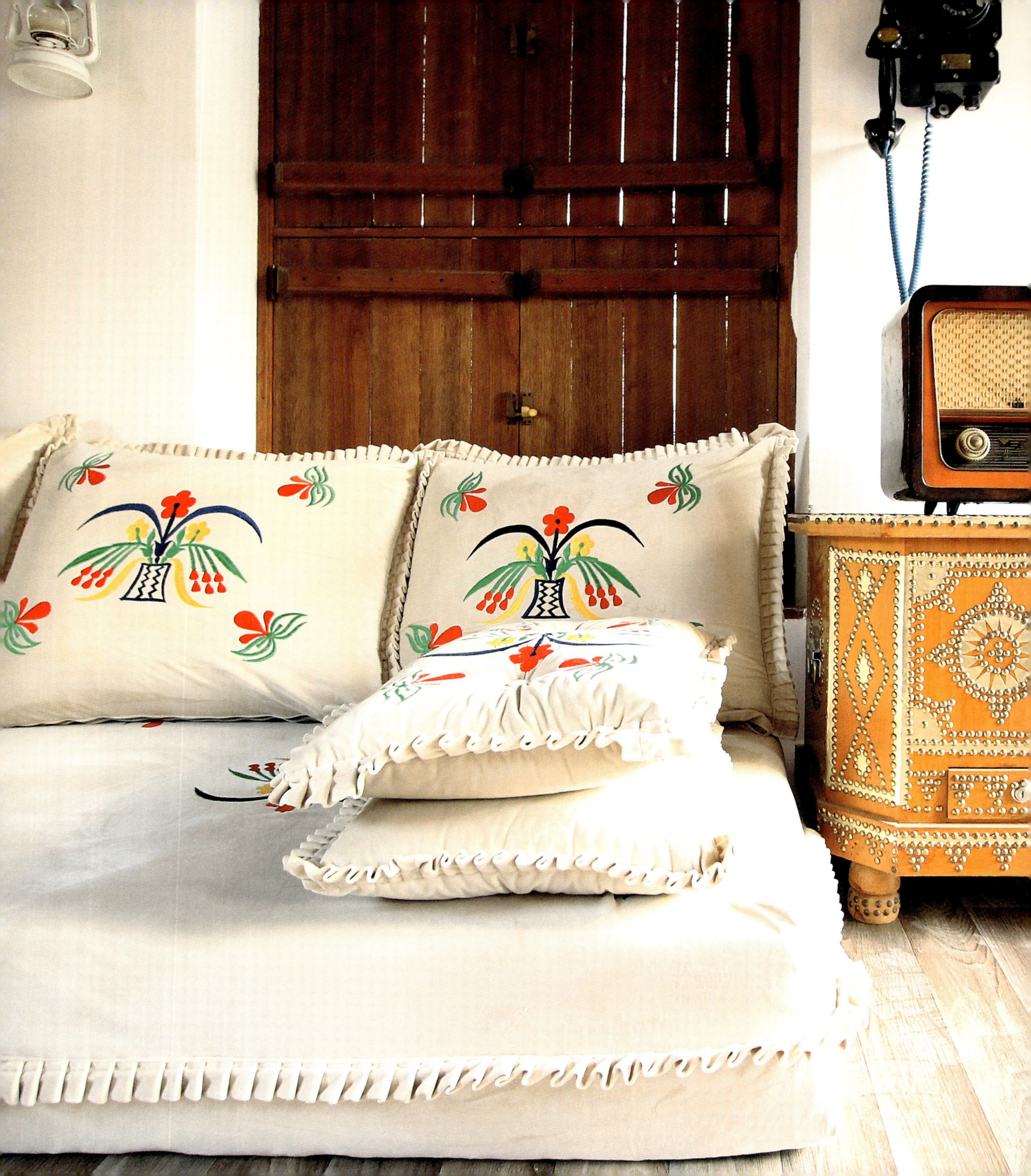

BOUHASHIM ALSAID MAJLIS

Abdulaziz AlBouhashim Alsaid's property is one that has kept its traditional essence in most of its aspects. The property is located 15 kilometers north of Doha in Umm Slal Mohammed. Numerous farms populate the settlement of Umm Slal Mohammed, since even before water infrastructure was brought to the area, a large rainwater reservoir that would naturally form during the rainy season was accessible to the farmers.

The property, landscaped with multiple indigenous *sidr* trees, is composed of a *maylis* facing the street that is separated from the single-story L-shaped residential house by a large courtyard. As part of the courtyard, there is an elevated seating area called a *dakkah* which is used during the pleasant weather in winter. In the old time, the *dakkah* used to have a floor of small seashells; nowadays, carpets are used instead. An outdoor kitchen is adjacent to the *maylis* and is decorated with dilapidated antique kitchenware. The falcons' mews are located opposite the residential unit, elevated on the site to make use of the natural topography. The owner takes great pride in his birds; for him, falconry provides a connection to the past and allows for a stronger engagement within the community. Moreover, falconry has been recognized as the intangible cultural heritage of the State of Qatar and as such was inscribed in the UNESCO list in 2016.

The rectangular *maylis* exhibits the typical traditional elements of the Qatari style. The ceiling seems to be an enhanced version of the traditional ceilings used in the pre-oil era. The materials were replaced with modern materials that are more durable. The floor-cushion seating runs around the room, typical of traditional *maylis*. But, unlike in some modern manifestations of the *maylis*, here windows reach the floor seating. The wooden windows have upper and lower sashes that open into the room. The split sash is used to allow the breeze while protecting the privacy of the room occupants. Rooms in pre-oil Qatar usually served multiple purposes based on the time of the day and the season. In this case, the *maylis* would be used at night for the children to sleep in. The floor seats would be turned into beds. The windows would then be half-closed for privacy. On the other hand, the double sash could be used to protect the seated persons from direct sunlight in the afternoon hours. The embroidery on the seating fabric is also a traditional design that was commonly used at the time.

The room is decorated with old items, some of which have been collected by the owner and some of which he inherited. One of the intriguing items in the room is the large *ṣandūq imbaīyt*, the wooden chest with the brass rivets. These wooden chests were traditionally brought from Zanzibar, India, or Southeast Asia and became an important element in wedding ceremonies. These chests would be filled with various items by the groom's family and would be gifted to the bride. After the wedding the chest was used to store valuables. The size of the chest usually indicated the social status and level of affluence of the groom's family.

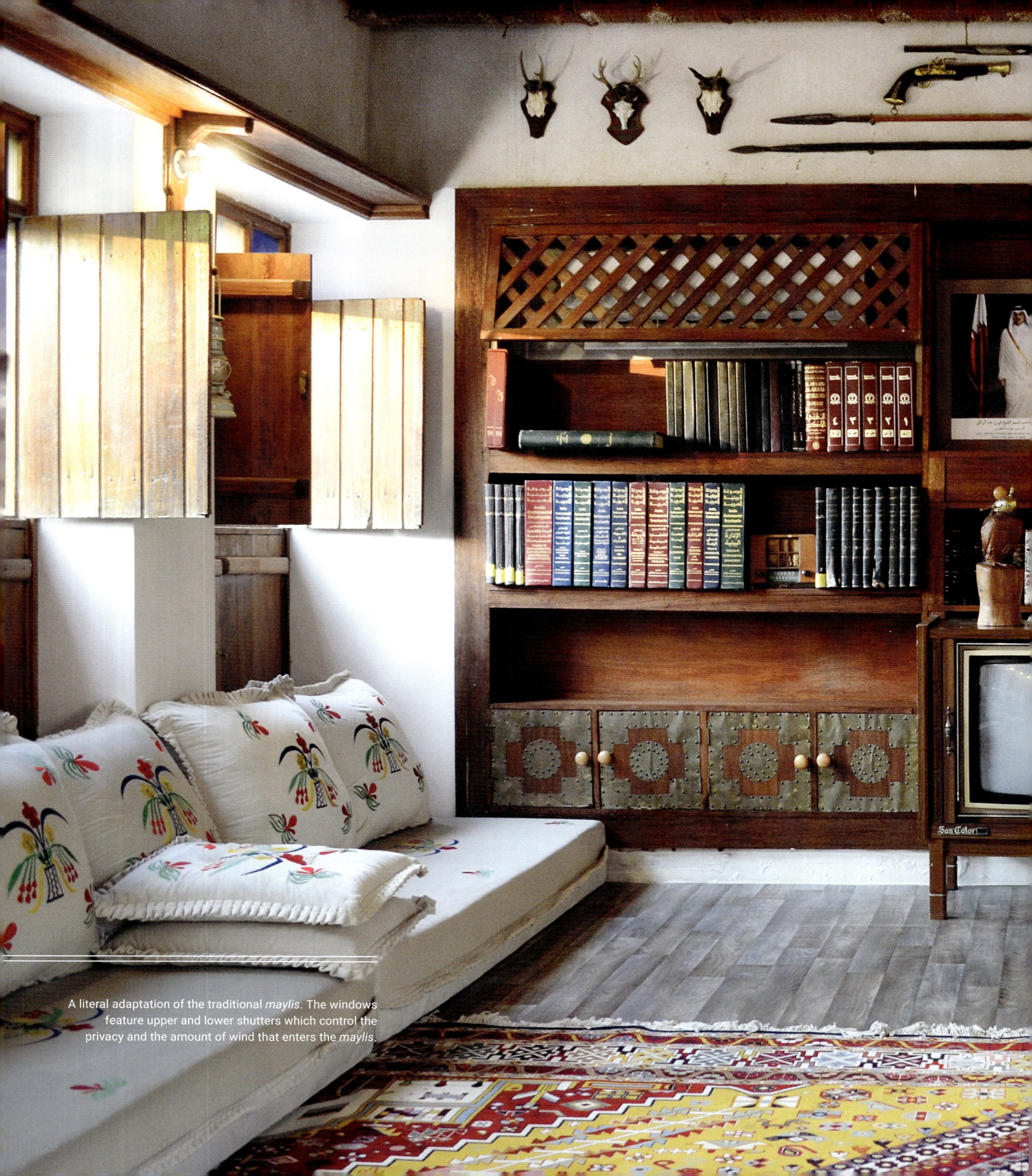

A literal adaptation of the traditional *maylis*. The windows feature upper and lower shutters which control the privacy and the amount of wind that enters the *maylis*.

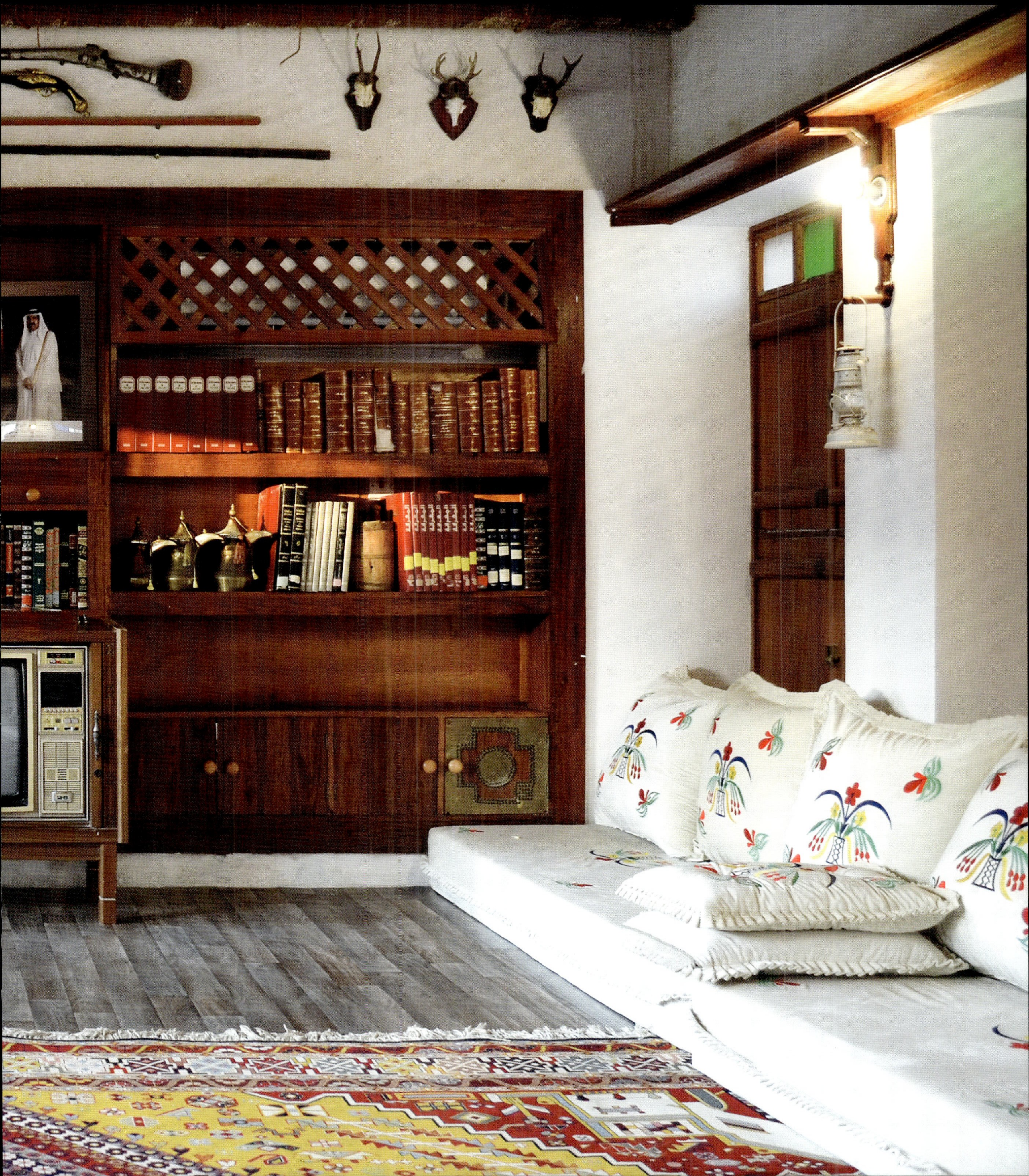

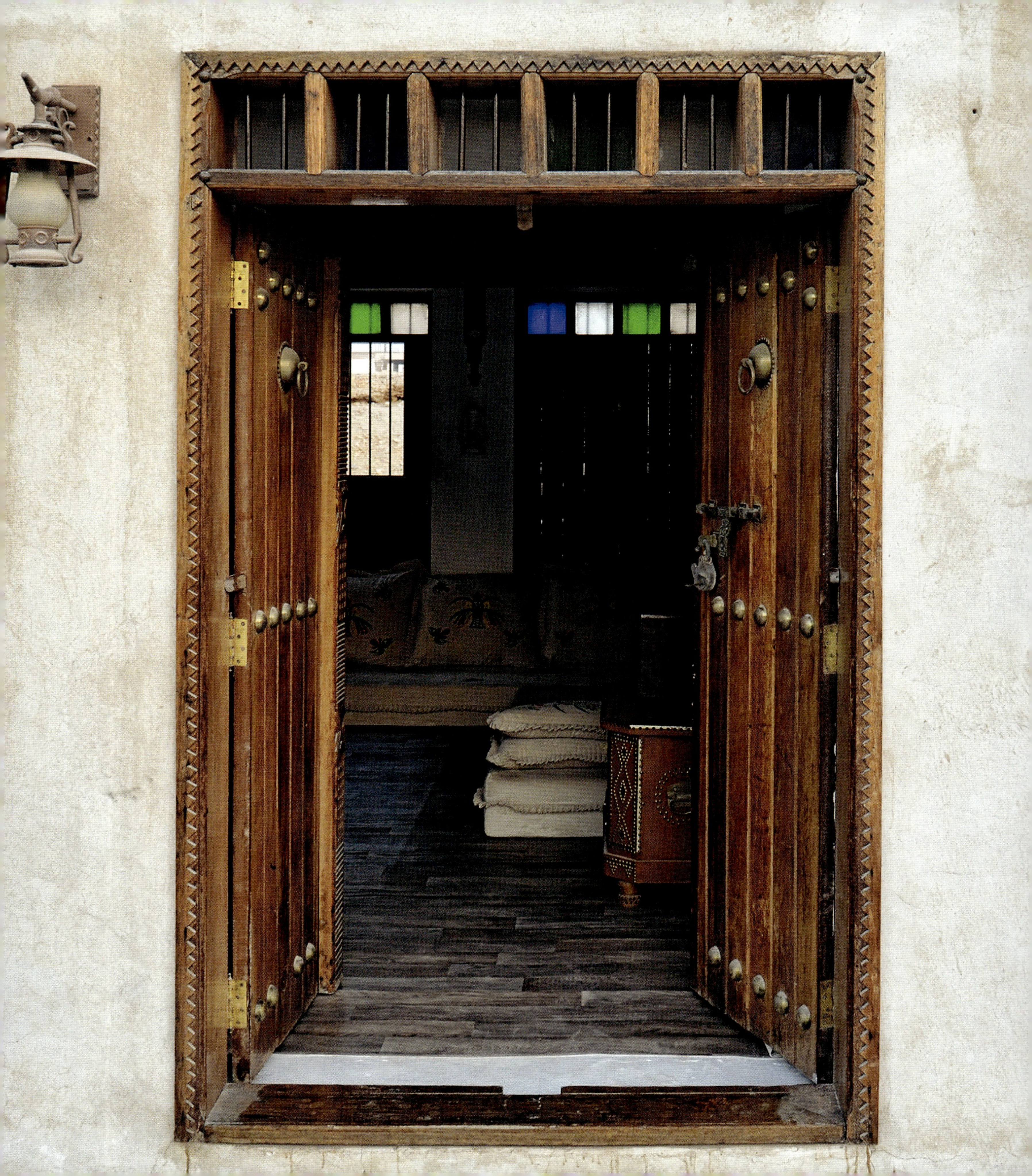

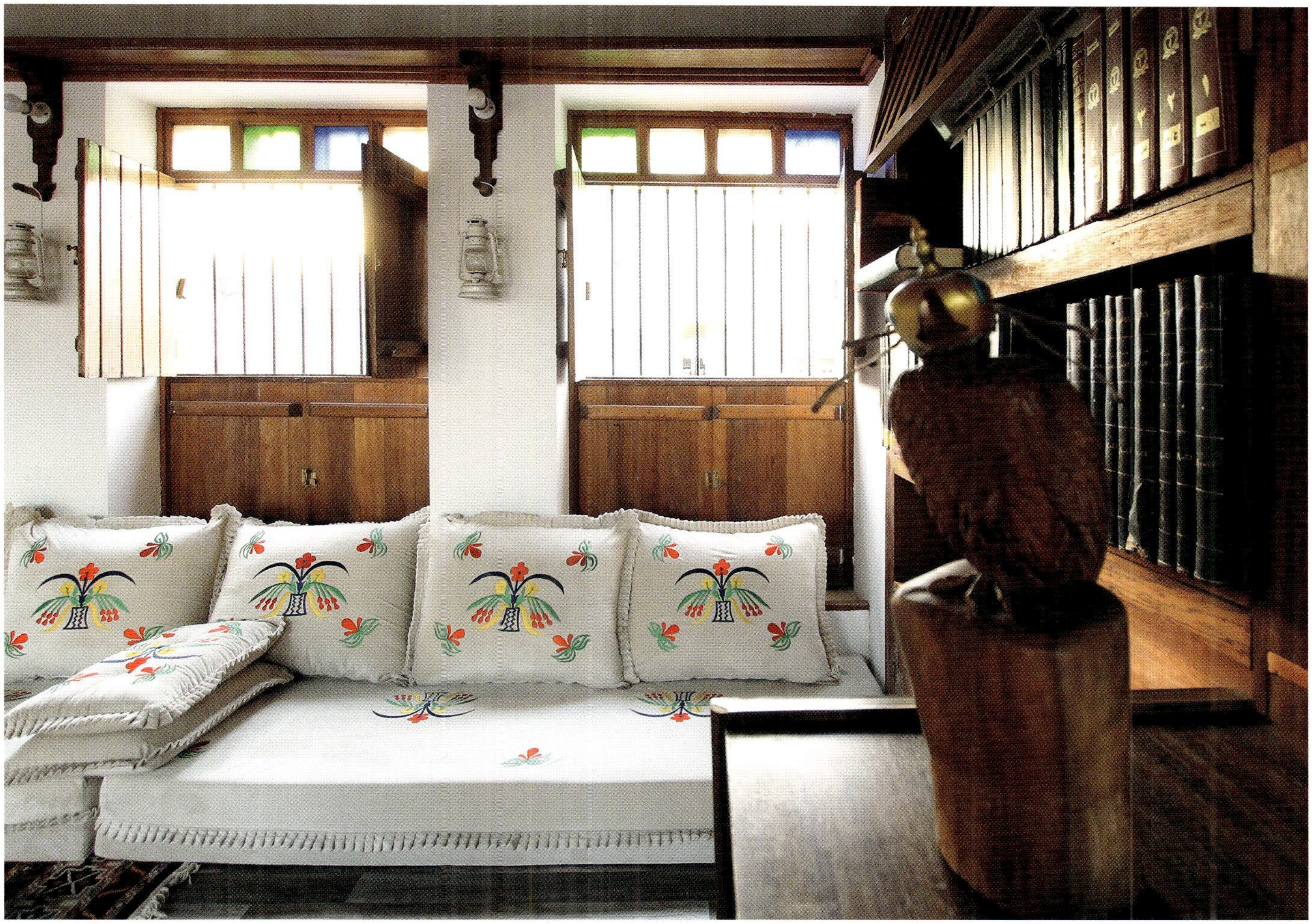

Above: The floor seating is more elevated than its traditional form and is slightly thicker for comfort.

Left-hand page: The entrance to the *maylis*. Colorful glass is frequently used at the top and allows dimmed light to enter when doors and window shutters are closed.

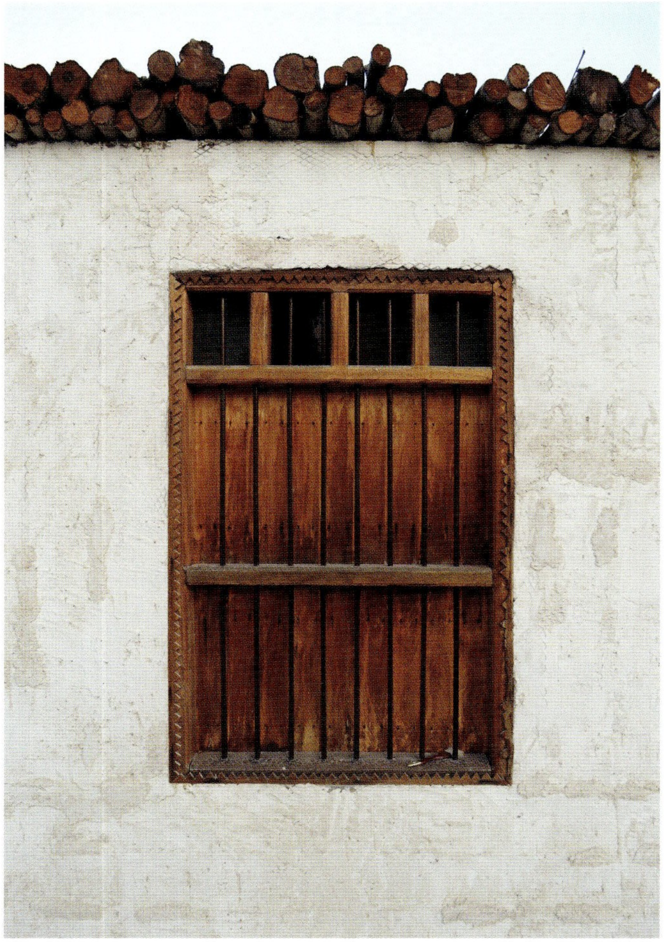

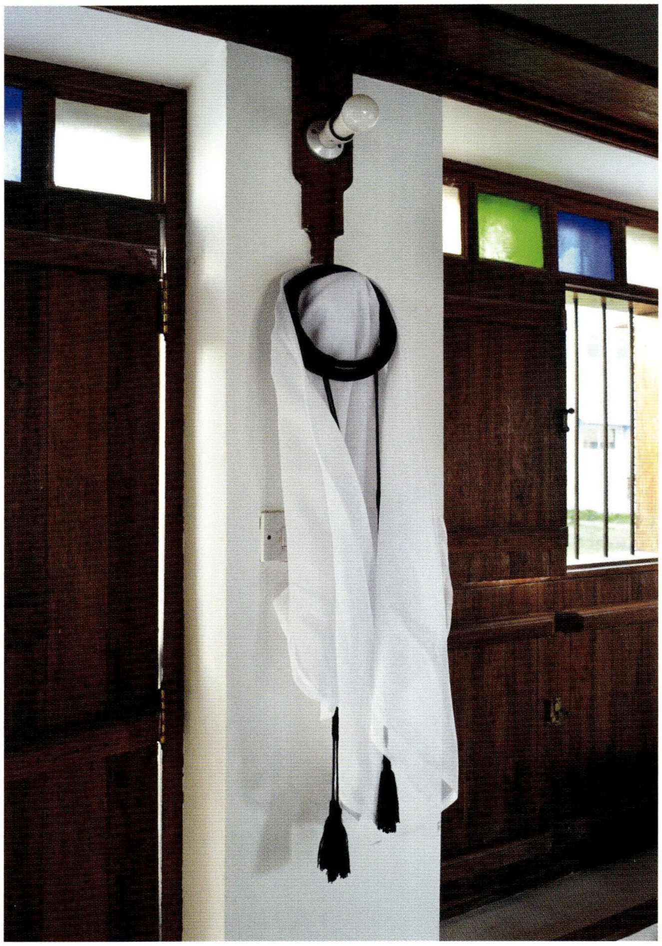

Above left: A traditional window—*dirīshah*—with a carved wooden frame and metal bars providing security.

Above right: Traditional men's headgear has been hung in the *maylis* as the owner goes about his day.

Right-hand page: A wooden bench fitted with traditional *sadw* is placed outside the fence of the *maylis* facing the street.

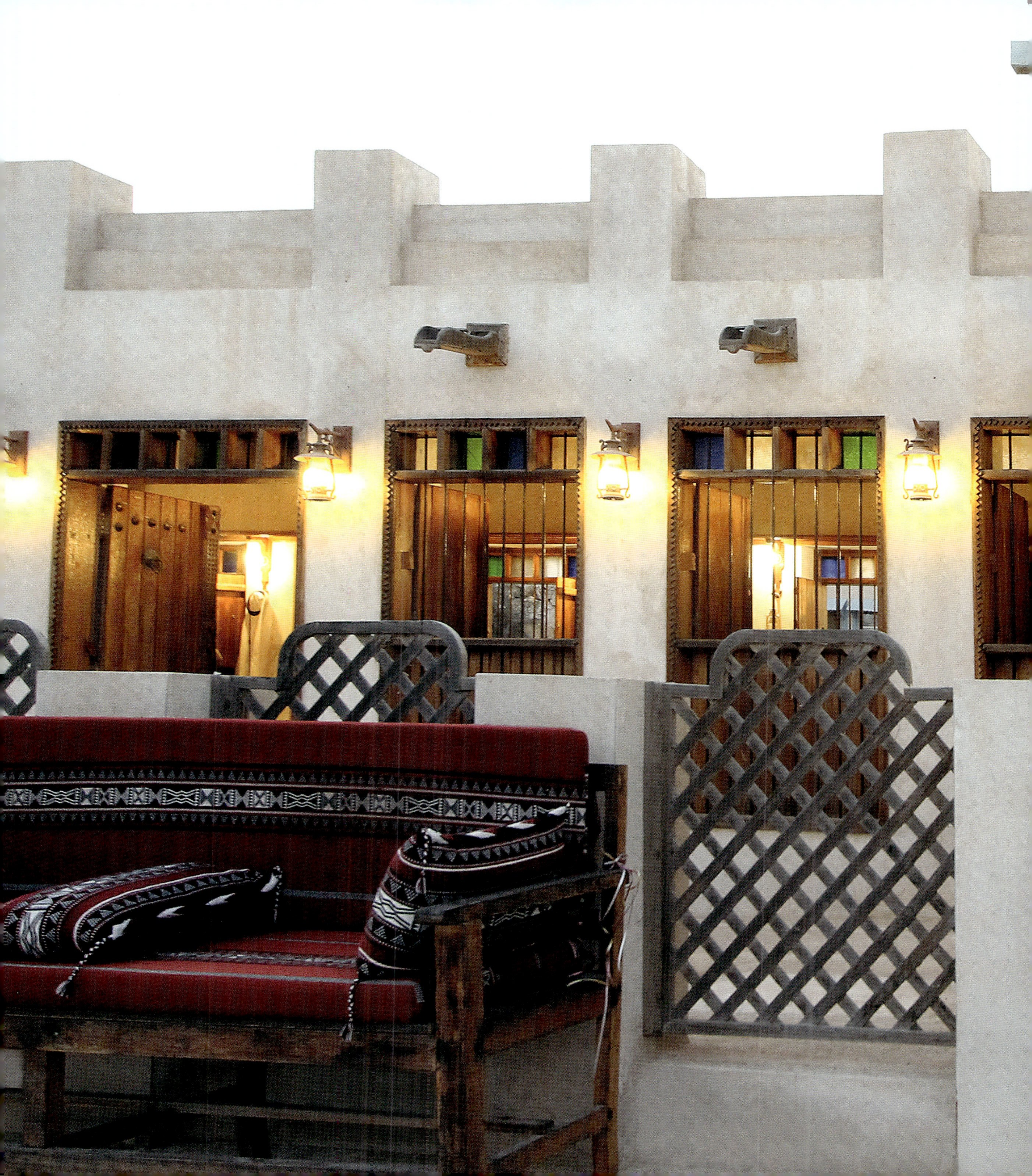

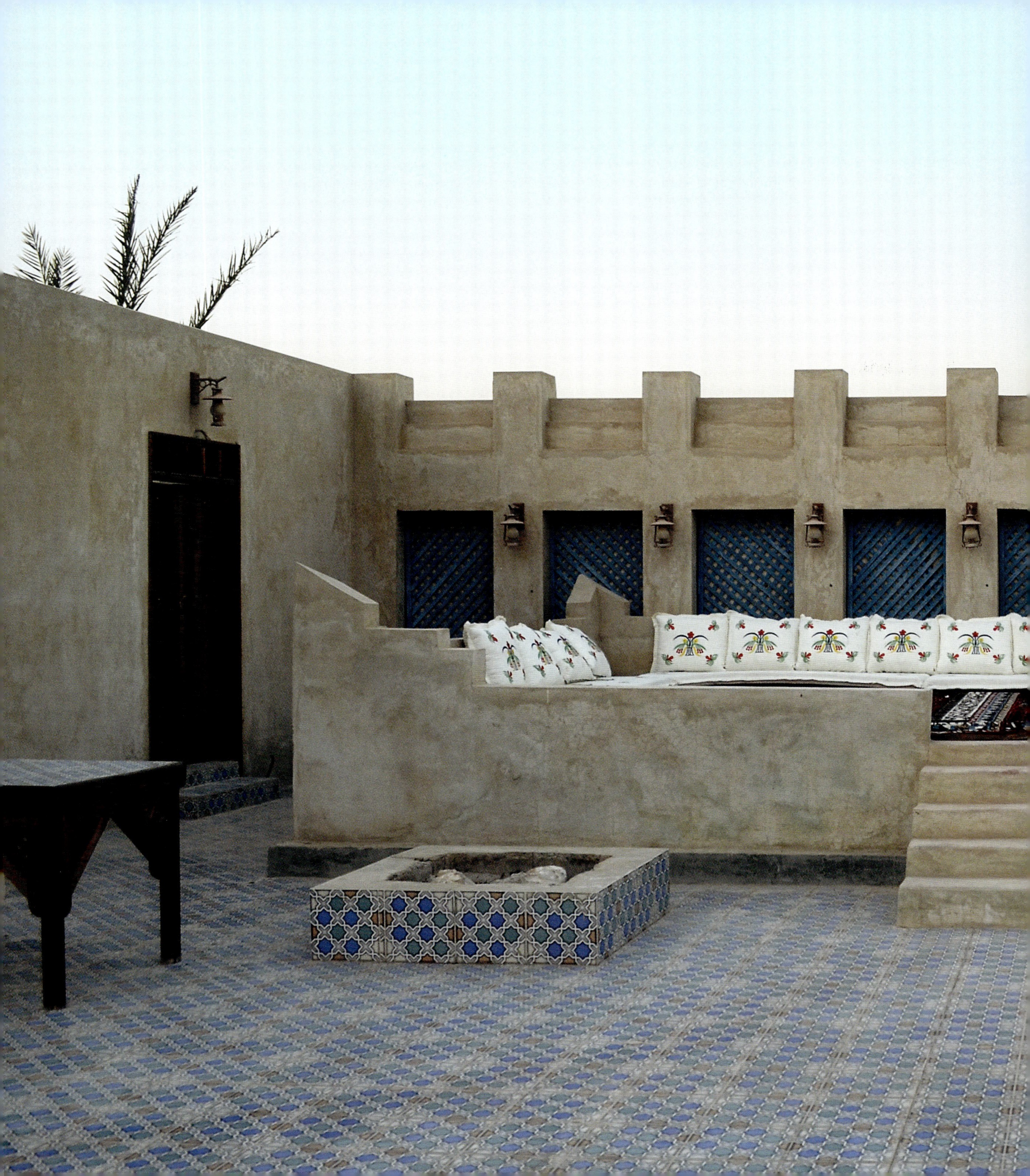

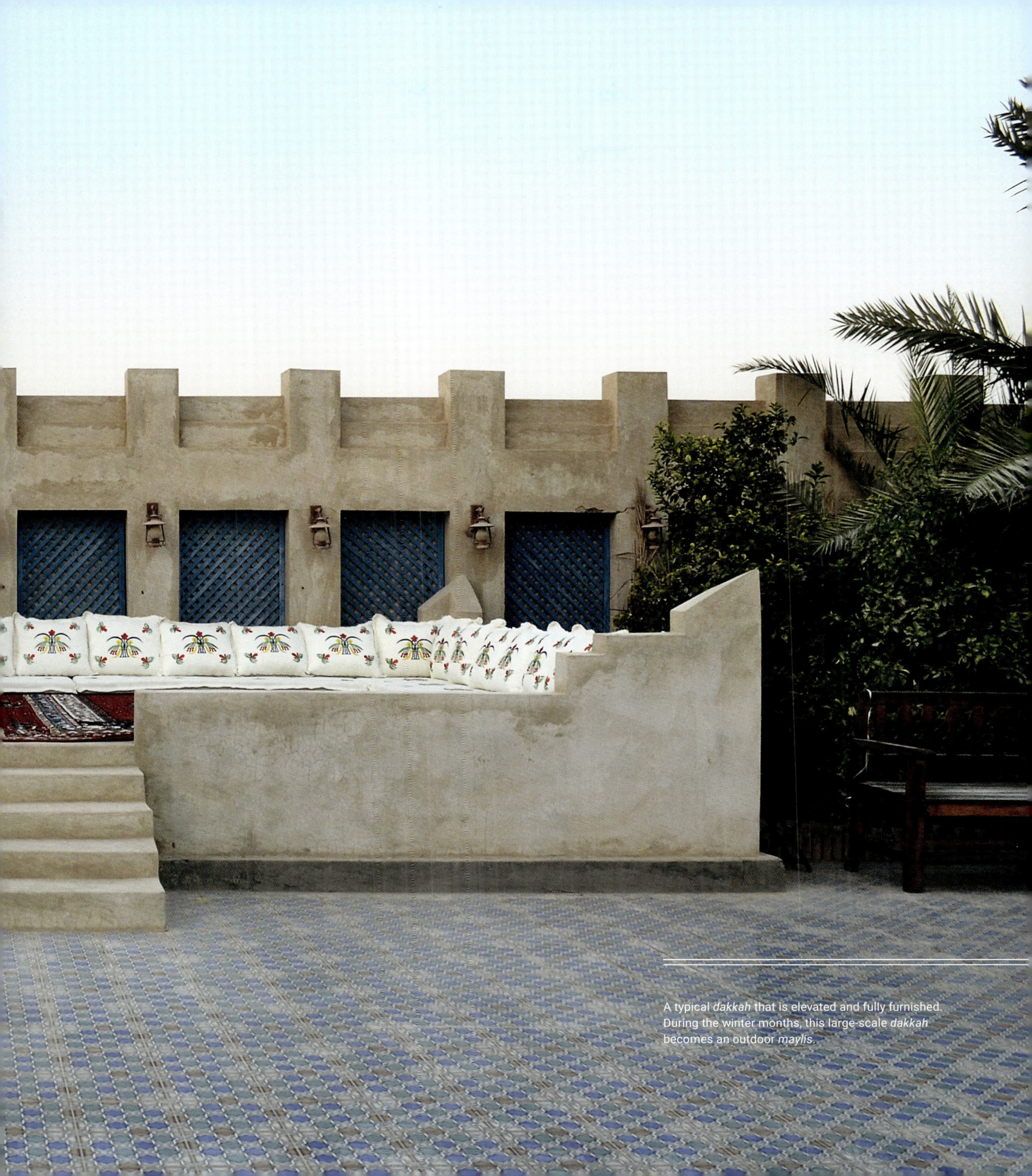

A typical *dakkah* that is elevated and fully furnished. During the winter months, this large-scale *dakkah* becomes an outdoor *maylis*.

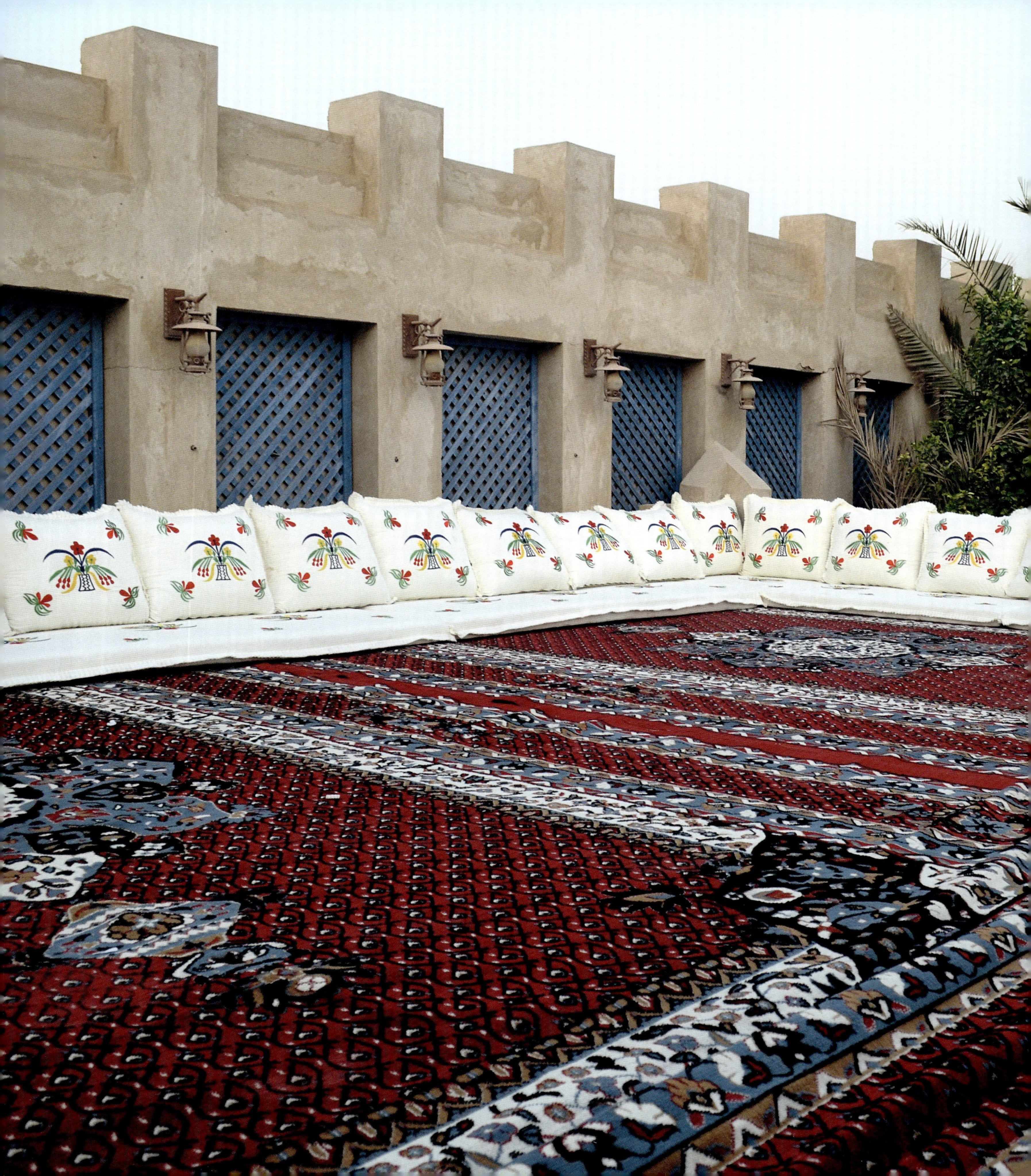

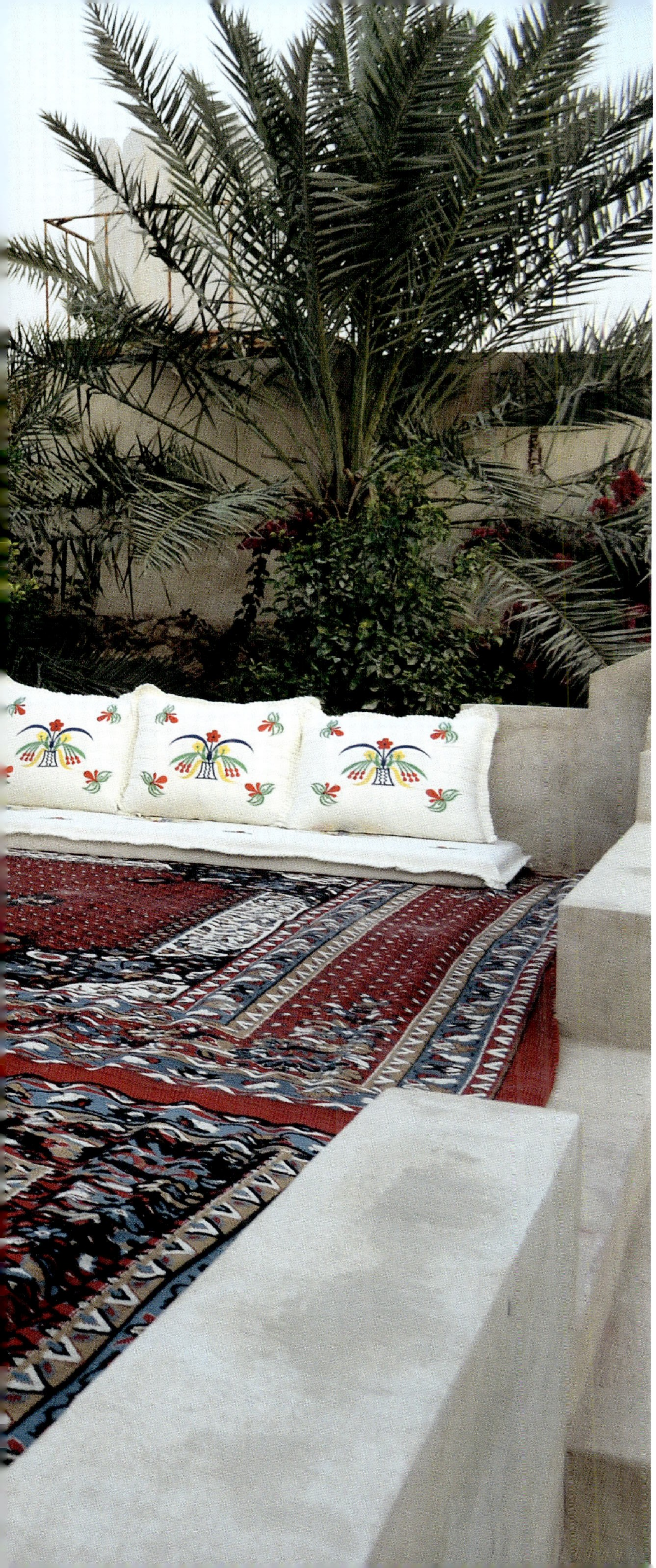

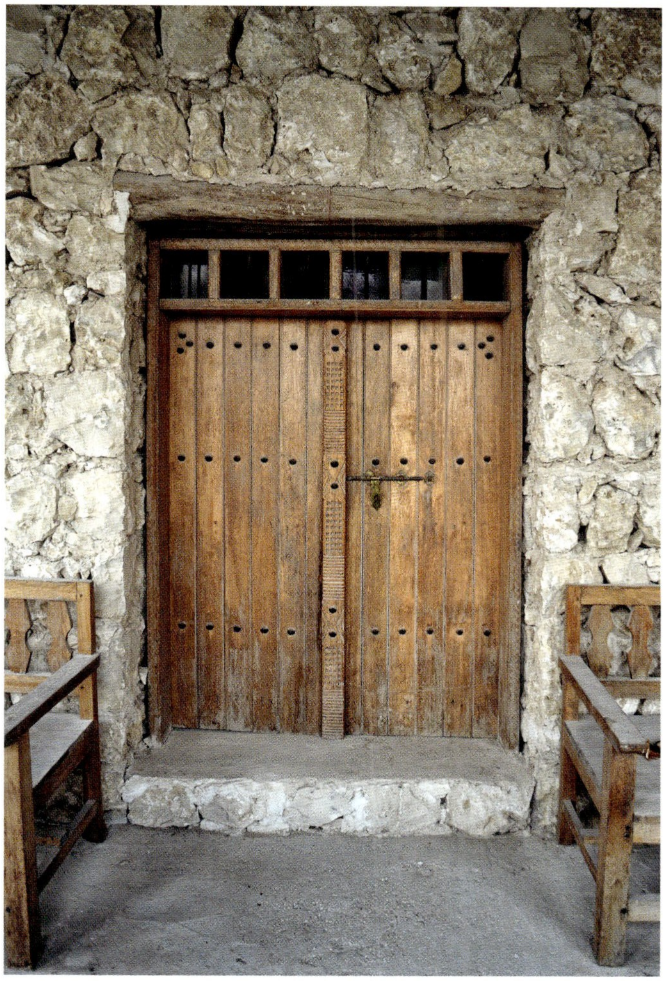

Above: Double wooden doors flanked by the wooden benches outside the falcons' mews.

Left: In the past, the floor of a large outdoor seating area like this one would have been covered with small seashells.

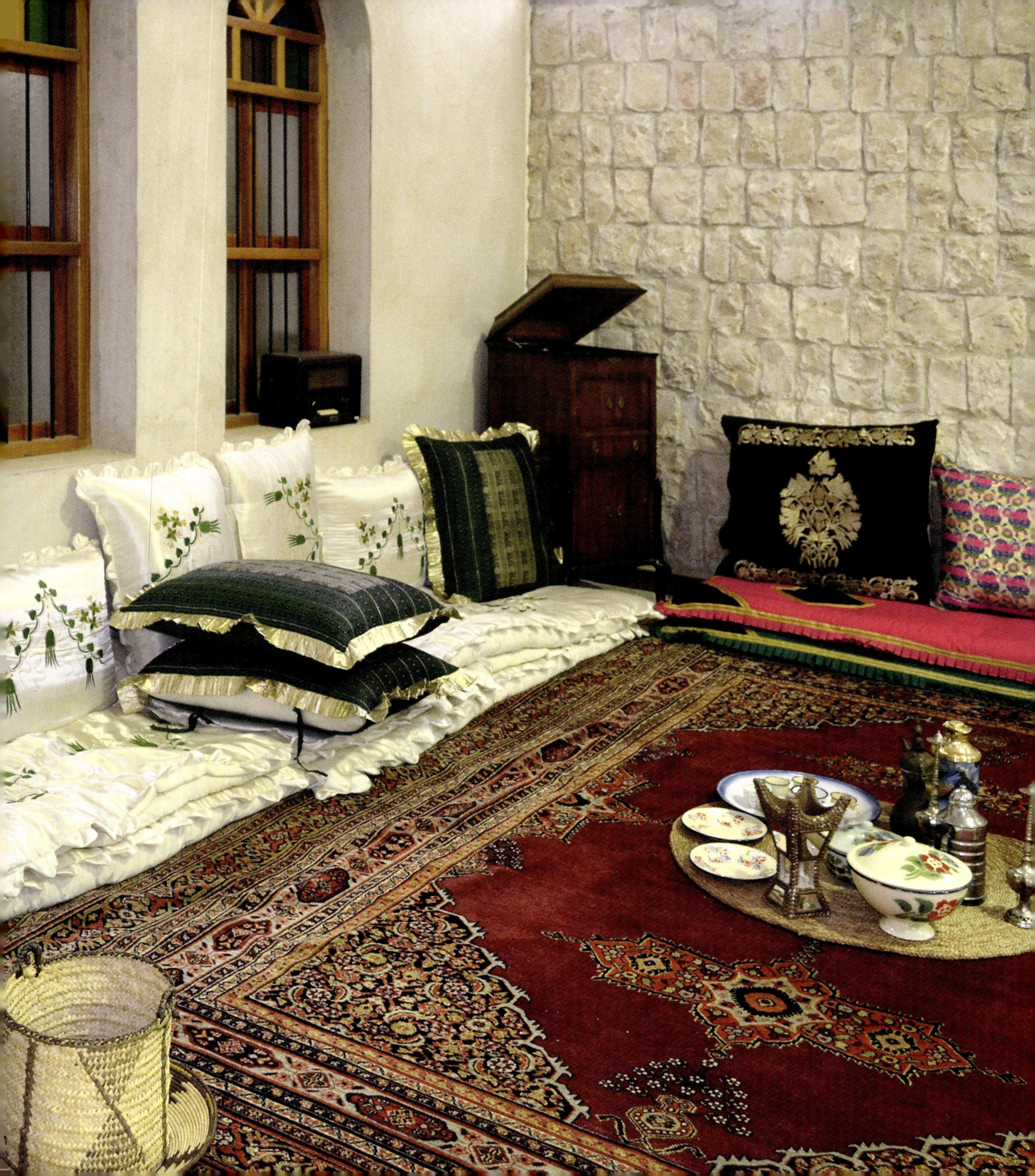

SHEIKH FAISAL BIN QASSIM MUSEUM

The Sheikh Faīsal bin Qassim Museum is located in the vicinity of Shahaniya Municipality, some 30 minutes' drive west of Doha. The unusual personal collection is estimated at around 15,000 artifacts from various periods and of various origins. One section of the museum is dedicated to the traditional Qatari lifestyle where various everyday objects are displayed in the context of an old house setting.

The notion of an old traditional house is conveyed by the use of *rūshanāt* and *darāīsh*. The common *darāīsh* in Qatar were rectangular with wooden shutters and stained glass; however here we see arched *darāīsh* that emerged with changes in the method of construction.

The artifacts displayed in this collection provide an excellent overview of the history of everyday life in Qatar in the past. Some of the items displayed are *tchoulah* (gasoline burner), *hisrān* (palm-frond mats), *jīfrān* (woven baskets), *gidw*, *yīḥal* (clay water pots) and *raḥāt* (grinders). The *raḥāt* were mostly used to grind flour and were an essential element of every Qatari household.

Apart from the kitchen items, the private living quarters are also recreated in the museum. There is a *kurfāyah* which is inspired by an Indian-style bed. The frame and structure are made from the rachis of palm-tree leaves. Alongside the bed displayed here is a dressing table of an affluent Qatari woman where she would typically keep her jewelry, perfumes, and *marash* with rose water.

The collection displays a set of traditional *dawāshig*, *masānid* and *sadw* carpets accompanied by the features of the welcoming culture of Qataris where *gahwa* and food is offered in the *maylis* at all times.

Interestingly, the central area of the exhibition space is occupied by old, traditional boats known as *sanābīk*, which were used for pearling and trading in Qatar during the pre-oil period. One of the *sanābīk* displays a typical boat set-up of the designated area where *nawākhzah* would sit as they had higher ranks than the divers and other crew members.

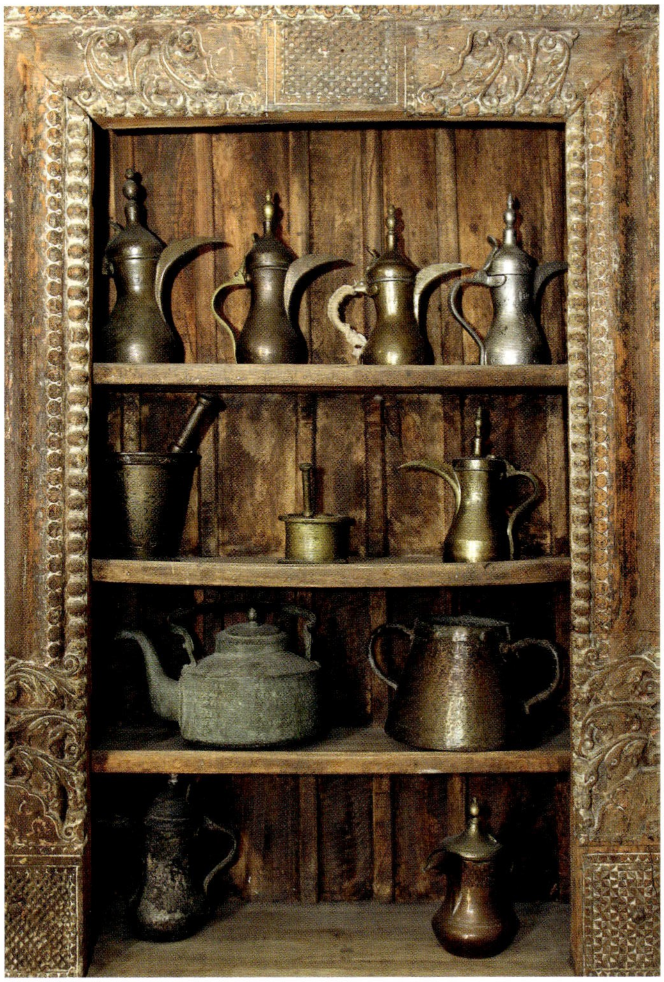

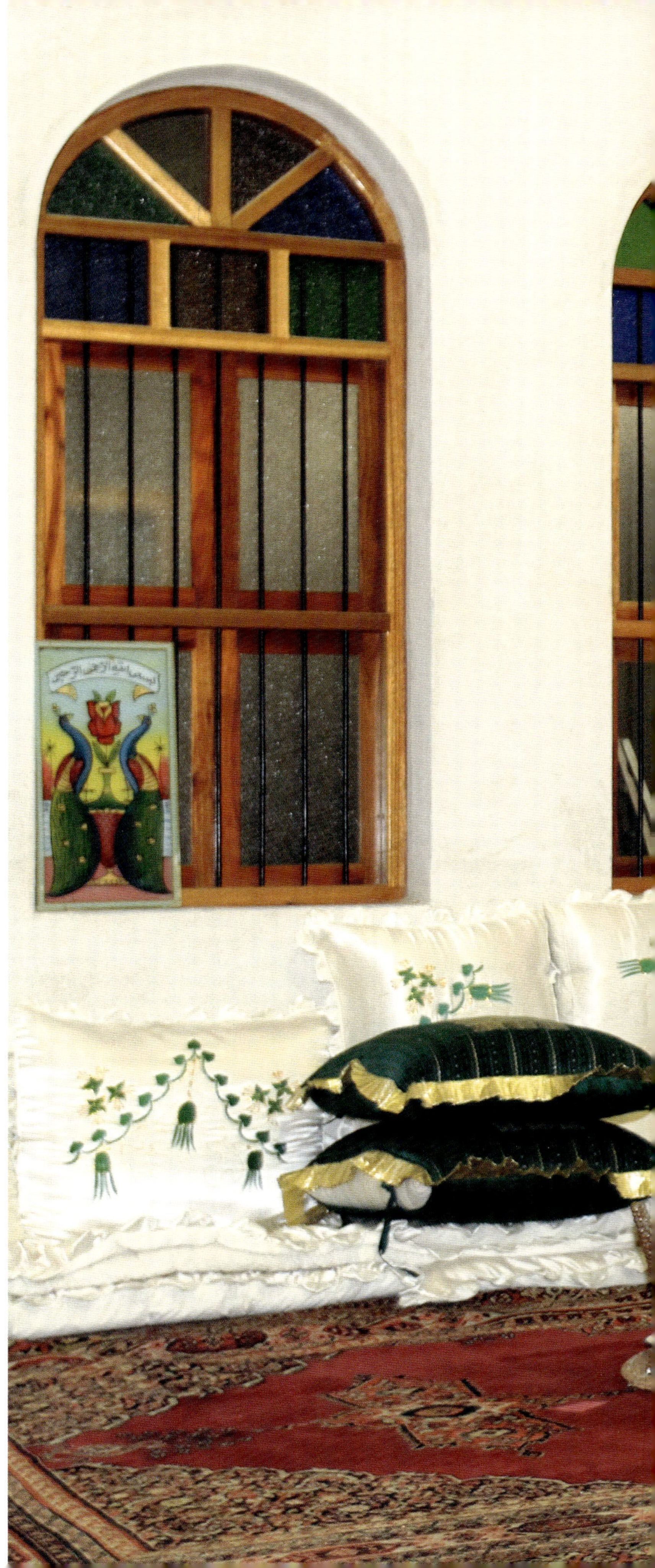

Above: In the Sheikh Faisal bin Qassim Museum, actual exhibition objects, in this instance a carved wooden cabinet, are frequently used as display cases.

Right: This exhibit shows an inner living room and a *maylis* for a family gathering and dining. A typical smaller living room is placed within the context of the museum's much larger exhibition space.

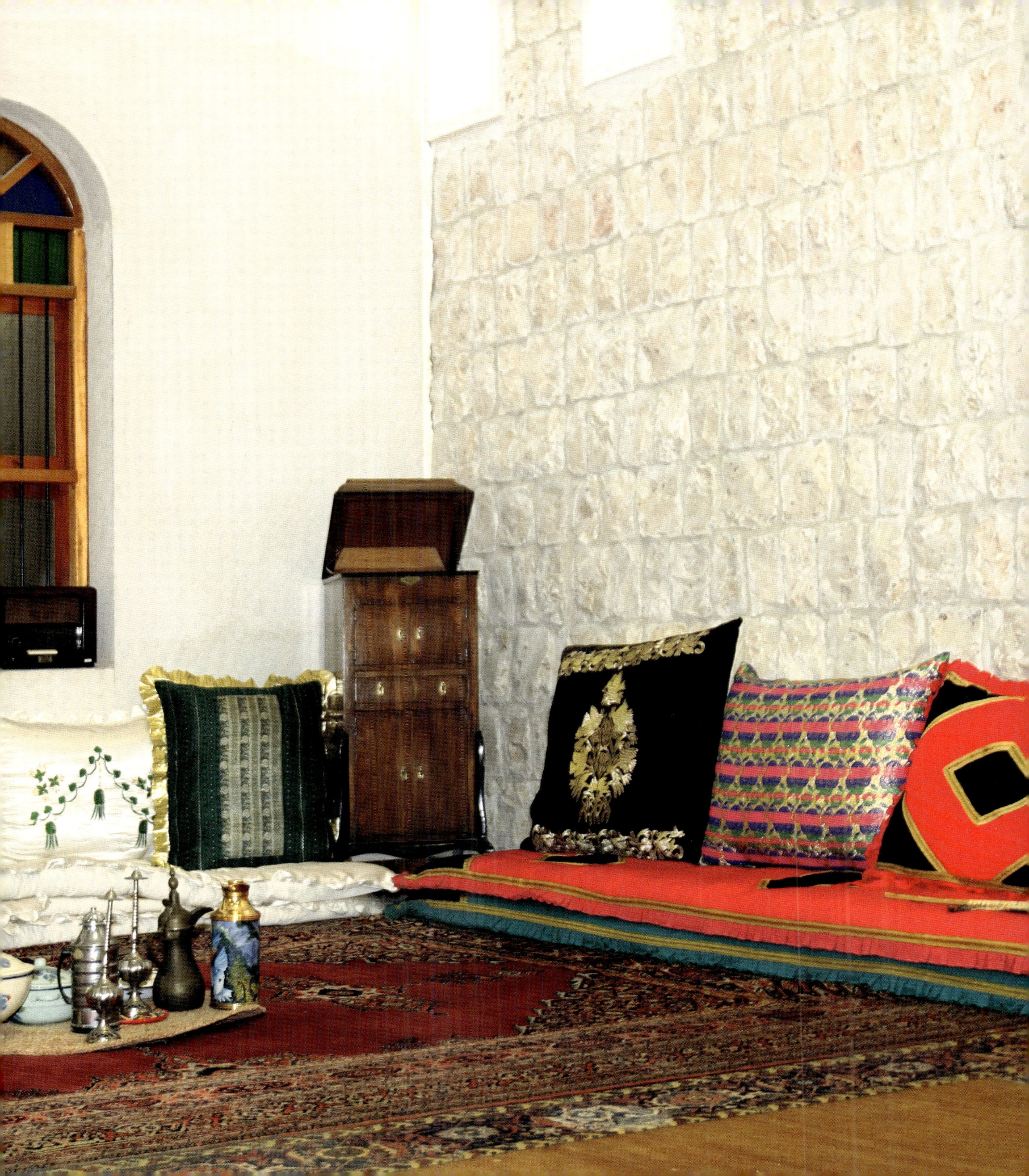

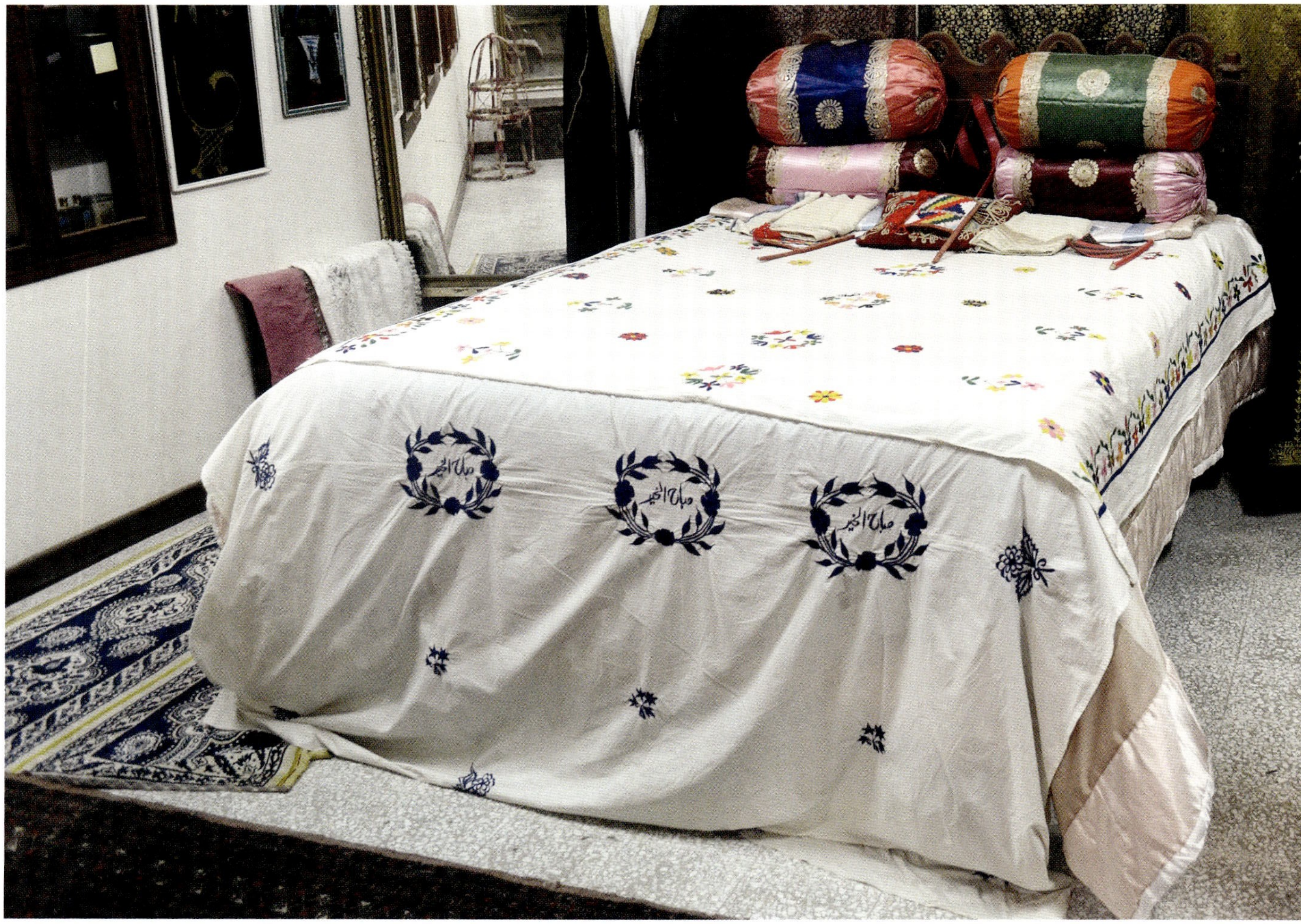

Above: This dedicated space in the Sheikh Faisal bin Qassim Museum shows a master bedroom featuring embroidered bedding, silk textile wall coverings, woollen carpets, carved wooden cabinets and a mirror.

Right-hand page: An eclectic collection of kitchenware and various photographs.

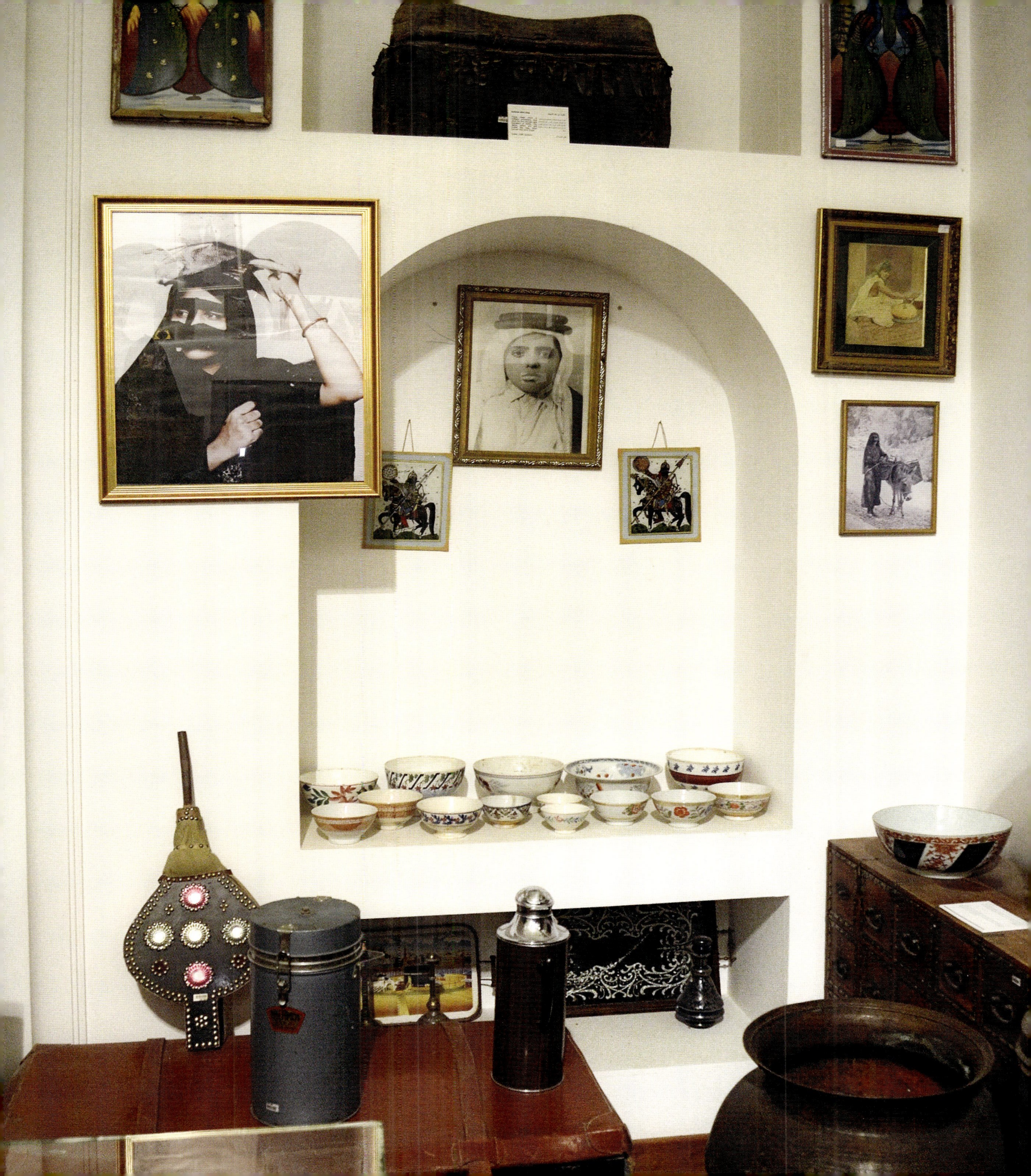

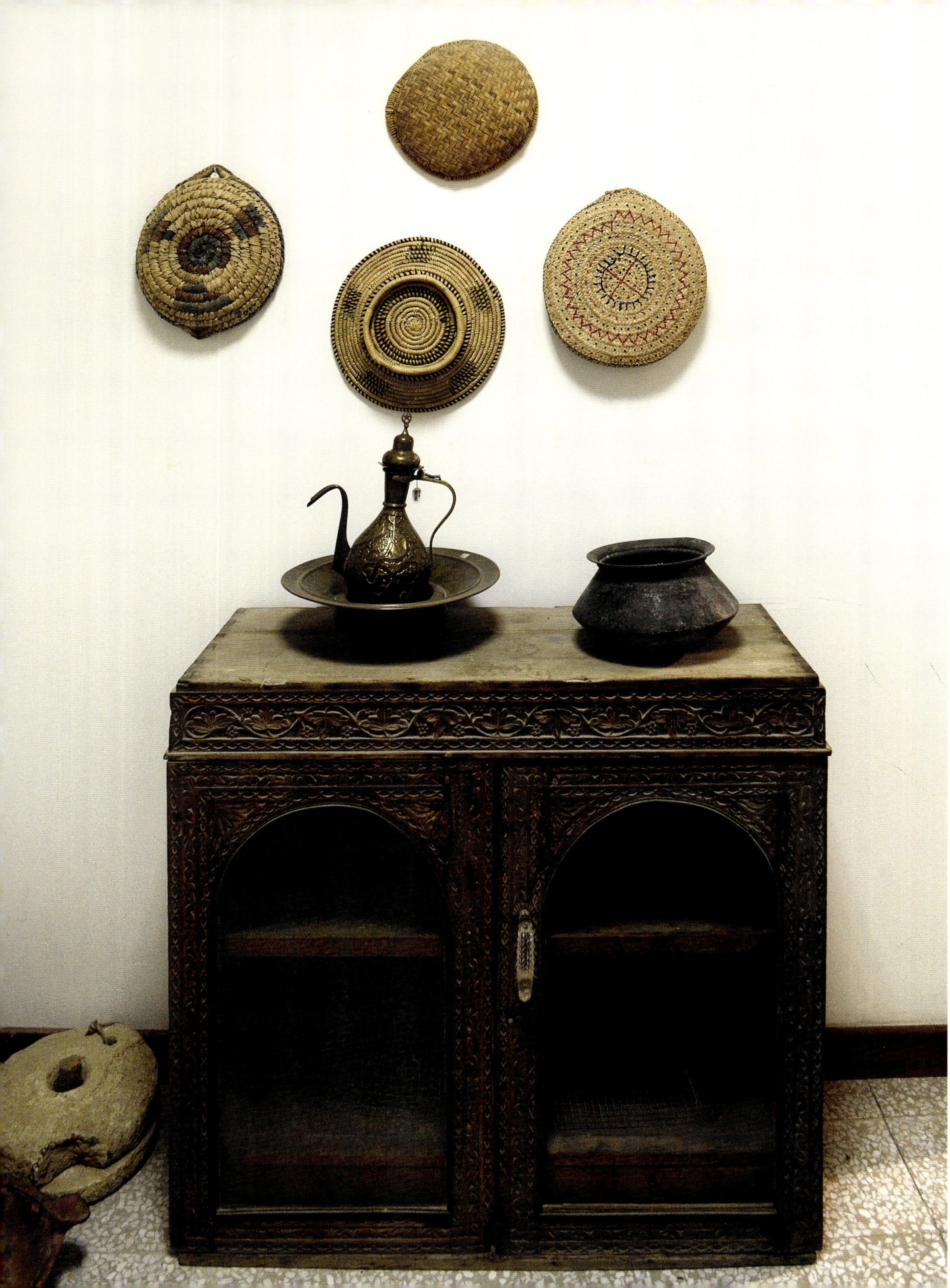

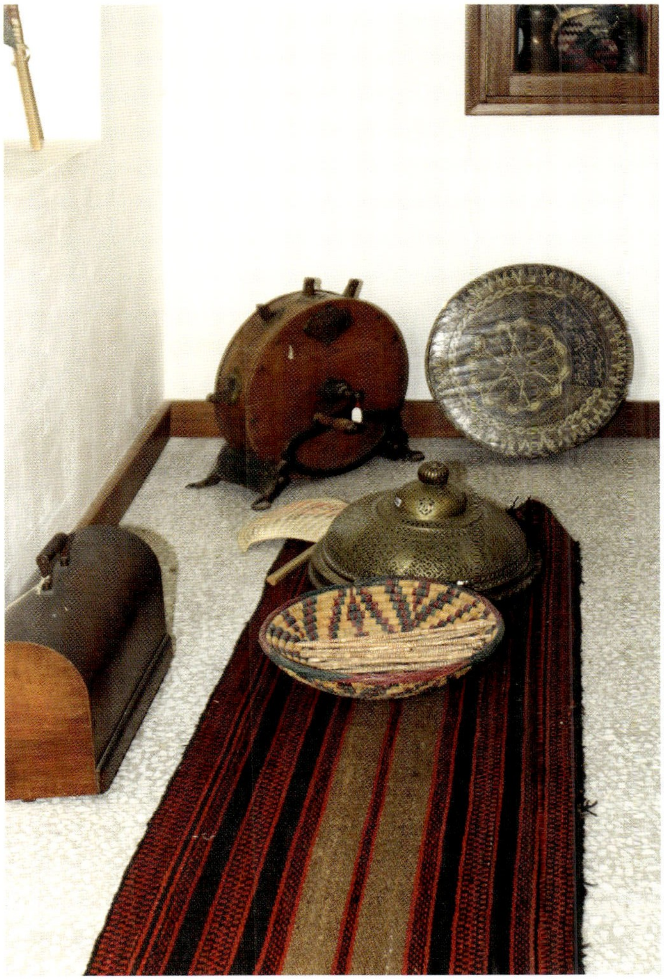

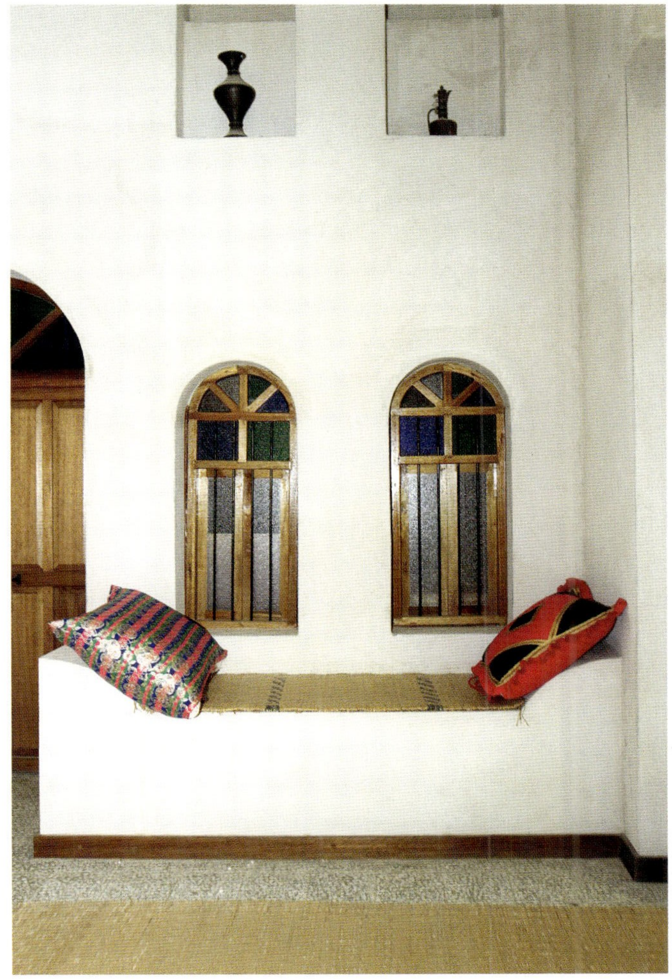

Above left: The Sheikh Faisal bin Qassim Museum's permanent exhibition includes a large personal collection. In a few instances non-related everyday objects are exhibited together. Although they do not tell a continuous story, individually they are a valuable source of information relating to the traditional way of living.

Above right: Over time, *dakkah* became a fixed element of many traditional Qatari houses. The elevated outdoor seating would usually be placed outside the living quarters and against the boundary wall.

Left-hand page: Copper kitchenware and *sufar* are exhibited on the carved wooden chest.

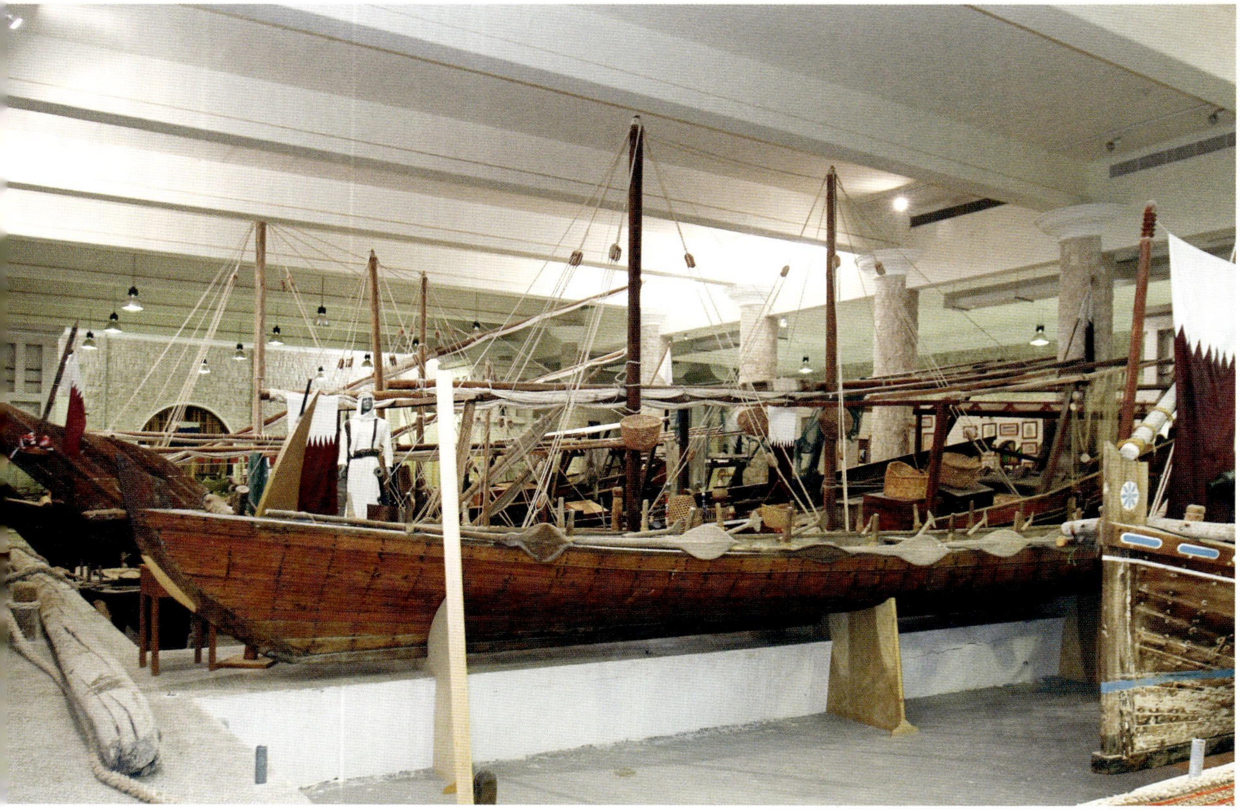

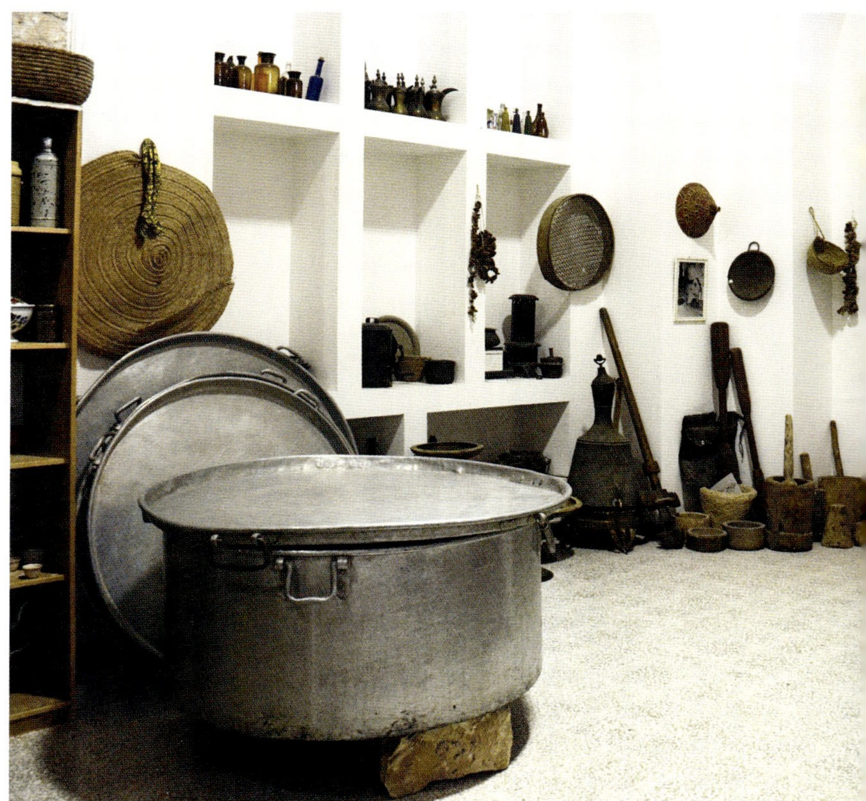

Above: A collection of Qatari boats.

Right: A large collection of traditional kitchenware collected over decades. Very large pots are used for preparing food for feasts and celebrations.

Far right: Serving Arabic coffee is a symbol of hospitality in the region. Here we see a selection of *dilāl*, coffee pots, on display alongside various manually operated grinders.

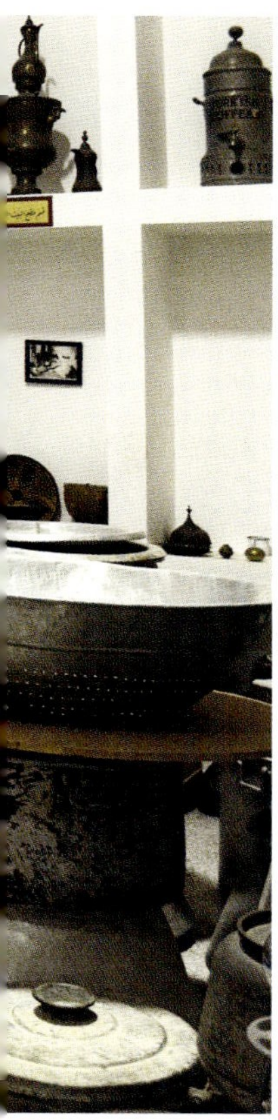

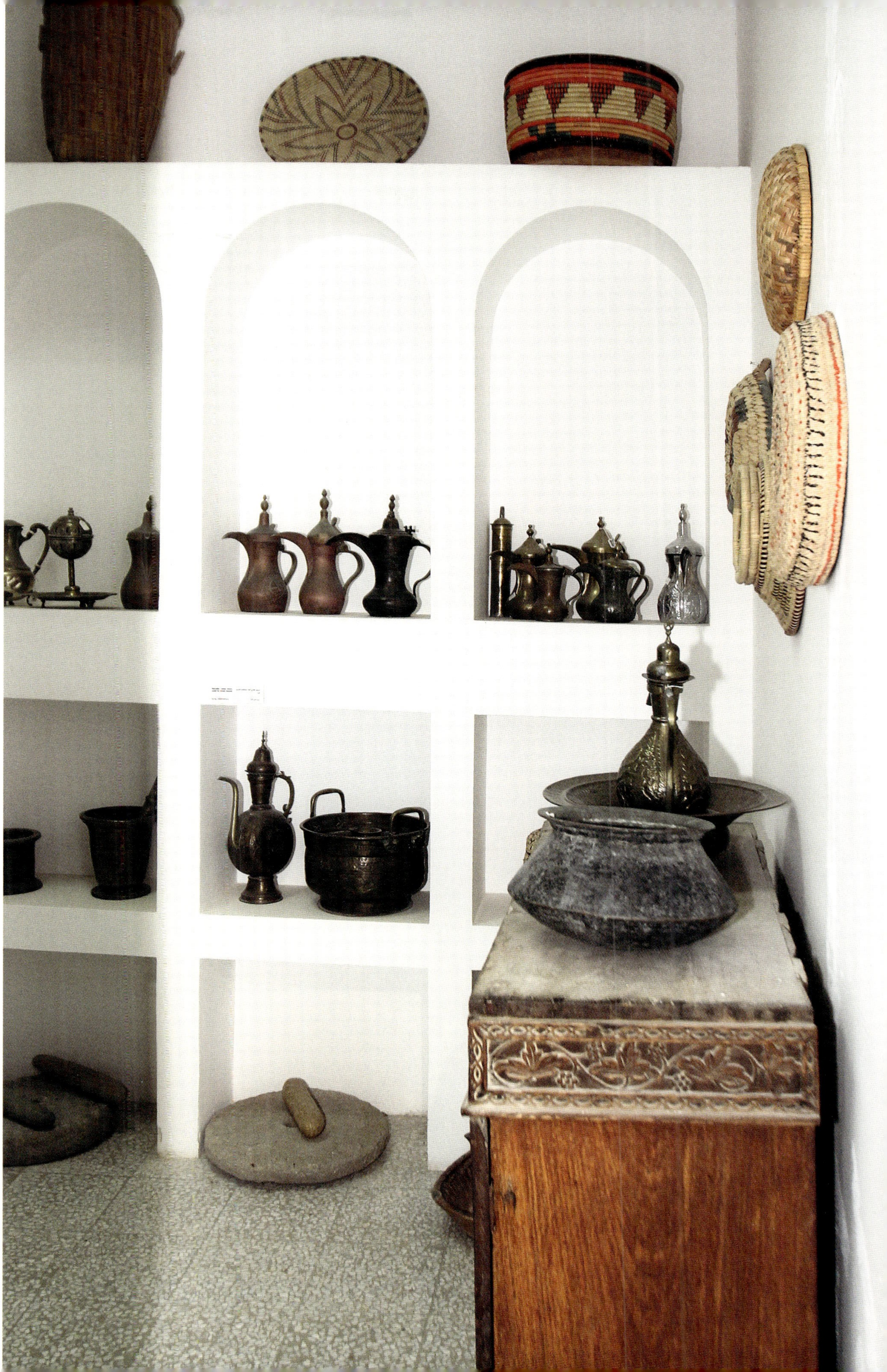

TRANSITIONAL

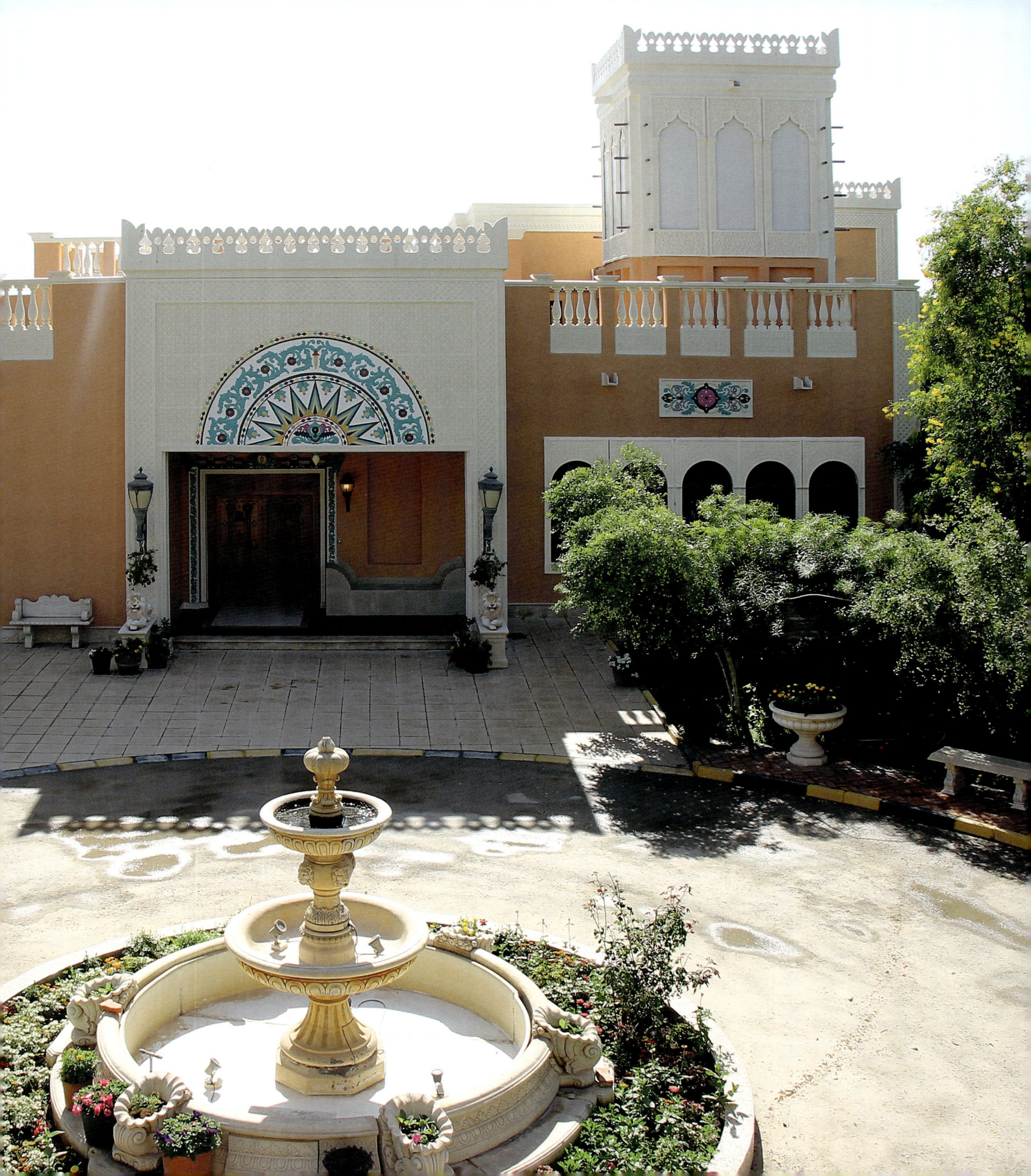

ALFARDAN TRADITIONAL HOUSE

The Traditional House, as the owner refers to it, is part of a much larger functioning family farm. Arab Engineering Bureau (AEB) was commissioned by the owner to design the luxurious traditional courtyard house.

A large wooden gate separates the traditional house from the rest of the property. It is intricately carved and does not conform with local traditions. The design of the relief of the gate can be traced back to the 1960s when architects from the other Middle Eastern countries started to practice in Qatar. These architects influenced the architecture in Qatar by presenting the market with elements that were common to their own home countries. Similarly, we see these patterns in Sheikh Mohammad Bin Hamad's *maylis* near the Amiri Diwan in the Al Bidda area in Doha. These gates were recycled by transferring them from another of the owner's properties; in the past only affluent families could afford such imported high-quality materials.

The interior of the house reflects a wealthy merchant's house from the past. It echoes the distinctive ambience of a well-travelled and affluent individual. The furnishings, carpets, and decorative elements look as if they were brought in from other countries by merchant seamen. For instance, the chandeliers seem to have come from one place while the tables and tapestries seem to have come from another. Some furnishings and decorative features required skilled craftsmen, which has rendered them expensive as well. For example, the patterned cornices were not a feature of a common Qatari traditional house.

The house creates a harmonious blend of many luxurious Middle Eastern styles under the roof of a traditional Arabic house with vernacular Qatari elements like the *danāshil* and *rūshanāt*.

The furnishing of the house incorporates items that were much coveted in the mid-twentieth century, such as the sideboards, cabinets, and doors that are all decorated using brass rivets, inspired by the *ṣandūq imbaīyt*.

The main dining hall and *maylis* are located on either side of the entrance doors and straight ahead is the main reception area. In evidence here are design trends of a specific period of the twentieth century in Qatar: peacock mirrors and wooden surfaces inlaid with hand-painted glass and tiles. The tables are decorated with tiles, a popular trend that grew over the years in Qatari houses as Qatari families started being able to afford such high-end items. Some of these elements have been lost over time, and now we are witnessing a trend where older people commission furniture designers to produce this style of table for its nostalgic value. The colorful peacocks and decorative tiles represented a whimsical element for the locals who lived in the neutral environment of Qatar.

Off the reception area are the master bedroom, which has a functioning wind tower, and two smaller bedrooms. Here, the beds with posts, *kūrāfi*, are influenced by designs seen in Zanzibar and India. They are elevated to allow for additional storage underneath, and are adorned in luxurious brocade.

While this is a fully functional house, it is not used by the owner as a place of residence, but rather as the visitors' center for his guests who are offered an opportunity to experience a rather different traditional Qatari setting.

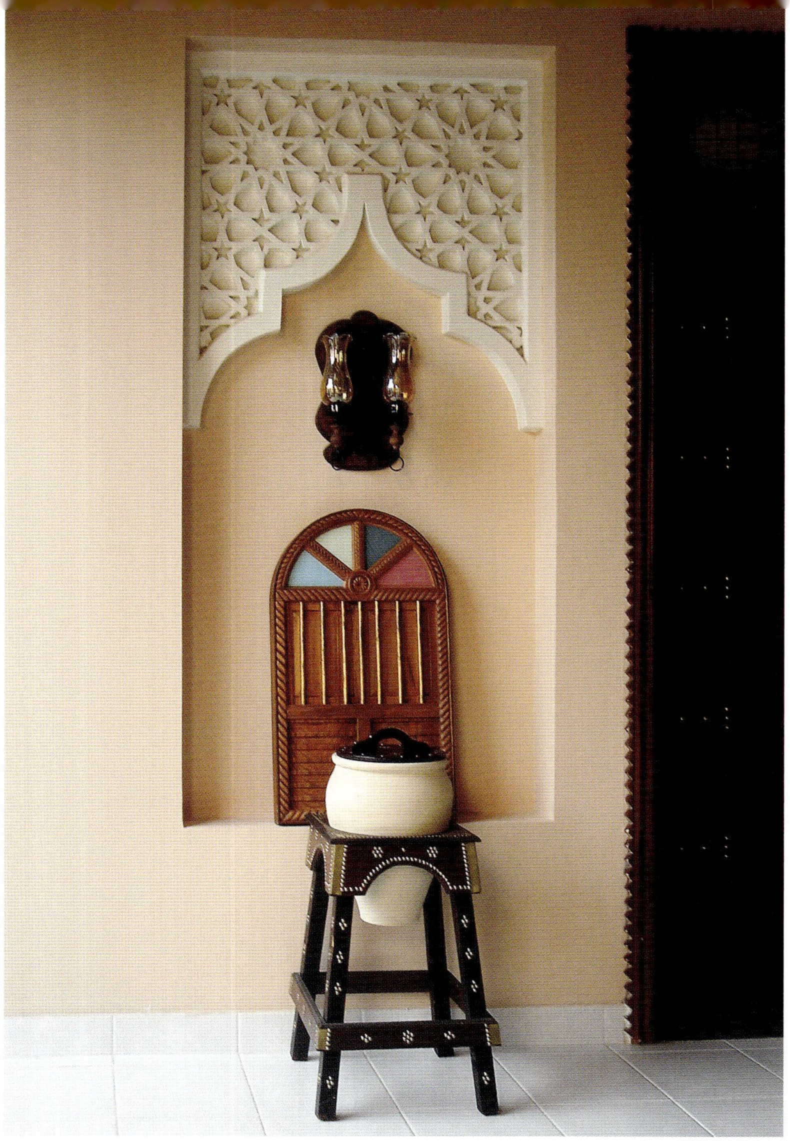

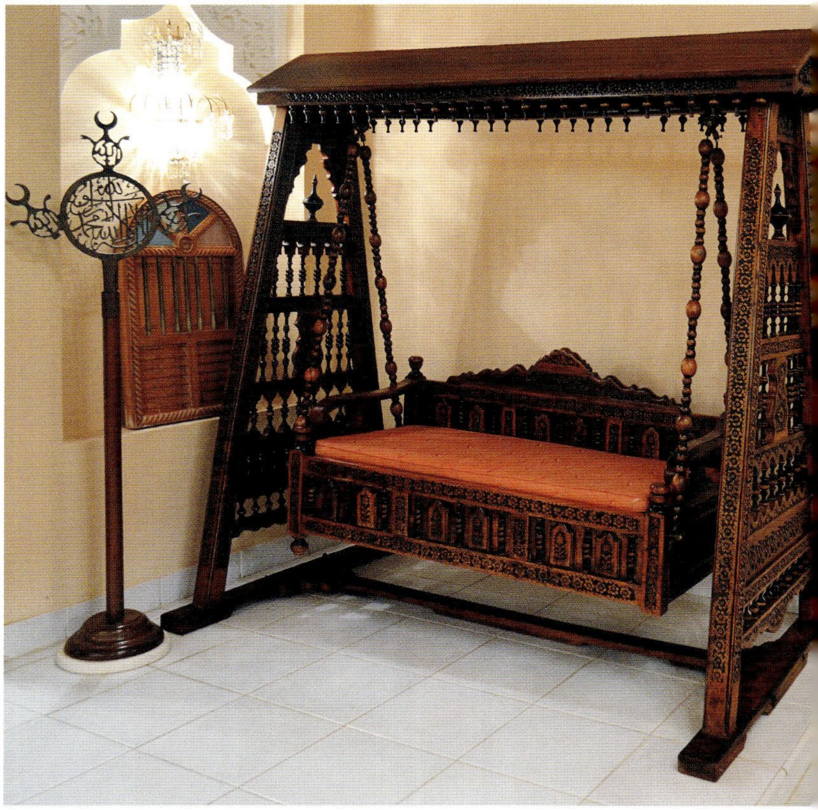

Above: The *yīḥlah* is elevated on a wooden structure that is decorated, unlike the more commonly found traditional simple wooden structure.

Right: An Indian style swing that recalls the trading tradition between Doha and Mumbai.

Right-hand page: The inner *ḥawsh* has a pergola which is an element foreign to the local design.

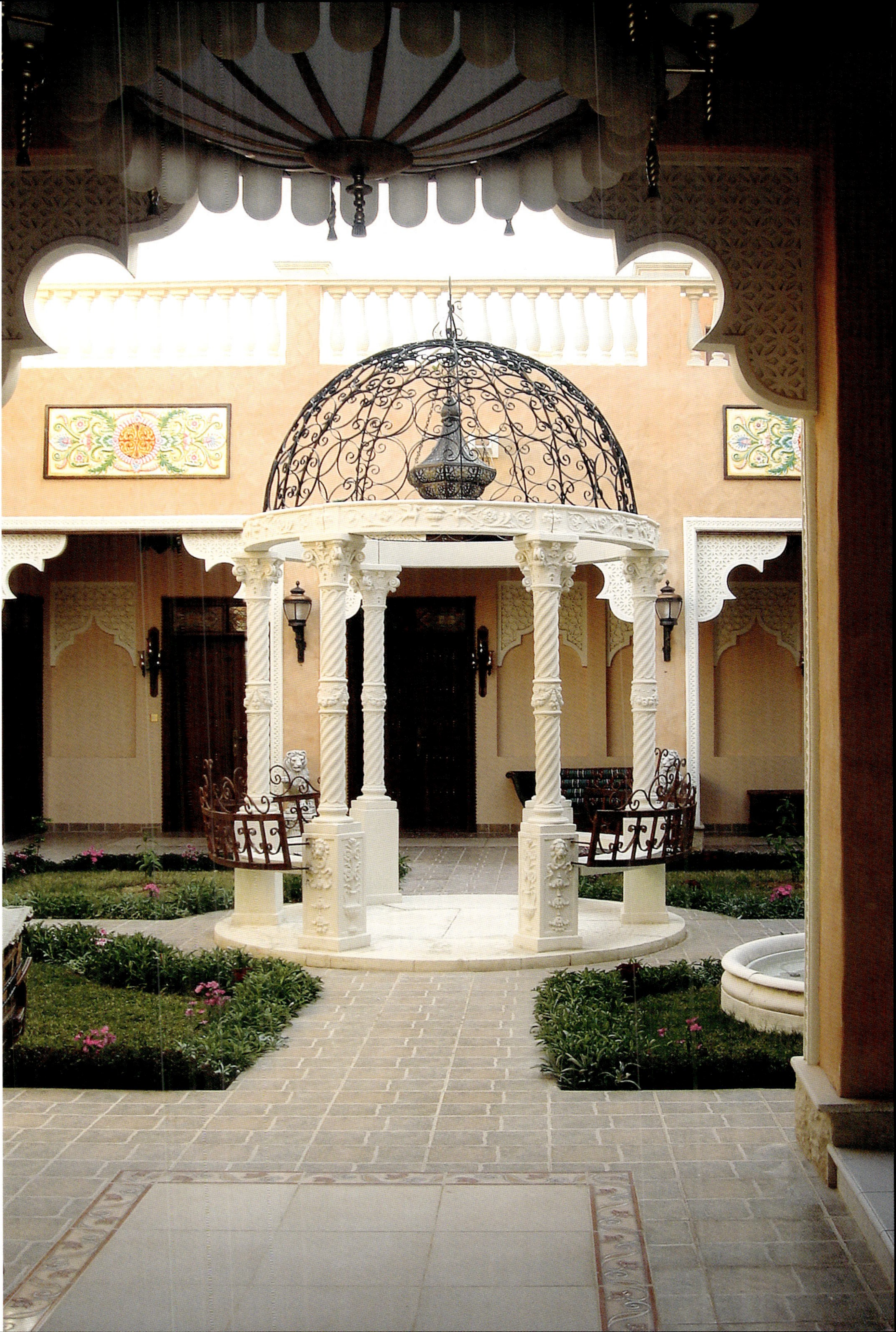

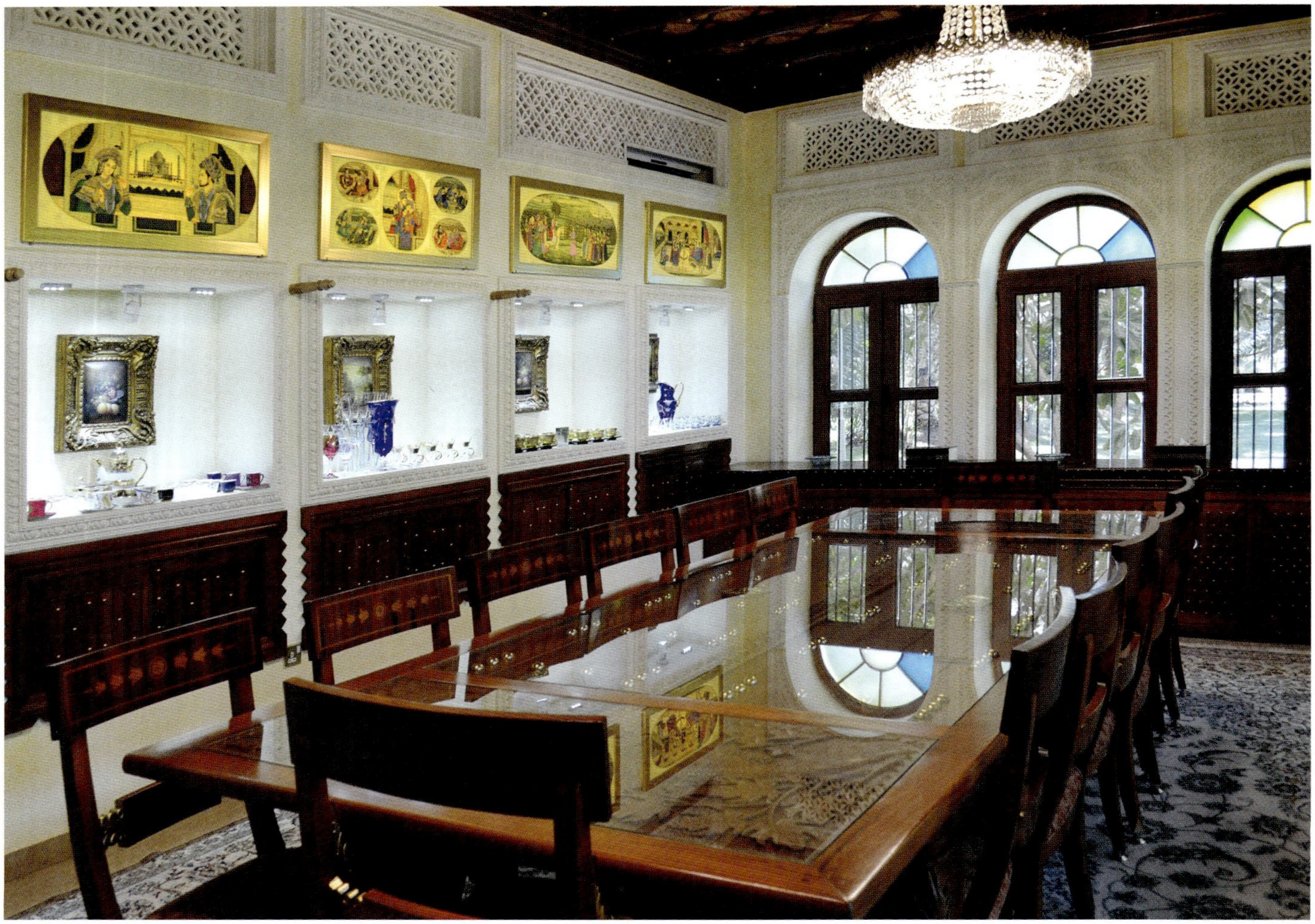

Above: The formal dining room features a unique collection of glassware. In addition to the traditional gypsum patterned panels, which in this instance are functional rather than decorative as they conceal the air-conditioning units, the room is adorned with intricate wooden paneling and back-lit glass paintings.

Right-hand page: The house showcases a selection of items collected by the owner while traveling for trade within the region. The result is a very fine example of a merchant's house from the past century.

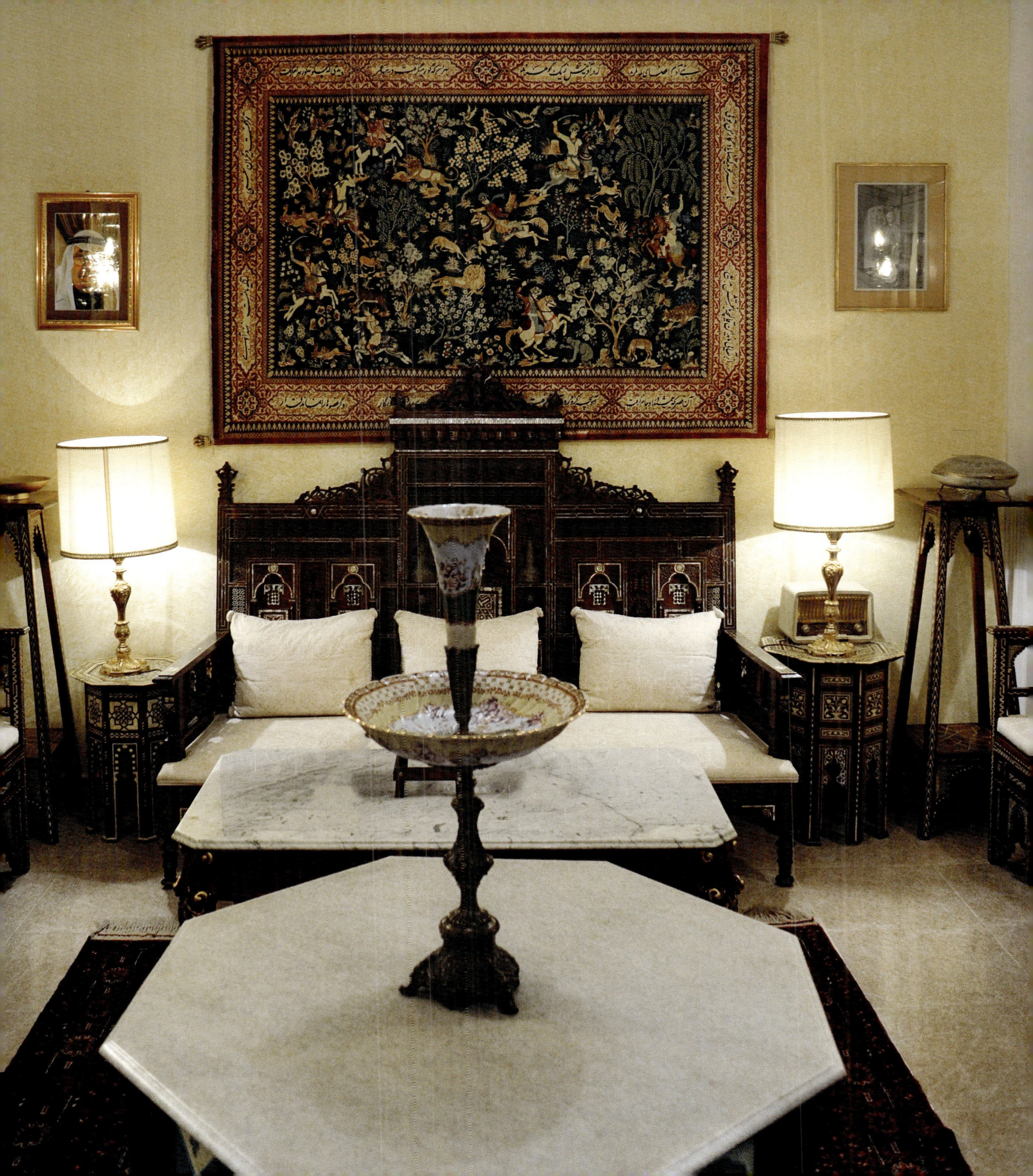

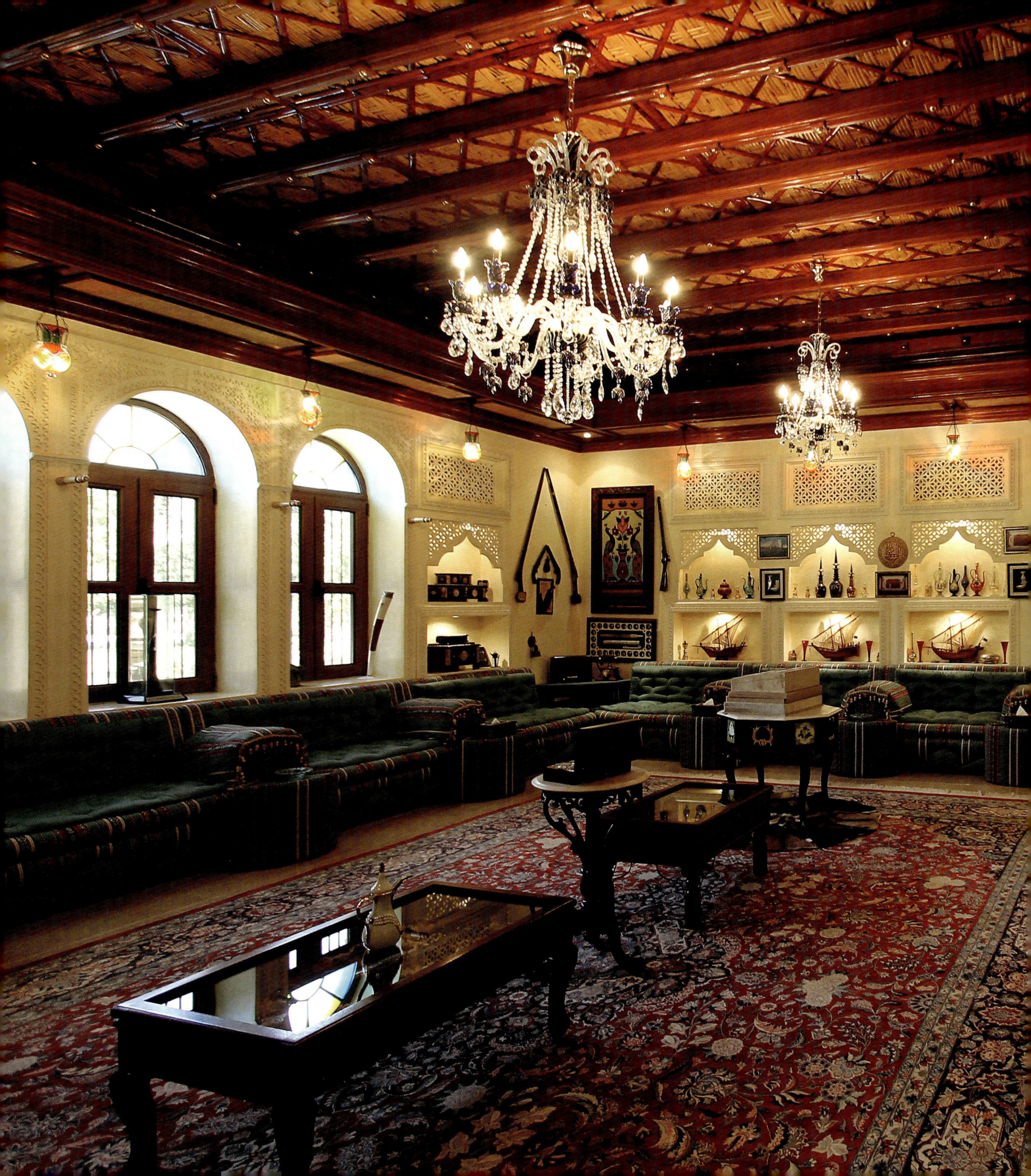

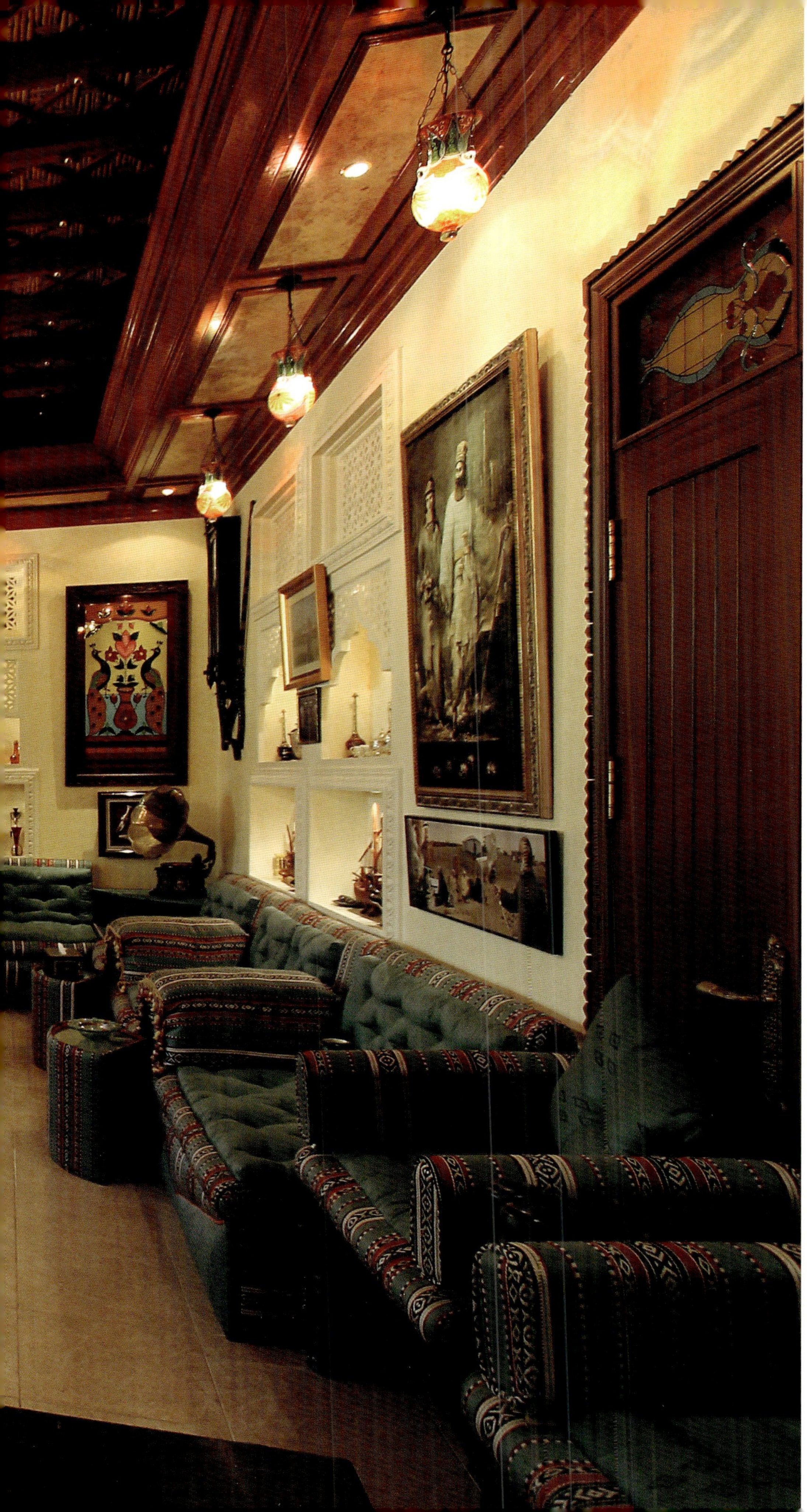

The formal *maylis* is furnished with elevated seating upholstered in green *sadw* fabric. A small private collection of various everyday items is also shown.

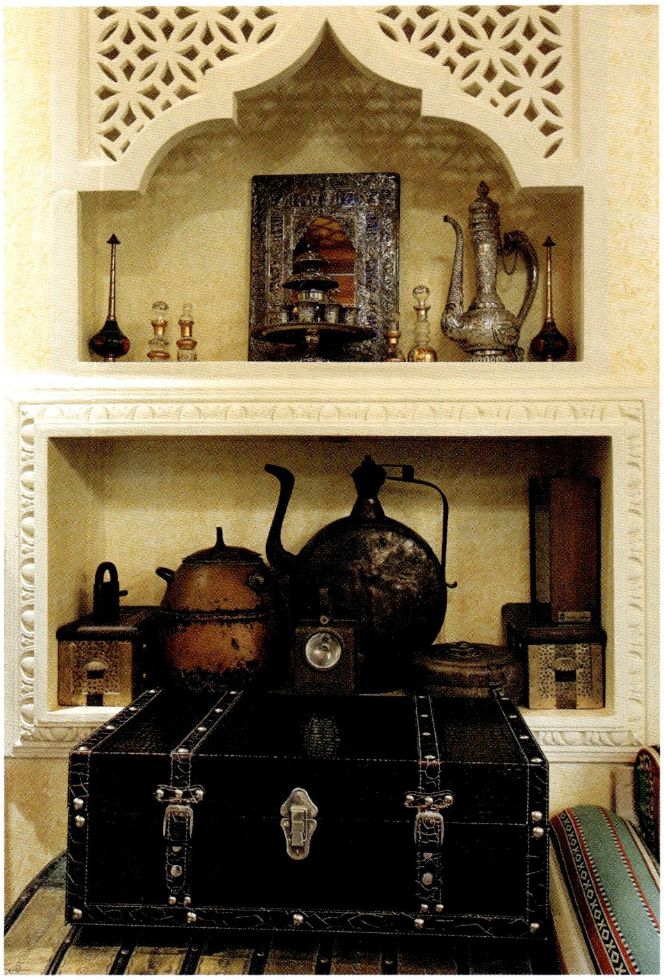

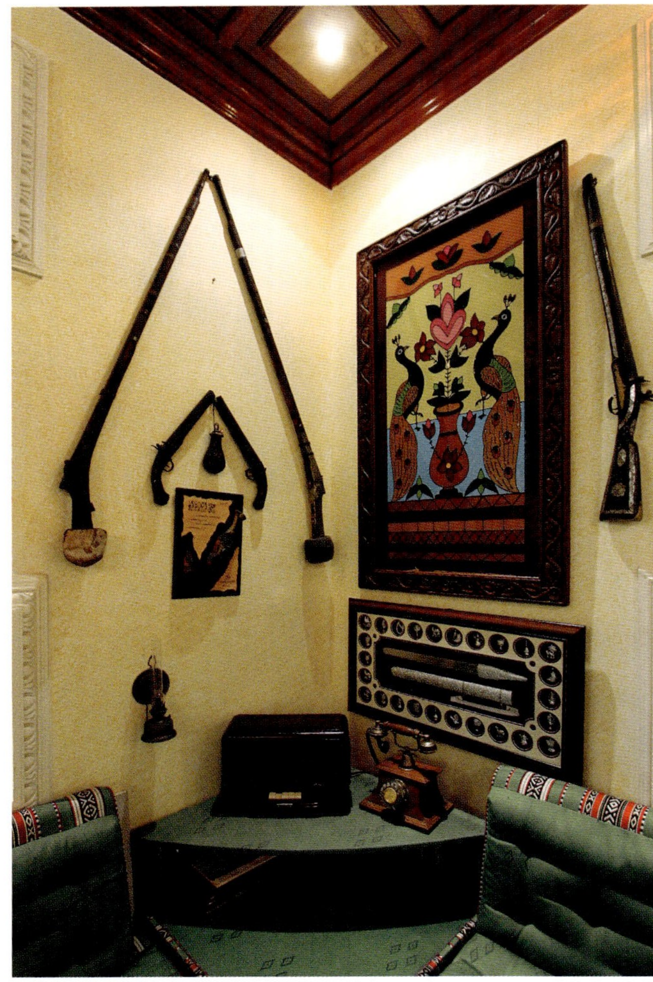

Above left: One of the *rūshanāt* in the *maylis* features perfume bottles, water pitchers and *ṣanādyq imbaīyt*.

Above right: Peacocks were a common decorative motif in Qatar in the mid-twentieth century. Here the motif is interpreted in a variety of ways, such as the wall tapestry shown here.

Right-hand page: *Rūshanāt* were purely functional components of traditional Qatari houses which enabled higher walls to be erected and were used as shelving. In more modern times, they became decorative features. Here *rūshanāt* are adorned with traditional Qatari gypsum patterns, and are used as shelving to accentuate the owner's prized collection.

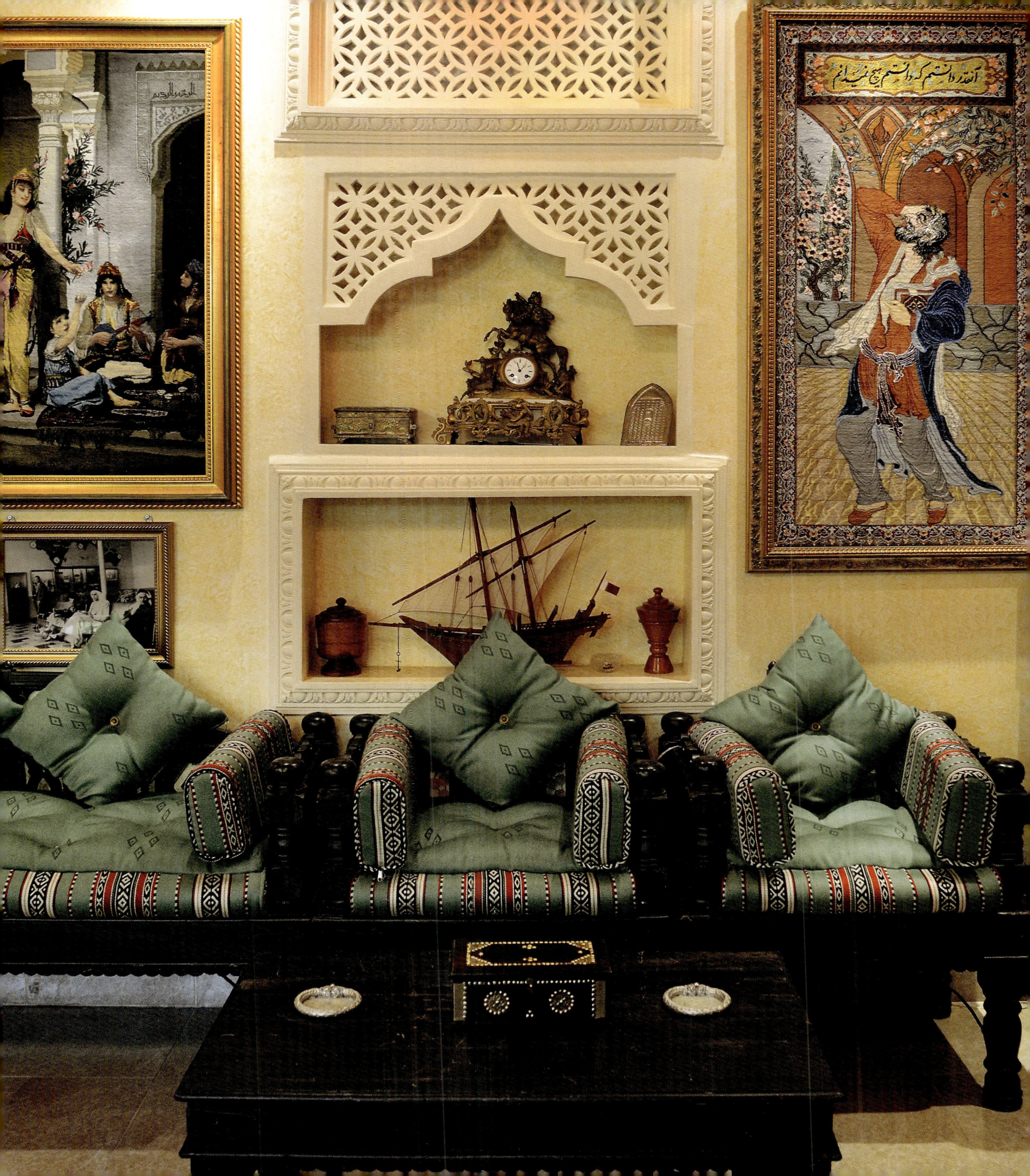

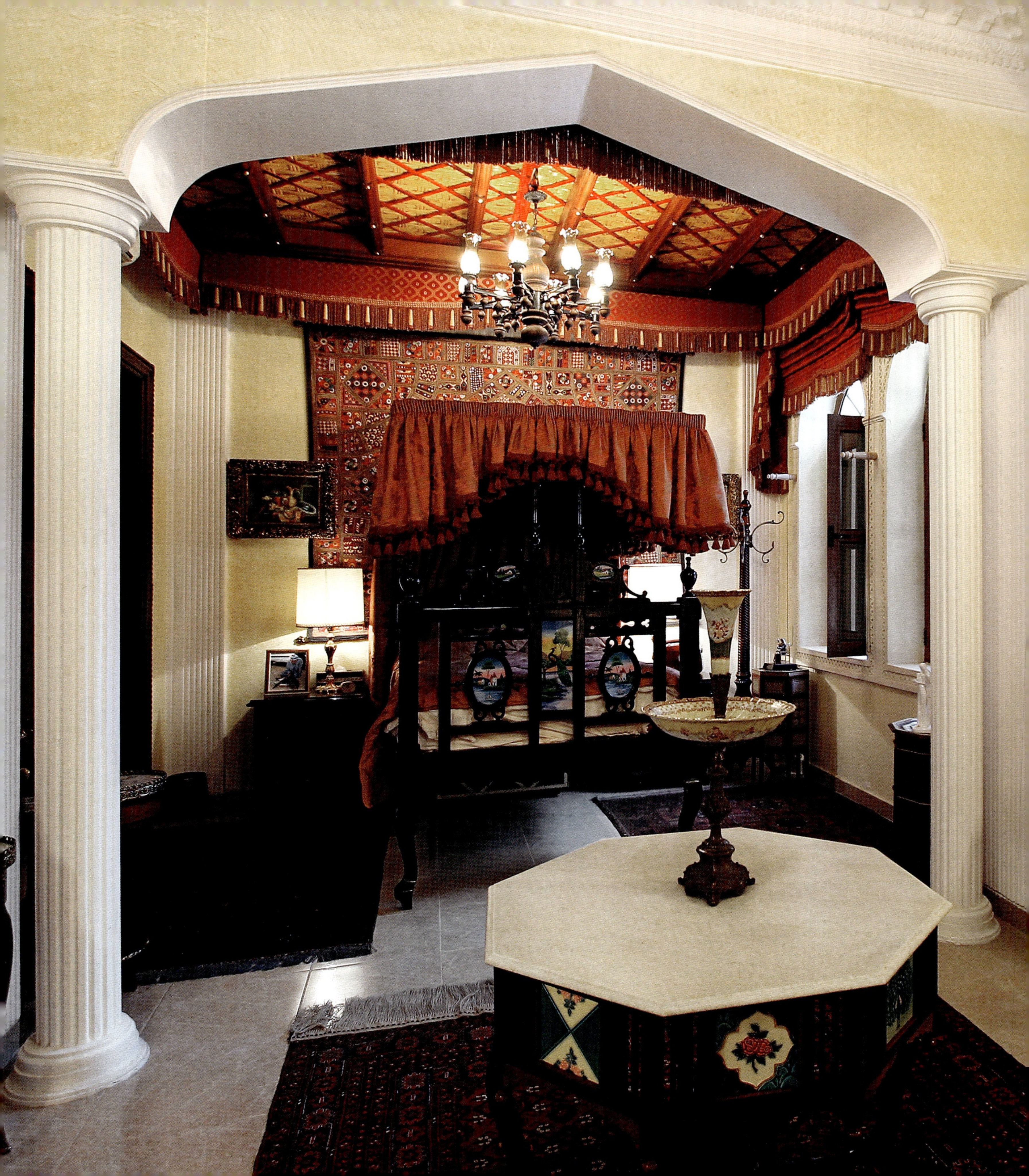

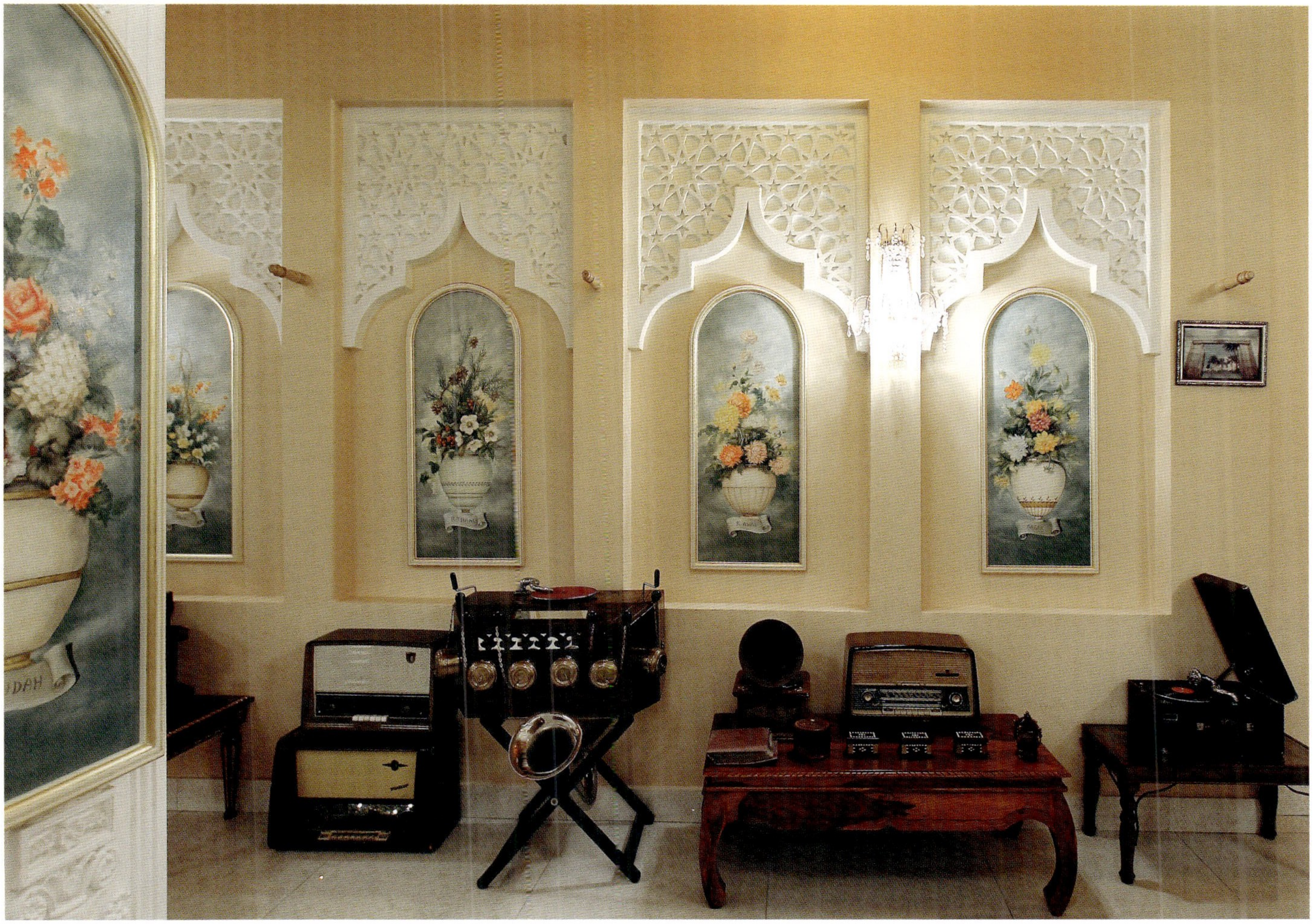

Above: The owner displays a collection of speakers, gramophones and record players from different eras showing a lengthy traveling tradition.

Left-hand page: The opulently decorated main bedroom is dominated by an adorned Indian-style bed.

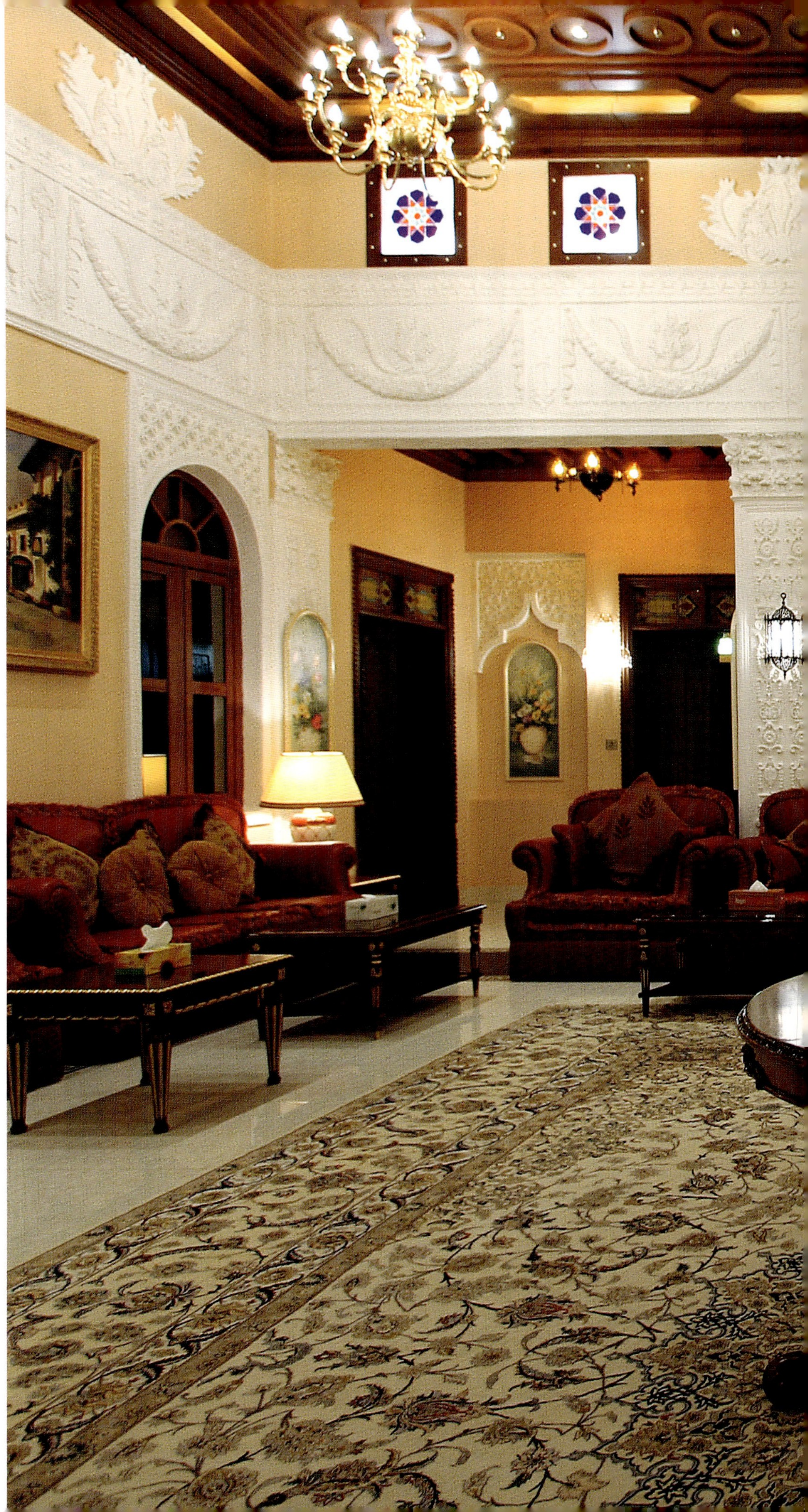

The main reception area combines furnishings and decorative details from various styles and eras.

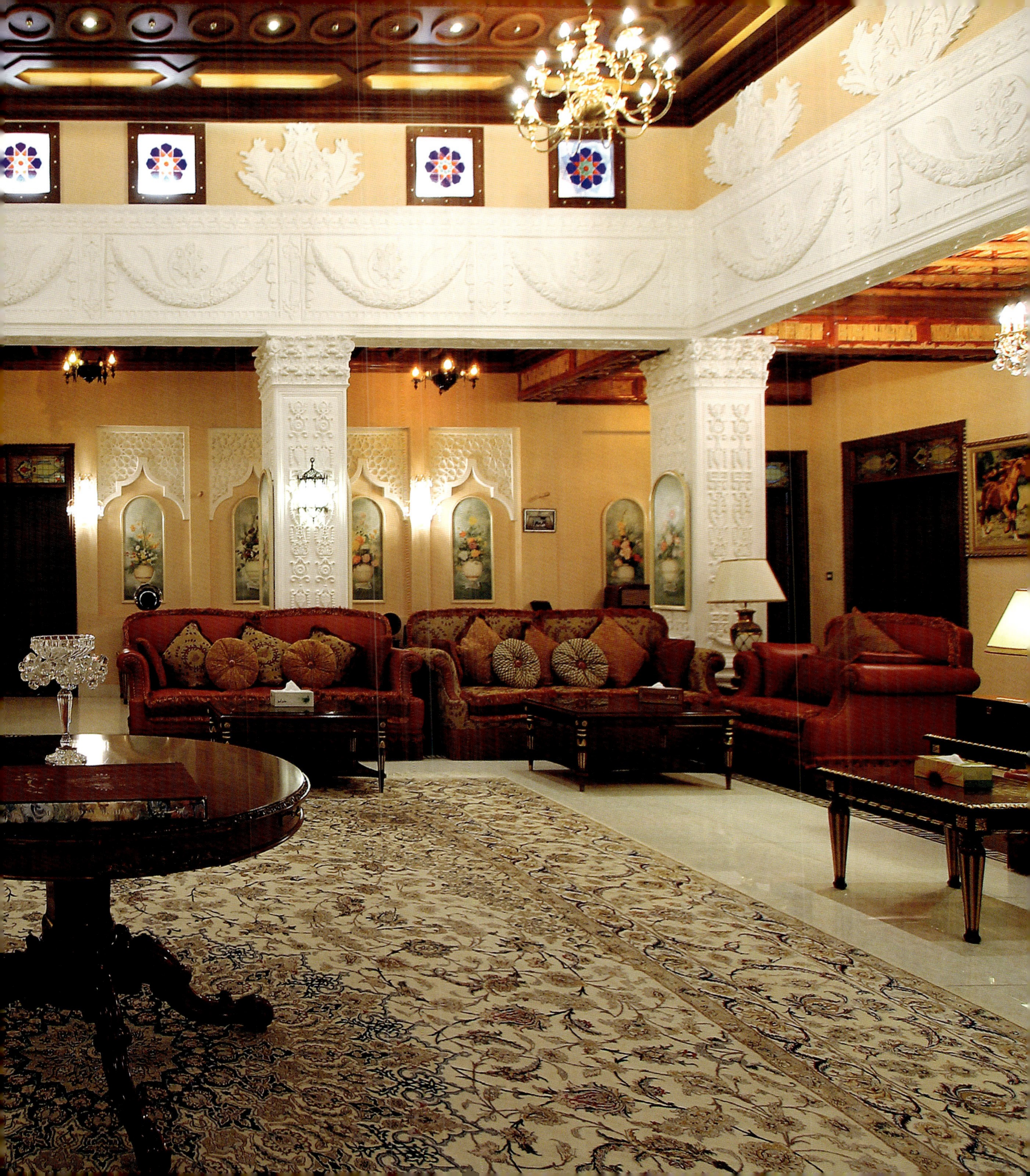

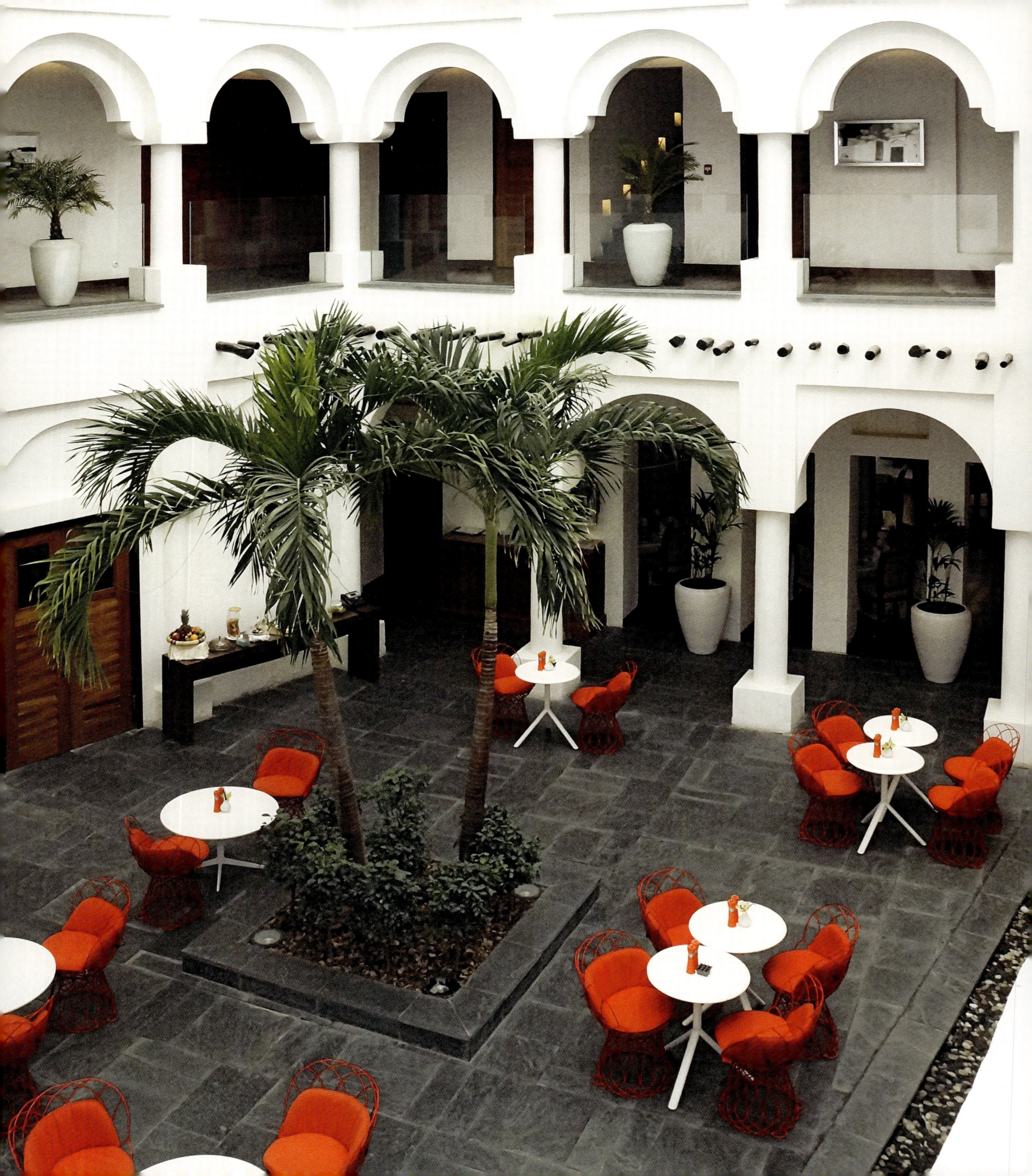

AL NAJADA HOTEL

Al Najada Hotel is situated in the south-west corner of Souq Waqif. Three traditional Qatari houses were connected and turned into a five-star hotel by the renowned architectural firm Legorreta.

The sense of a typical traditional house has been retained and local vernacular elements dominate its interiors. The hotel's main entrance is adorned by traditional wooden doors, carved in the pattern much favored by the locals in pre-oil times. The traditional design elements were established with wood and the contemporary elements are provided by the furniture in contrasting colors. The traditional interiors of the Qatari house and *maylis* are characterized by bright colors in contrast with the neutral environment. In Al Najada, rough white walls are intercepted by the wooden windows covered with *lūziāt* for privacy. The rooms are quite minimalistic, lacking any traditional ornamentation and rather functional, but at the same time rich in color.

The hallways of the hotel recreate multiple traditional *lawāwīn*. Exploring further, you realize that Al Najada reflects a micro *firīj*, a traditional neighborhood, where multiple units are arranged around a courtyard or public space, in this instance the hotel's restaurant. The public areas of the hotel are lit by indirect natural light, while white canopies are stretched to create shade. Common areas are also adorned by a number of water features which were used to transfer the salt water wells commonly found in courtyards of the traditional houses. We can imagine falling into a nostalgic mood while sipping Arabic coffee in the early morning or the late afternoon, sitting in the naturally lit courtyard and enjoying the babbling of the water interspersed with the sounds of bustling Souq Waqif.

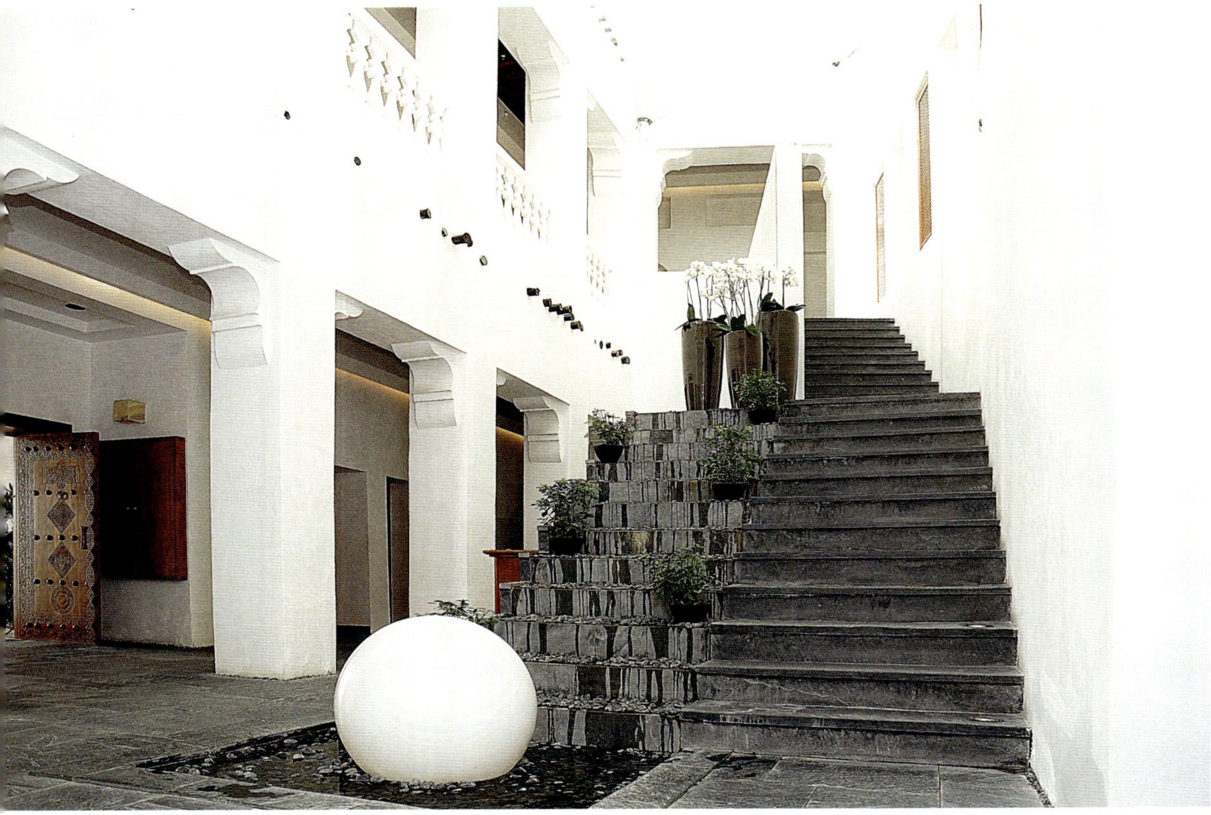

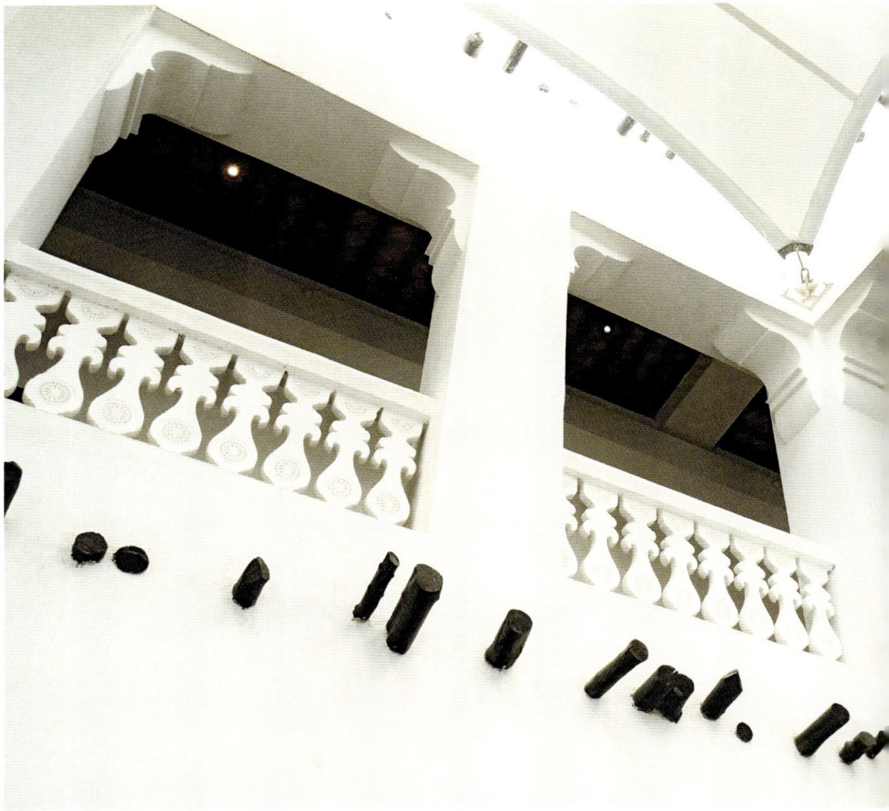

Above: The water feature in the lobby of the hotel blends with the design of the stairs.

Right: The upper *lawāwīn* surround the lobby, in this instance occupying the central courtyard —*ḥawsh*—of one of the houses forming the hotel.

Far right: At the entrance to the hotel are large wooden doors carved in various geometric and floral patterns featuring Arabic calligraphy.

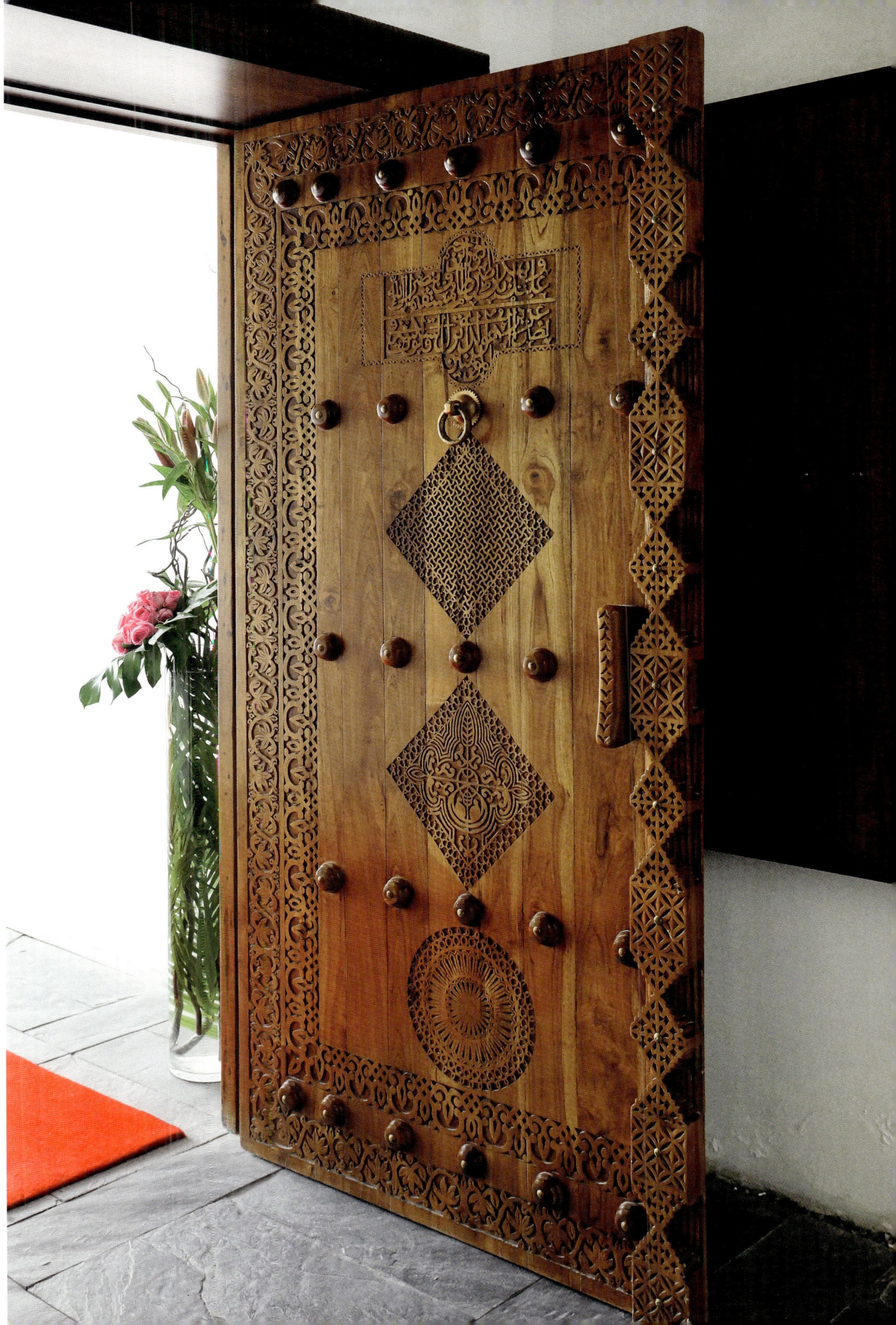

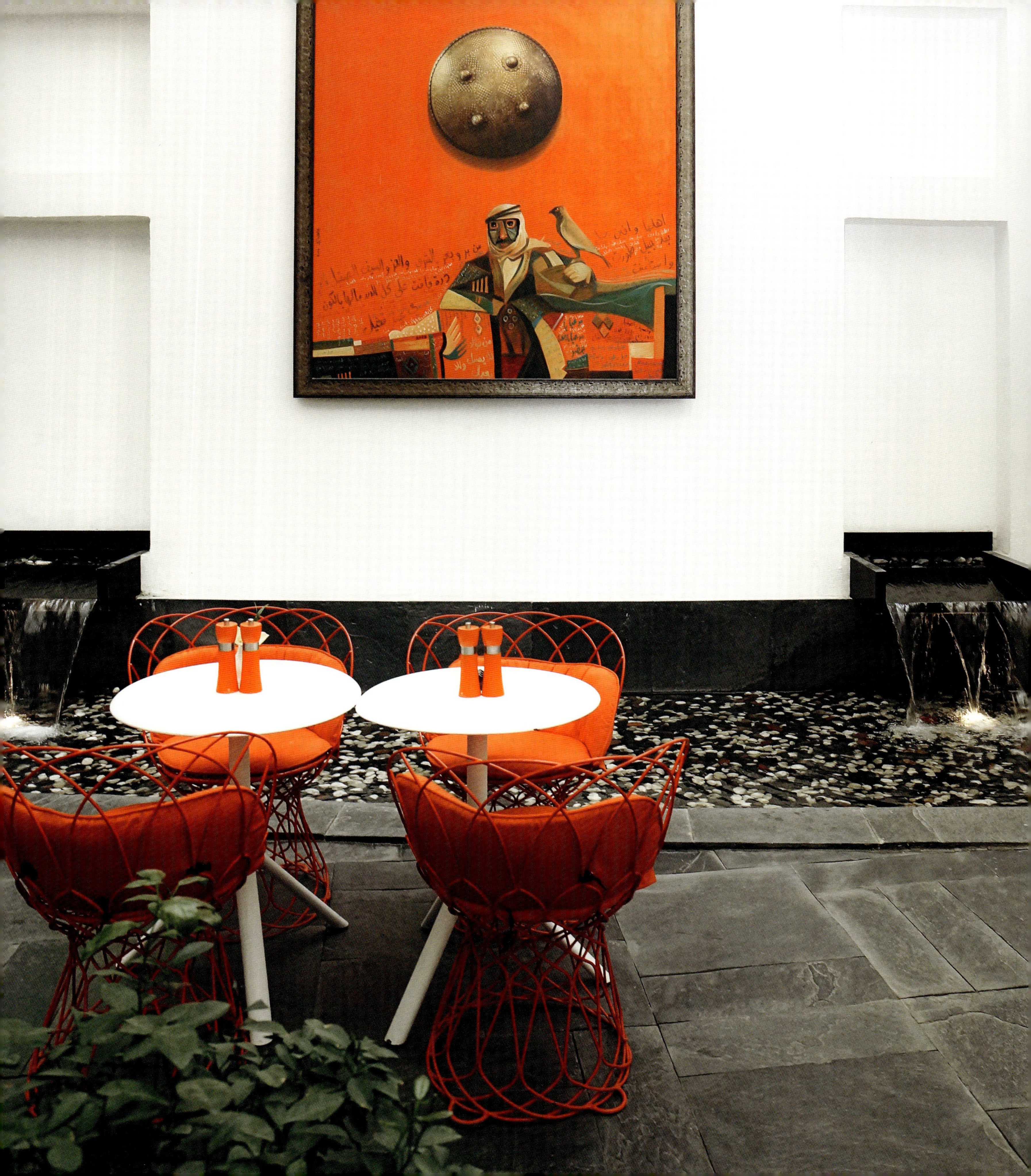

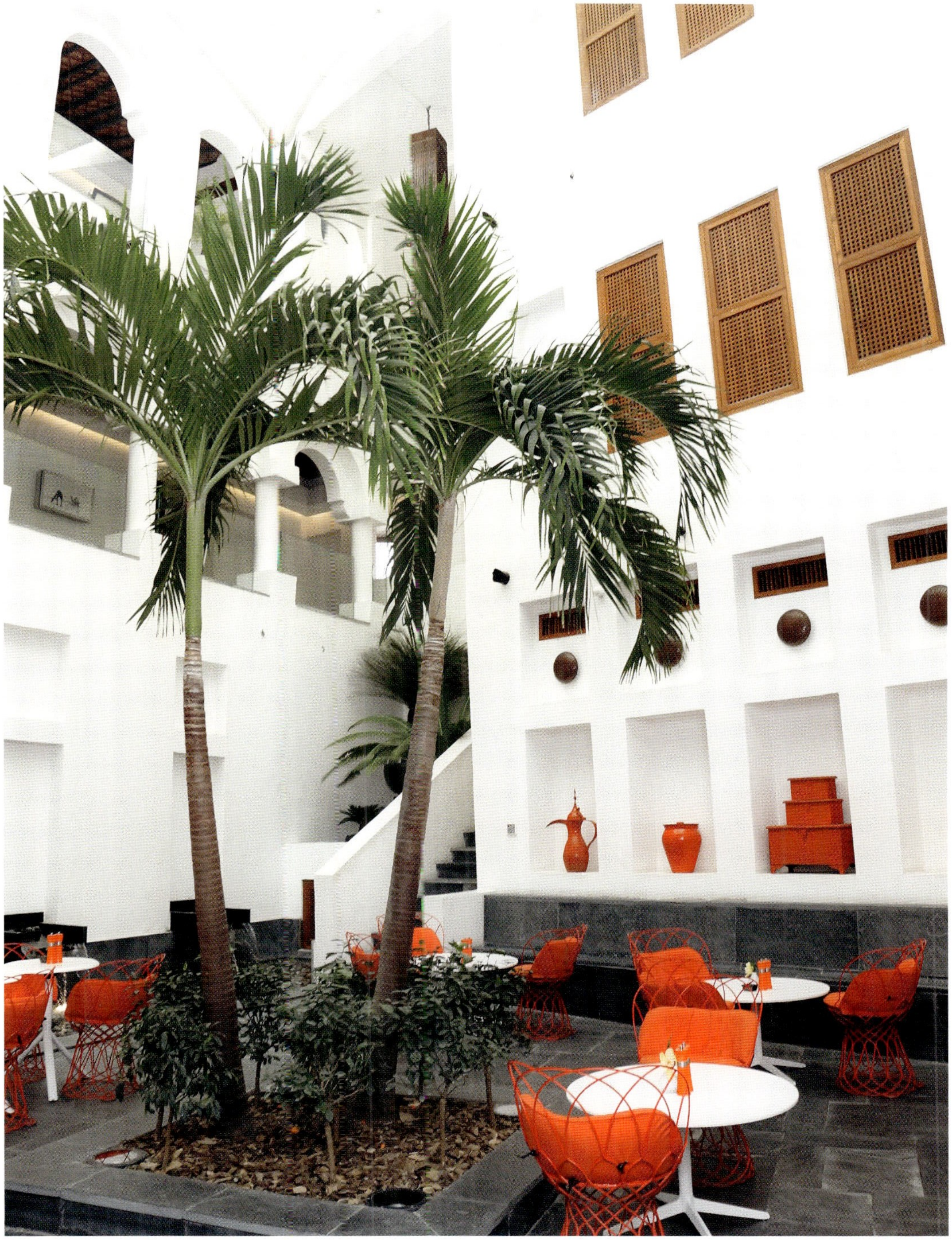

Above: A creative way of re-adapting the central courtyard, which in this instance serves as one of the restaurants in the hotel.

Left-hand page: Bright furniture and decorations contrast with the white walls.

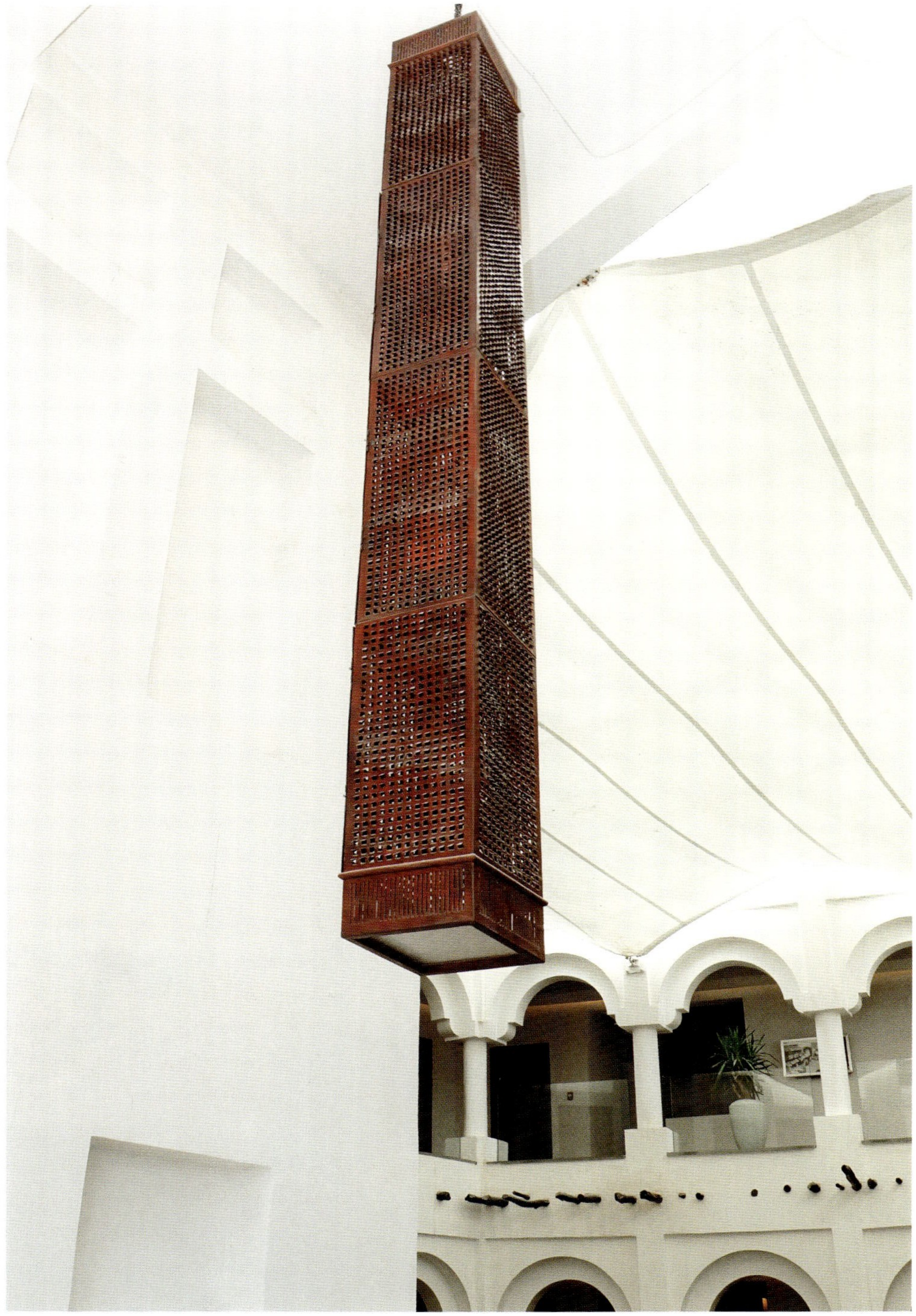

Above: Wood is used throughout the hotel in a variety of ways such as the window shutters and lighting fixtures which soften bright white walls.

Right-hand page: A contemporary *lūzīah*.

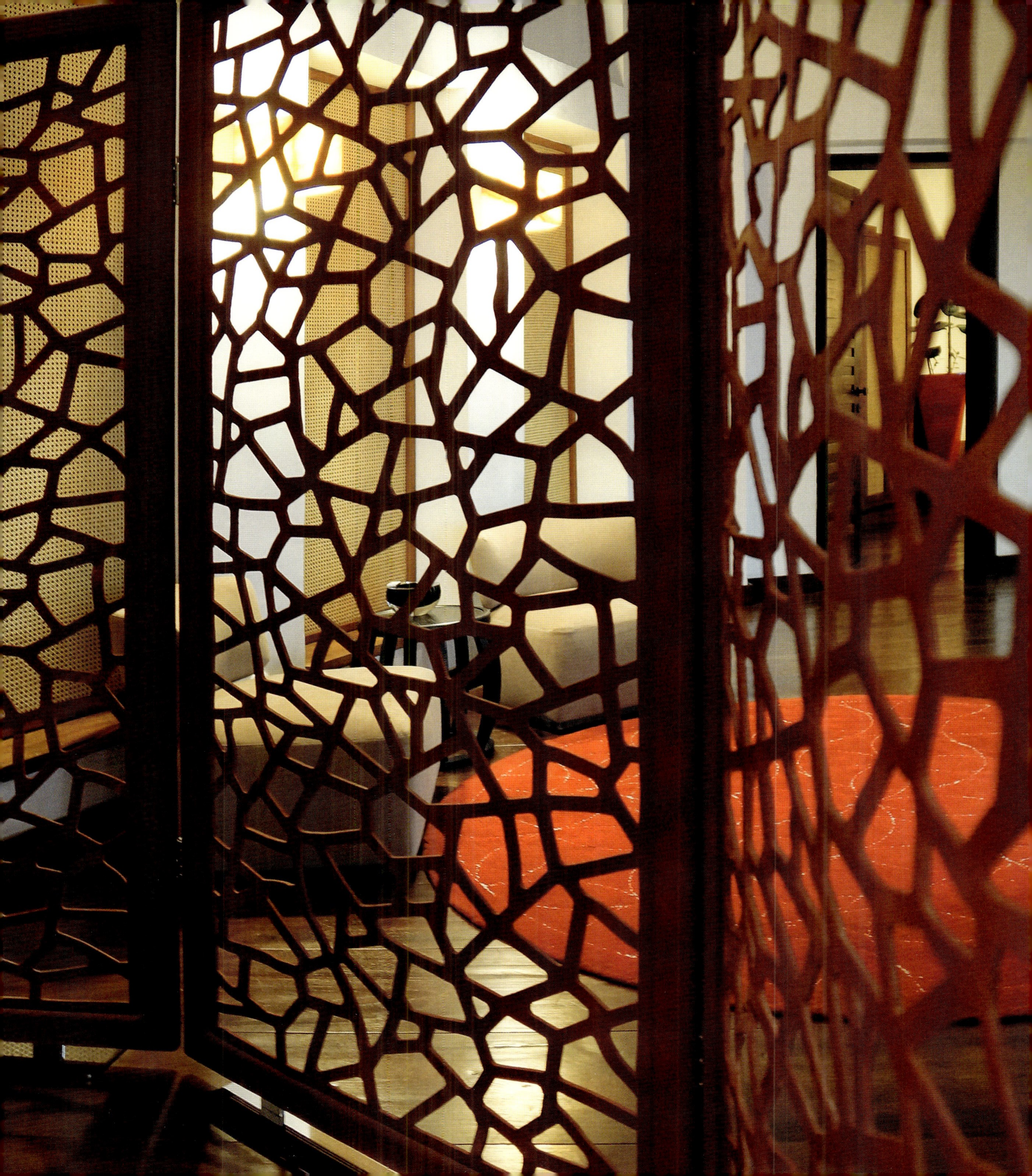

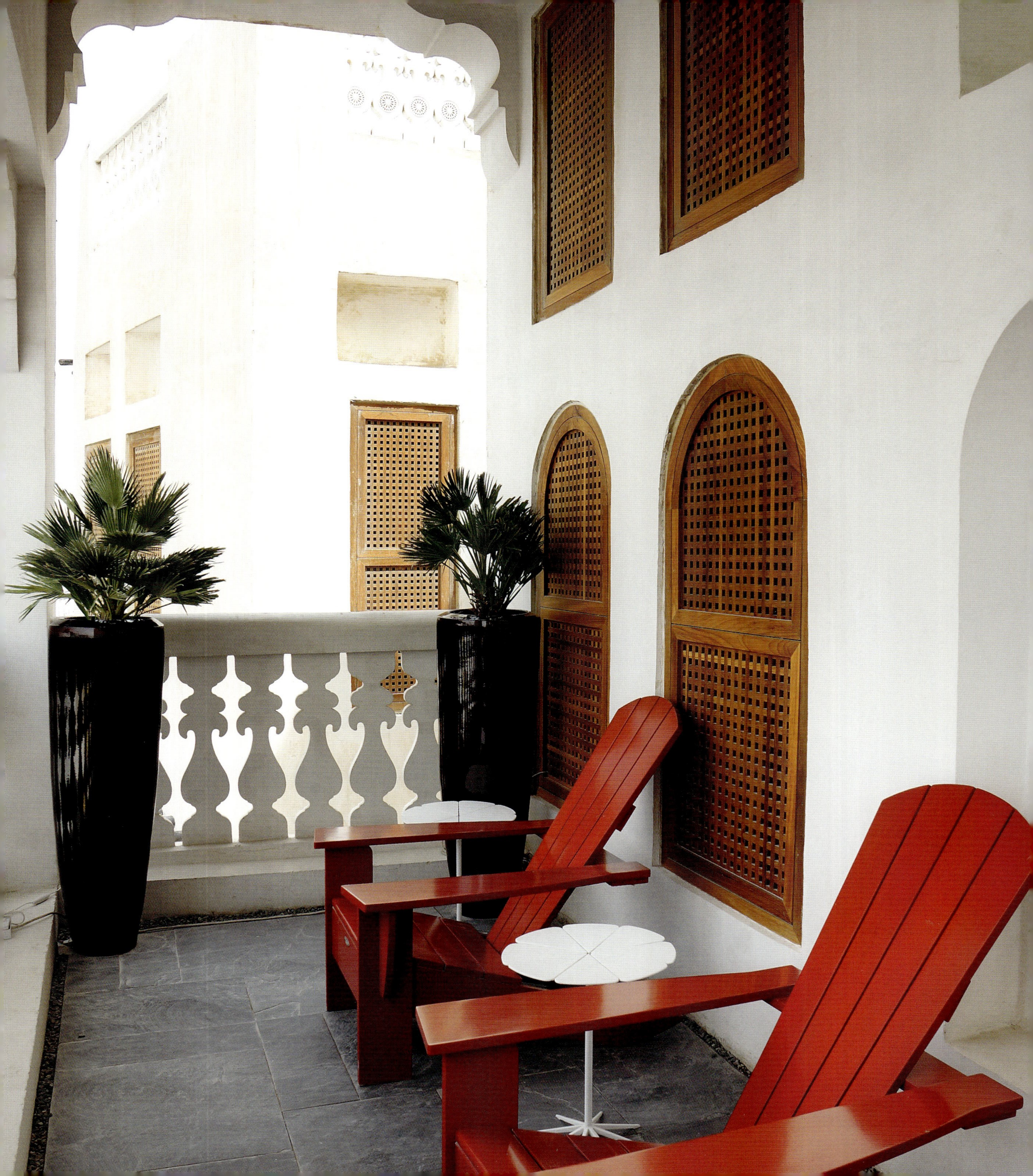

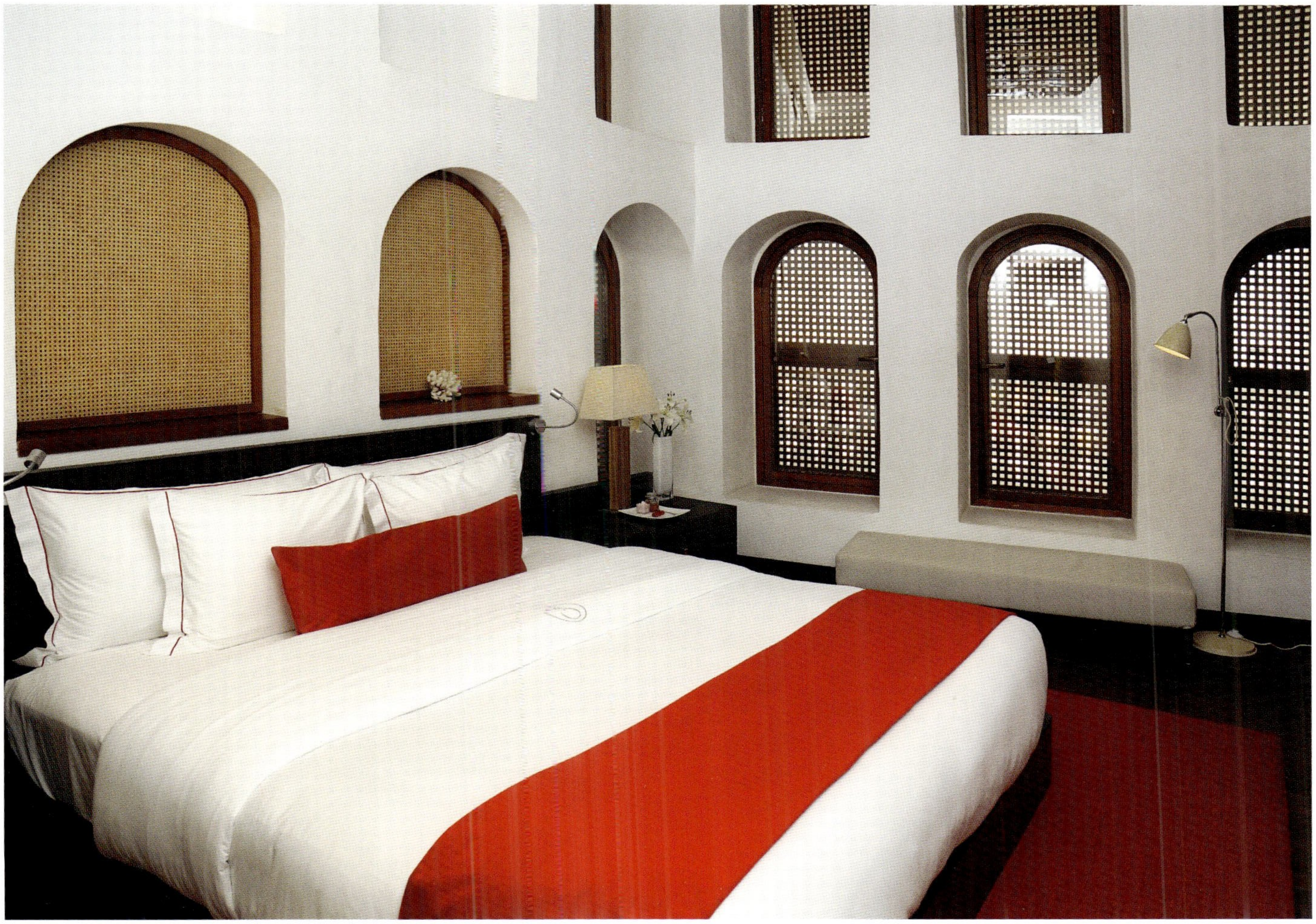

Above: This simply styled bedroom features numerous *lūzīāt* and *rūshanāt* accentuating the high ceiling and allowing for maximum light while providing privacy for the guests.

Left-hand page: Contemporary outdoor furniture is juxtaposed with traditional architectural elements.

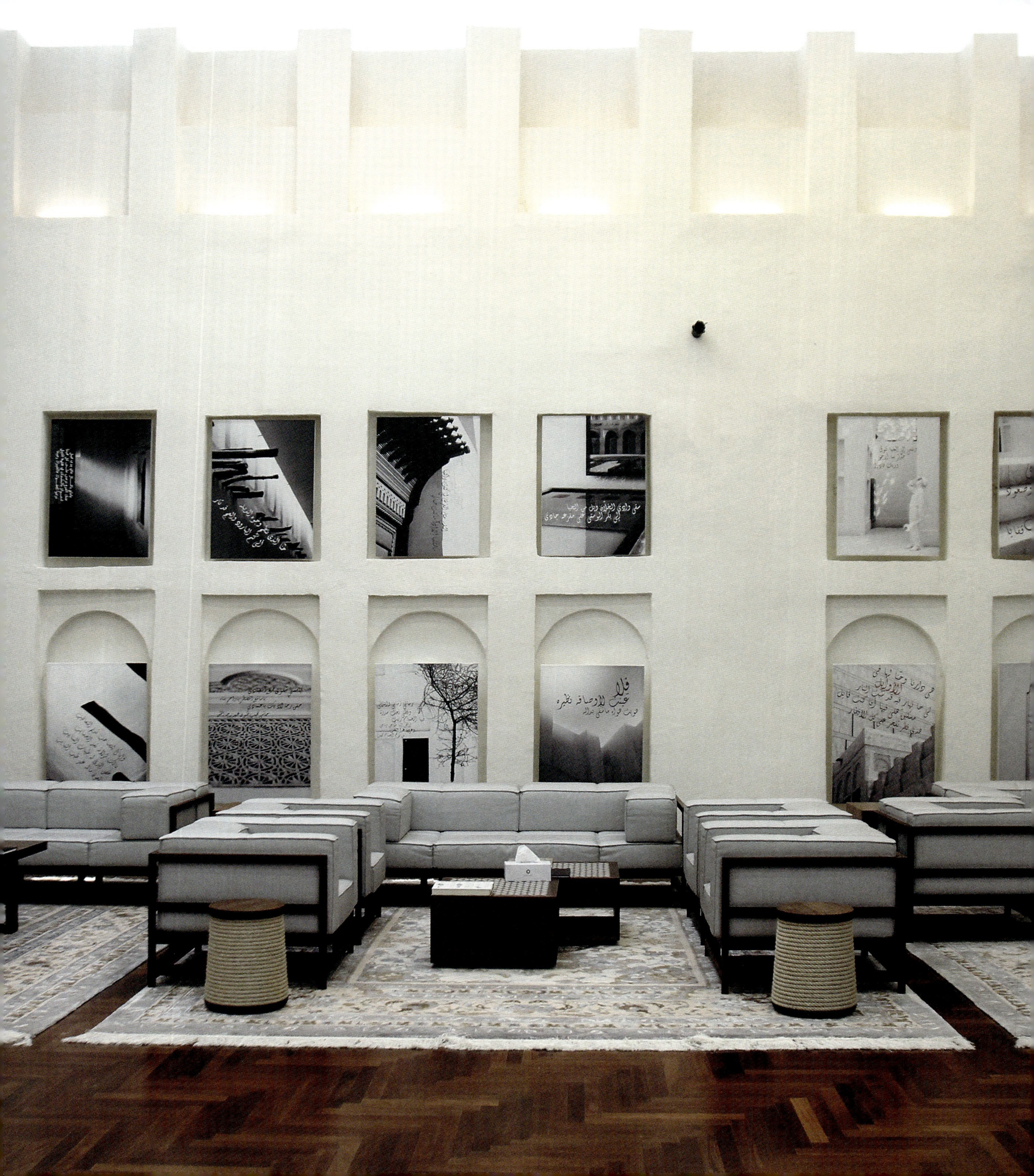

BIN JELMOOD HOUSE

Bin Jelmood House is the largest of four houses that comprise the newly opened Msheireb Museums.

Bin Jelmood House was once a house owned by Doha's most prominent slave trader. He was named Jelmood, which means "rock" and implies that he was a hard-hearted character. Now Bin Jelmood House is a testament to slavery in the Indian Ocean and an acknowledgement of the influence of once-enslaved people on the development of Qatar's modern society.

Architecturally speaking, Bin Jelmood House is a typical example of a traditional Qatari courtyard house. Its former residential quarters have been turned into the exhibition galleries, a small library that is run in collaboration with Qatar National Library, a learning and education center and a multi-purpose hall.

The main hall was originally open, but the unusual ceiling was added to create a larger indoor space for the museum. The ceiling in the main hall creatively admits natural light which blends beautifully with the features of the simple traditional architecture.

The house has been further adapted into a museum by focusing on the arcades, *lawāwīn*. Originally, the *līwān* is a transitional space between indoor and outdoor spaces. It shades the windows and doors of the house which face the inner courtyard. As a part of a residential building, the *līwān* is usually a habitable space in which the residents could carry out many activities. Here multiple *lawāwīn* have been partially closed to create smaller galleries within the museum.

The recesses in the walls, *rūshanāt*, have also been retained. These recesses relate to the old methods of construction. Having *rūshanāt* resulted in lighter walls which allowed for building them higher without structural beams. Over time, these recesses became a decorative feature and a space where items could be displayed. The design of the cornices on the walls is one that was originally used in the old National Museum's *maylis*. Recently, this pattern has become a typical Qatari cornice as it has been used in museums and traditional-style buildings like Al Dana Club. However, it might not be original to this building as the use of cornices became popular after the discovery of oil in the region, unlike the rest of the structure.

The ceilings show a reuse of *mangharūr* and bamboo wood with joyful streaks of enhanced color. The wooden teak doors of the museum seem to be identical to a door in the pre-oil era.

The minimalist furniture echoes the welcoming and simplistic mood of vernacular Qatari architecture using solid-color pale fabrics and wood.

What makes this museum unique is that the building is not simply a space for display, but it also forms part of the exhibit. The curators were successful in preserving the old structure while adapting it to its new function as a museum with all the required facilities. The adaptation was carried out in a way which successfully preserved the harmony of the interiors.

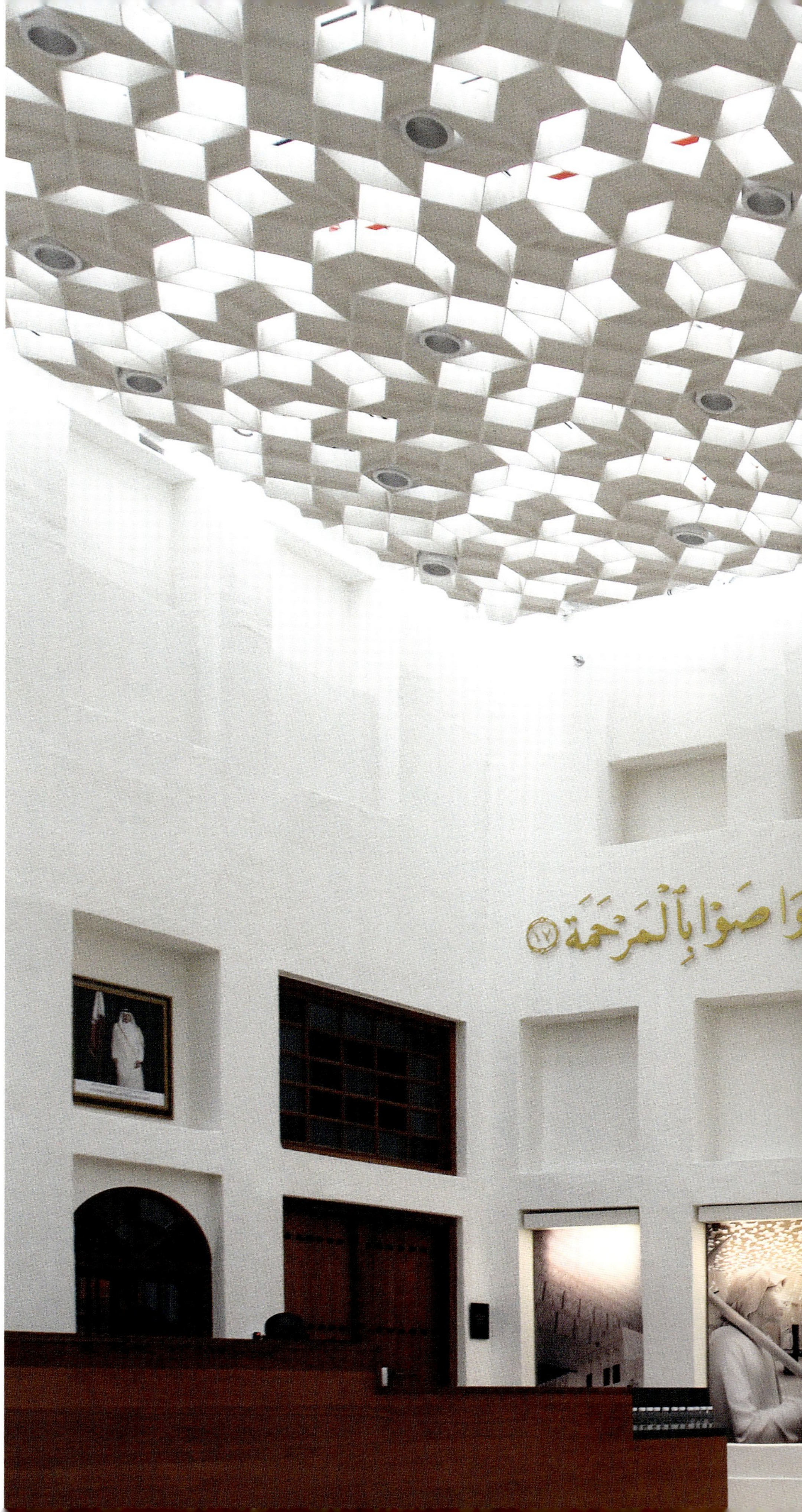

The contemporary geometric ceiling enclosing what would have been an open courtyard is in harmony with traditional architectural features. Enclosing the courtyard in this way reduced the glare of the sun while still providing an outdoor feeling.

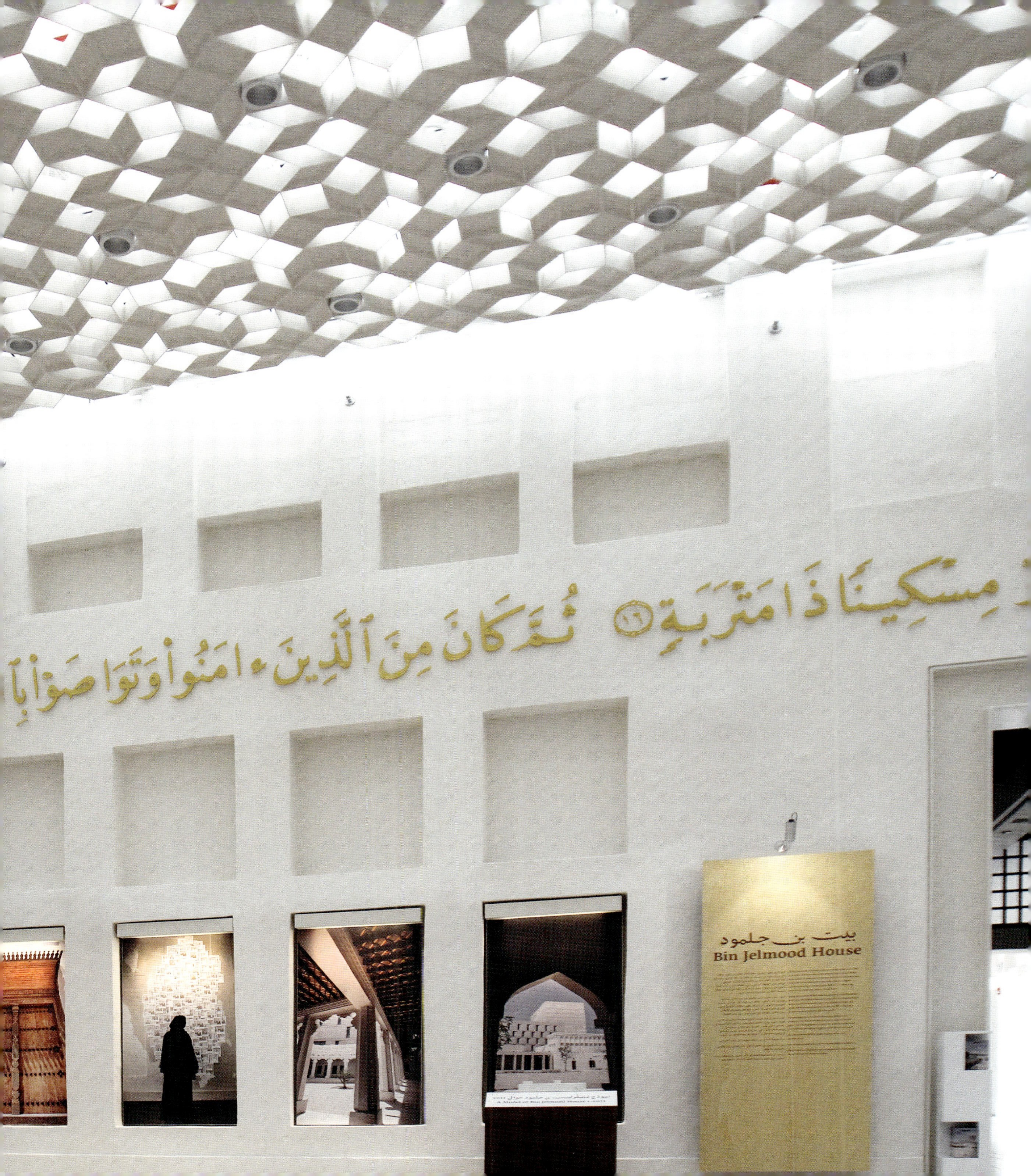

بيت بن جلمود
Bin Jelmood House

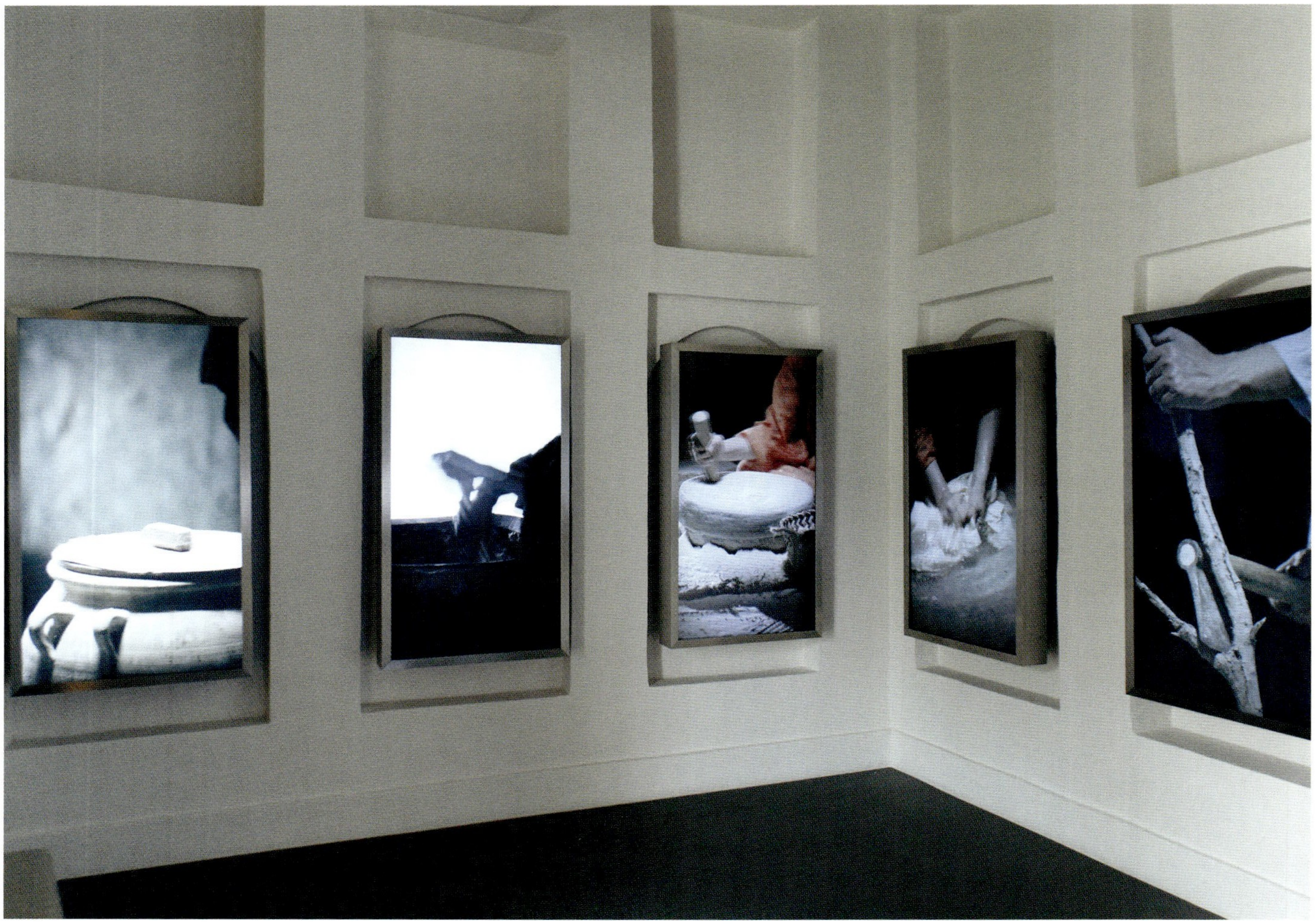

Above: Although the museum space is traditional in shape, its display methods take advantage of the latest technology.

Right-hand page: During the renovation the doors and *darāīsh* were reproduced to reflect their traditional look.

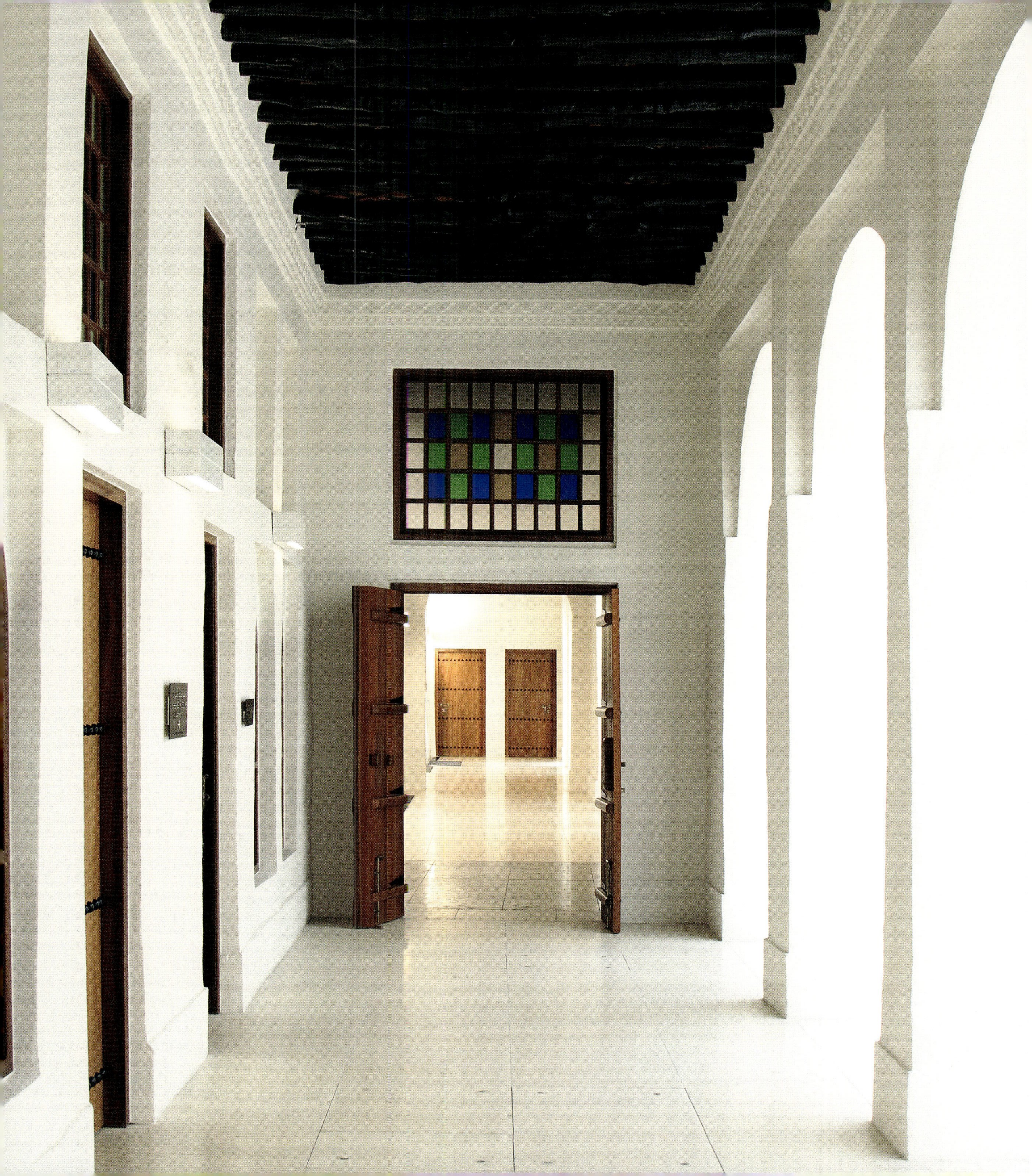

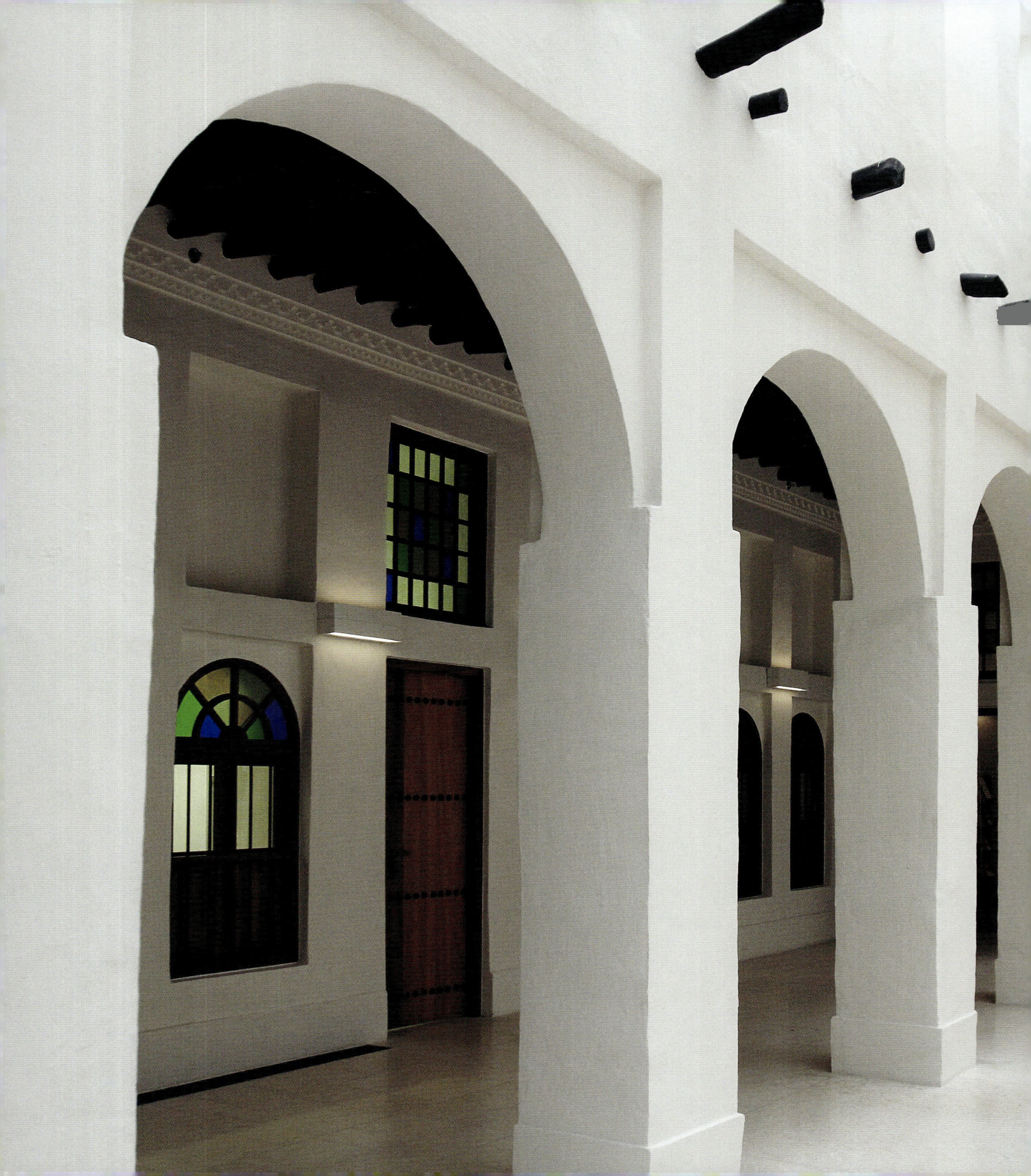

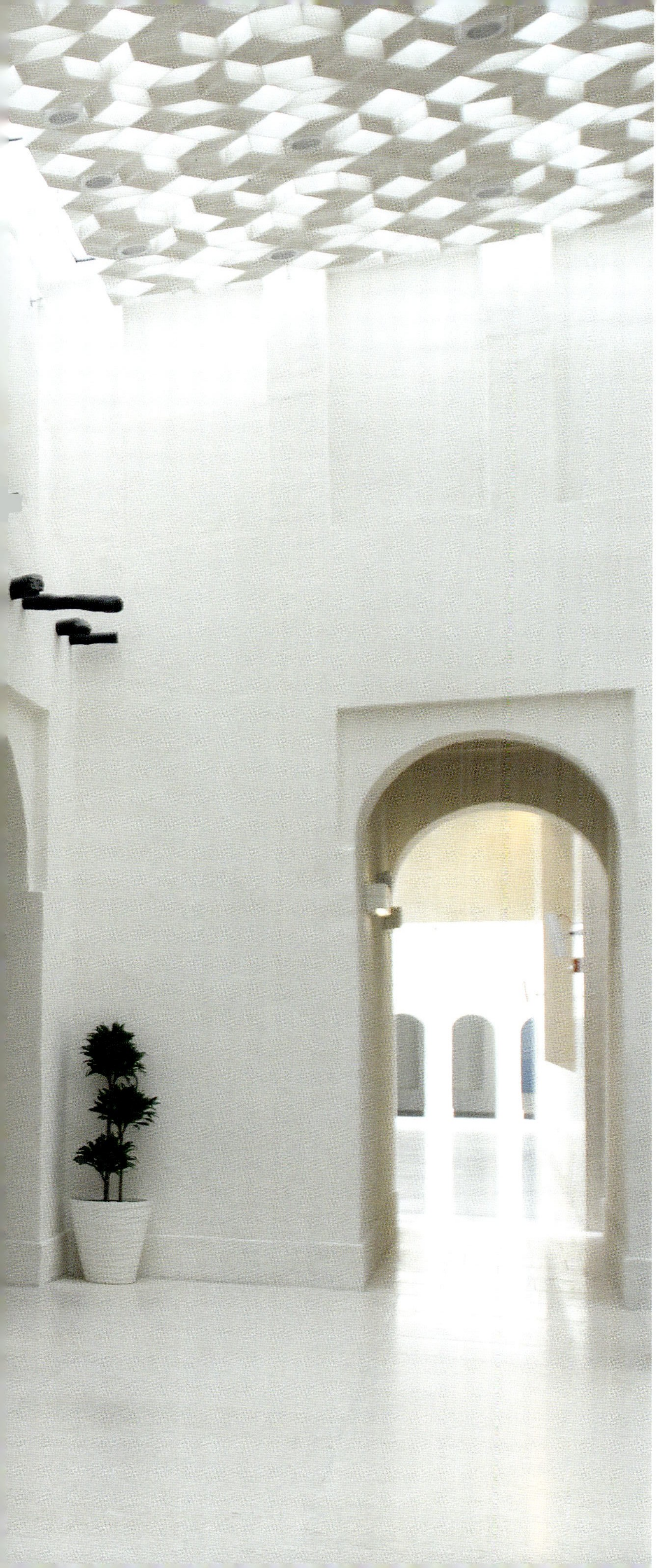

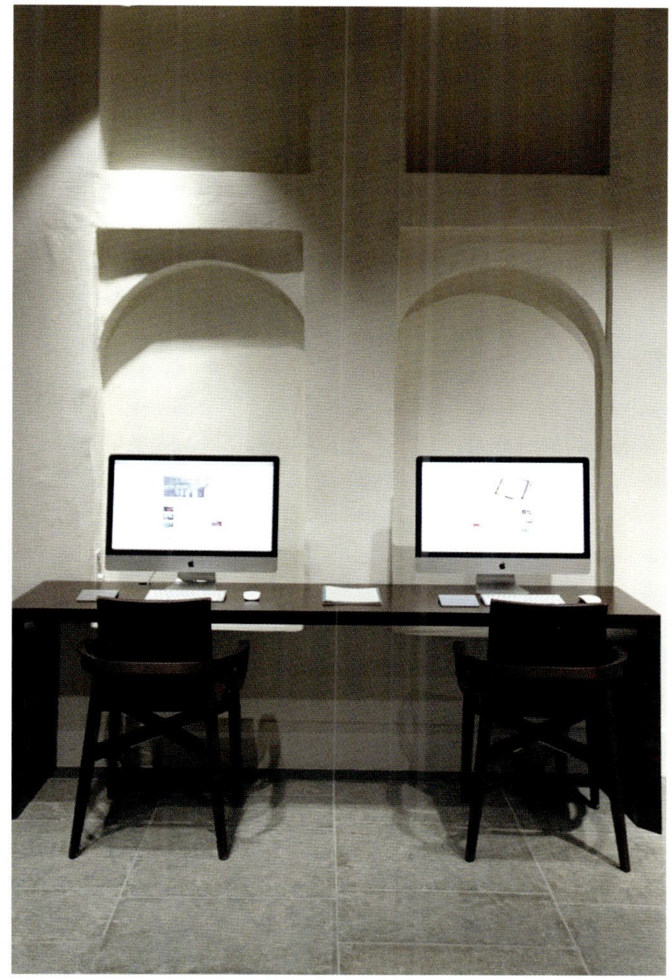

Above: A reading nook with access to the online records of Qatar National Library.

Left: Although the *līwān* became superfluous once the courtyard was fully enclosed, it remained in the house to maintain the authenticity of the space.

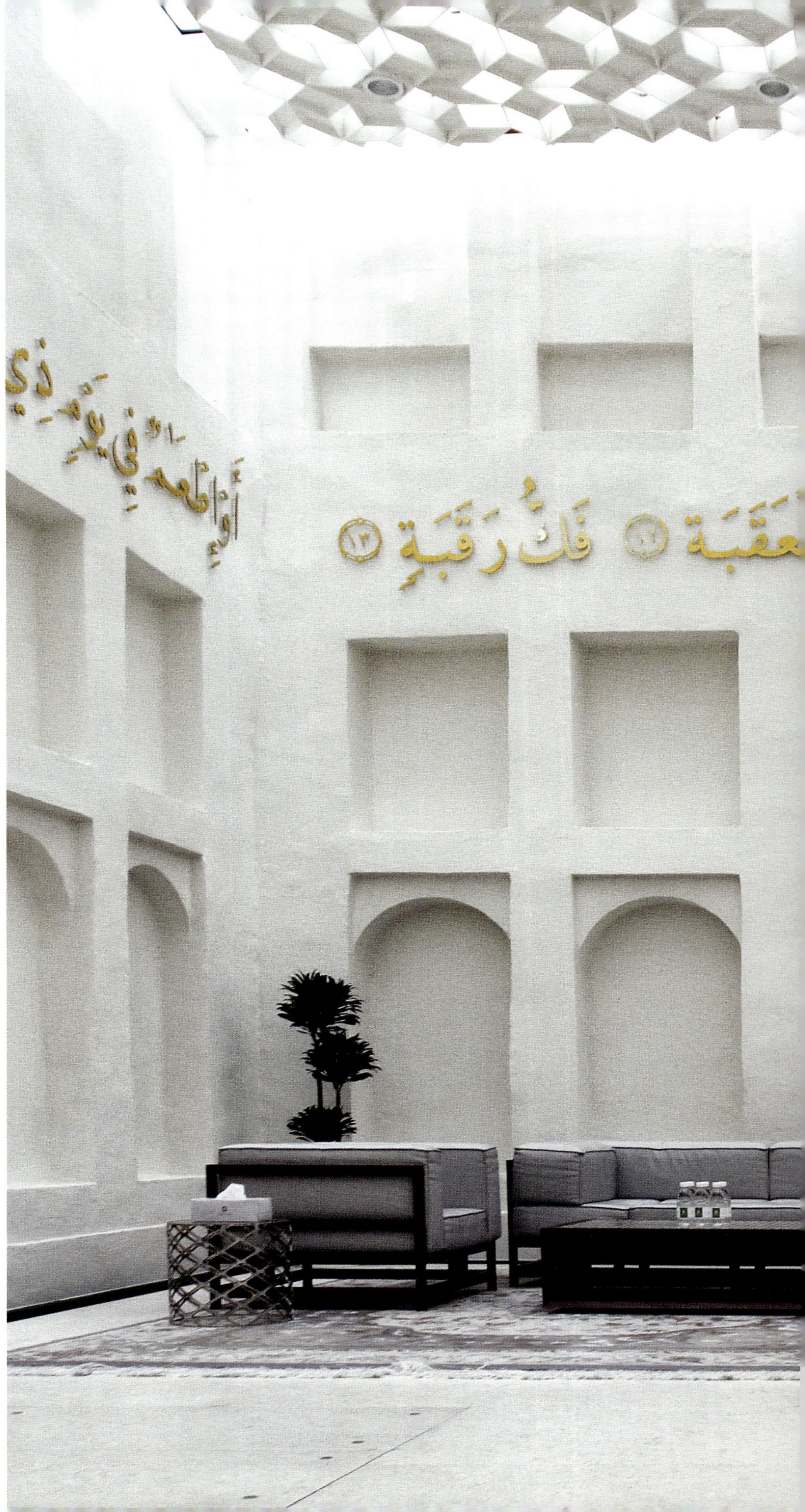

Verses from the Qur'an that essentially translate to:
"Yet he has not embarked upon the uphill task.(11)
And how will you know what is the uphill task? (12)
[It is] the freeing of a slave, (13)
or feeding [the needy] on a day of starvation, (14)
or an orphan among relatives, (15)
or a needy man in desolation, (16)
while being one of those who have faith (17)
and who enjoin one another to patience,
and enjoin one another to compassion. (18)"
Sūrat Al-Balad

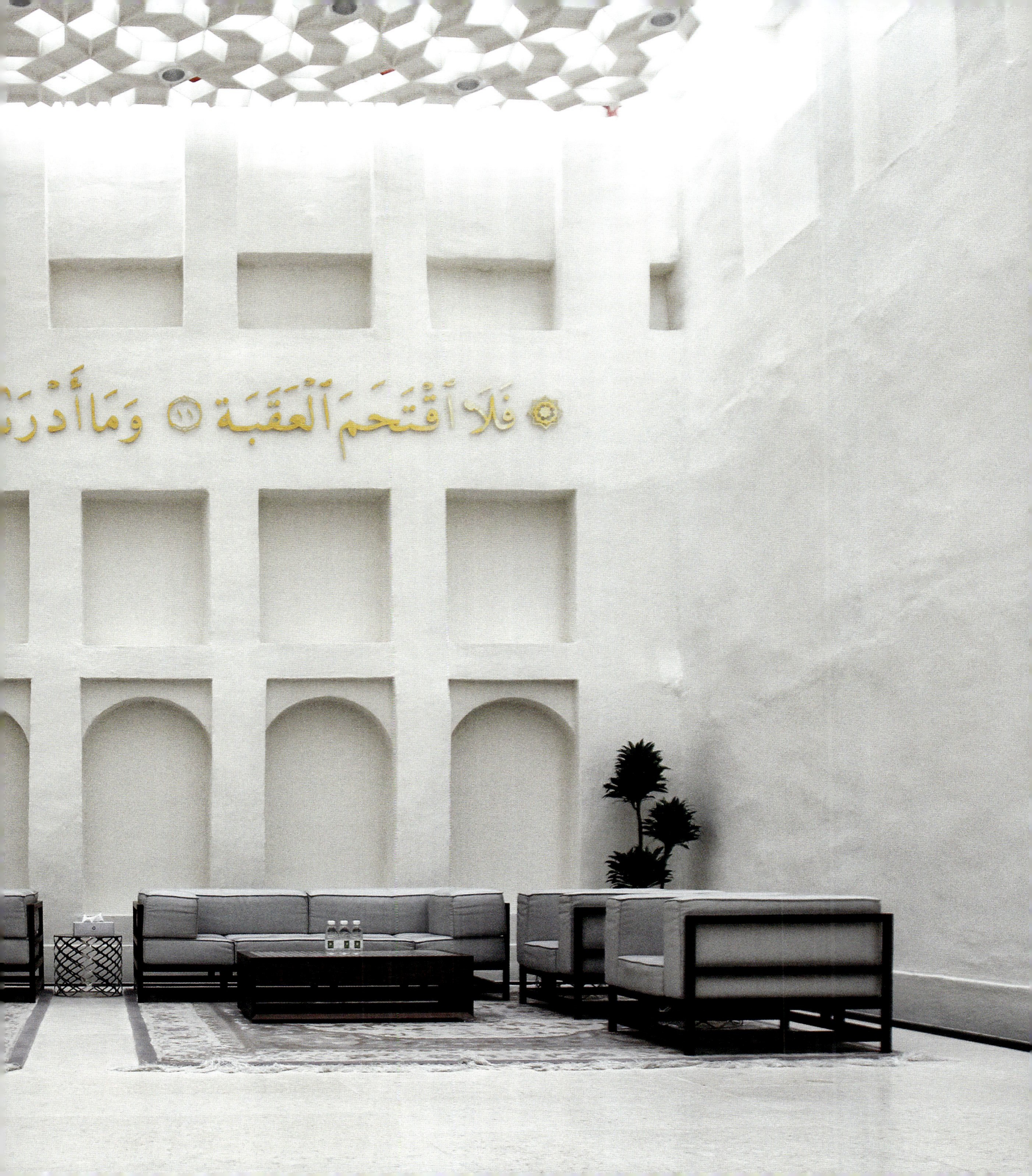
فلا اقتحم العقبة ١١ وما

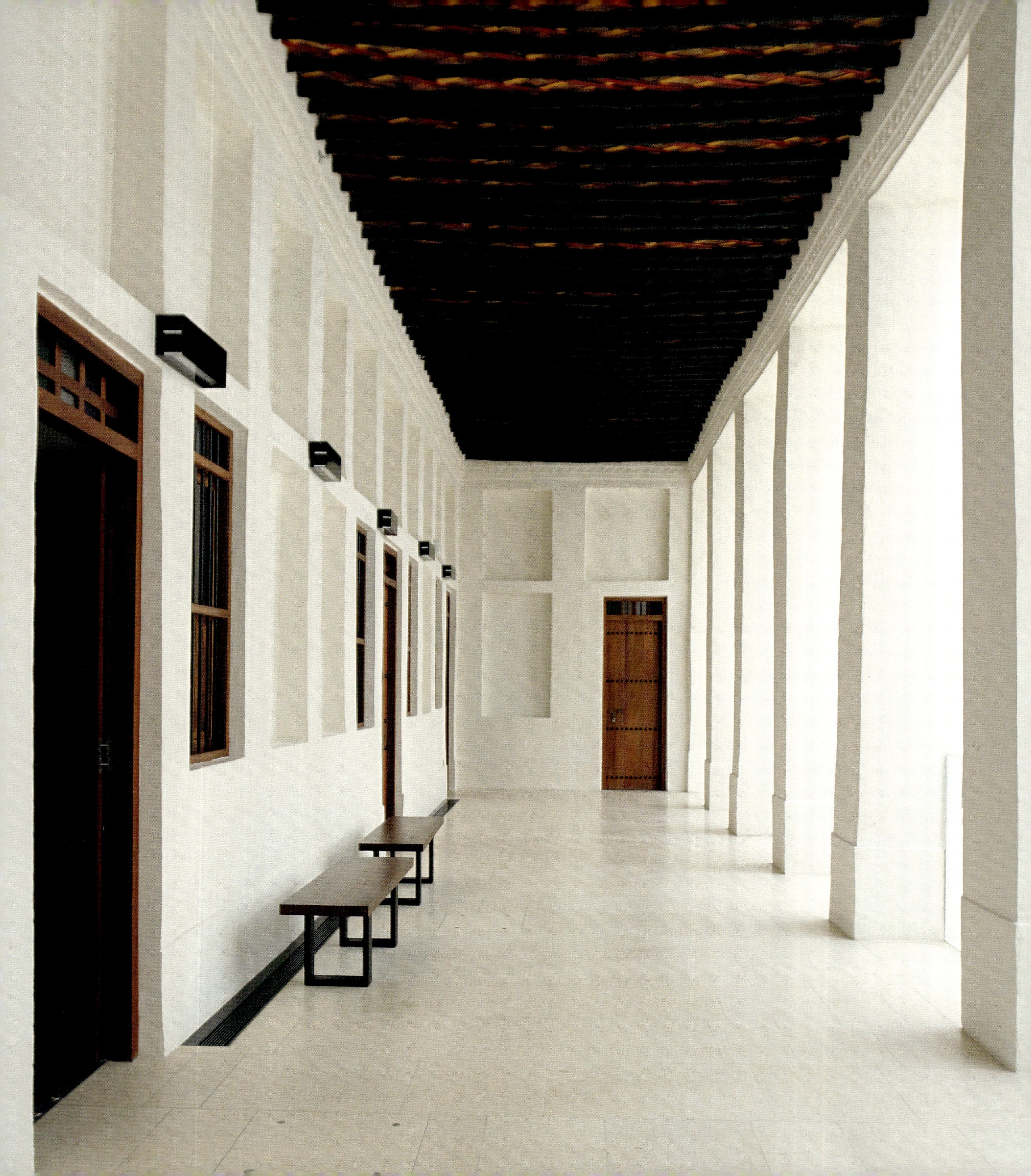

COMPANY HOUSE

The Company House is the smallest of the four Msheireb Museums and is located between the Radwani and Bin Jelmood houses.

The house itself represents a turning point in the country's economic history. It dates to the early twentieth century, and has served as the headquarters for Qatar's first oil company where Qatari men were recruited for jobs in the oil industry following the decline in pearling.

Company House was renovated and reconstructed during the rehabilitation of the Msheireb Downtown Doha project. The original layout of the house remained but the design team has closed off the courtyard and turned it into a functional exhibition space. The courtyard was enclosed by glass with modern metal *lūzīah* that allows a lot of natural light into the space. A modern metal façade decorates the main entrance and the exhibition design inside continues the industrial theme. Many of the traditional architectural elements remain such as *rūshanāt* and *danāshil*. Traditional *rūshanāt* are used for exhibiting objects, text panels and in a few instances digital screens have been installed in the wall recesses. The furniture used in the museum is scarce but functional, and is intended for the museum's visitors. It is simple and does not distract the visitors' attention.

Company House celebrates Qatari men who were the first employees in the oil industry. These pioneers of Qatar's major industry and their stories are a testament to modern-day Qatar.

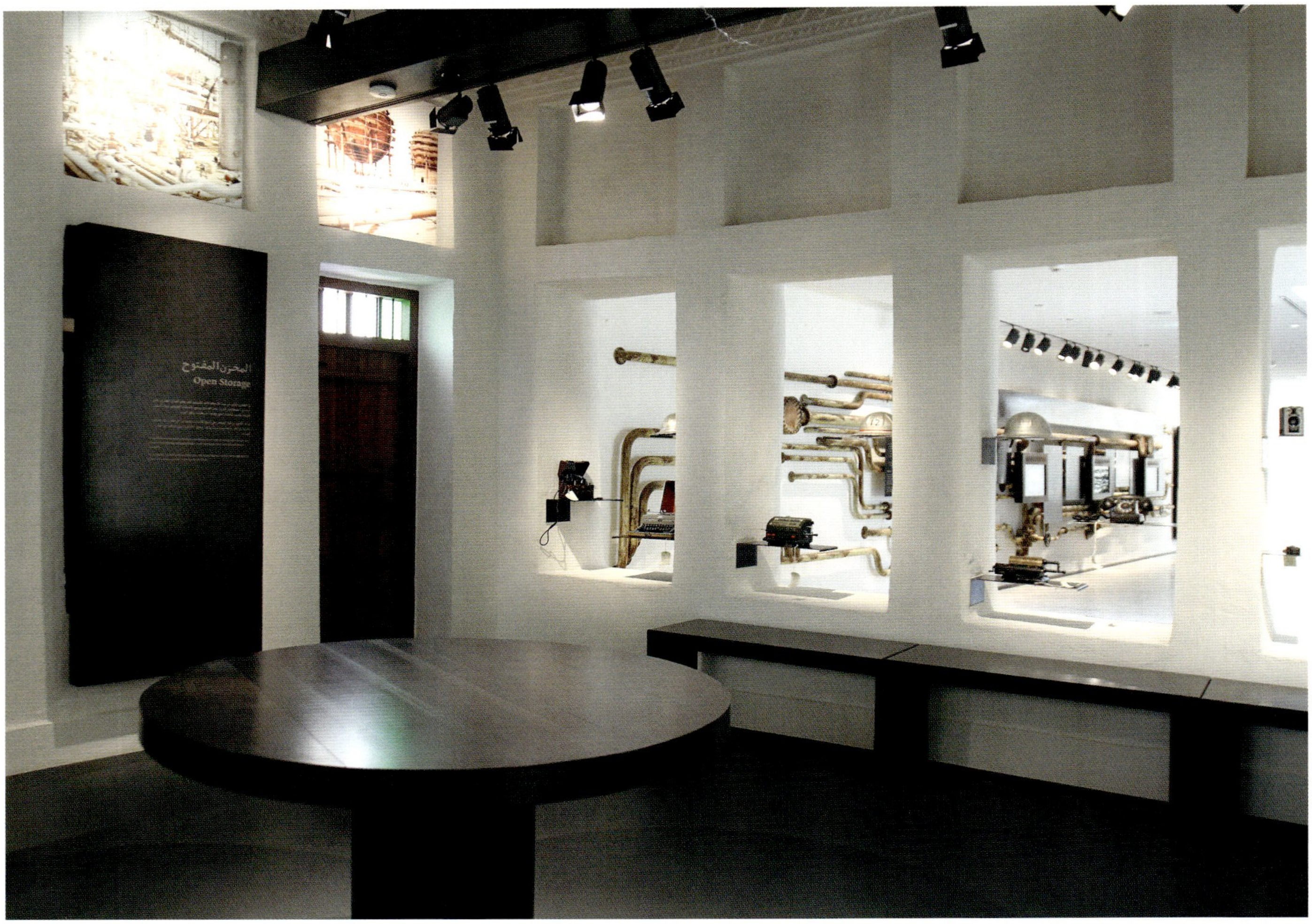

Above: The architecture of the house allowed for generous exhibition spaces.

Right-hand page: The exhibition lighting was incorporated into the existing space without neglecting existing architectural elements.

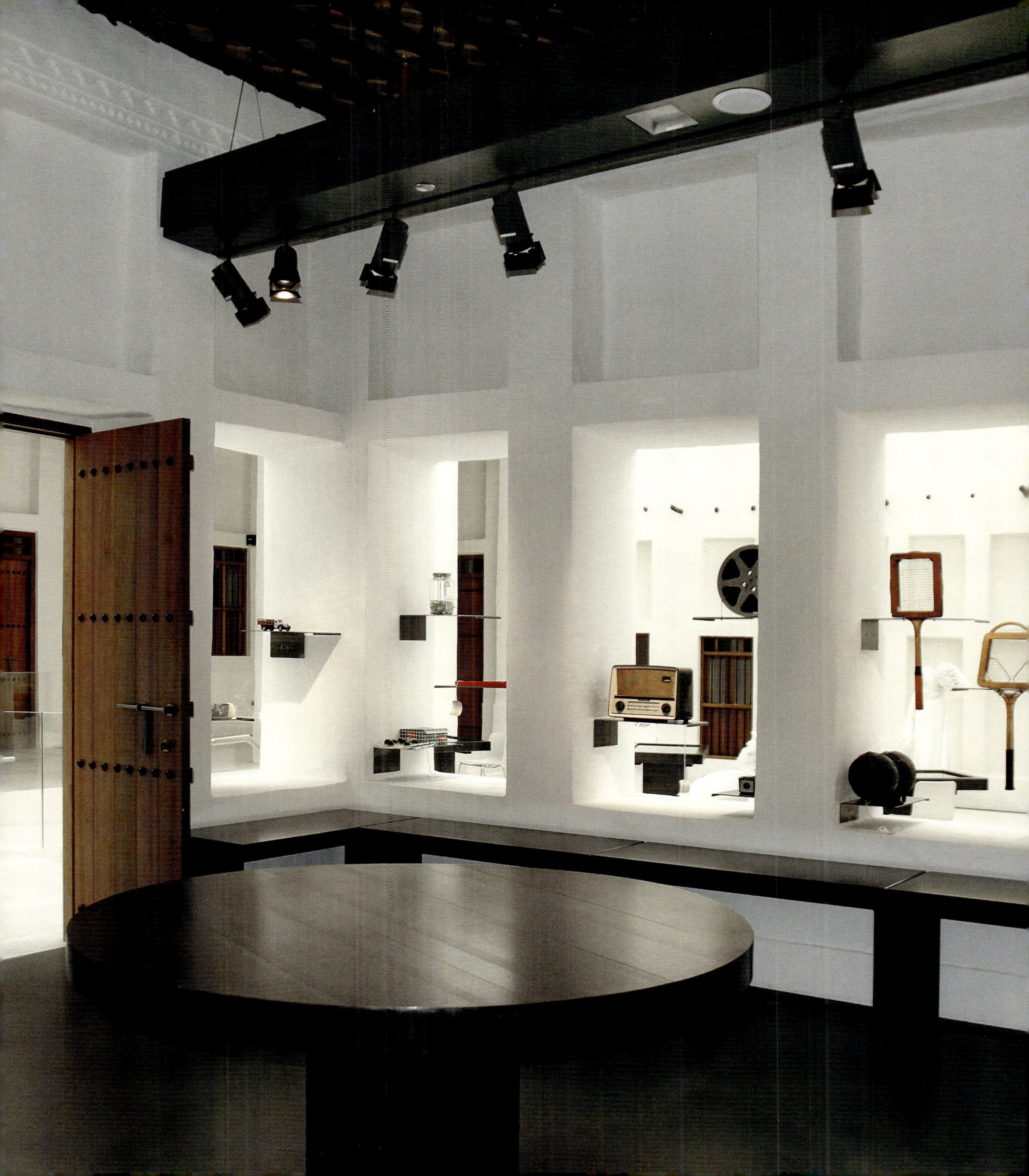

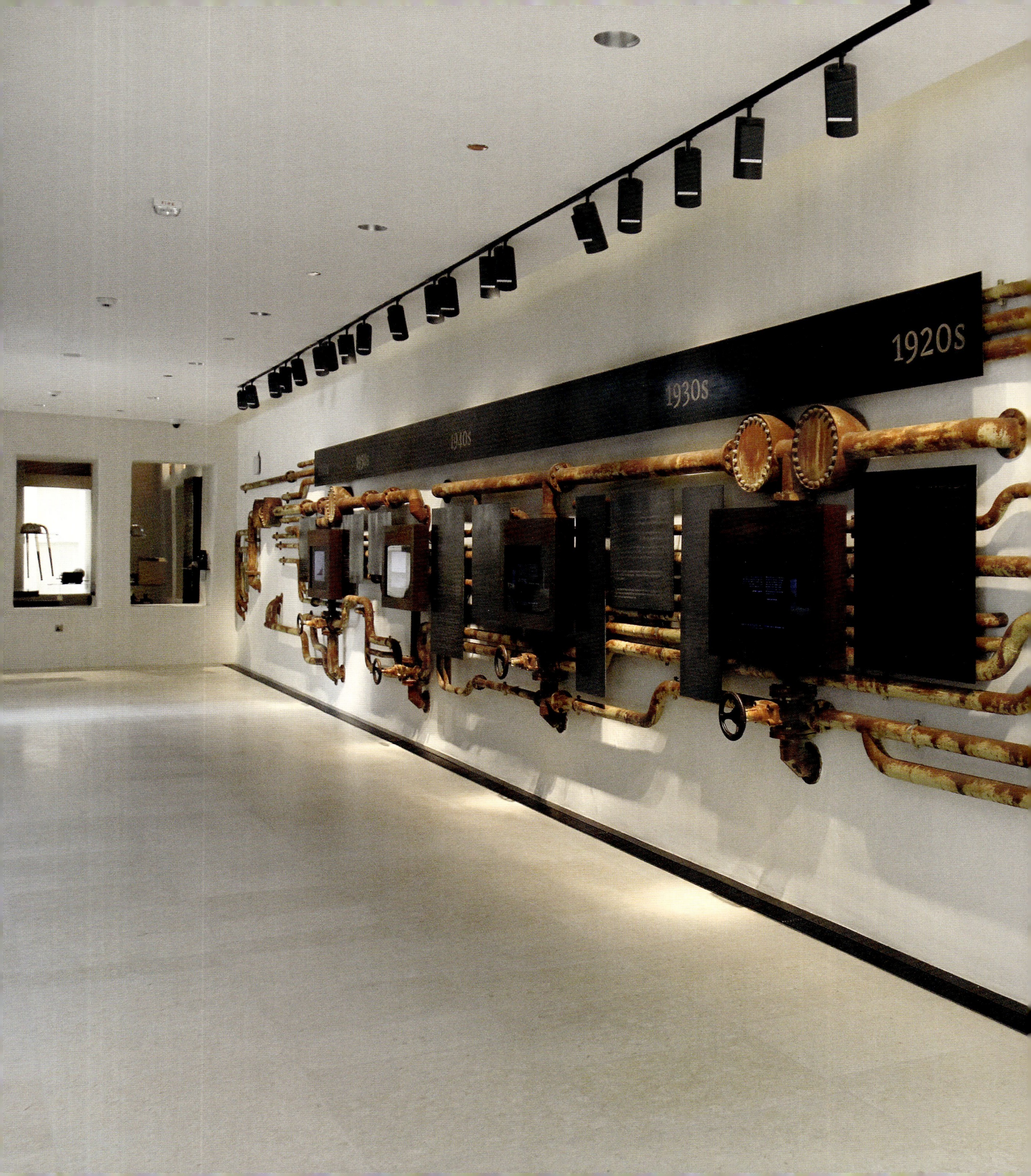
1920s
1930s
1940s

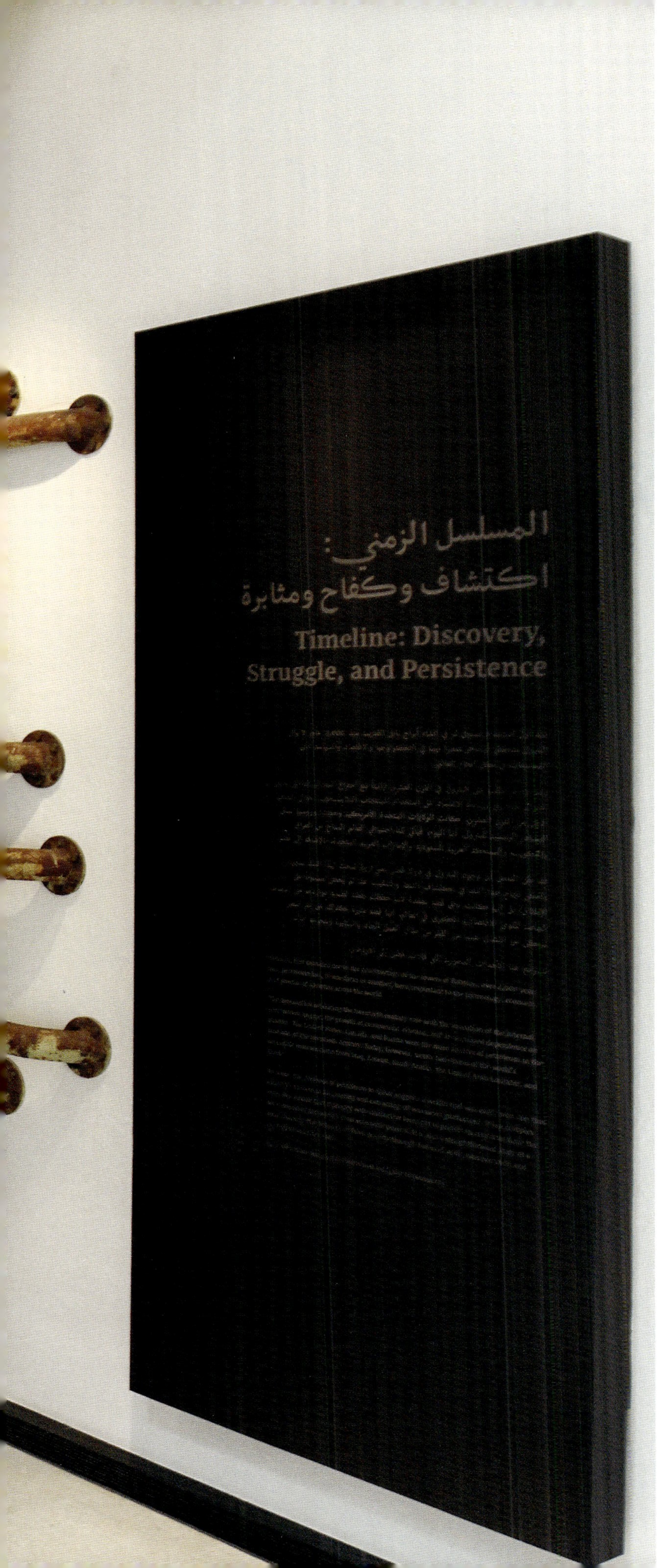

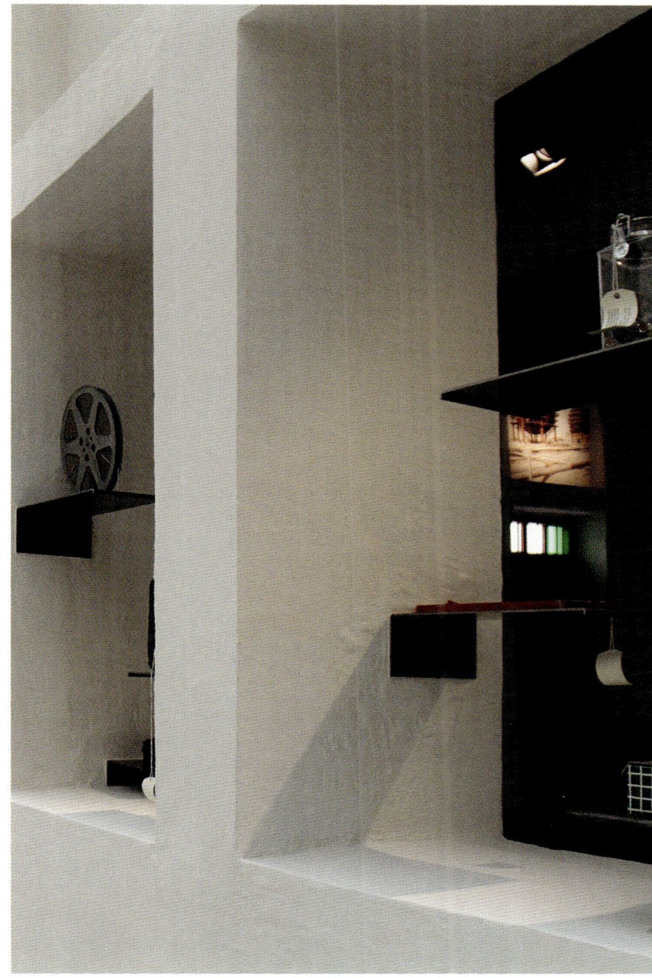

Above: Wall recesses and openings are used differently in the Company House. Here the designers have created multi-level displays within a single opening.

Left: The newly built annex to the traditional Company House is simple and does not vie with the original architecture. In Company House even the display methods relate to the museum and its permanent exhibition. The interactive pipe installation tells the history of the oil industry in Qatar.

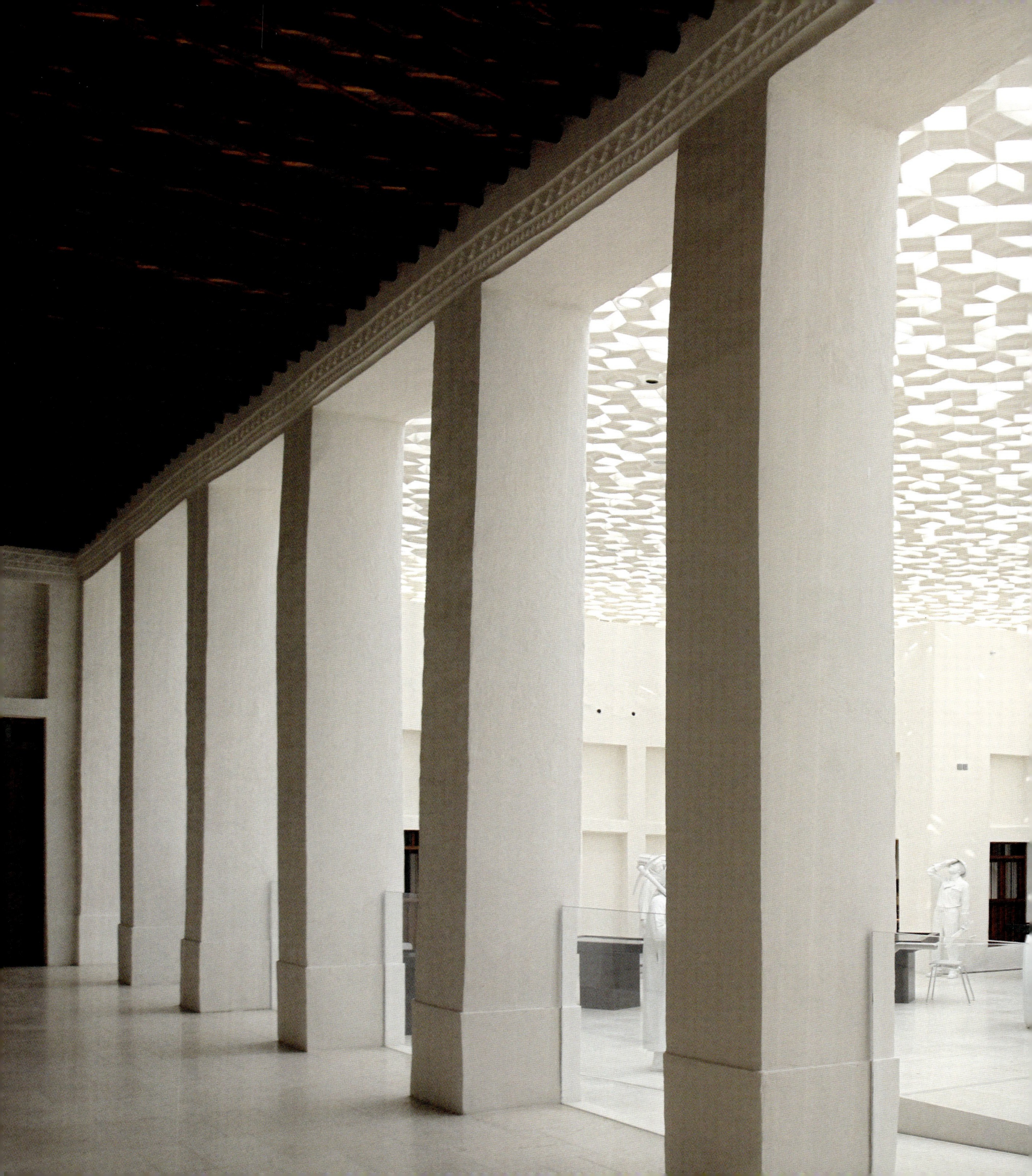

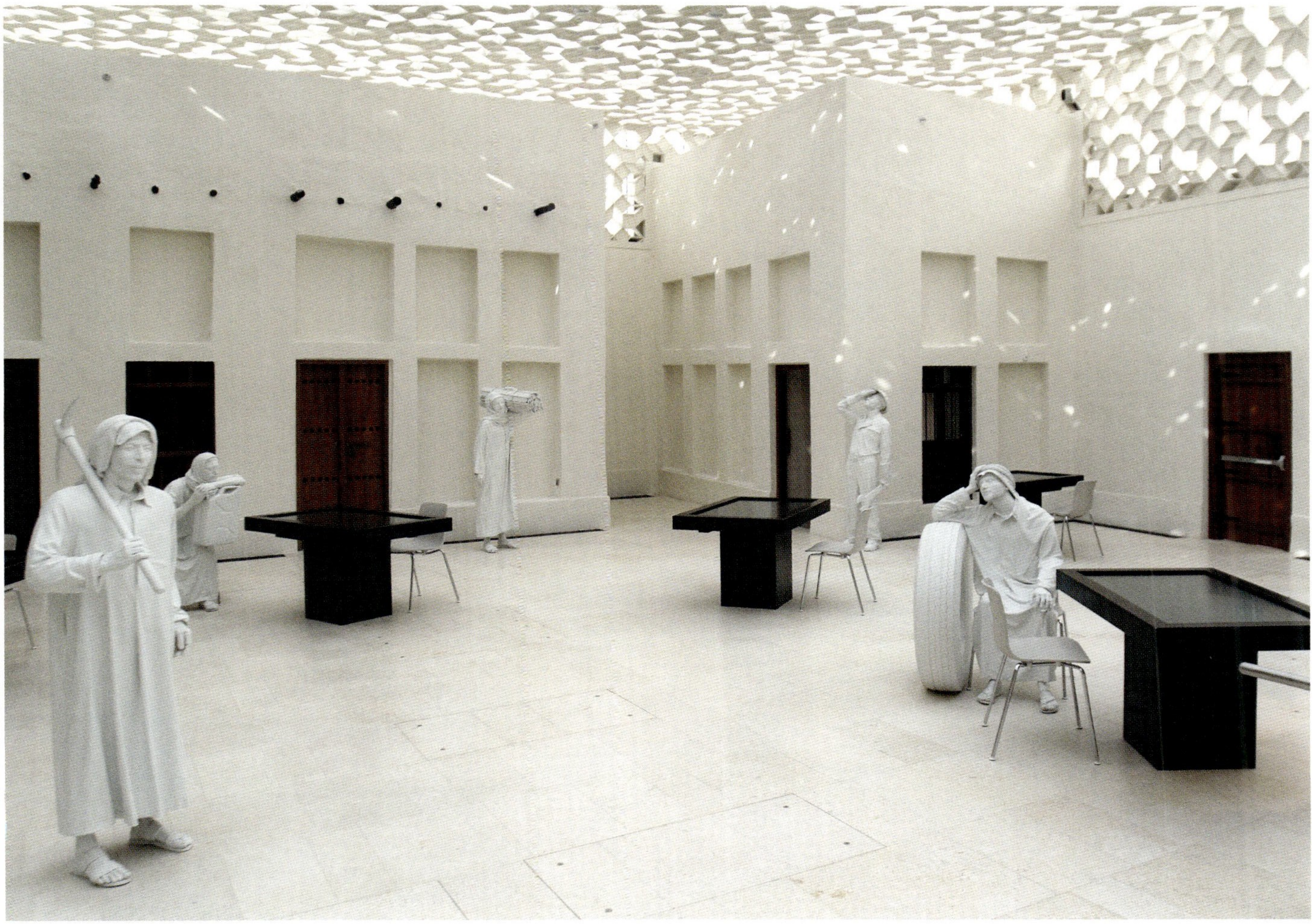

Above: As in Bin Jelmood House, here the central courtyard was enclosed by the use of a contemporary geometric aluminum ceiling.

Left-hand page: The Company House maintained all of its original traditional architectural features; hence we can see *lawāwīn* and *danāshil* in their original locations.

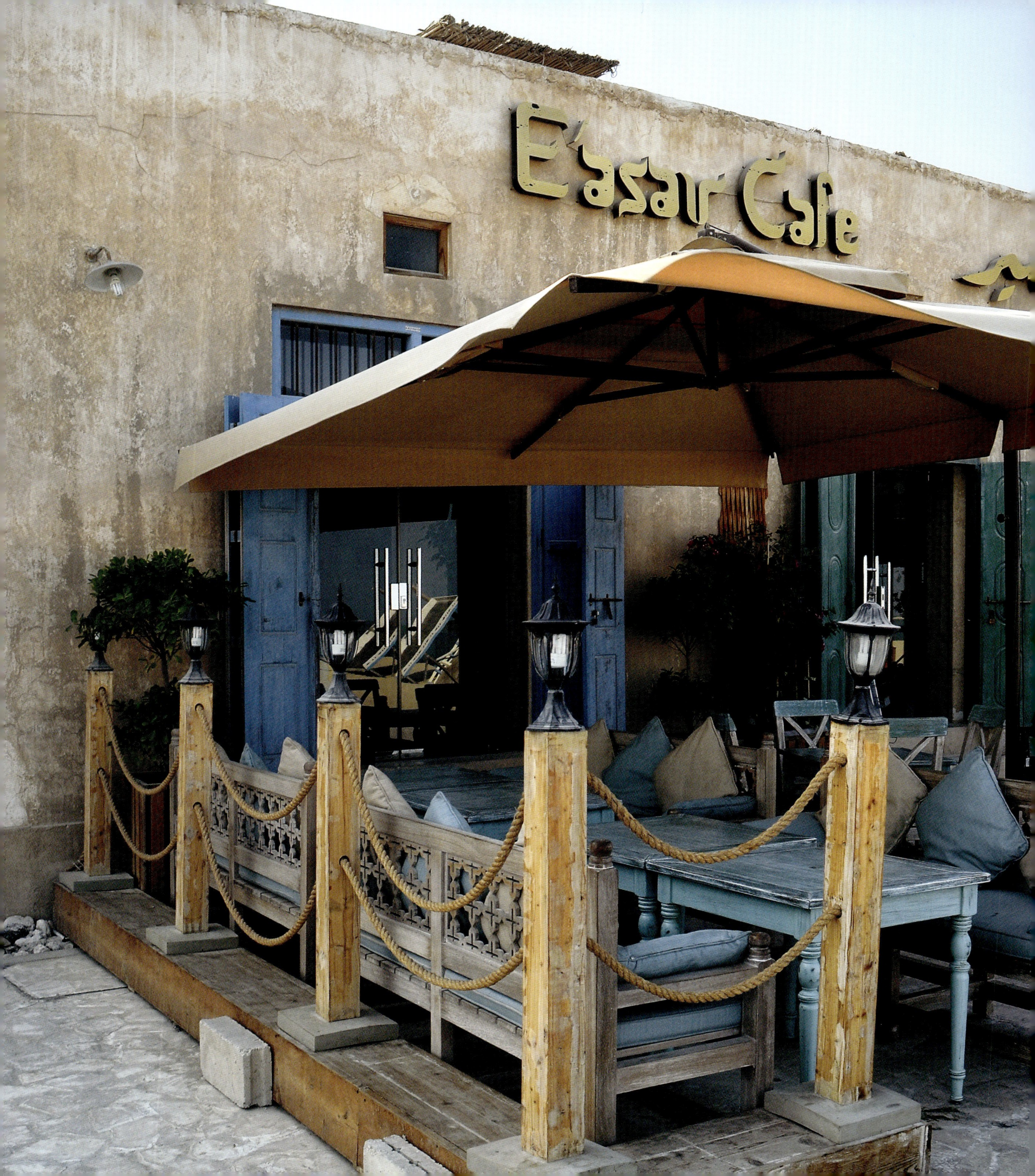
E'asar Cafe

EASAR CAFÉ

Easar Café at Al Wakrah Souq subtly blends farm and coastal styles. The thick ropes usually used for mooring the *sanābīk* are used here to suspend the lighting fixtures. Ropes not only echo the boating history but are a reflection of the café's location facing the sea. The use of colorful tiles on the floor, rustic furniture and light wood recalls a farmhouse interior style. In this instance even the traditionally dark *danshal* was painted in a light color to suit the overall color scheme of the café. The farmhouse style is taken further in the use of wooden fruit and vegetable crates also known as *ṣaḥārāt*. In the 1970s wooden crates were not only used to transport farm produce but also for planting and shelving. Hence in Easar Café, in addition to the traditional *rūsharāt*, the designer has used the crates for the display of various memorabilia while also honoring their traditional use as planters by using them to contain flowerpots.

The walls of the café are painted in a style that is common in vernacular Qatari architecture. In the late 1970s, wall stamps like the ones used here became a trend in combination with the faux plaster finish of the wall paint. The combination of sand yellow and rustic mint blue colors present in both walls and furniture further enhances the concept of the duality of the locations from which the inspiration is drawn. The seating arrangements against the wall are an elegant reinterpretation of the 1970s *maylis* interiors. Long benches alongside the wall are lined with *dawāshig* and numerous pillows are used as replacements for traditional *masānid*.

It is important to note here that in Qatari culture, the outdoor seating is of social significance. In the old days, it was the place for daily gatherings. Every *firīj* or neighborhood had one or more cafés to accommodate men who would meet for *tchāi* and *gahwa*. This is also where people exchanged greetings and daily news. One main feature of this seating area was the high wooden benches. In the outdoor area of Easar Café, the same type of seating is used, but with modified backs where Islamic geometric patterns are evident.

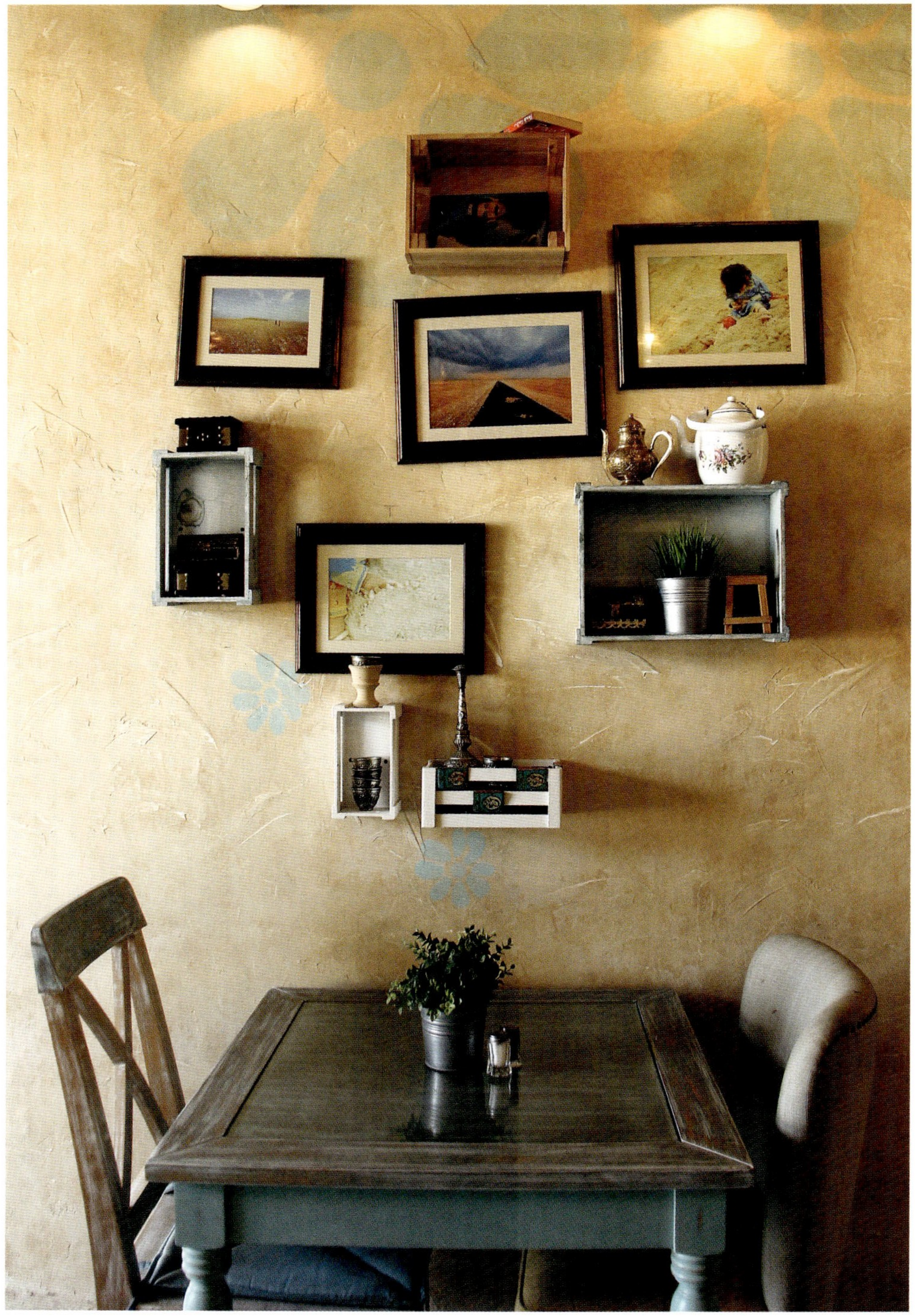

Above: The plastered wall has been decorated with photographs and non-traditional tea-pots.

Right-hand page: The space was re-adapted to suit the design concept of the café. Dark *danāshil* have been painted in a lighter color.

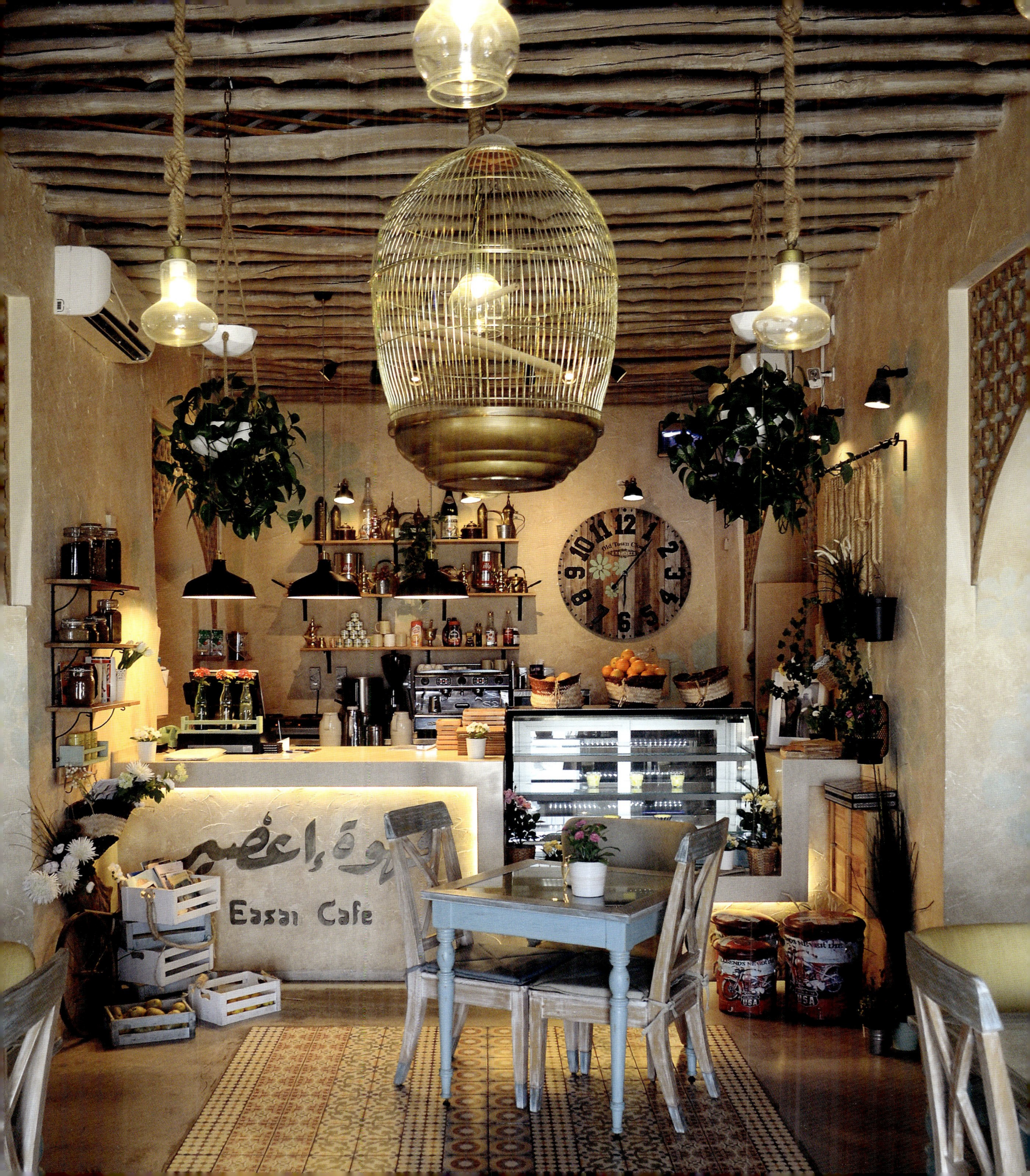
Easai Cafe

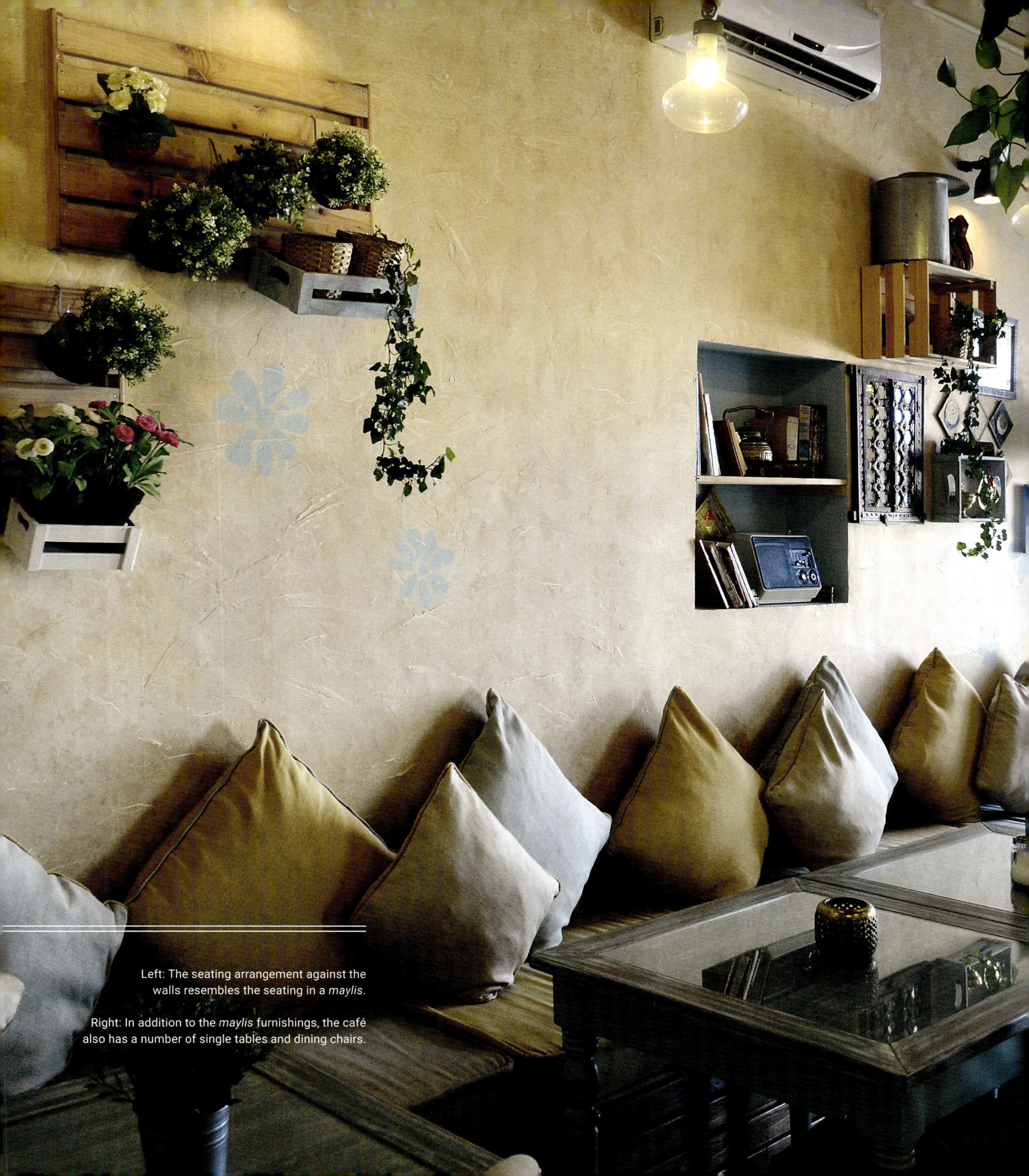

Left: The seating arrangement against the walls resembles the seating in a *maylis*.

Right: In addition to the *maylis* furnishings, the café also has a number of single tables and dining chairs.

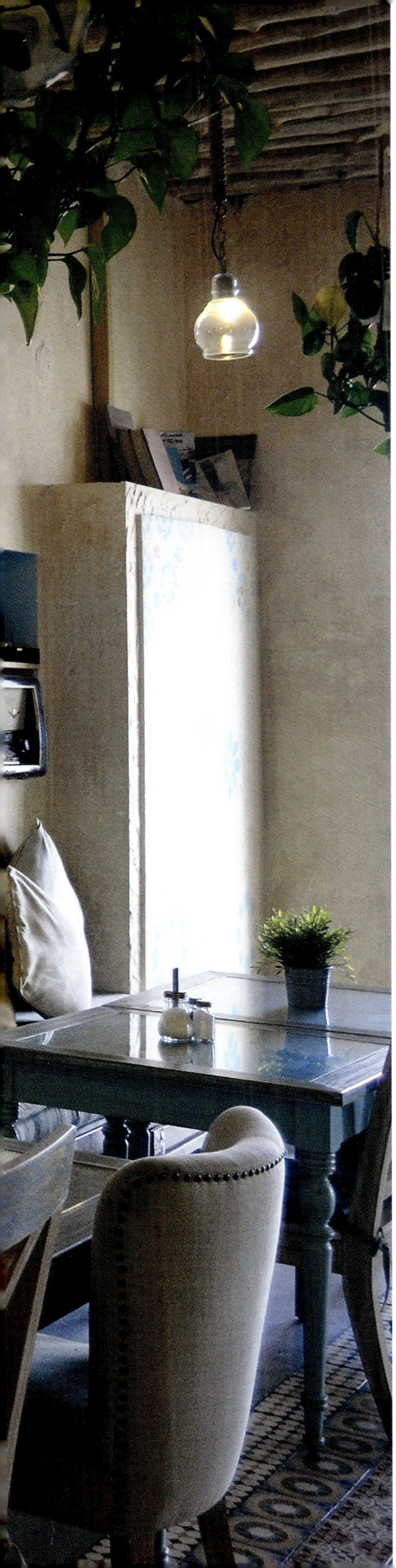

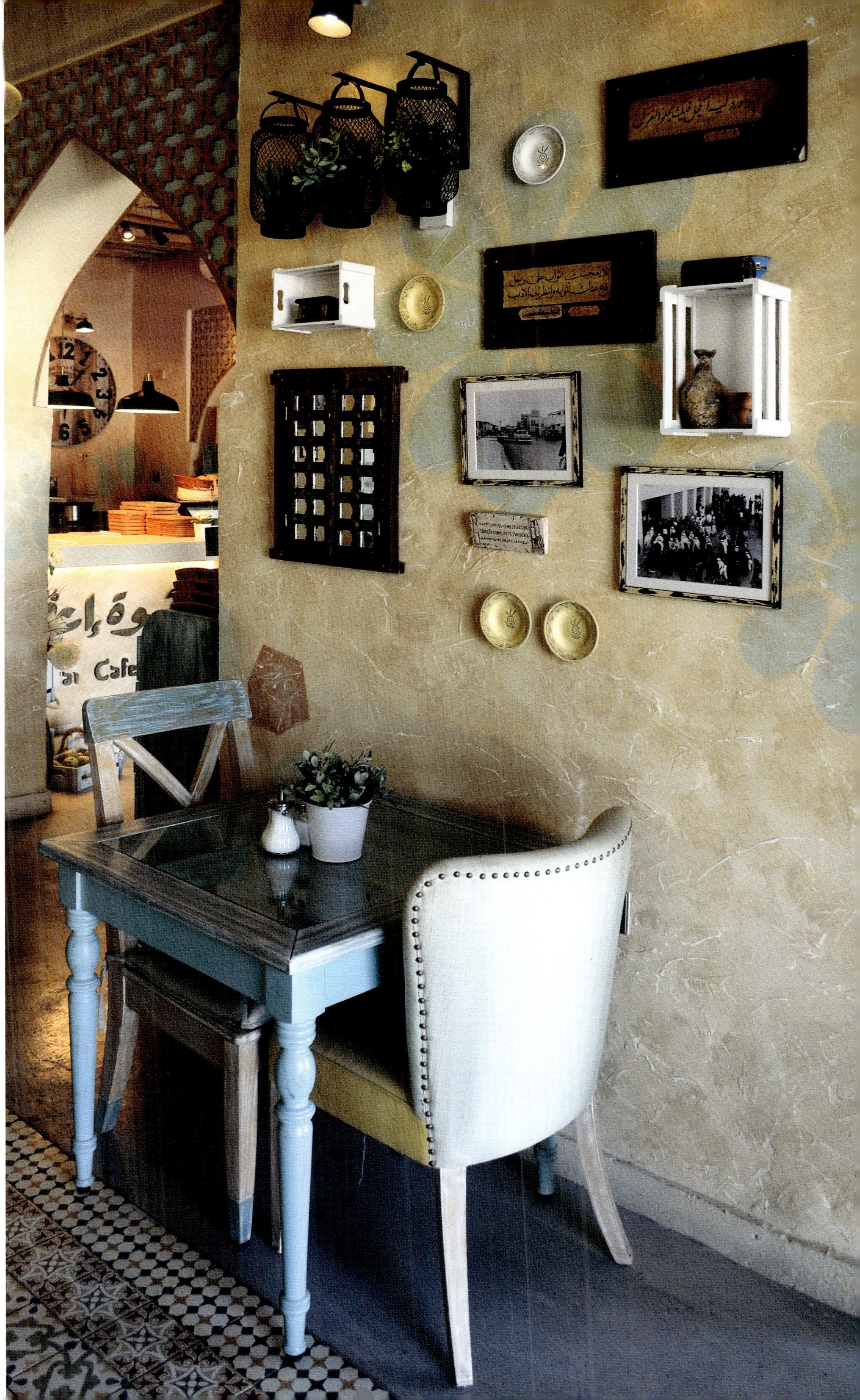

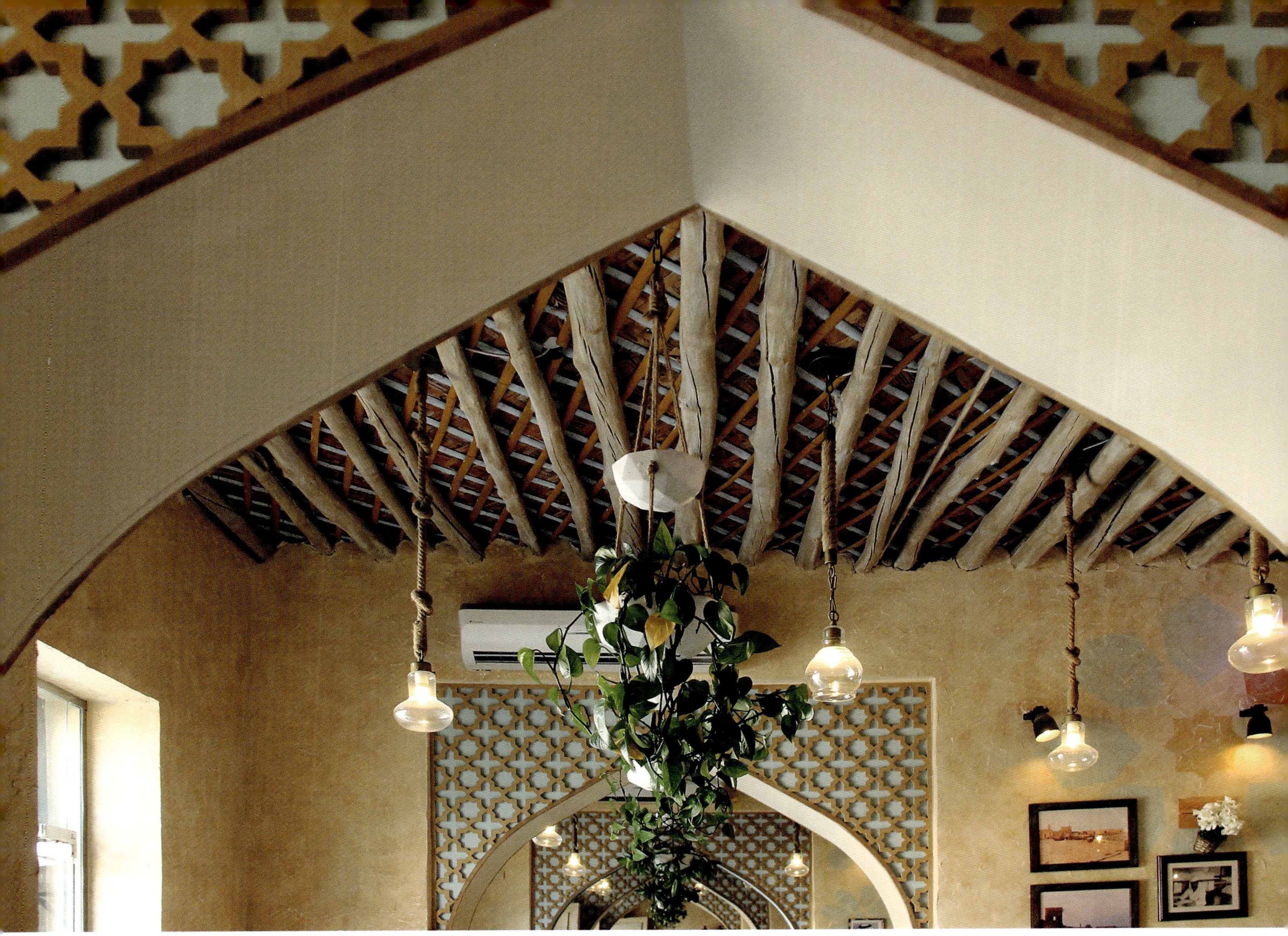

Above: Traditional *danshal* is present in the entire café and while traditionally it was a functional architectural feature, here it is used as a decorative element.

Right-hand page: Re-purposed vegetable crates and *jafīr* decorate the central counter.

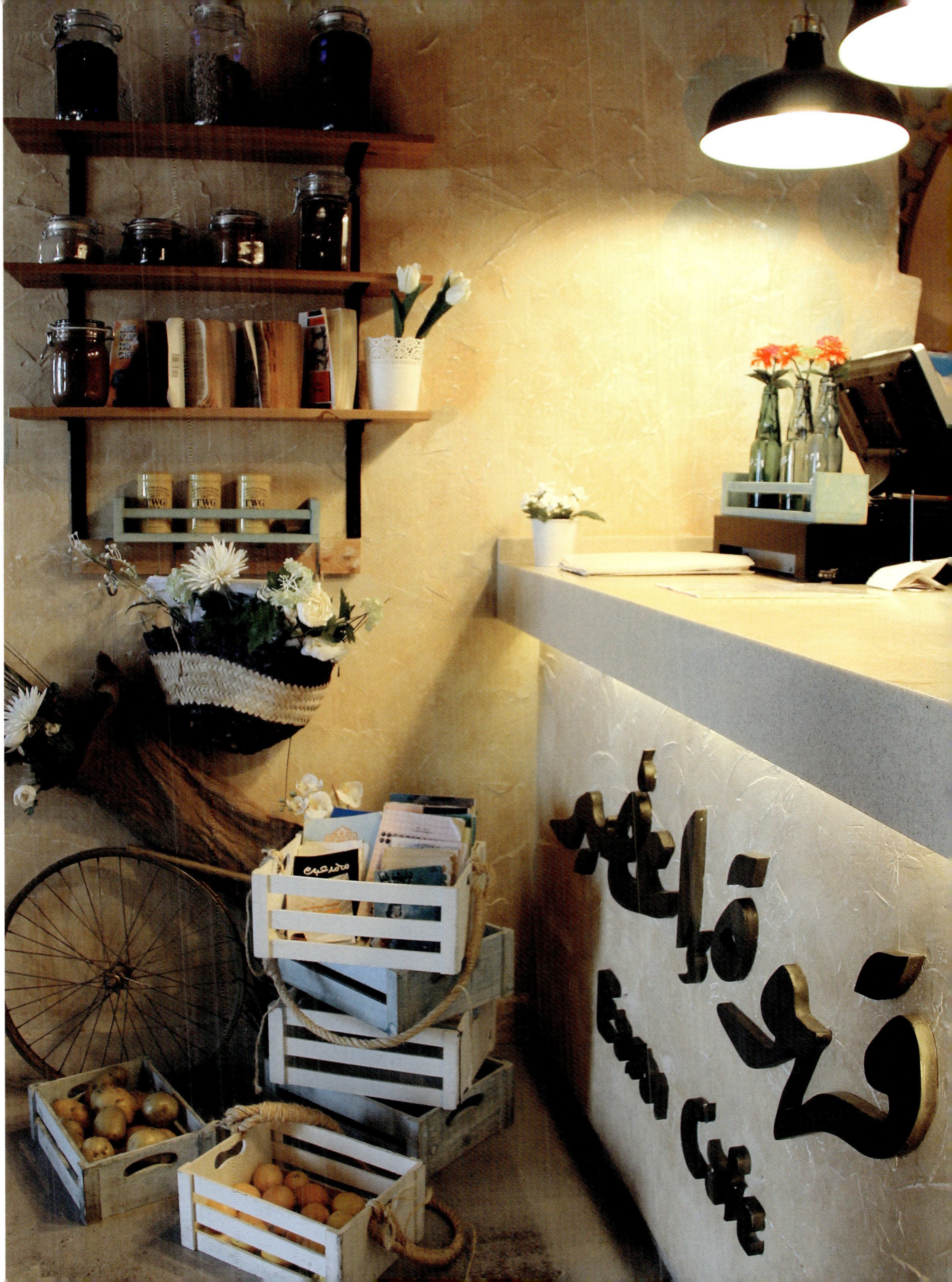
TWG
TWG
TWG

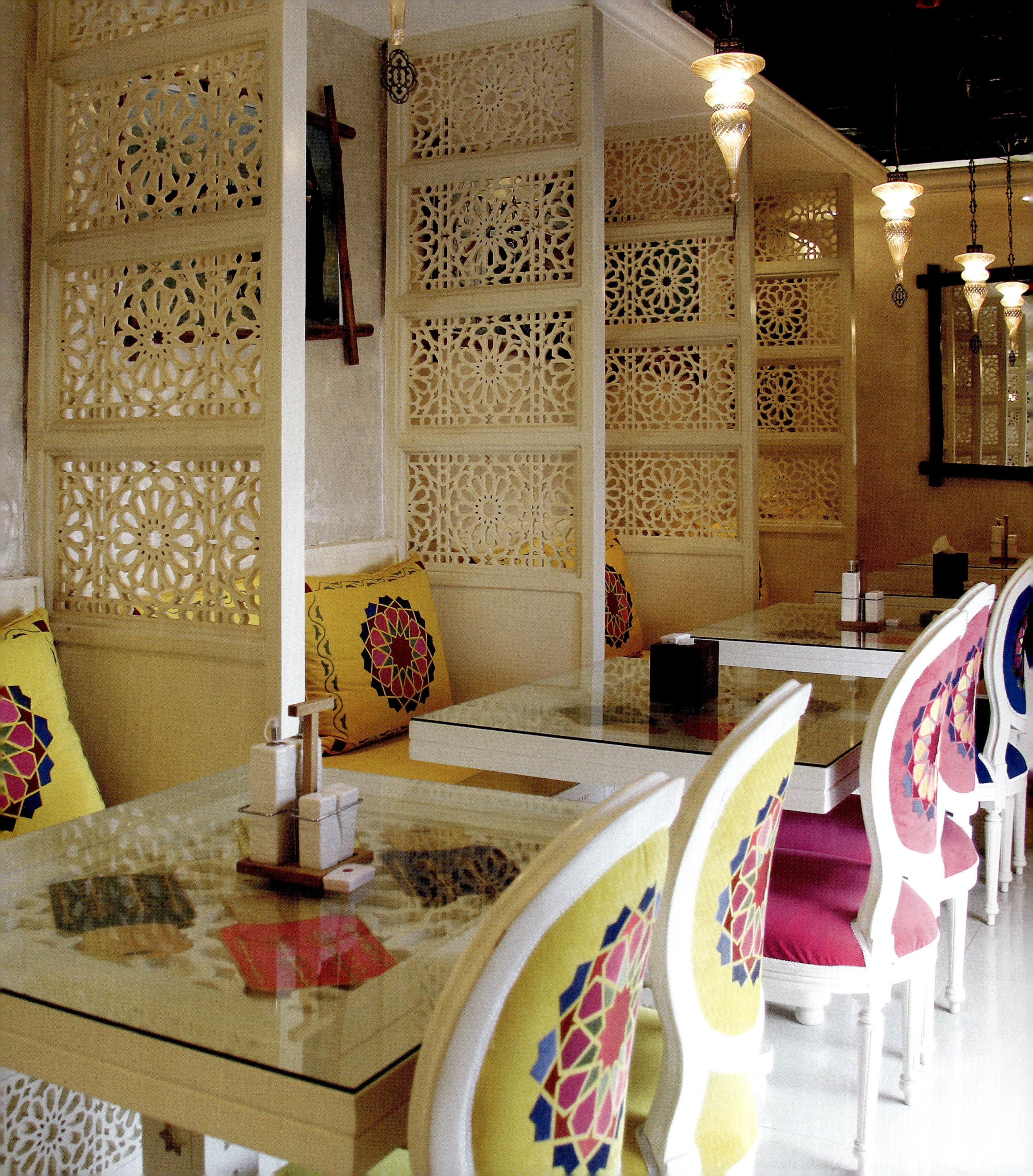

AL NOUKHAZA RESTAURANT

The name of the restaurant originates from the title of the captains of the pre-oil period *sanābīk* who were referred to as *nawākhzah*. This restaurant is composed of three distinctive spaces.

Firstly, facing the beach is the front of the restaurant that is fitted out in rustic white wooden chairs with colorful mosaic backs and simple tables.

Secondly, the interior space of the restaurant is very different than the outdoors seating area. The seating furniture is upholstered in bright colors such as yellow, blue, and pink, and is juxtaposed with whitewashed walls and white wooden furniture. Private areas are created using *lūzīāt*. Traditional *danāshil* are complemented with rustic non-uniform wooden frames for the mirrors and paintings. Wall recesses, *rūshanāt*, are also present, but here these are even in size and consist of framed rectangles.

Thirdly, there is the back outdoor area. The narrow space between the restaurant's main building and the outer wall of the property creates a private outdoor space that is secluded from curious passers-by. Evident here is an interesting use of the *dakkah* where there are no backs for the faux built seating. Some semi-private areas in the corner of the space are distinguished by wooden structures, complementing the rustic *danshal* that protrudes onto the outside of the building. The exterior walls of the restaurant in this area are decorated with *danāshil* and *sufar*, while the tables are decorated with a modern interpretation of the *fnāra*.

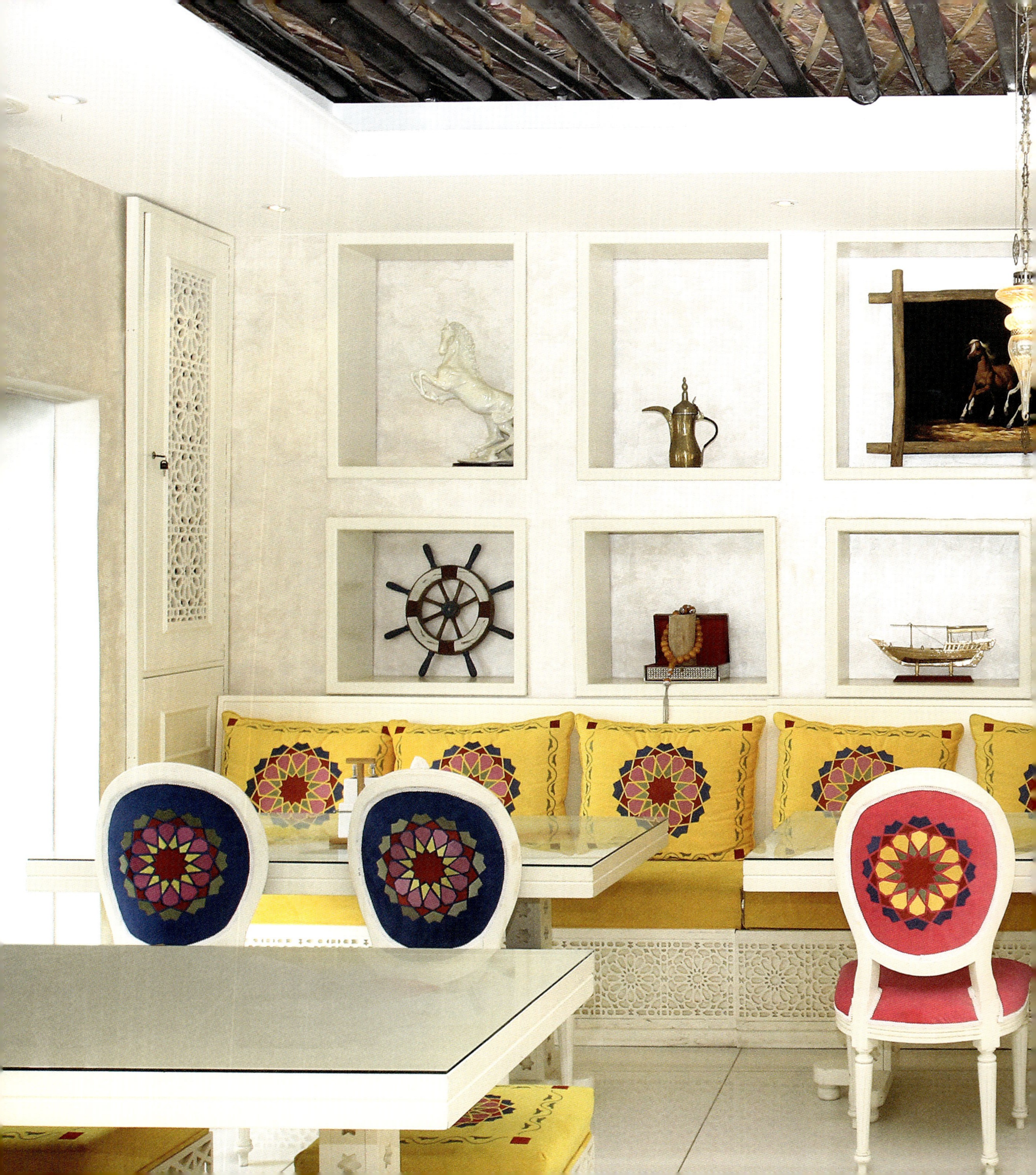

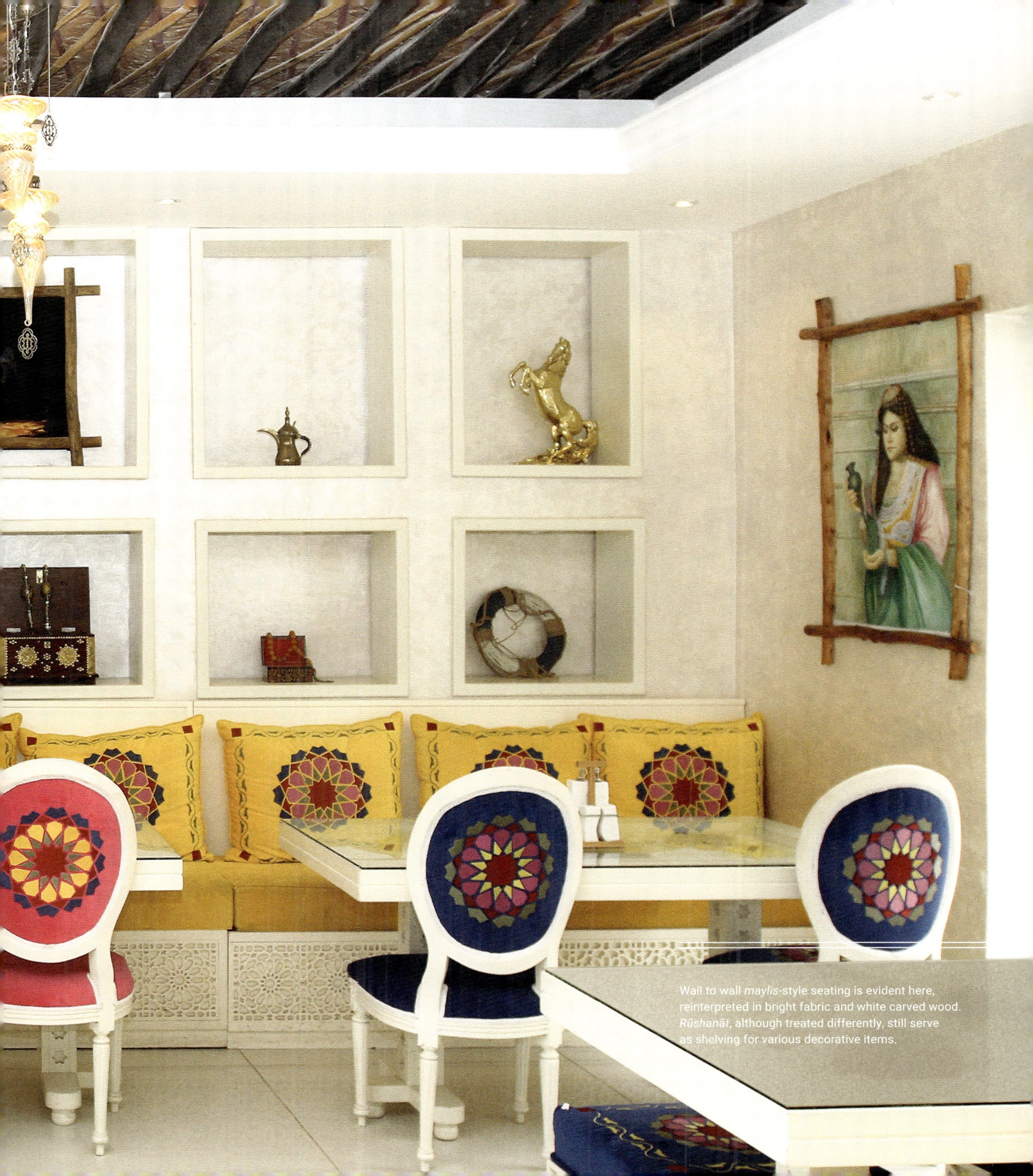

Wall to wall *maylis*-style seating is evident here, reinterpreted in bright fabric and white carved wood. *Rūshanāt*, although treated differently, still serve as shelving for various decorative items.

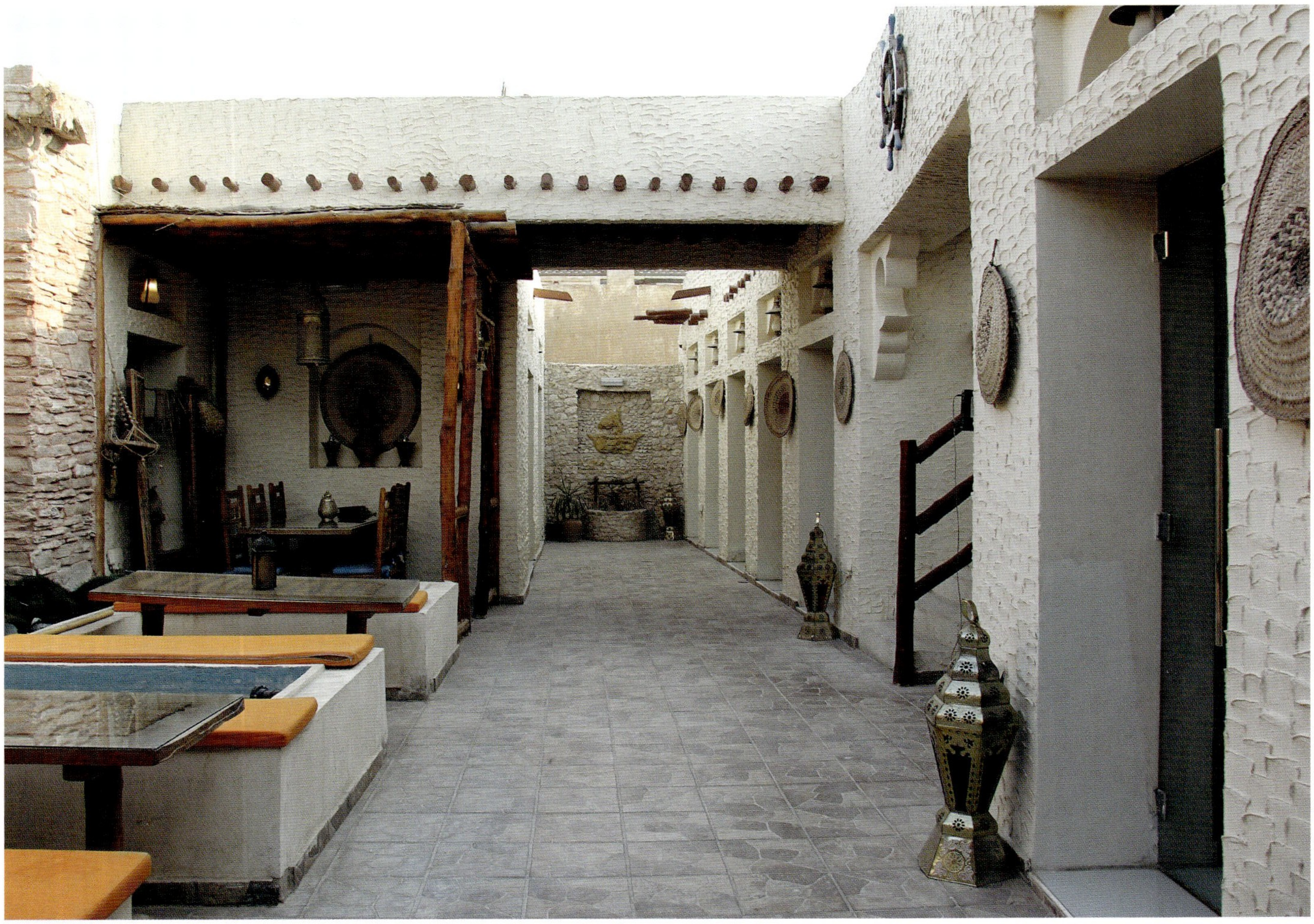

Above: An outdoor seating area at the back of the restaurant features what could be a modern reinterpretation of *dakkah*.

Right-hand page: There is a more secluded seating area under the rustic wooden structure against the rough plastered wall.

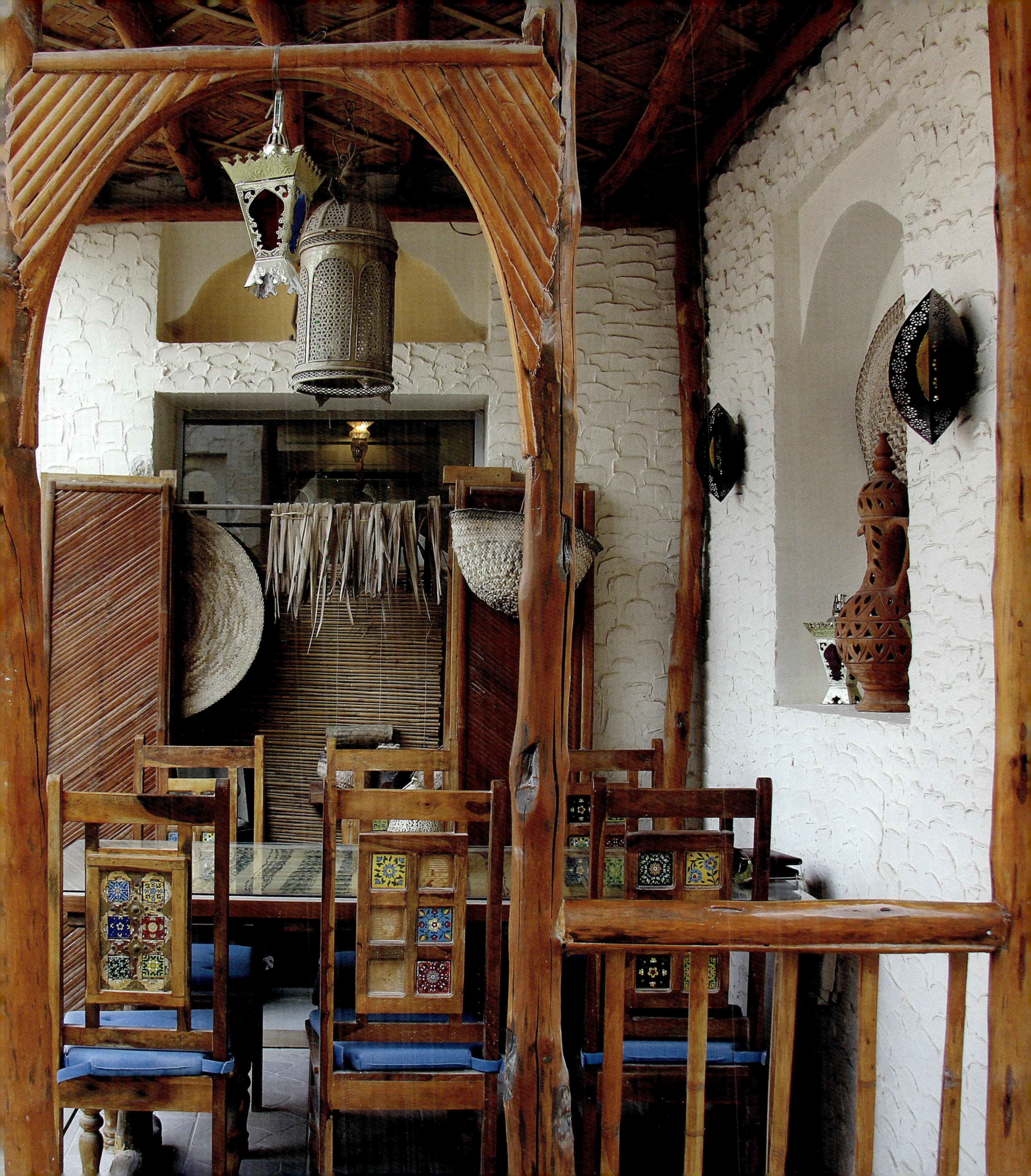

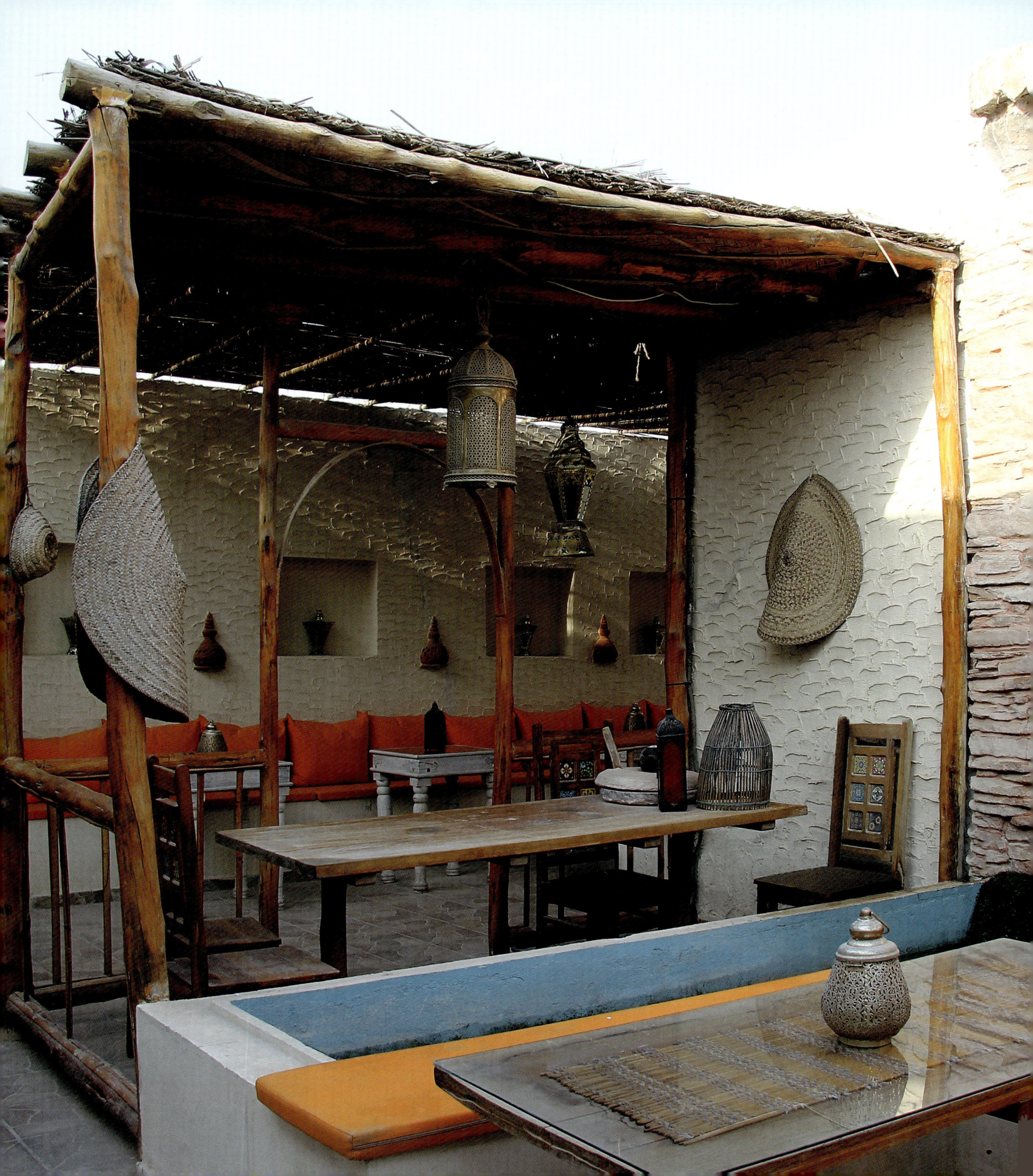

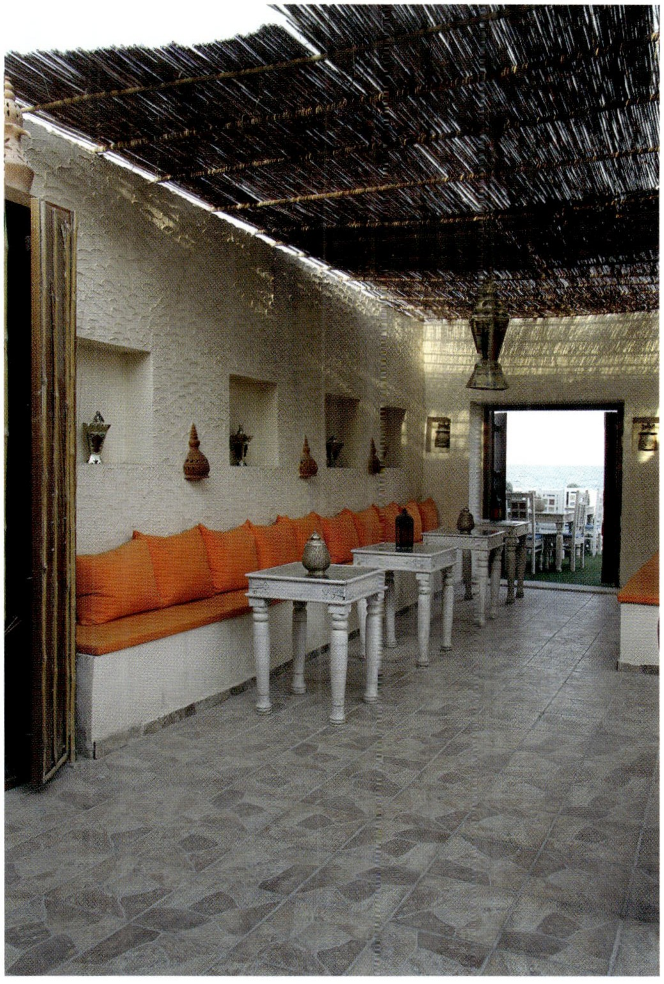

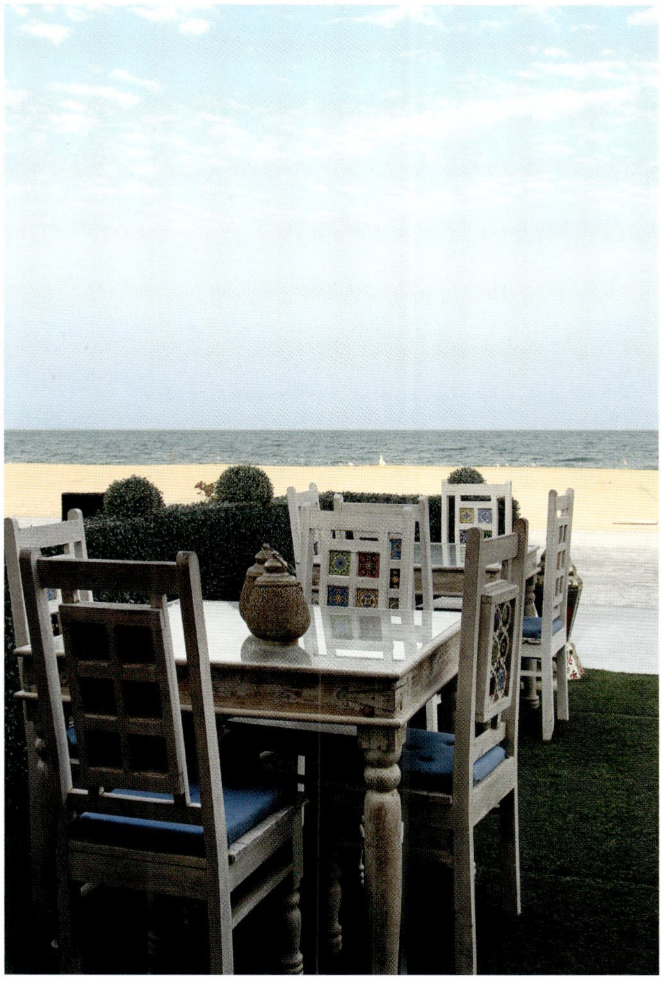

Above left: *Dakkah*-style seating runs alongside the outside wall of the café.

Above right: Beach-front outdoor seating.

Left-hand page: Colorful textiles are used in combination with washed-out wood set against an imitation of a hand-plastered wall.

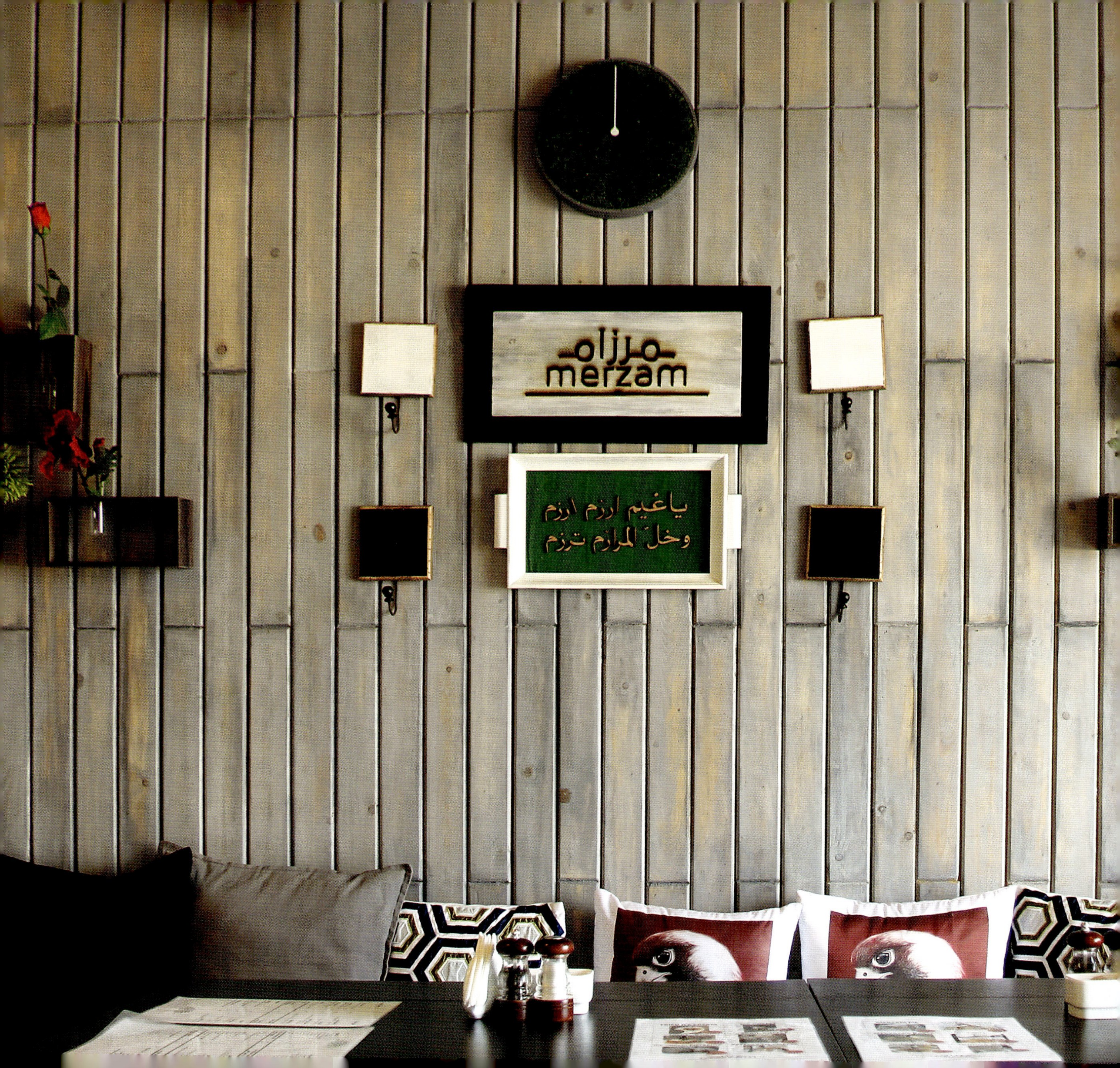
مرزام
merzam
ياغيم ارزم ارزم
وخلّ المرازم ترزم

MERZAM CAFÉ

The name Merzam or *mirzām* refers to the roof gutter of the typical structure dating to pre-oil Qatar.

Designed by a young Qatari woman, the interior of the café shows a fusion between modern design and local symbols. The overall color scheme is neutral and calming, but with the warm maroon details spread out across the hanging decoration and cushions. The relatively small space has been extended vertically by the use of wooden tiles from floor to ceiling, giving a more modern touch to the café but also allowing for space so that it feels more open, warm and inviting. Looking more closely at the decorations, there is elegance in the choice of details. The designer chose a red and yellow array of single flower vases. The cushion covers draw on a direct and literal influence of Qatari culture portraying a falcon, a national symbol and pride, and a woman with a black head covering wearing a *baṭṭūlah*. Similarly, the wooden crates holding the letters for the word "Qatar" displayed on the wall show the charming youthful patriotism of a modern woman.

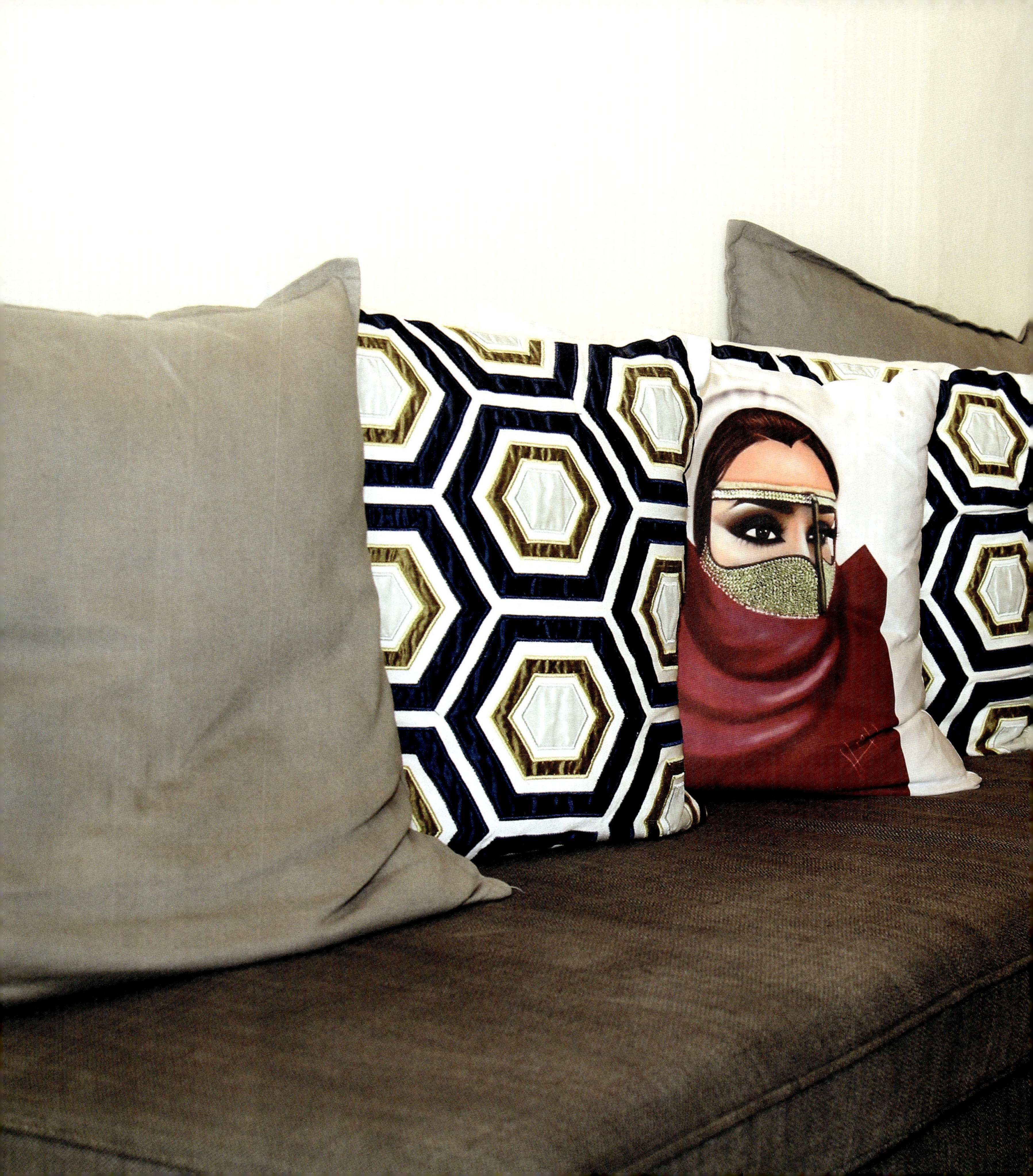

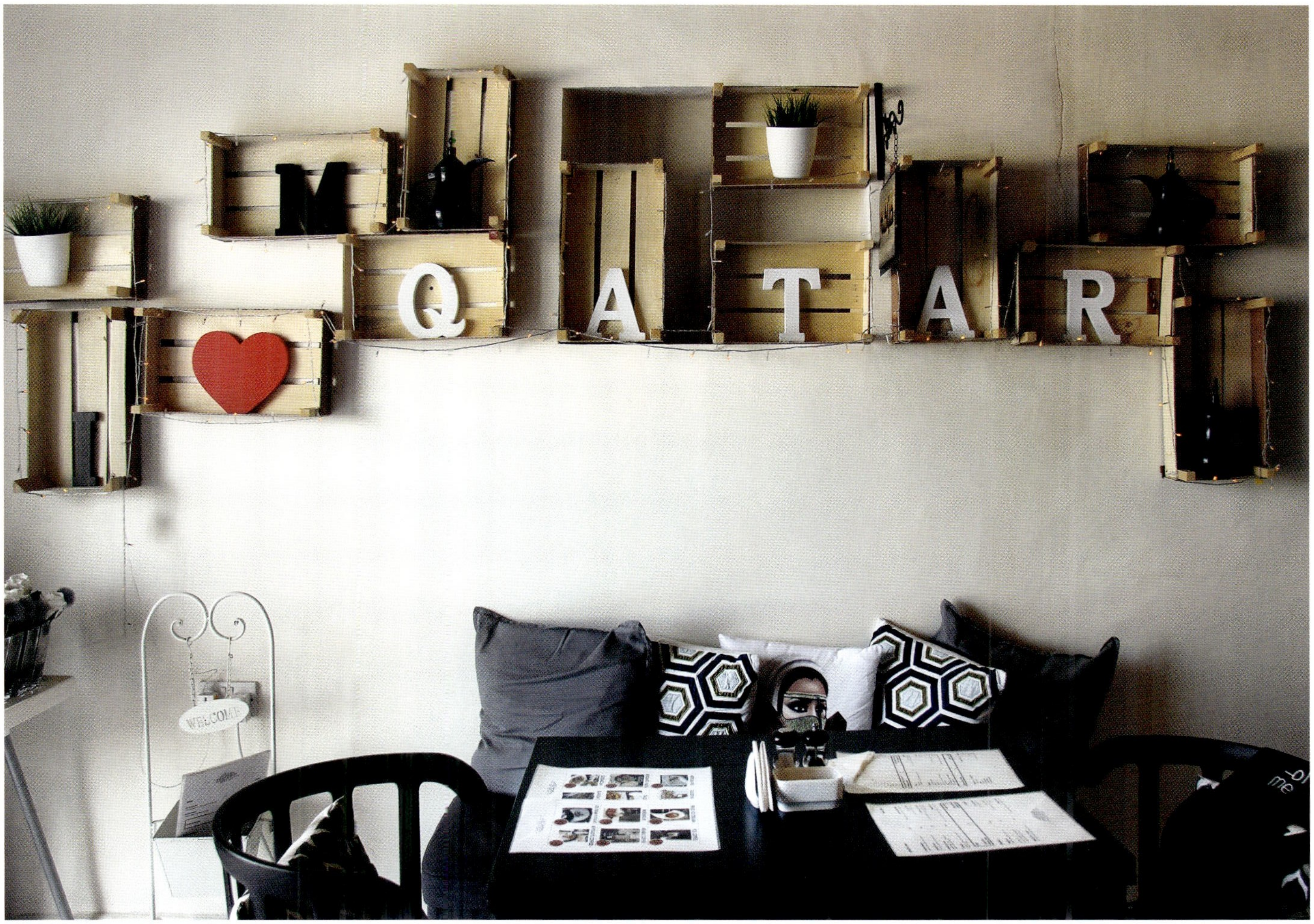

Above: Wooden crates are used as the shelving instead of the *rūshanāt*.

Left-hand page: Unlike many other adaptations of the traditional style where bright textiles are used, here we see a more contemporary color palette of warm grays accentuated with shades of maroon and navy.

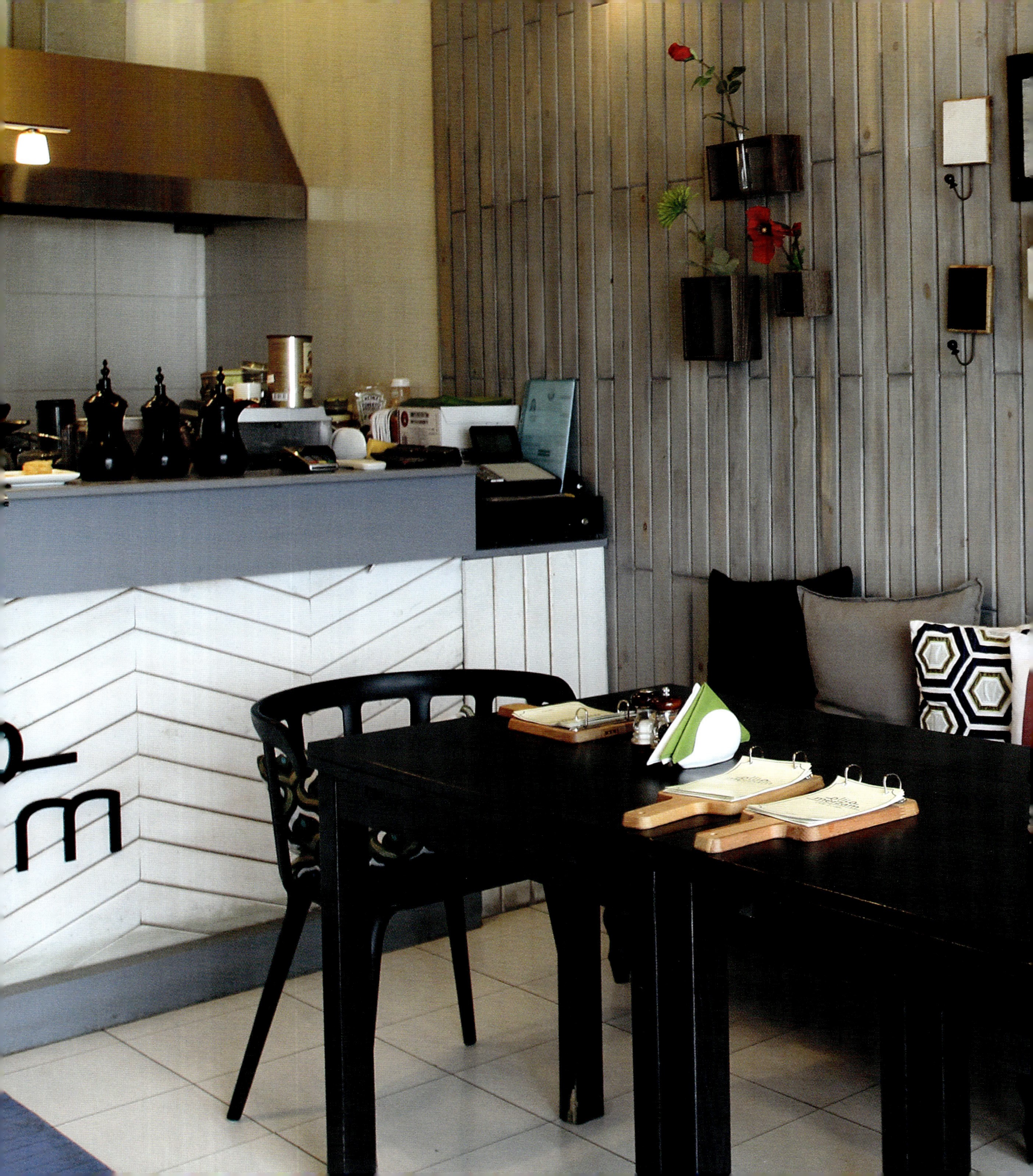

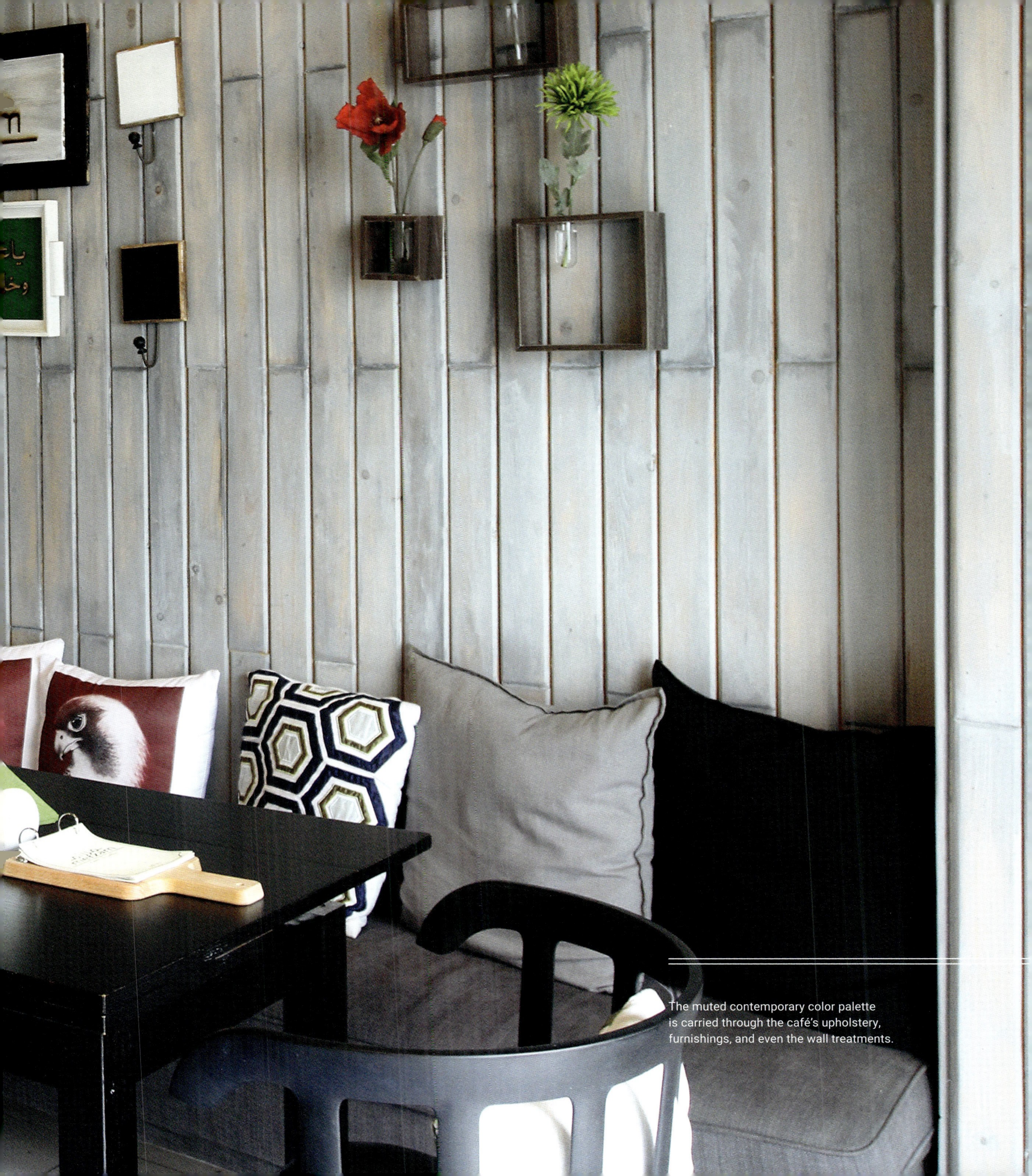

The muted contemporary color palette is carried through the café's upholstery, furnishings, and even the wall treatments.

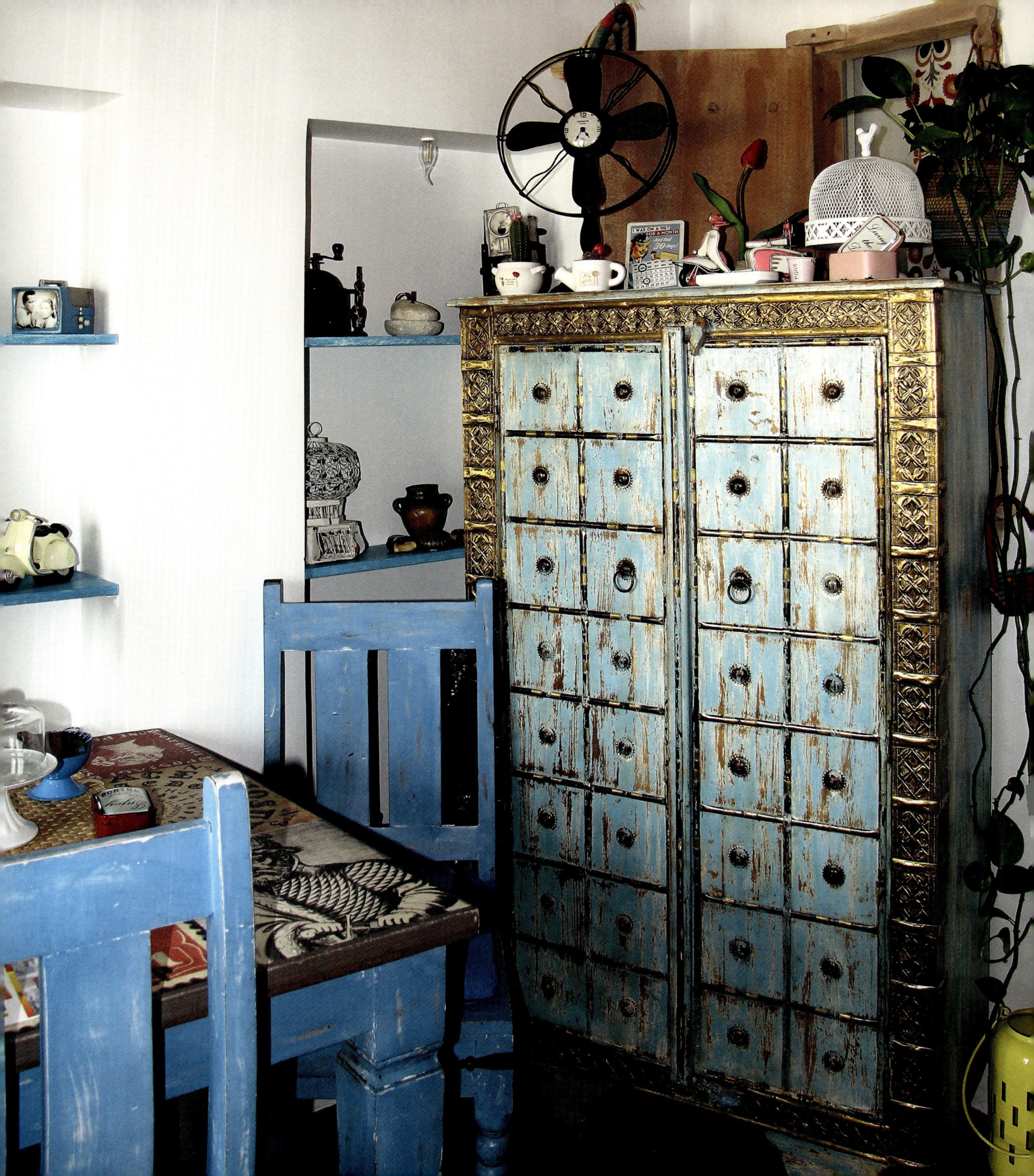
I WAS ON A DIET
FOR A MONTH
And lost
30 days!

AL MENA RESTAURANT

Al Mena translates as "The Port," and its interior design is inspired by the name itself. The details of this small but charming restaurant feel like the collection of a voyager settled in the coastal town. They fit the location—Al Wakrah, a traditional Qatari fishing village. The wooden beams across the ceiling are reminiscent of the inside of a sailing boat. The restaurant is furnished with bright blue furniture and the washed-out wood treatment echoes the presumed mature wear and tear.

Every corner seems to take the guests to a different place, while the inclusion of nets in the interior paired with the extensive use of blue tell the story of fishermen and the sea. The designer also gives charm to the lighting within the space by using colorful recycled jars, providing a further nostalgic echo of the collection of a voyager and local explorer preserving items from the world beyond the sea.

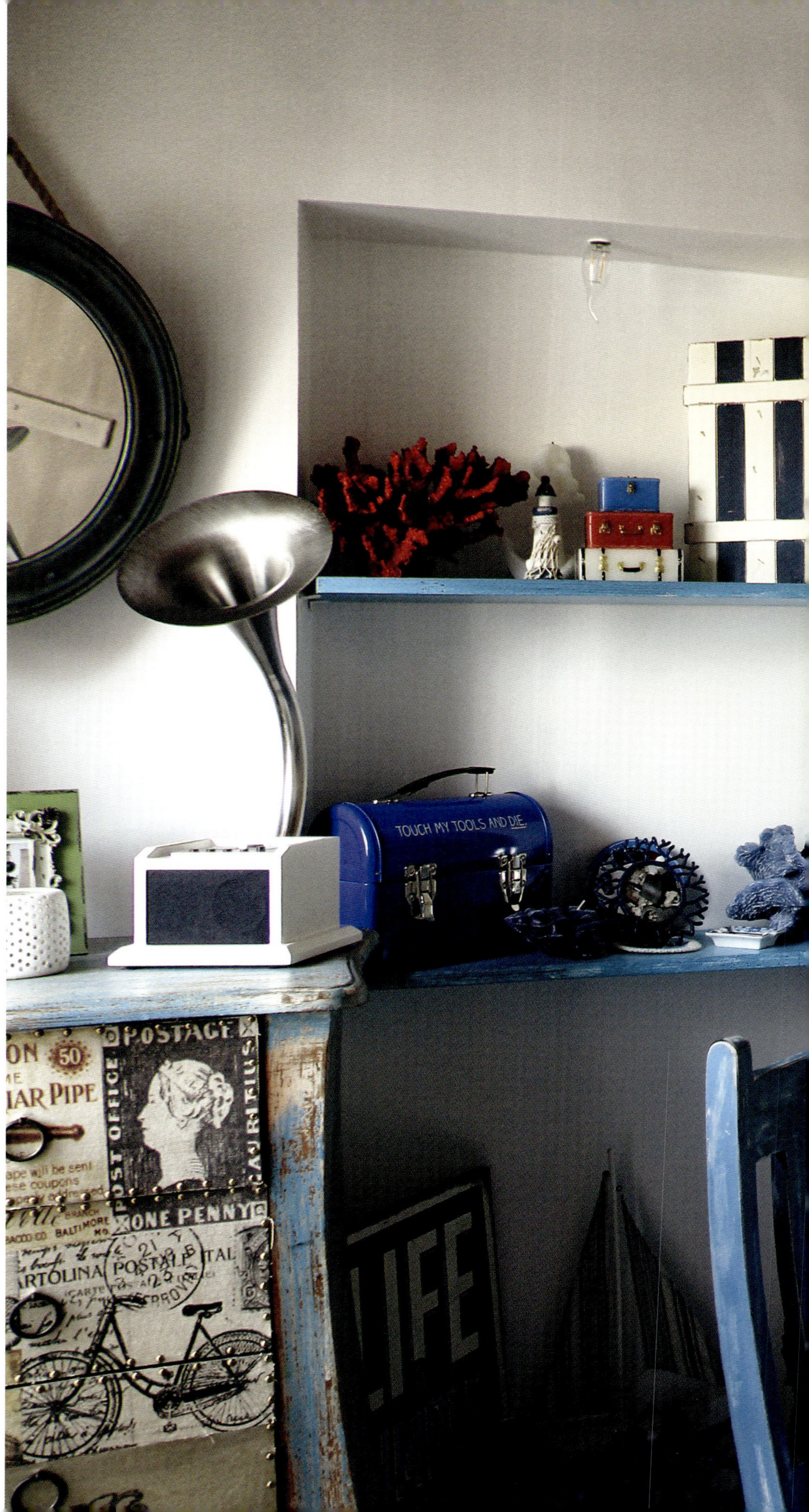

Displayed here is a collection of objects dominated by shades of blue and with a focus on the themes of sea and travel.

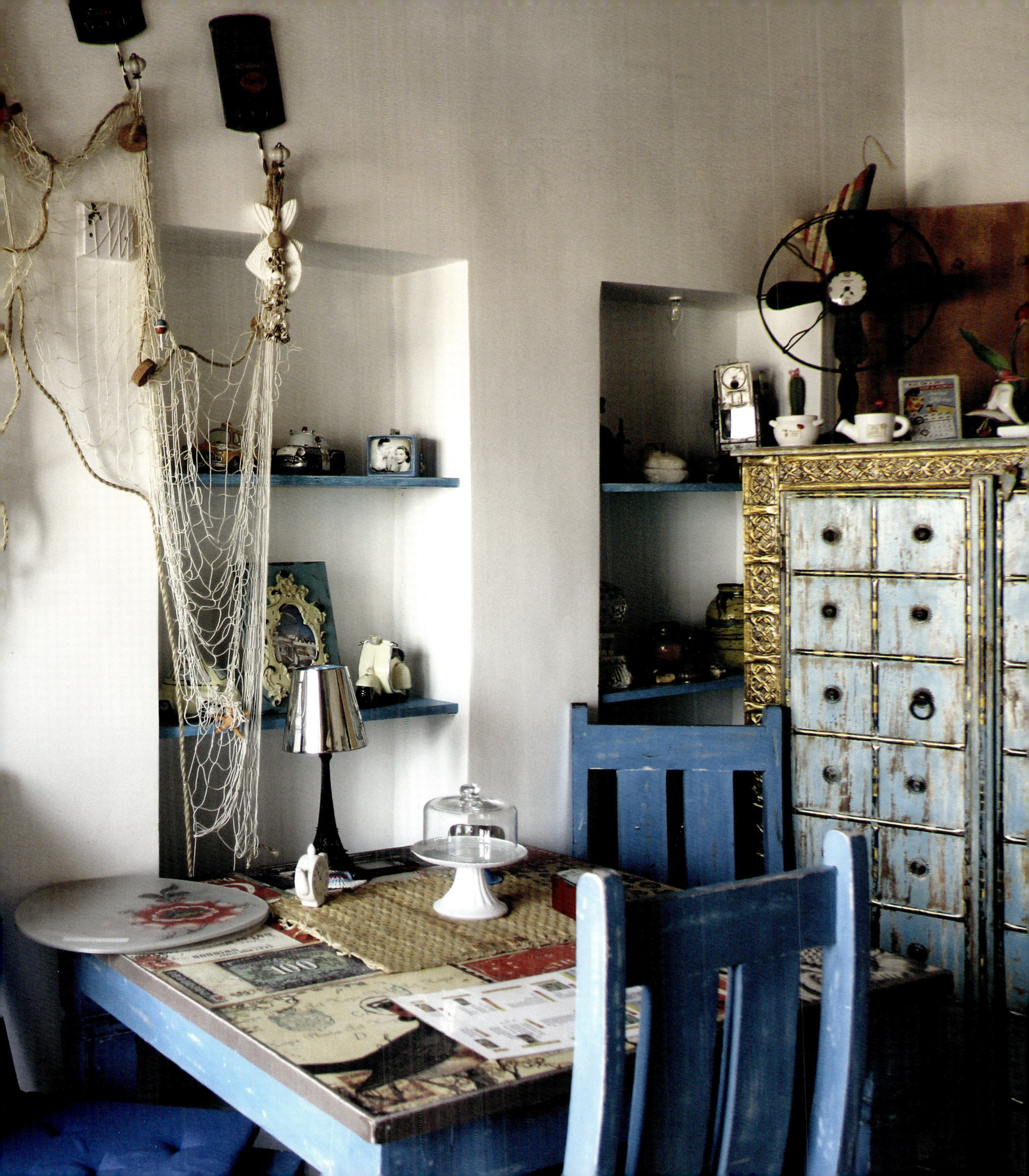

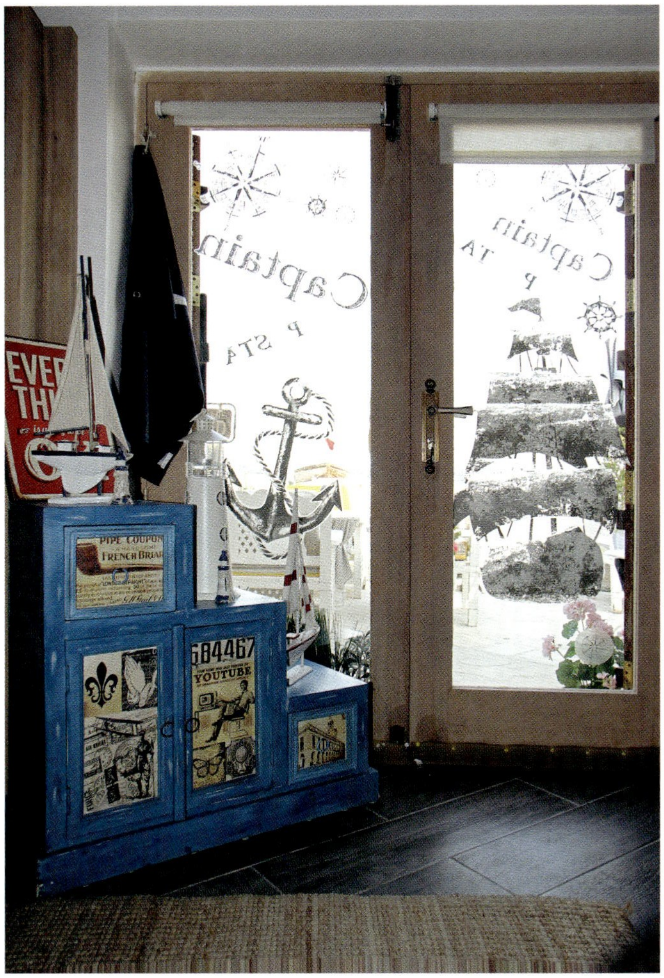

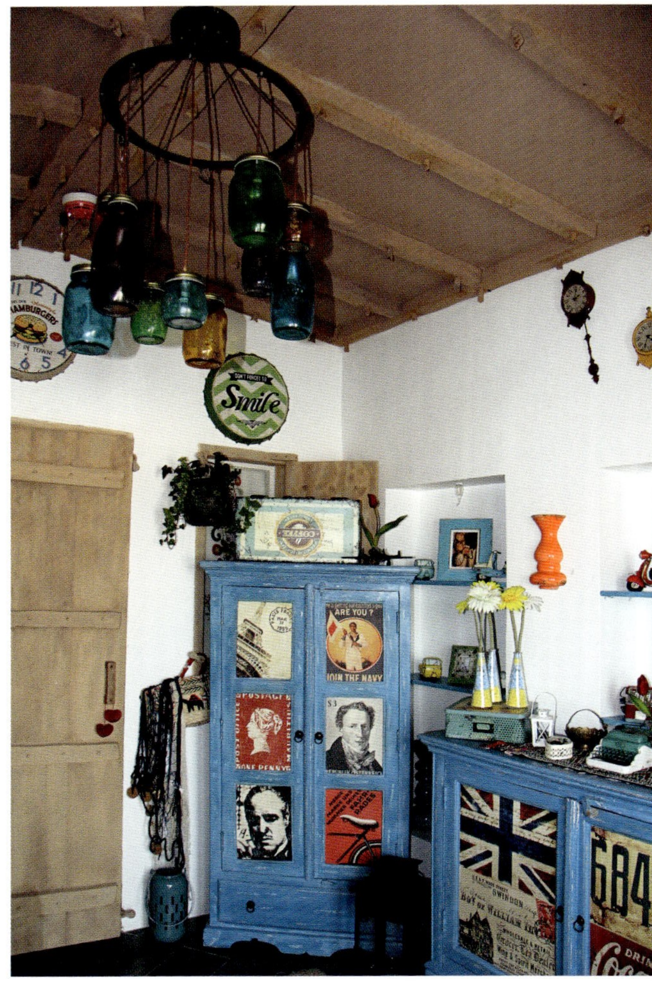

Above left: The furniture is decorated by numerous images of European travel destinations, referring back to the time when Qatar was a British protectorate.

Above right: In addition to what looks like refurbished furniture, the lighting fixtures are also re-purposed from colorful jars.

Right-hand page: Evident in this café are numerous storage units which are not used for their intended purposes but rather as decorative elements.

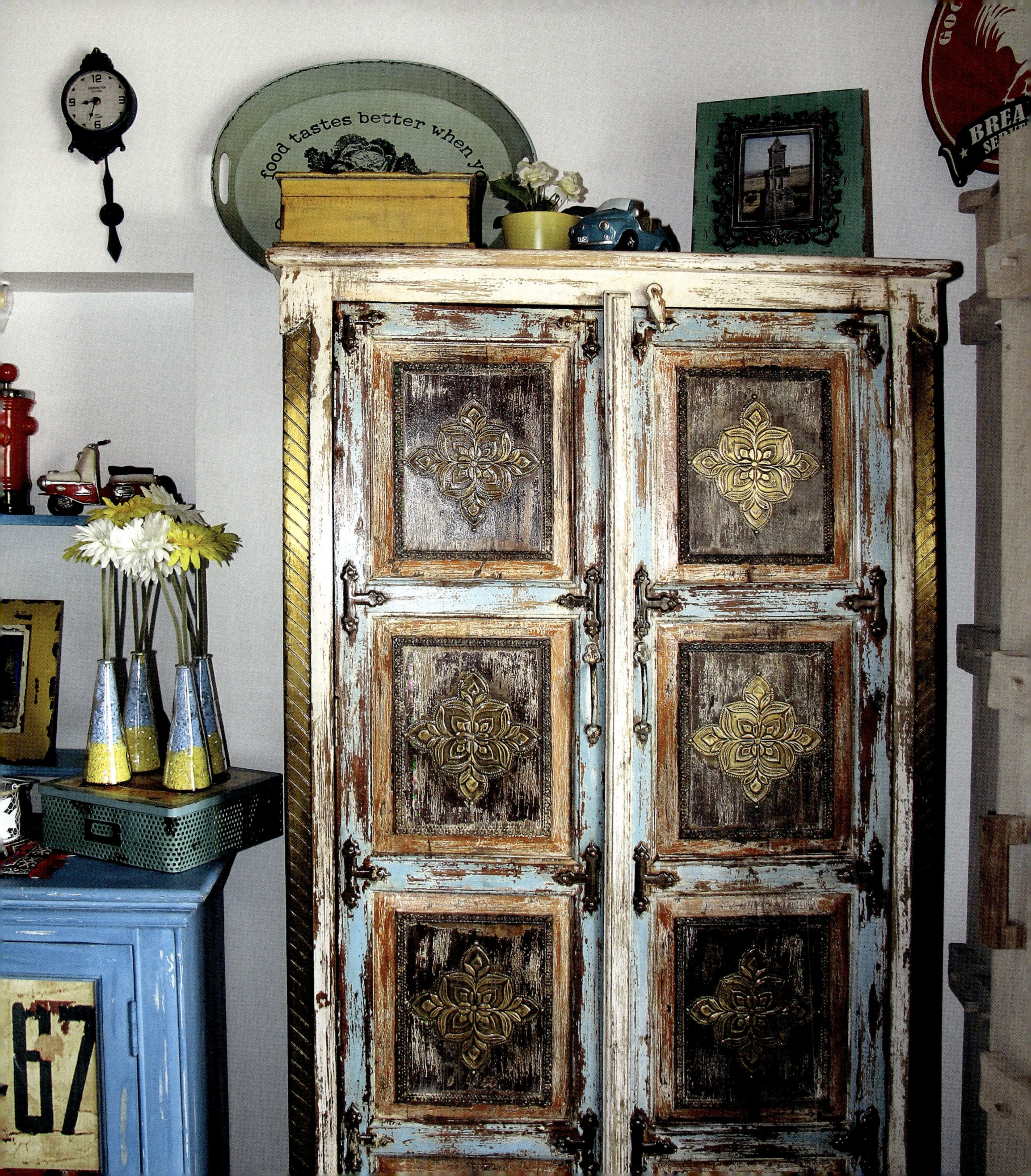
food tastes better when
67

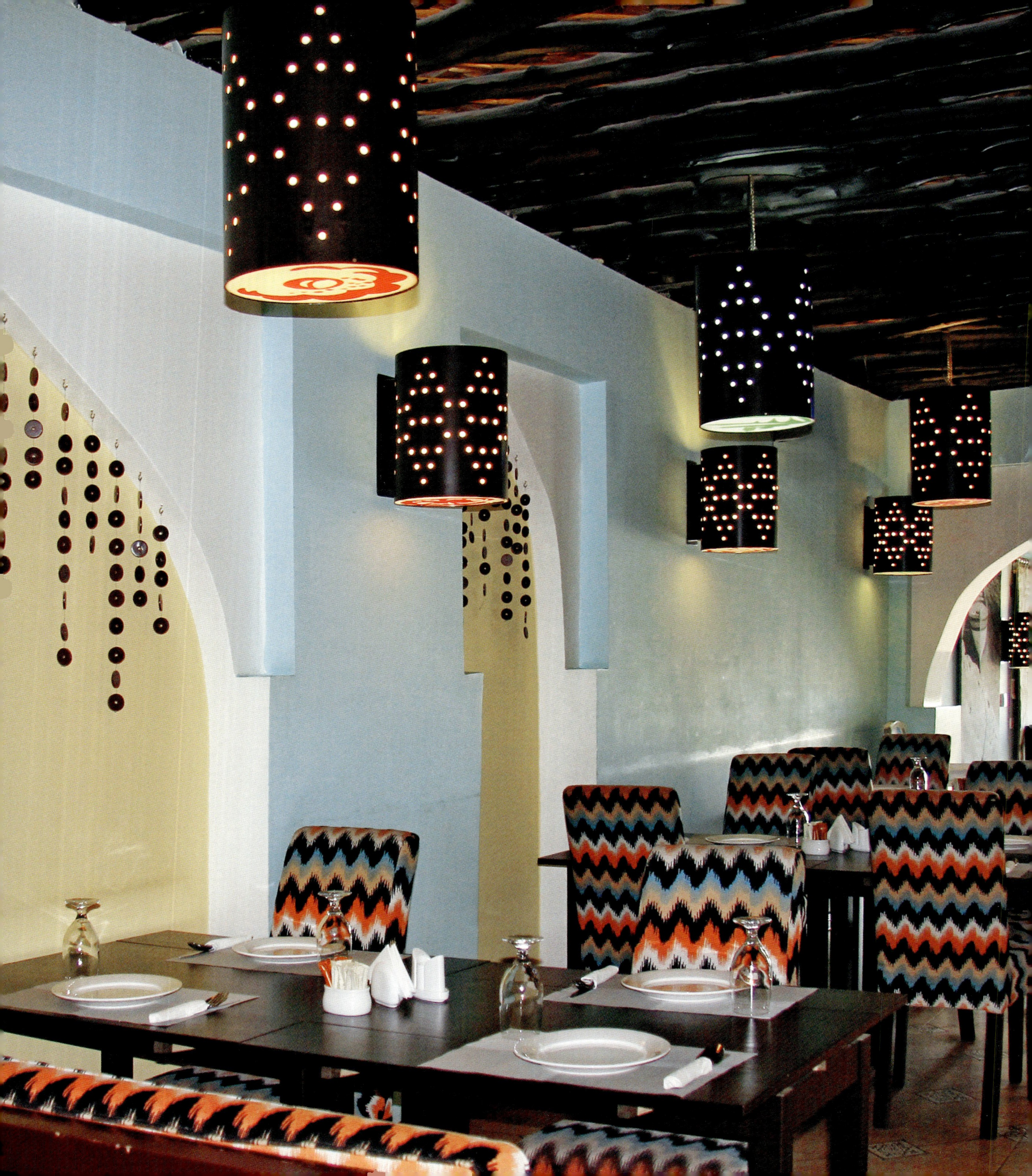

COAST CAFÉ

Like most of the public space in Souq Al Wakrah, Coast Café has a traditional *danshal* ceiling. Here we see the use of other architectural and design elements which refer to the Arabic and Qatari styles, such as pointed arches, *lūzīāt, sadw,* and *rūshanāt*. The seating along the longer wall is recessed in the arches and elsewhere the illusion of arched areas is created by the geometric wooden *lūzīah*. The seating is covered in fabric that is very abstract and displays a modern interpretation of *sadw*. However, the influence of the *sadw* extends beyond the textile design. It is evident in the chevron-patterned wall coverings on the accent wall. The same wall houses three *rūshanāt*. Unlike traditional *rūshanāt*, here wall recesses are wrapped in wood and are also back-lit. However, like the traditional *rūshanāt* these recesses are used as shelves and hold decorative items.

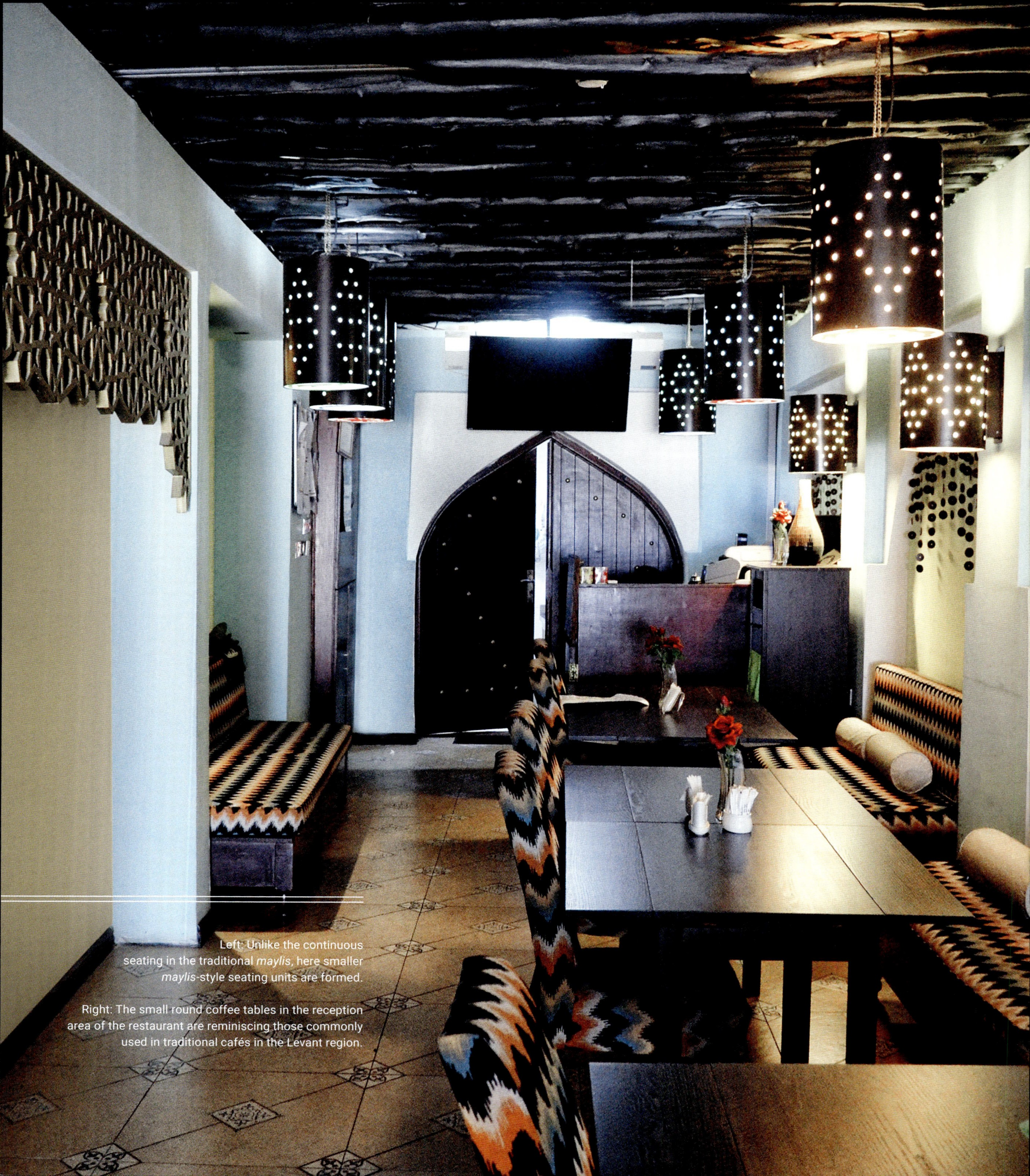

Left: Unlike the continuous seating in the traditional *maylis*, here smaller *maylis*-style seating units are formed.

Right: The small round coffee tables in the reception area of the restaurant are reminiscing those commonly used in traditional cafés in the Levant region.

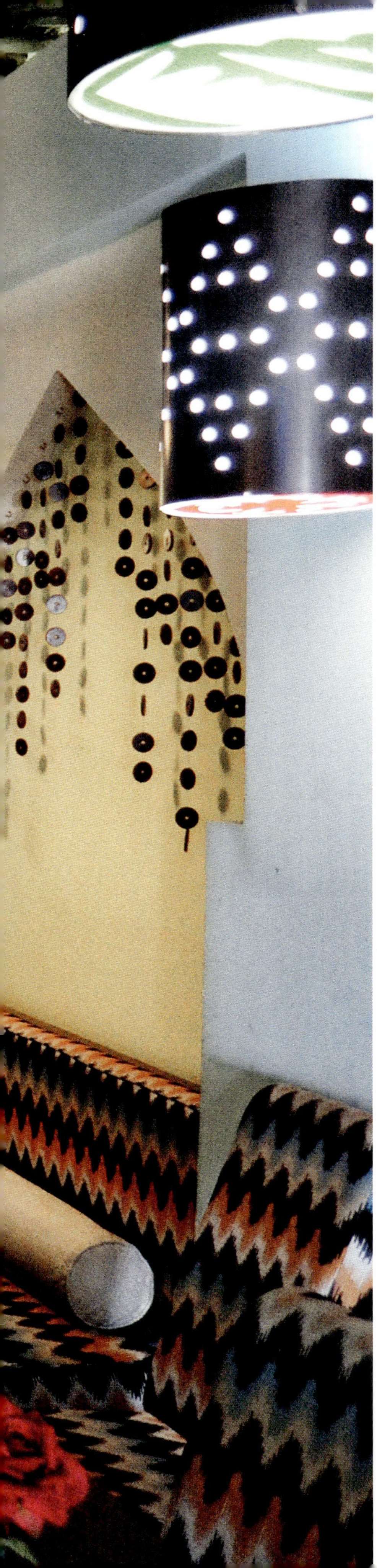
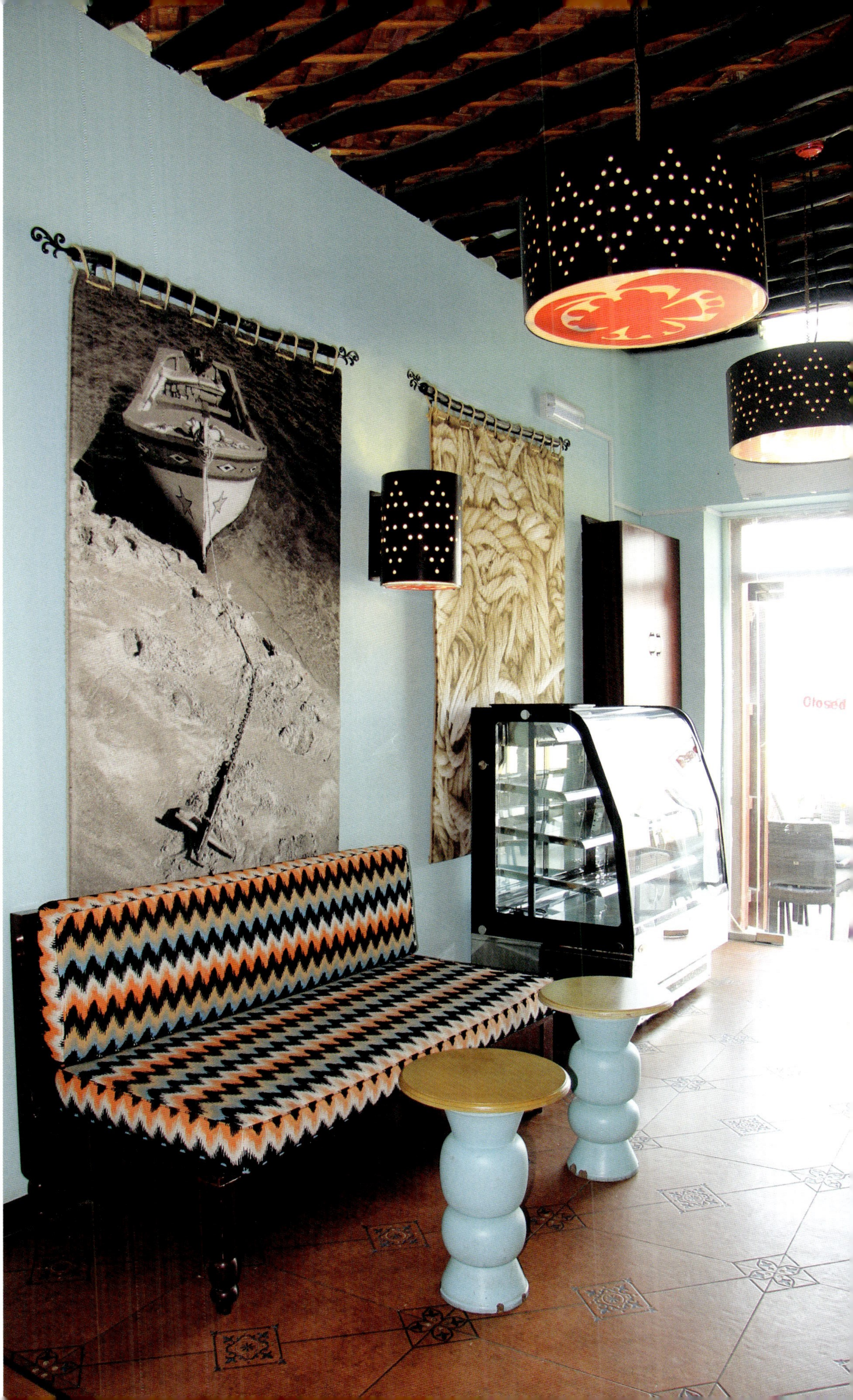

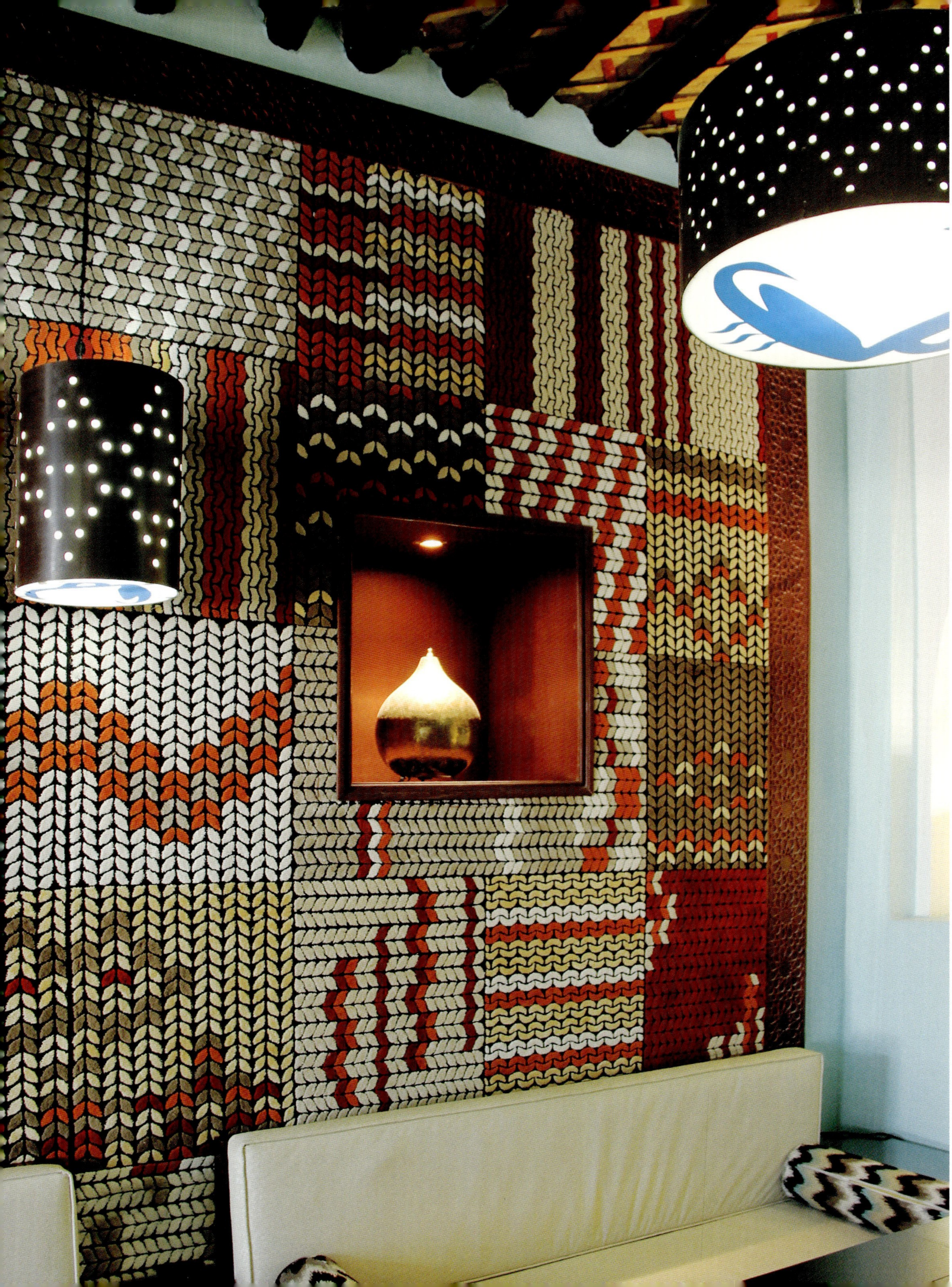

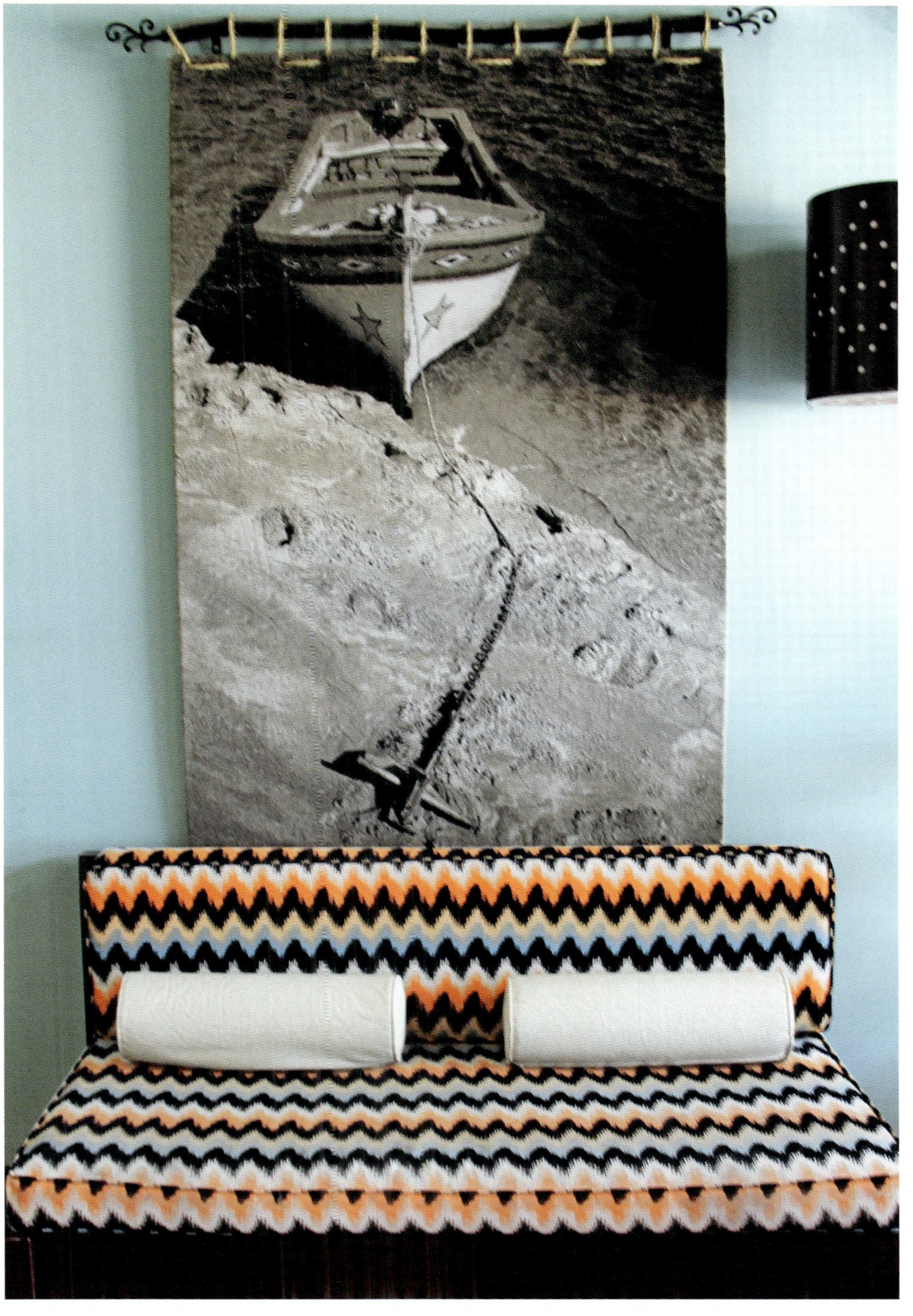

Above: The coastal themed artwork displayed in the reception area has a direct visual reference to the name of the café.

Left-hand page: Wall finishes in this section of the restaurant resemble traditionally woven *sadw* fabric.

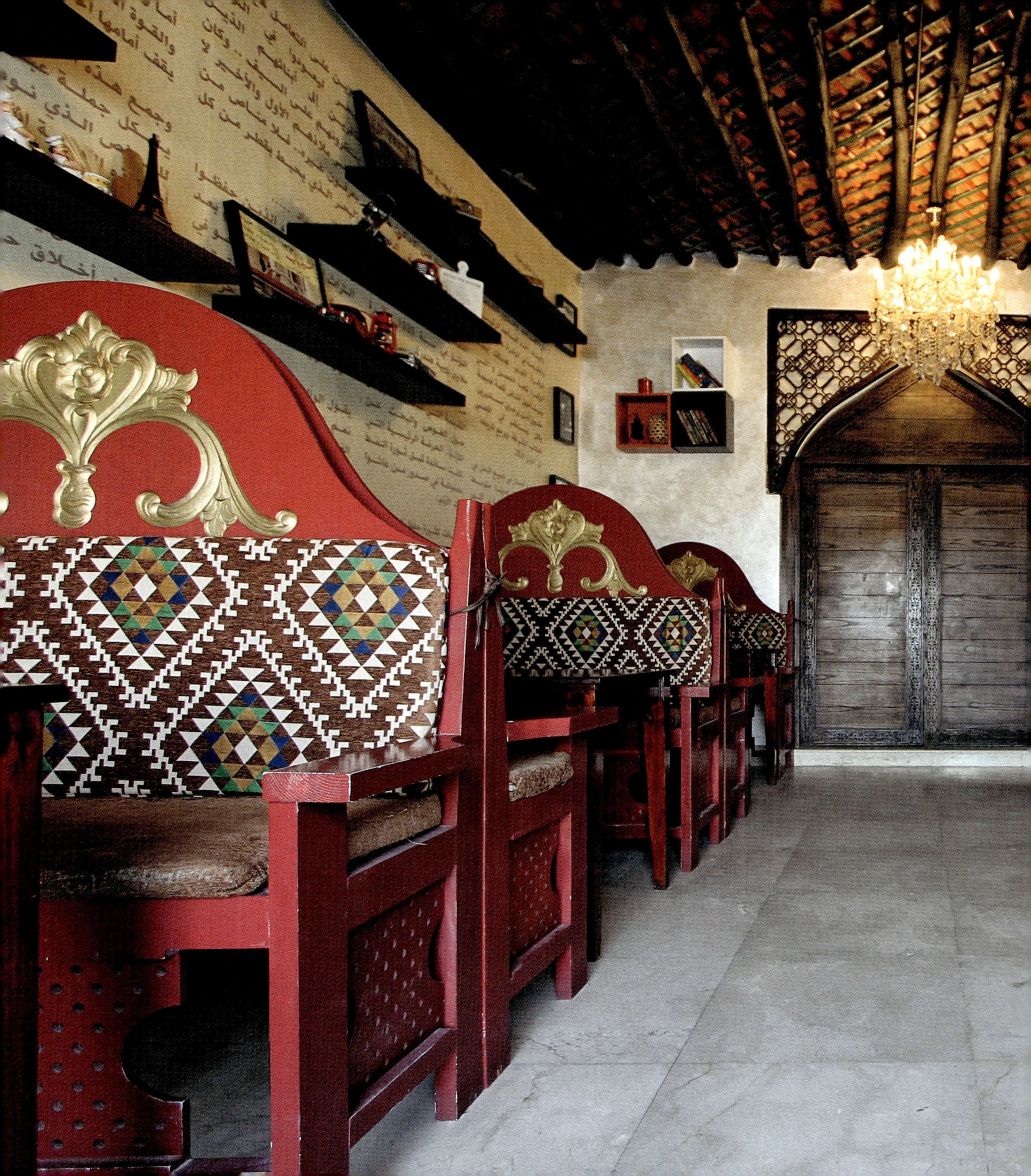

HABAT REEH

The interior of Habat Reeh restaurant in Al Wakrah Souq is permeated with eclectic influences. Evident here is a direct influence from vernacular Qatari architecture in the use of *danāshil* and *rūshanāt*. Both elements are complemented by contrasting and more contemporary objects. A lavish crystal lighting fixture is suspended from the traditional ceiling, and floating shelving contrasts with the traditional *rūshanāt*. The design of the seating is influenced by the traditional elevated seating *dakkah*, and the textiles are directly influenced by *sadw*. However, the seating furniture also appears to be influenced by the pan-Asian style, as can be seen in the gold details of the arched design on the chair backs.

The walls are covered in custom-made typographic wallpaper. Arabic texts relating the history of Qatar are printed on the off-white paper to match the surrounding walls. The text is arranged in columns so that the wallpaper as a whole is reminiscent of newsprint. Vintage objects on display like a radio, typewriter, and photographic and video cameras continue the idea of storytelling. In turn, these objects are paired with less explicable and random everyday items such as a chef's chopping board, vintage toy cars and a miniature Eiffel Tower. All these exhibits are then paired with traditional hunting rifles, *dilāl* and *ṣanādyq imbaīyt*.

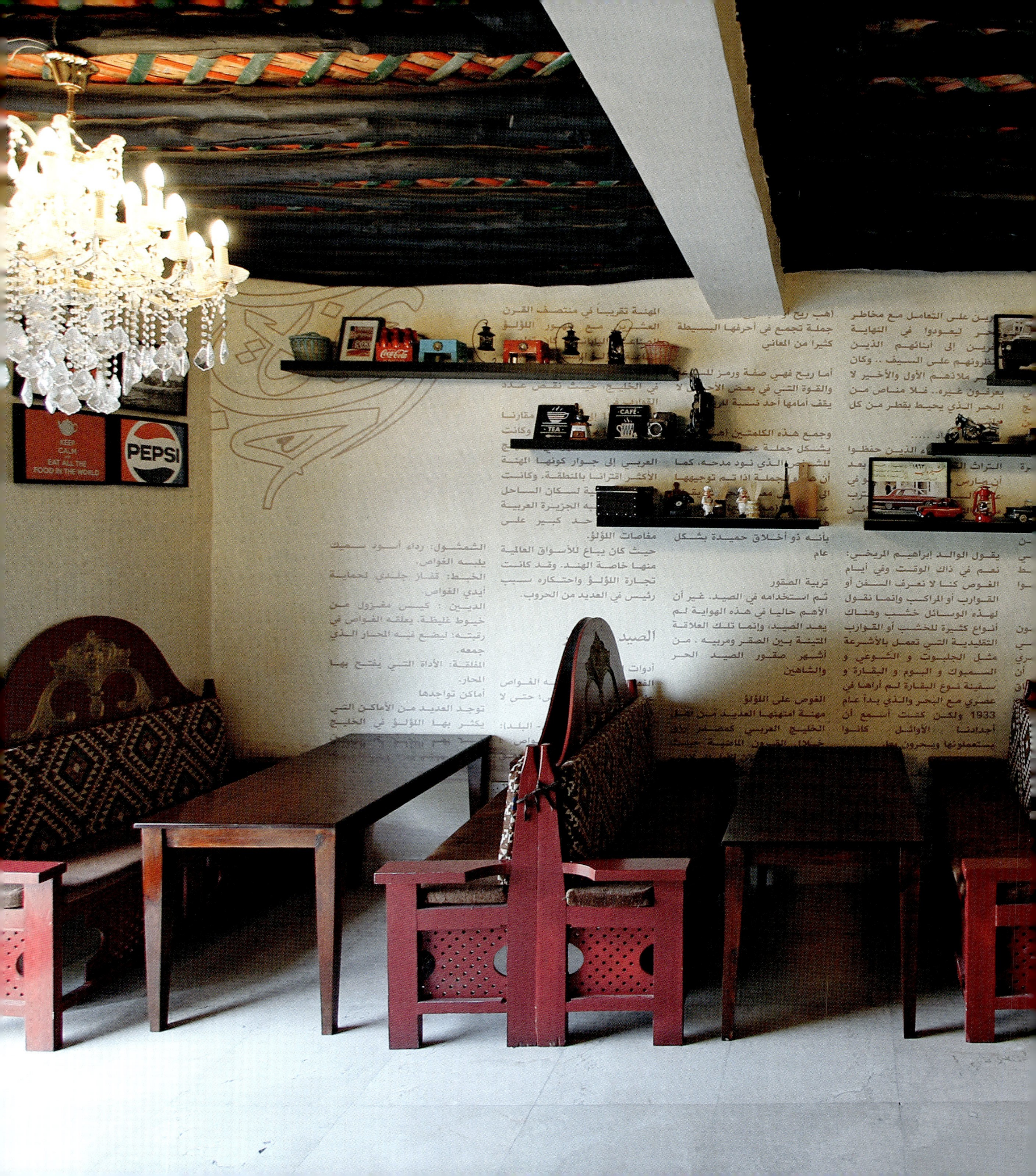
PEPSI
KEEP CALM AND EAT ALL THE FOOD IN THE WORLD

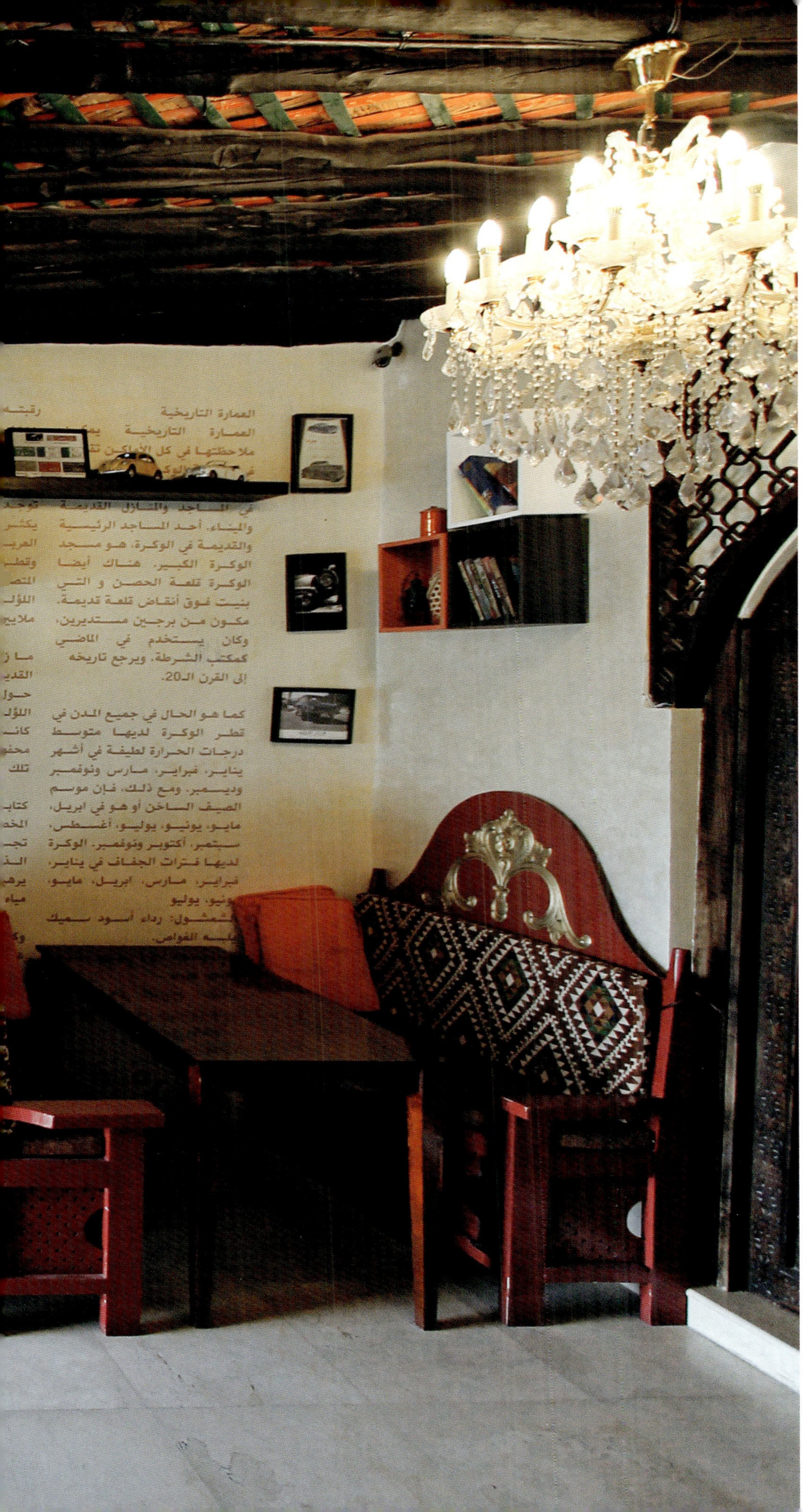

Elevated seating resembling *dakkah* with *sadw*-influenced textiles. Custom-made typographic wallpaper forms a main point of interest in the restaurant.

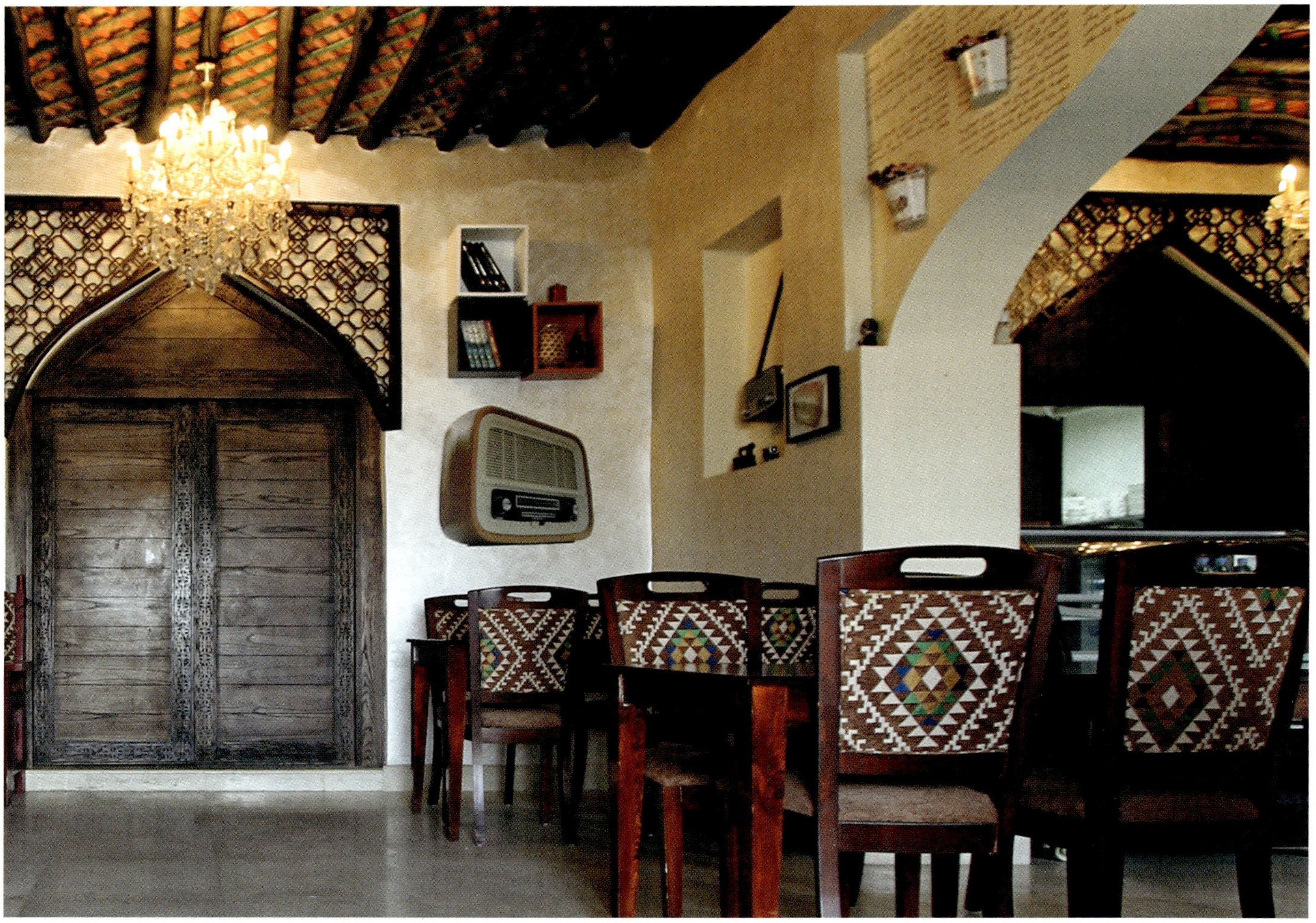

Above: A direct reference to pan-Arab style is seen in the wooden doors.

Right-hand page: An unusual pairing of collectibles: *dilāl*, *ṣandūq imbaīyt*, and *jafīr* are displayed in addition to ceramic cups with social media logos printed on them.

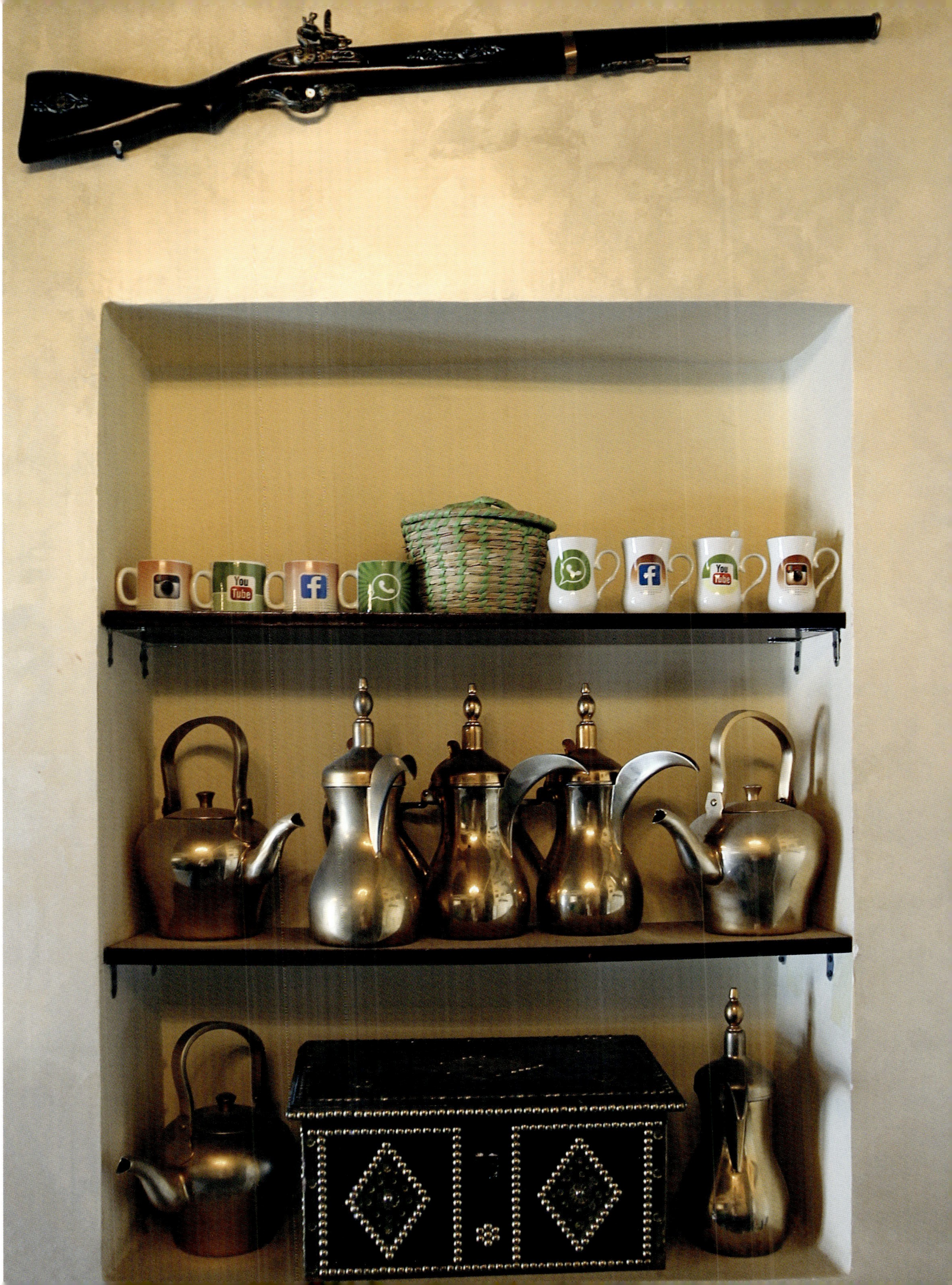
You Tube
You Tube

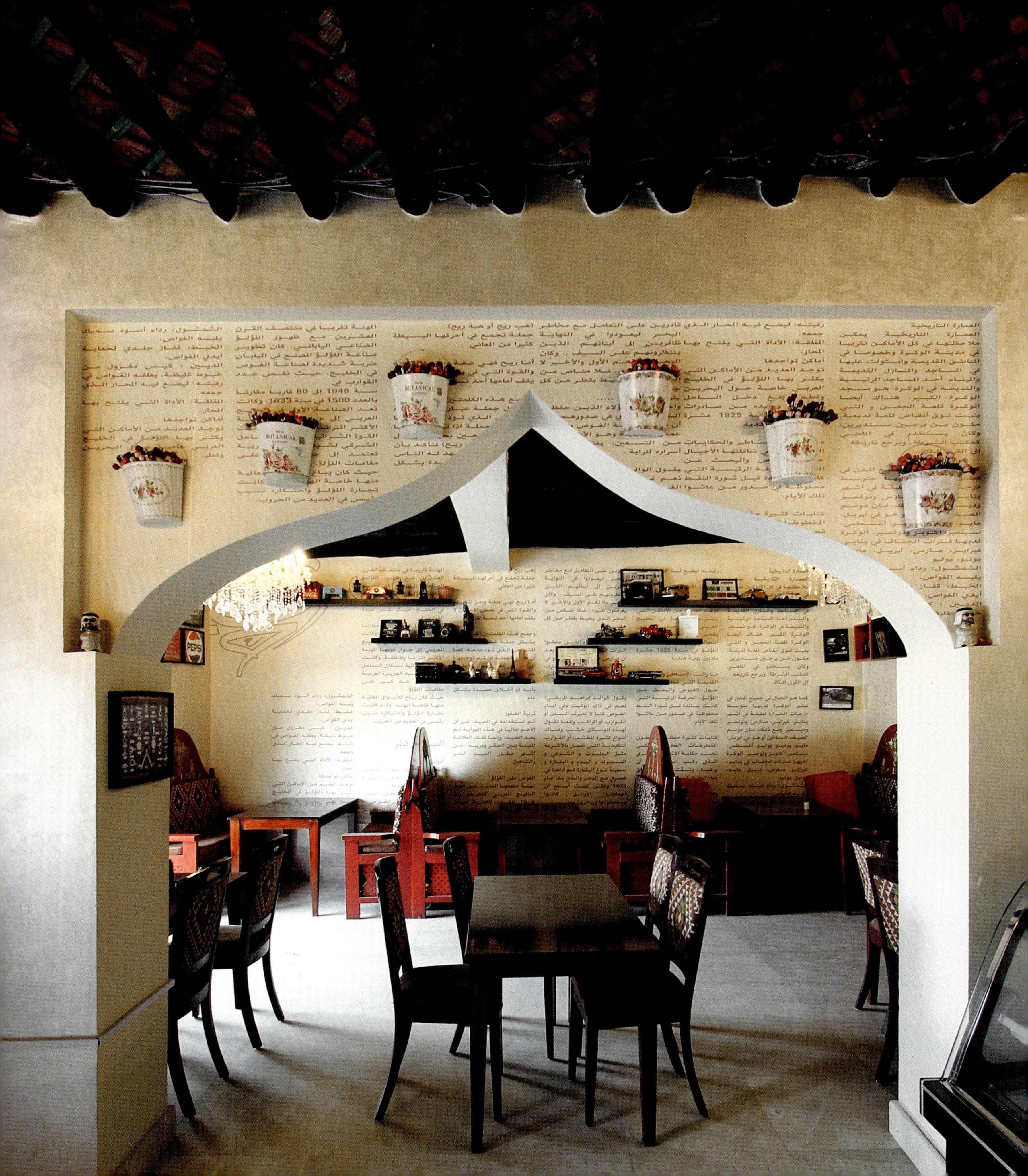
BOTANICAL
PEPSI

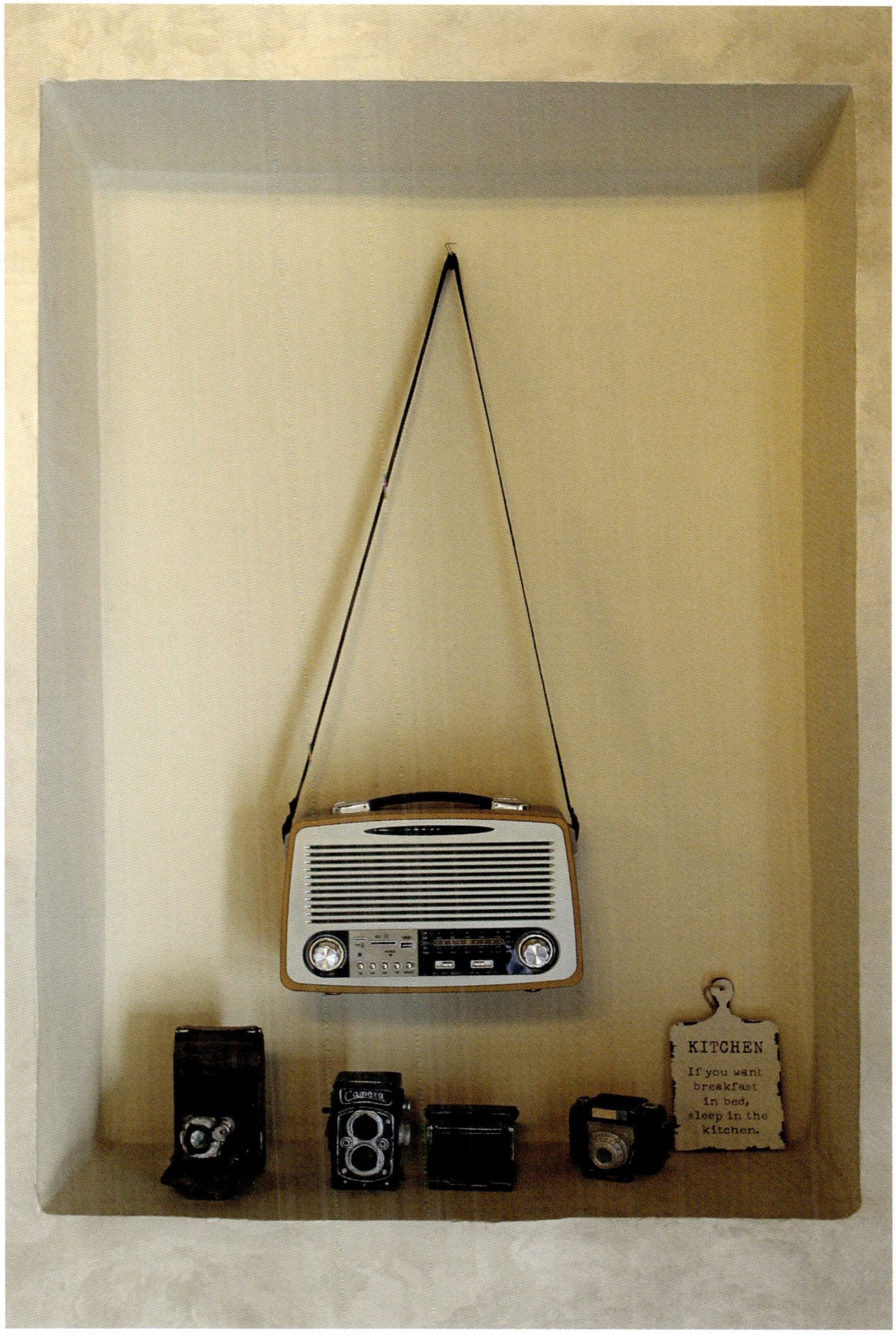

Above: Vintage items displayed in a *rūshanah*.

Left-hand page: The *danshal* ceiling is paired with pointed arches reflecting the local and pan-Arab influence.

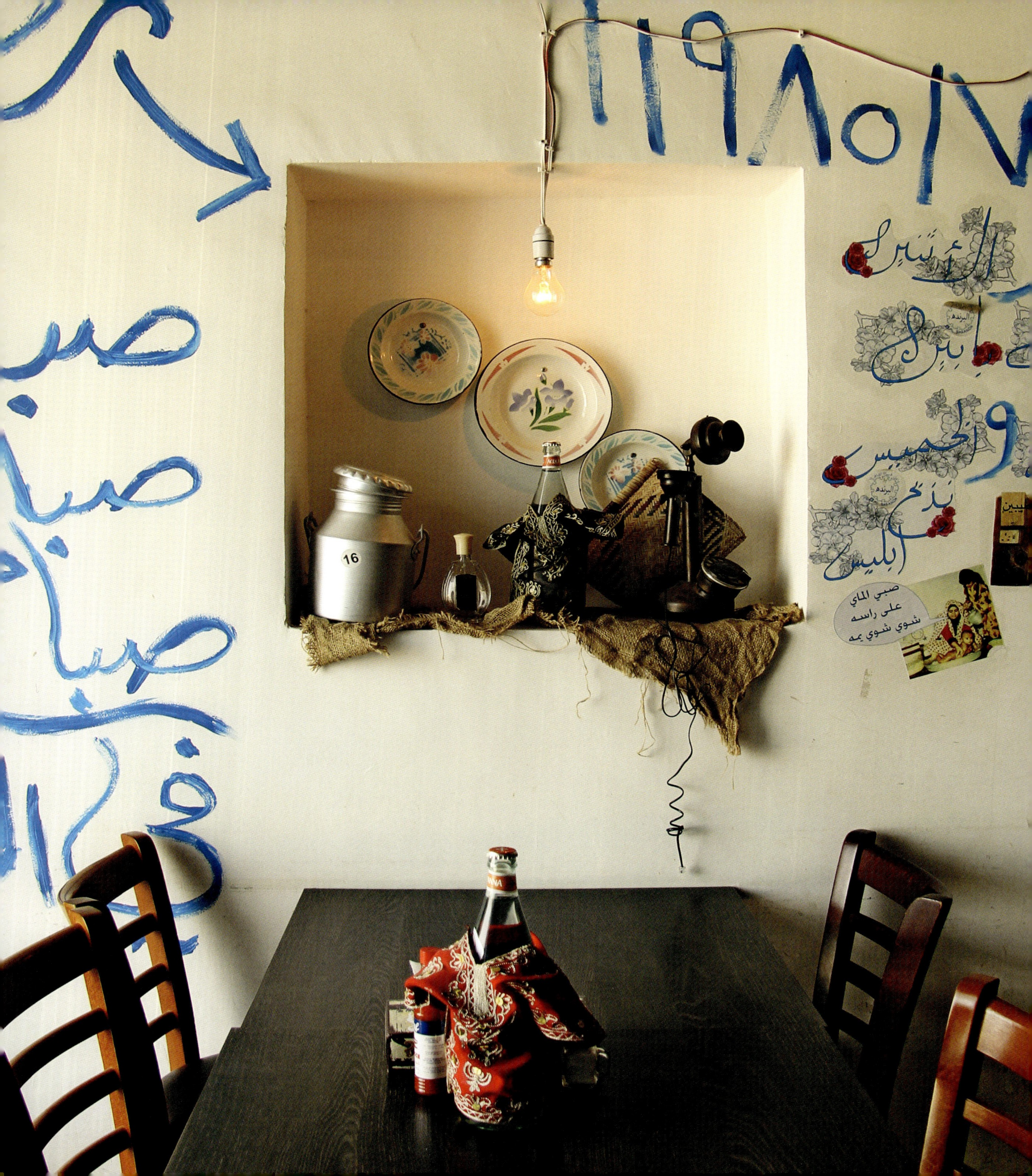
صبي الماي
على راسه
شوي شوي يمه

AL BARANDA RESTAURANT

Al Baranda replicates a neighborhood eatery of the 1980s. Use of *danshal* is evident in the ceiling which gives it a typical traditional look. The ceiling is festooned with many old *fnāra* which have been adapted as lighting fixtures. The finishes on the wall and furniture are completely unpolished, giving the restaurant the feeling of a place of transit.

The seating in the restaurant barely seems to belong together as chairs of assorted styles are grouped around single tables. This array of disparate furniture is set against white walls that are adorned with textual graffiti with phrases exclusively in Qatari dialect. Blue is the dominant color used and is evident in the graffiti, wooden doors and window blinds.

Numerous old photos and news clippings decorate the walls alongside the graffiti. An assortment of mismatched metal plates reminiscent of every household of the mid- to late twentieth century is also displayed across the restaurant. The rectangular *rūshanāt* serve as a non-curated space for numerous collectables such as toys from the 80s and also antique items such as *mirashīh* and *madākhin*.

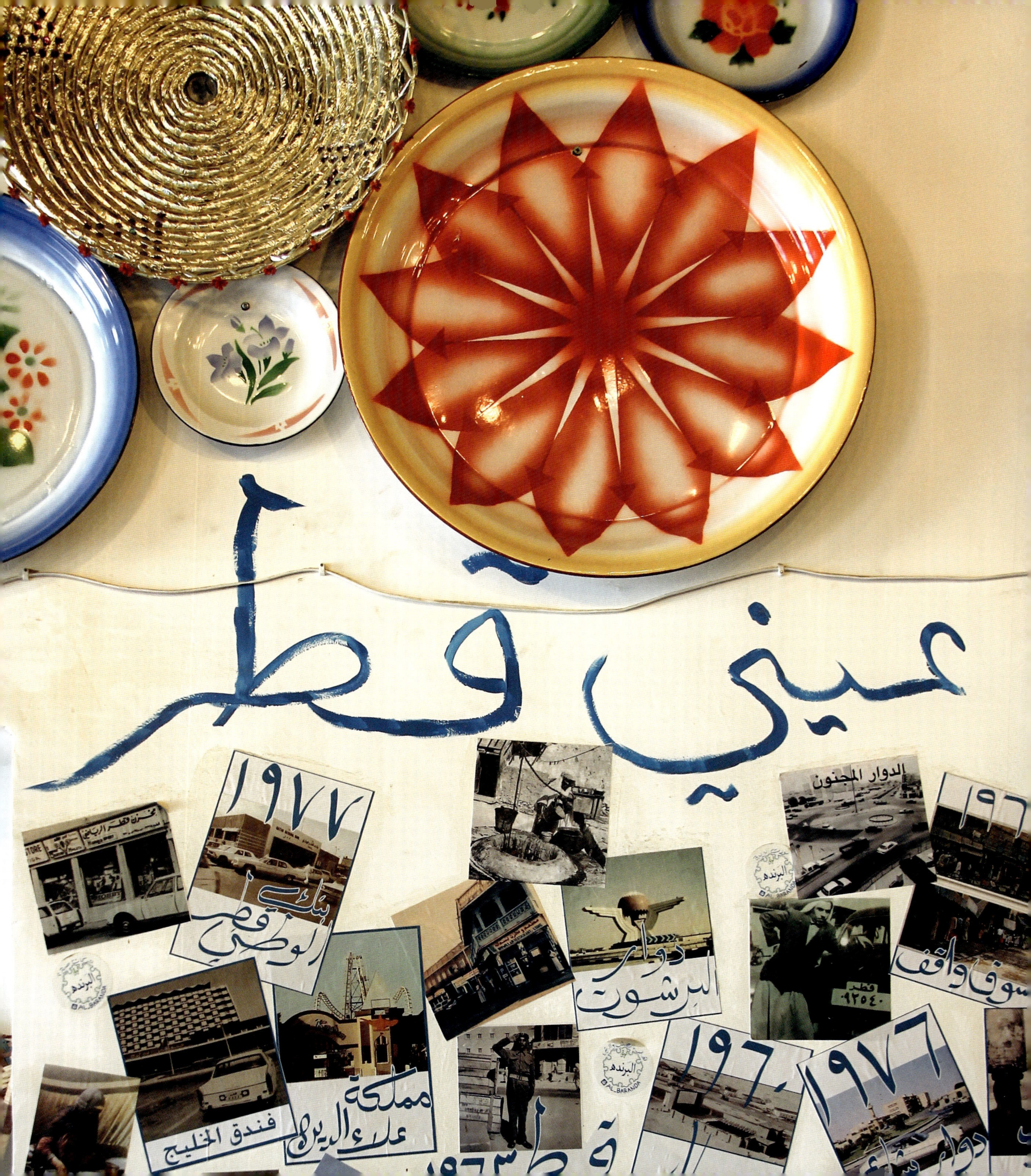

عيني قطر
١٩٧٧
بنك قطر الوطني
الدوار المجنون
دوار البرشوت
فندق الخليج
مملكة علاء الدين
١٩٧٦

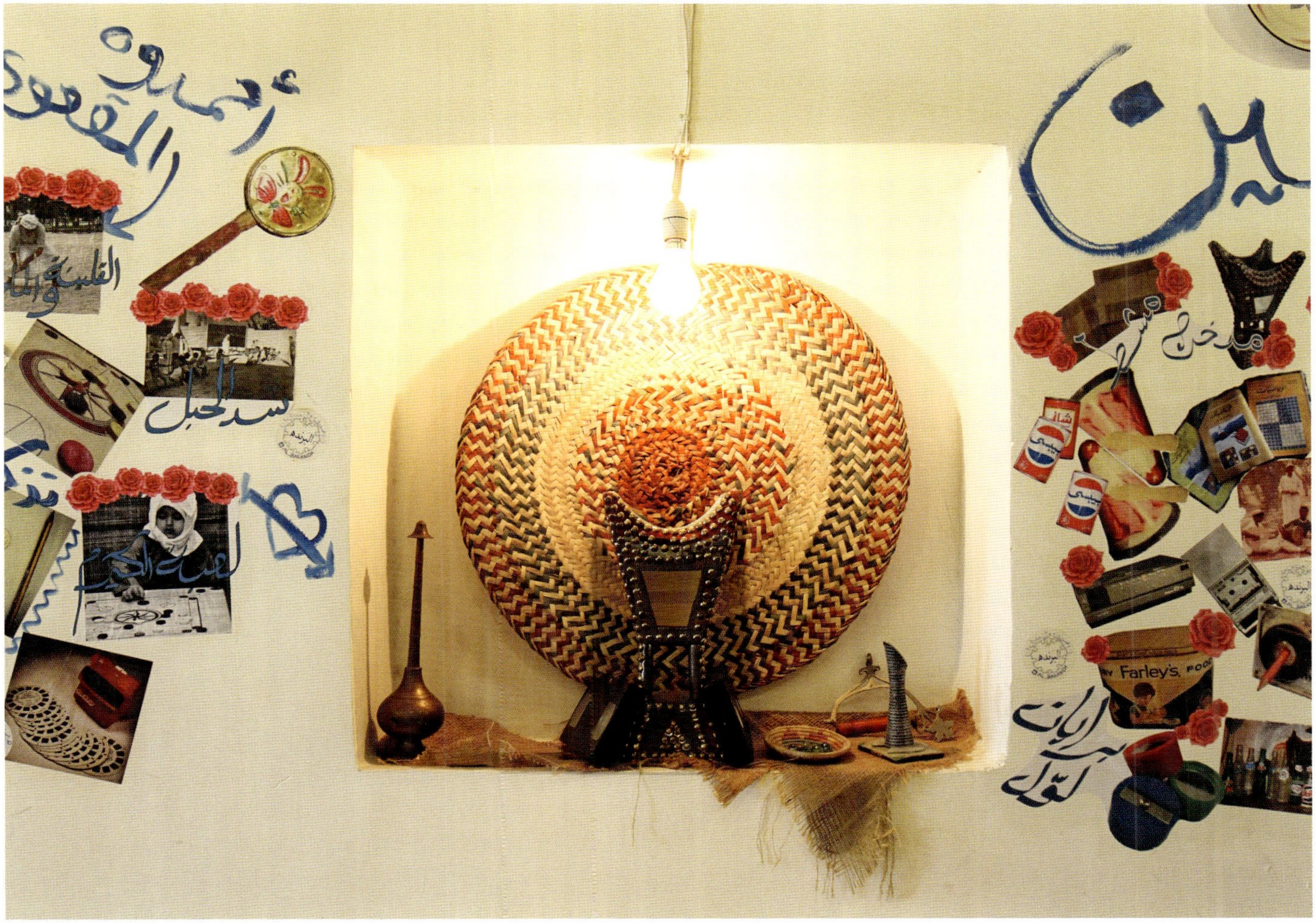

Above: A selection of easily recognizable everyday items such as a *mirash*, a *sufrah*, and a *mibkharah* are displayed in the wall recess.

Left-hand page: The walls of the restaurant are decorated witha variety of kitchenware and photos of Qatar dating back to the 1960s and 1970s.

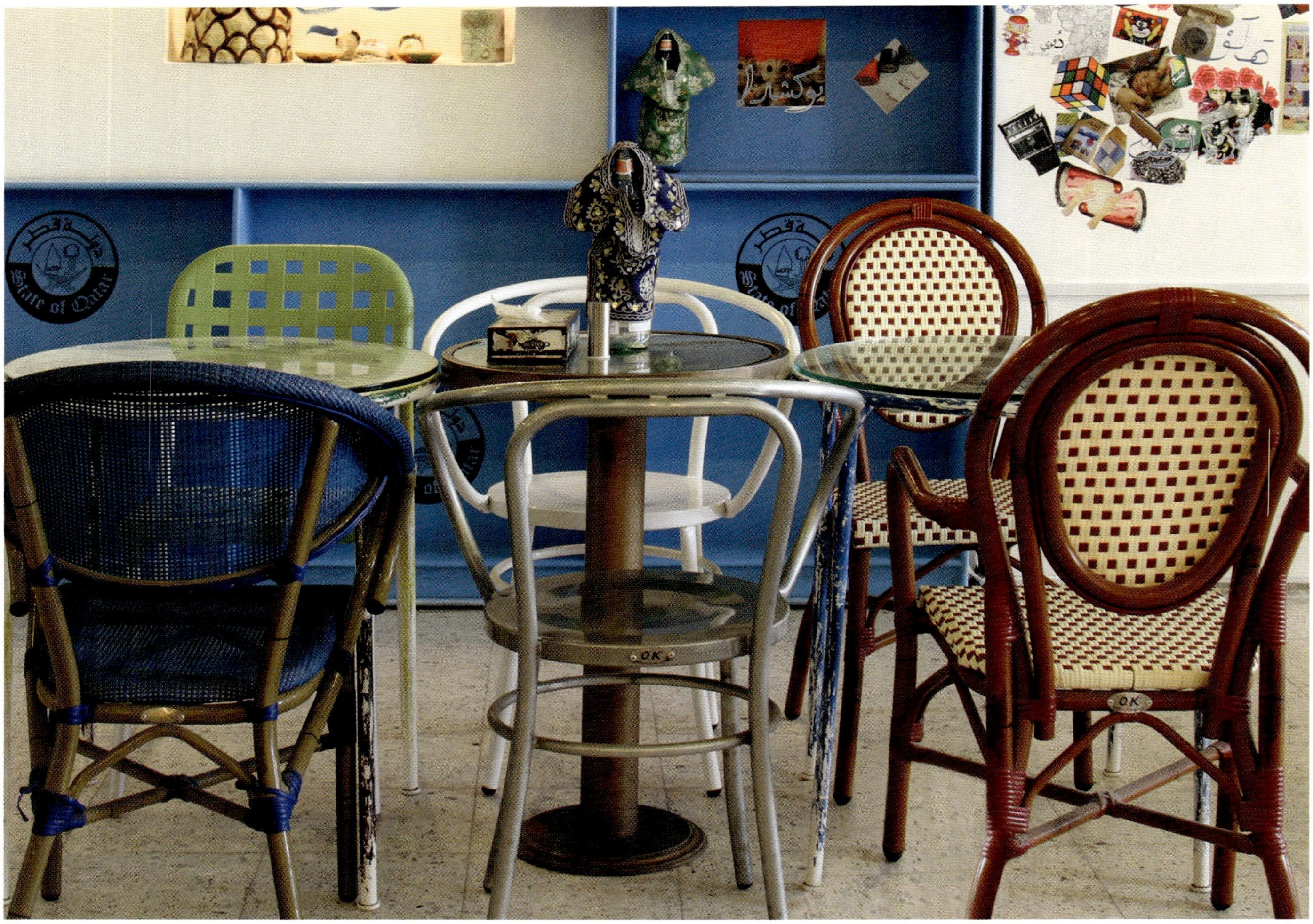

Above: An unusual arrangement of mismatched furniture.

Right-hand page: It is evident that the focal points of this restaurant are its walls. They are ornately decorated while the remainder of space is kept free of any non-essential items.

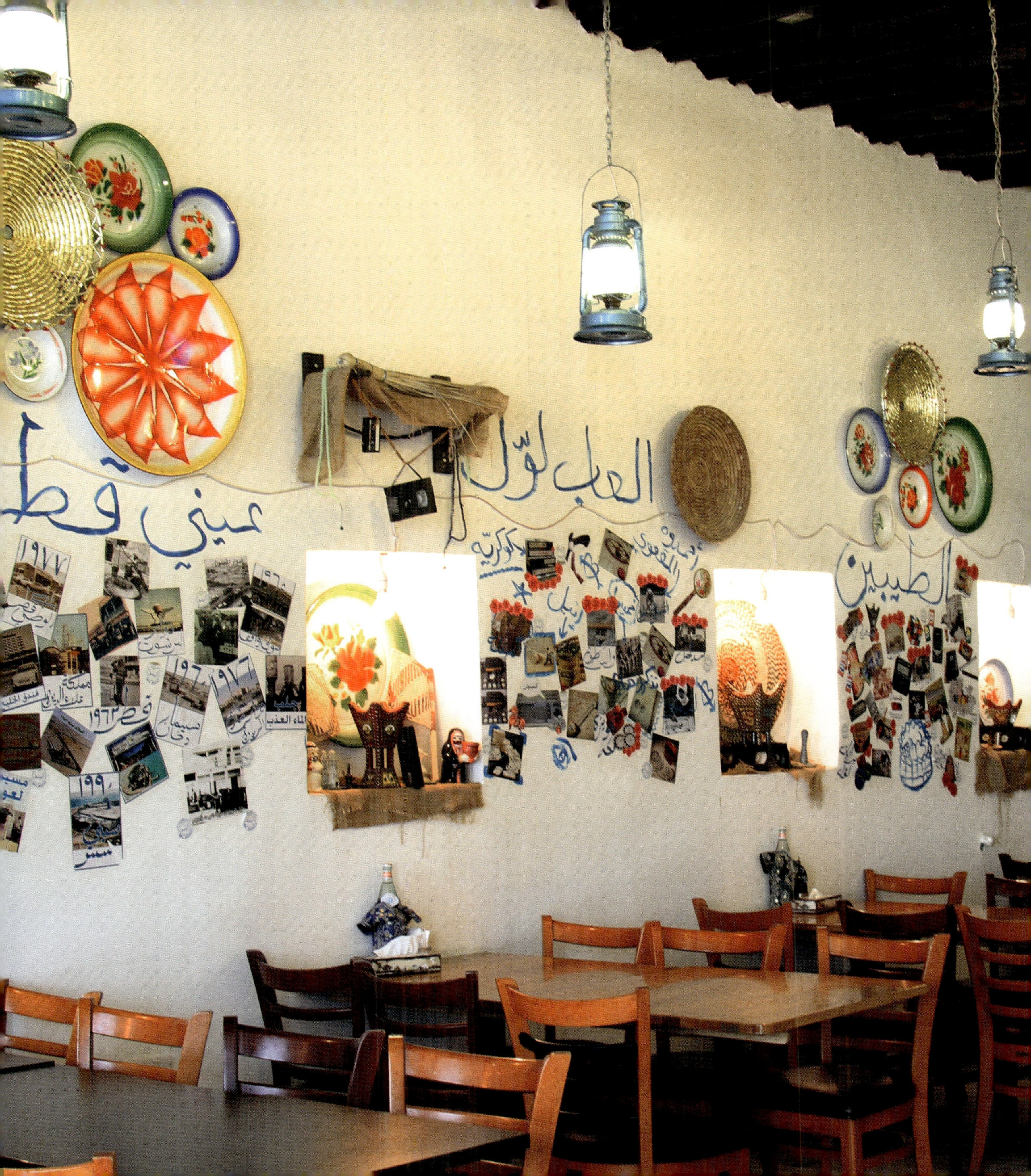
العب لوّل
الطيبين

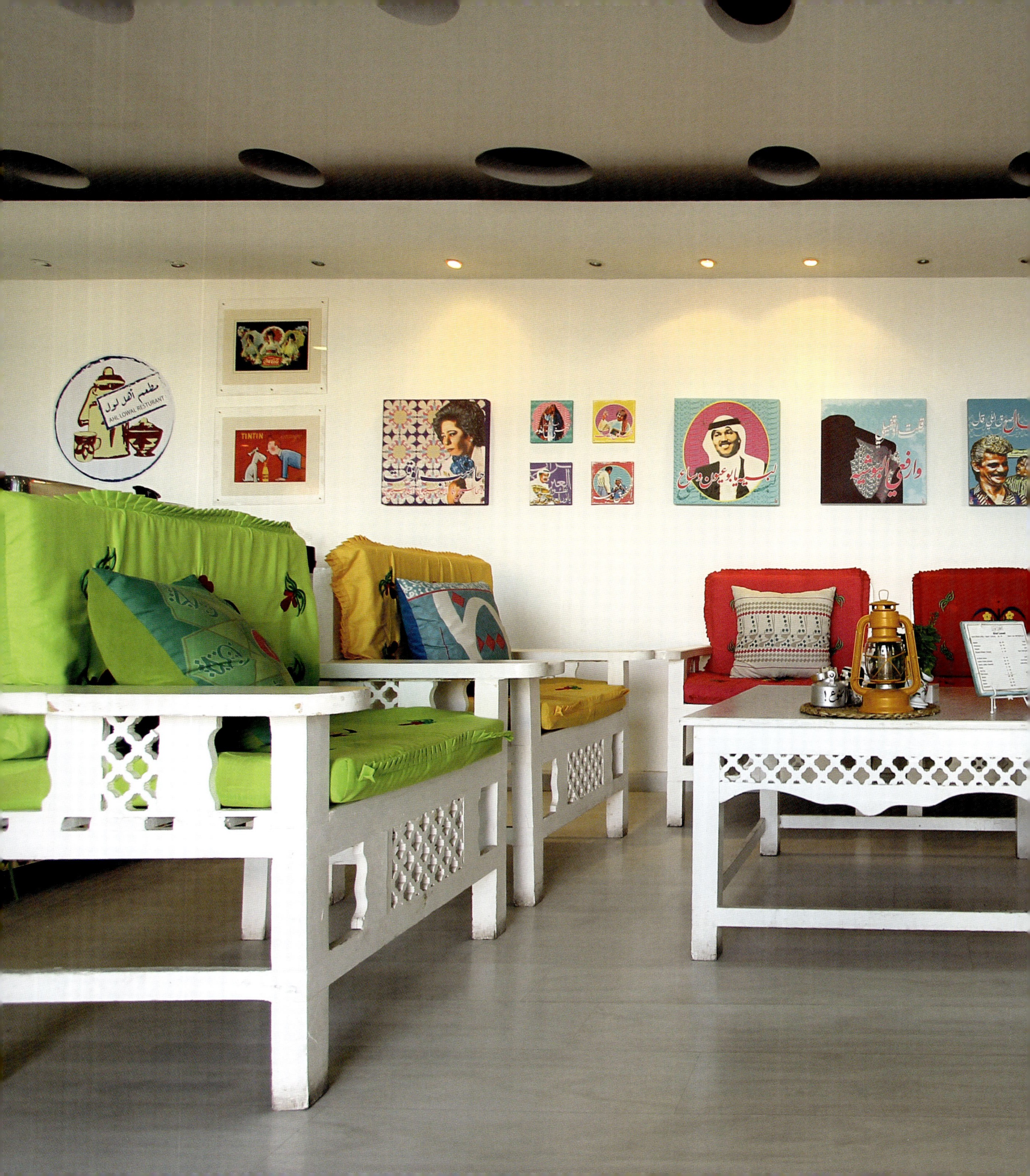
مطعم أهل لول
AHL LOWAL RESTURANT
TINTIN

AHL LAWAL

Ahl Lawal restaurant is located within Katara cultural village. The space reflects the interesting period of the 1970s–1980s and echoes the local pop culture of the time.

The ceiling treatment is quite modern and complements the contemporary interpretation of the traditional seating cushions, which were used for the floor seating in the past. Circular pigeon holes, commonly found in Qatari houses, are evident across the ceiling, bringing traditional exterior building elements inside.

The items displayed are purely decorative and reflect the influence of sea travel and trade. The arrays of artifacts exhibited in Ahl Lawal were picked up from India, China, and other popular travel and trade destinations during the mid-to-late twentieth century. The *ṣanādyq imbaīyt* (metal boxes) on the shelves were brought from Pakistan and India in different sizes containing various items such as letters or, most commonly, valuable gifts for the bride. Interestingly, these items have gained such popularity among the locals that they have become part of the local modern inheritance.

The walls are decorated with frameless artworks that portray expressions easily recognizable to middle-aged audiences as they are taken directly from popular Arabic plays, music and television shows of the 70s and 80s.

Here, various design features in the establishment—color, artifacts and collectibles—show a creative attempt at lifting the modern local style into a contemporary dimension.

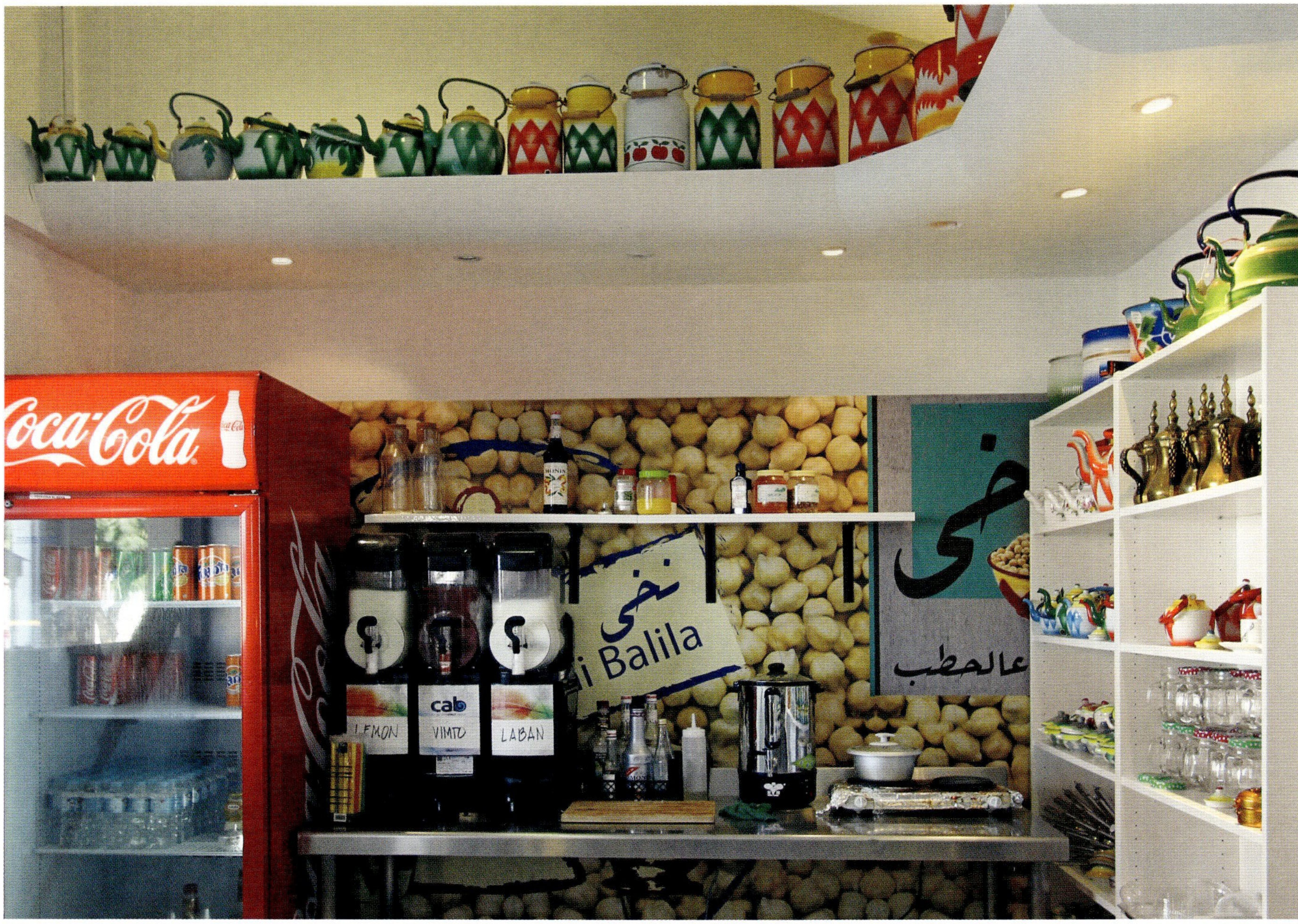

Above: Coffee and tea pots of various shapes and sizes form a display in the restaurant.

Right-hand page: Embroidery was a common way of decorating textiles in Qatar. Cushions used throughout the restaurant are embroidered with styles and patterns typical for early twentieth-century Qatar.

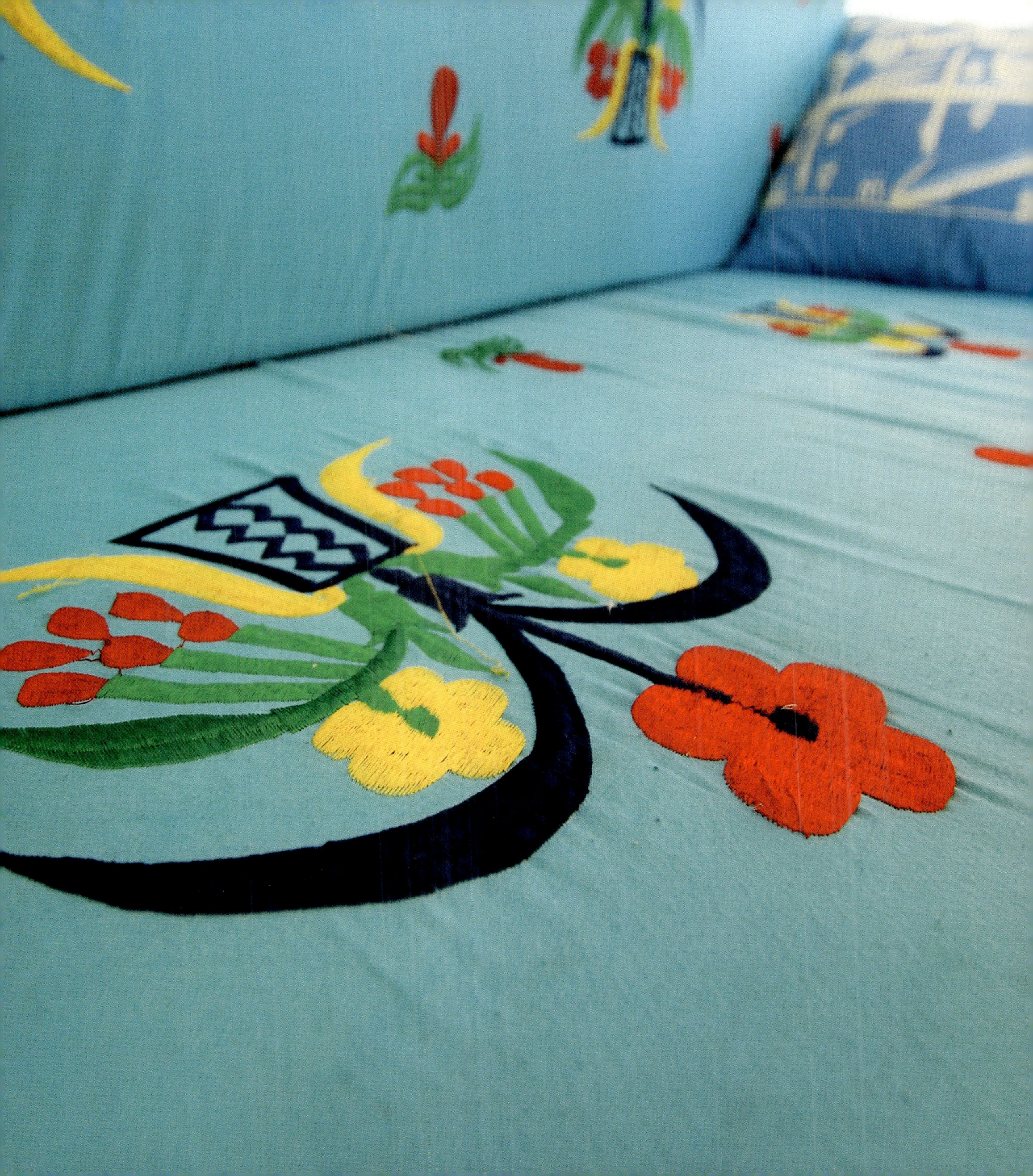

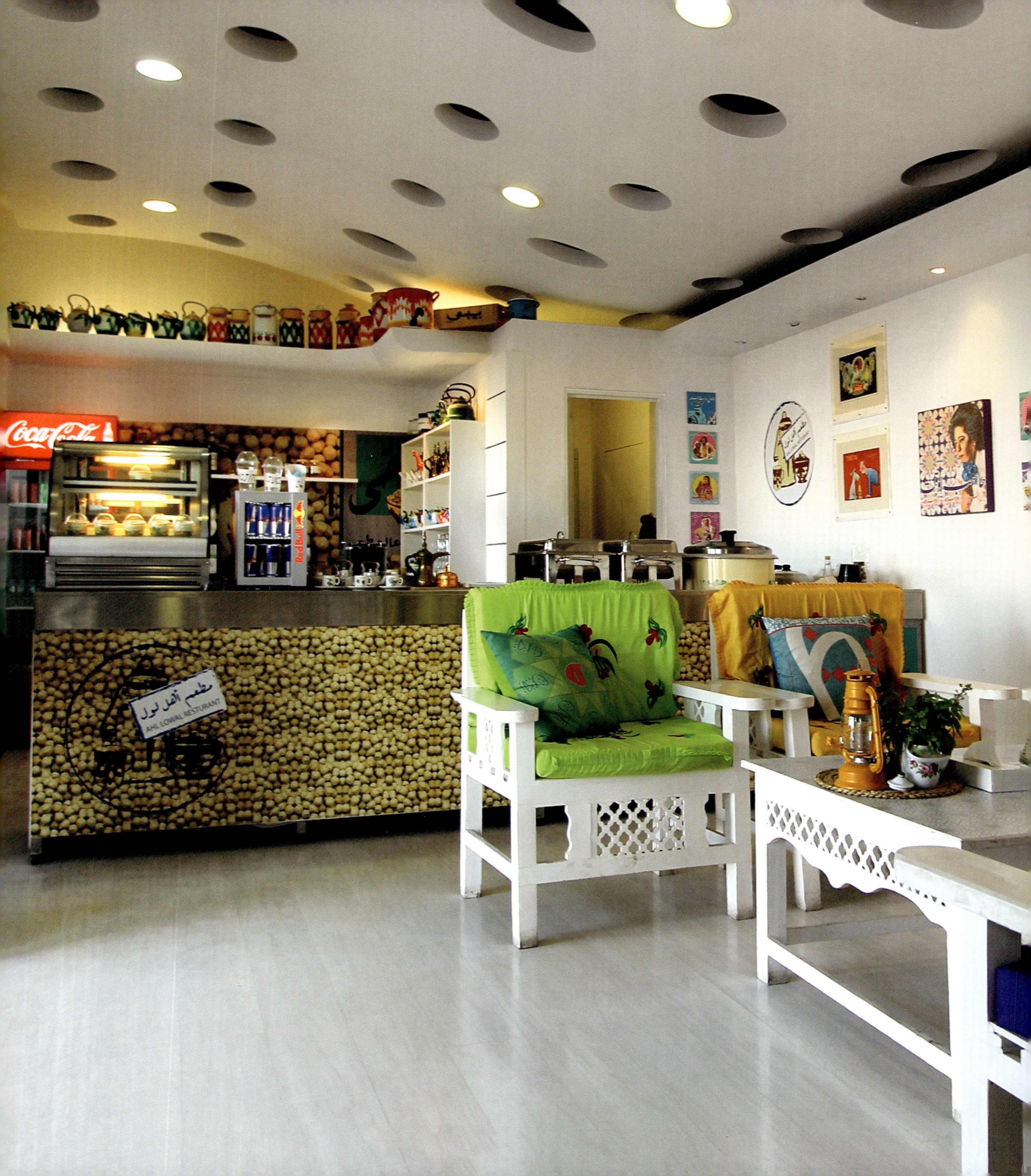
Coca-Cola
Red Bull
مطعم أهل لول
AHL LOWAL RESTURANT

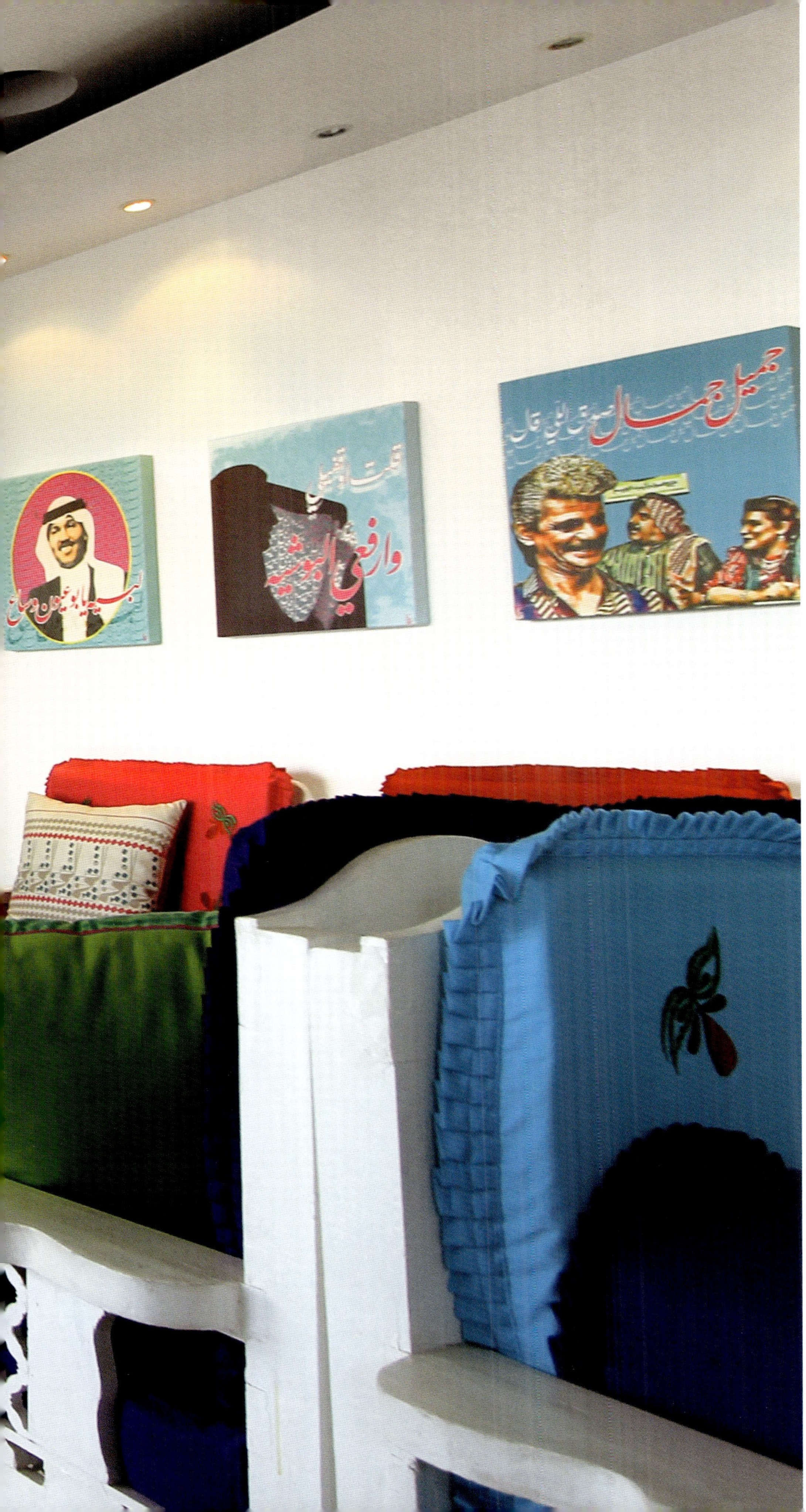

Neutral walls, floor and wooden seating are contrasted with colorful textiles and artworks. The ceiling here is not the traditional *danshal*; instead, it is a contemporary interpretation of pigeon holes that were a common feature in many traditional Qatari houses.

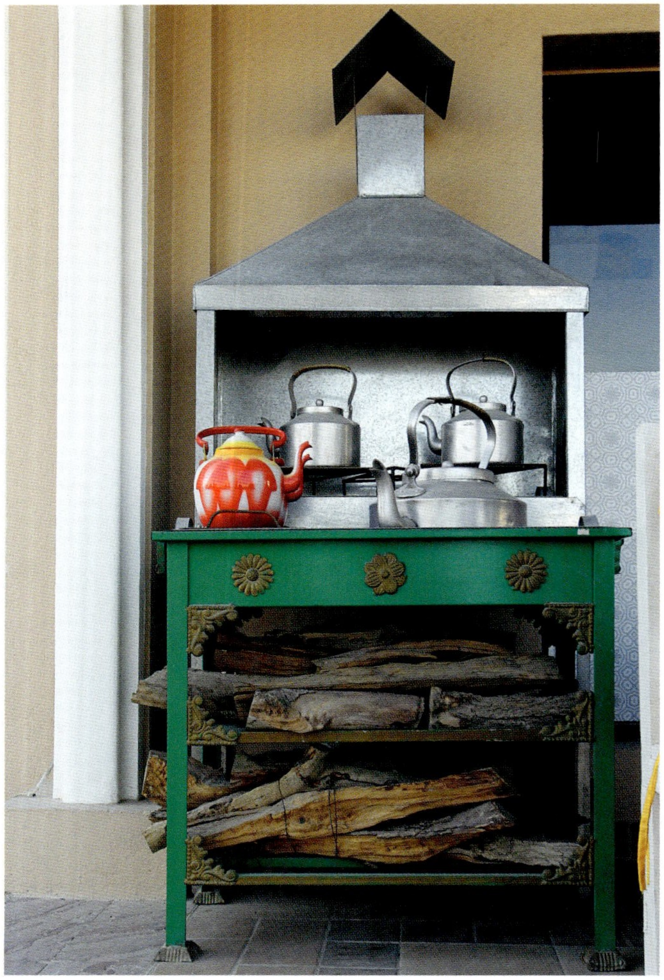

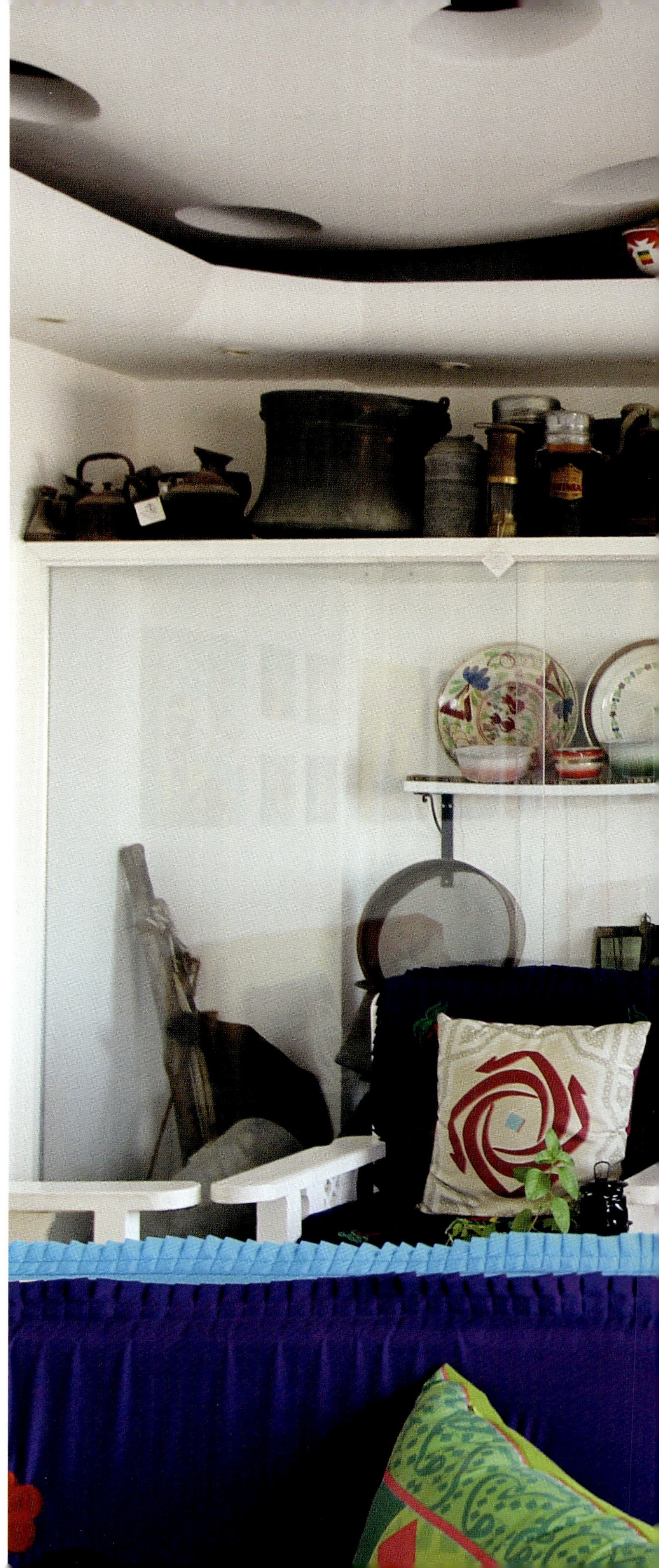

Above: A non-functional fireplace reminiscent of the traditional *dūwah* is used as a decorative element in the outdoor seating area.

Right: More prized antique collectibles are kept in an enclosed glass display cabinet and form a feature wall.

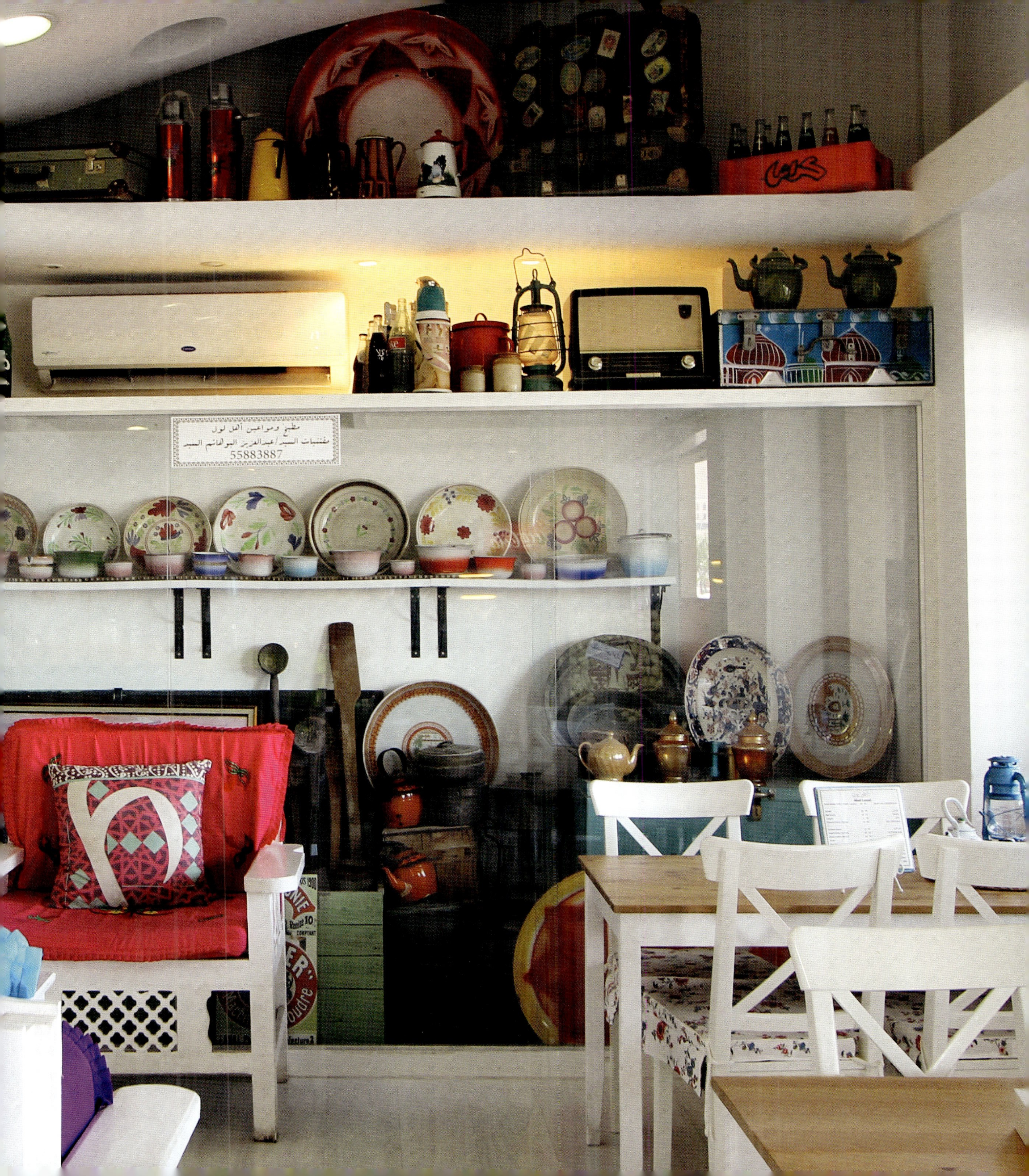
مطبخ ومواعين أهل لول
مقتنيات السيد/عبدالعزيز البوهاشم السيد
55883887

CONTEMPORARY

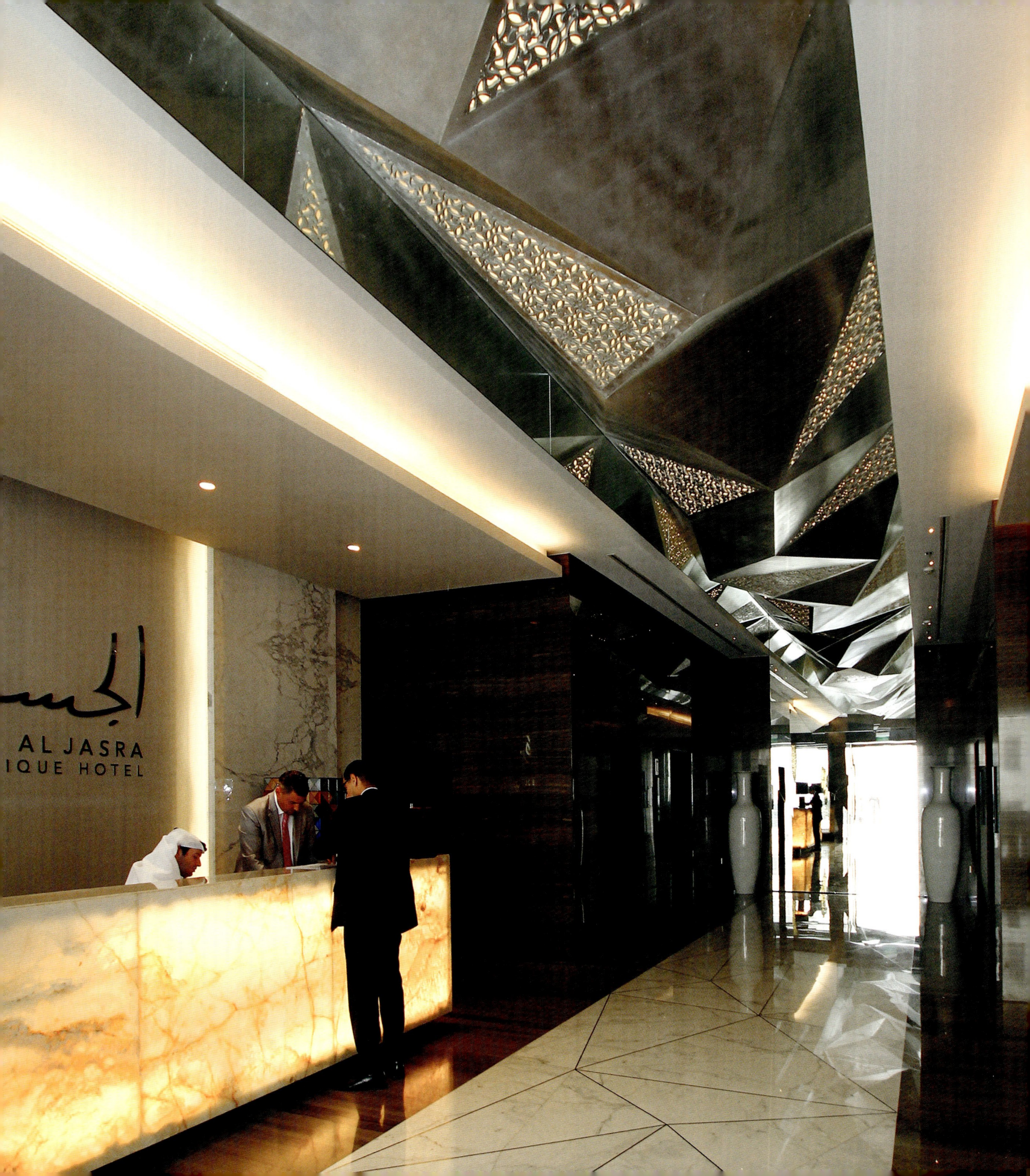
AL JASRA
IQUE HOTEL

AL JASRA HOTEL

Located in the old neighborhood of Al Jasra, after which it was named, this hotel is now part of the Souq Waqif and is adjacent to the Falcon Souq. Since its opening Al Jasra hotel has succeeded in becoming one of the most coveted home-grown brands, reaching international standards of hospitality. Internal public and private areas are furnished with opulent furniture pieces, many of which recall the late 1980s style of furnishings in Qatar. Highly polished wood with ornate metal details is in evidence throughout the hotel. However, there are also some more contemporary furnishings in the public areas such as the orange wire mesh bench.

The fountain forms a focal point in the lobby as you cross from the core hotel building into the restaurant area. While the hotel's lobby and rooms are influenced by a specific period, the restaurant areas take on a more themed design approach. Here, local identity is immersed in the broader Arabic-style vocabulary. In addition to the reference to a wider Arabic identity, the design also relates to the Qatari identity using specific patterns which are most prominently evident in the triangular geometry of the ceiling. Moreover, unlike other spaces where many everyday objects would be on display, here we only see *dalah*, which is a symbol of local hospitality.

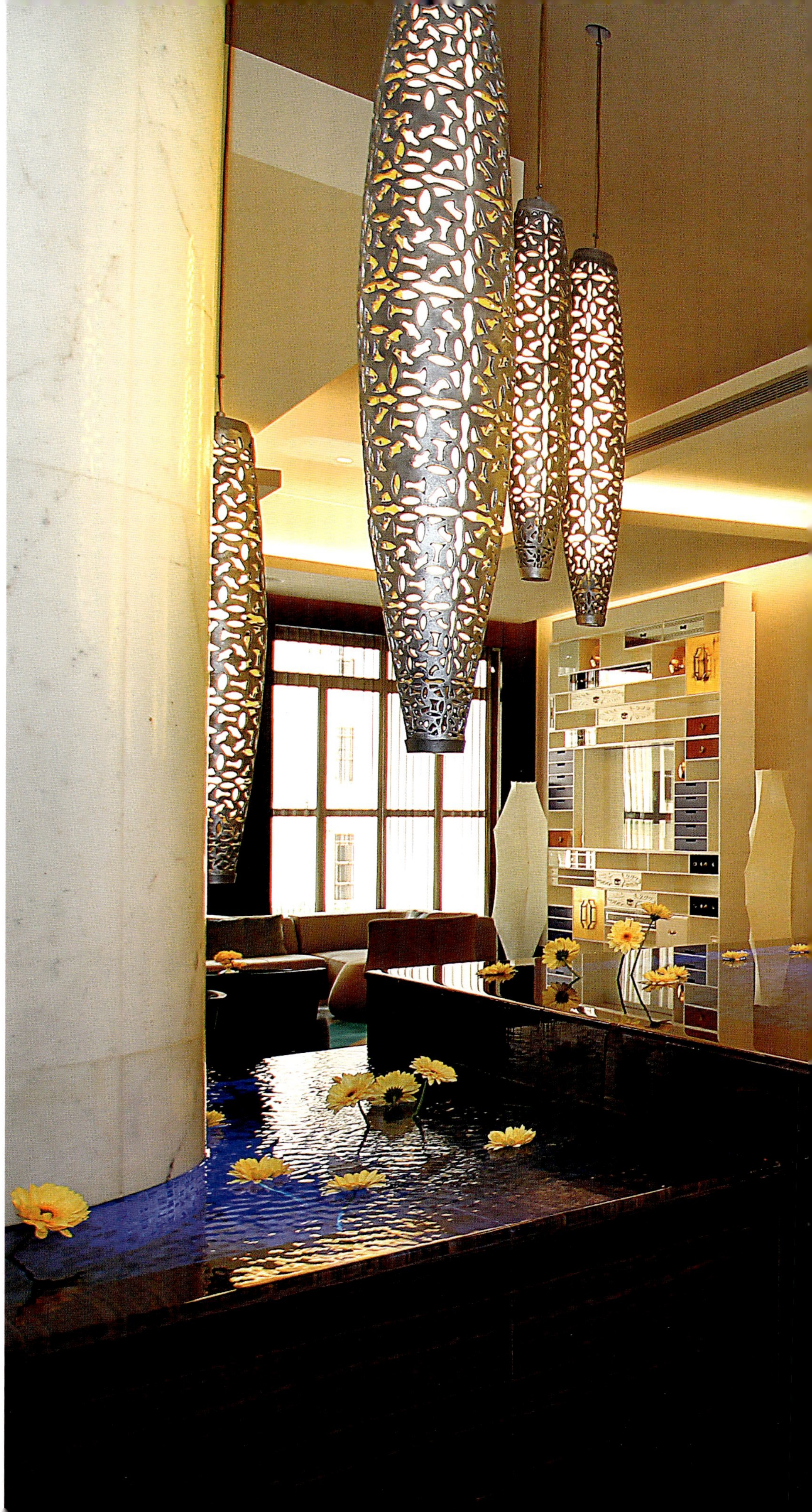

The interior design of the Al Jasra hotel relies heavily on the use of various geometric patterns that can be seen in the ceiling, the floor coverings, and even the lighting fixtures.

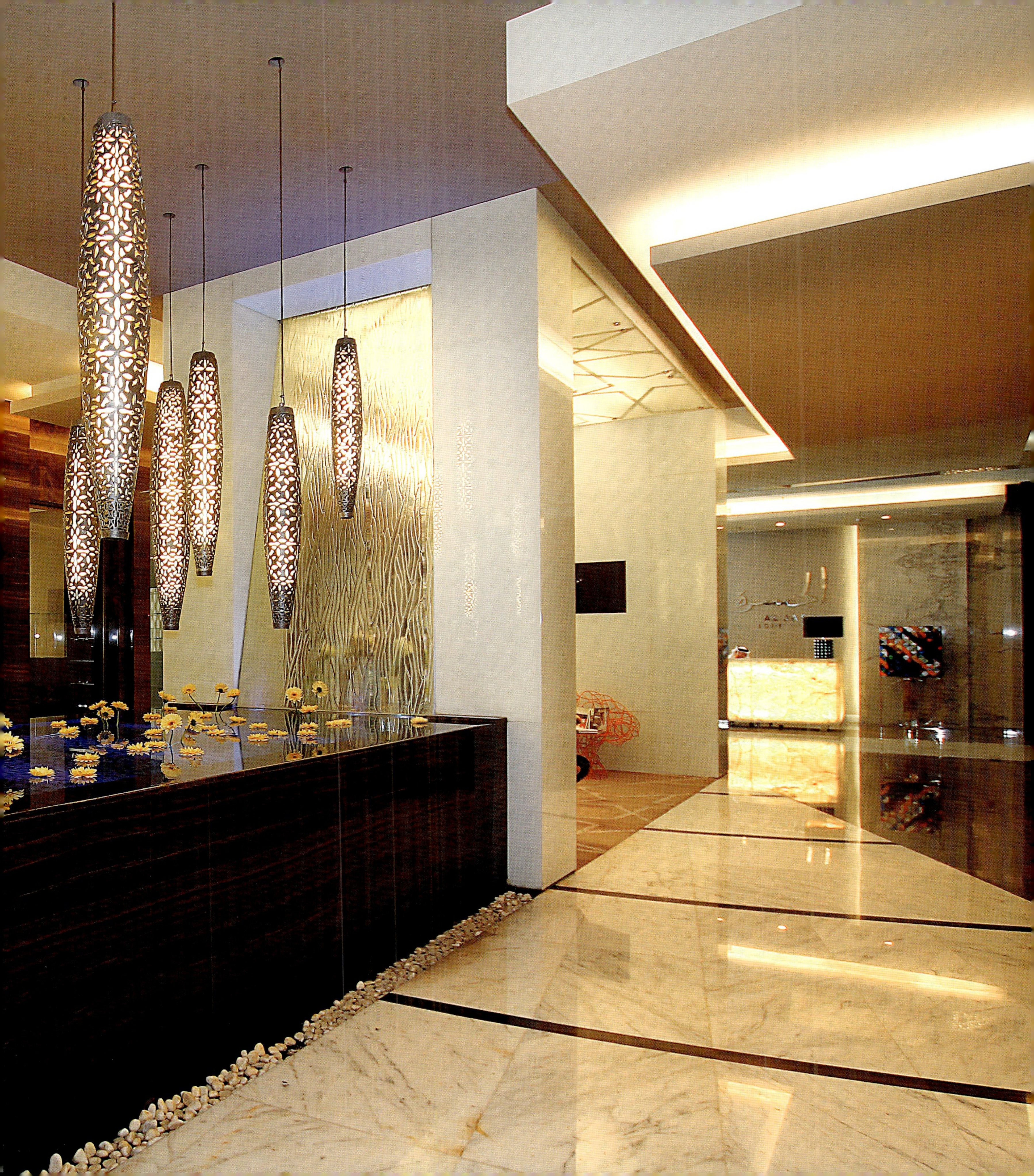

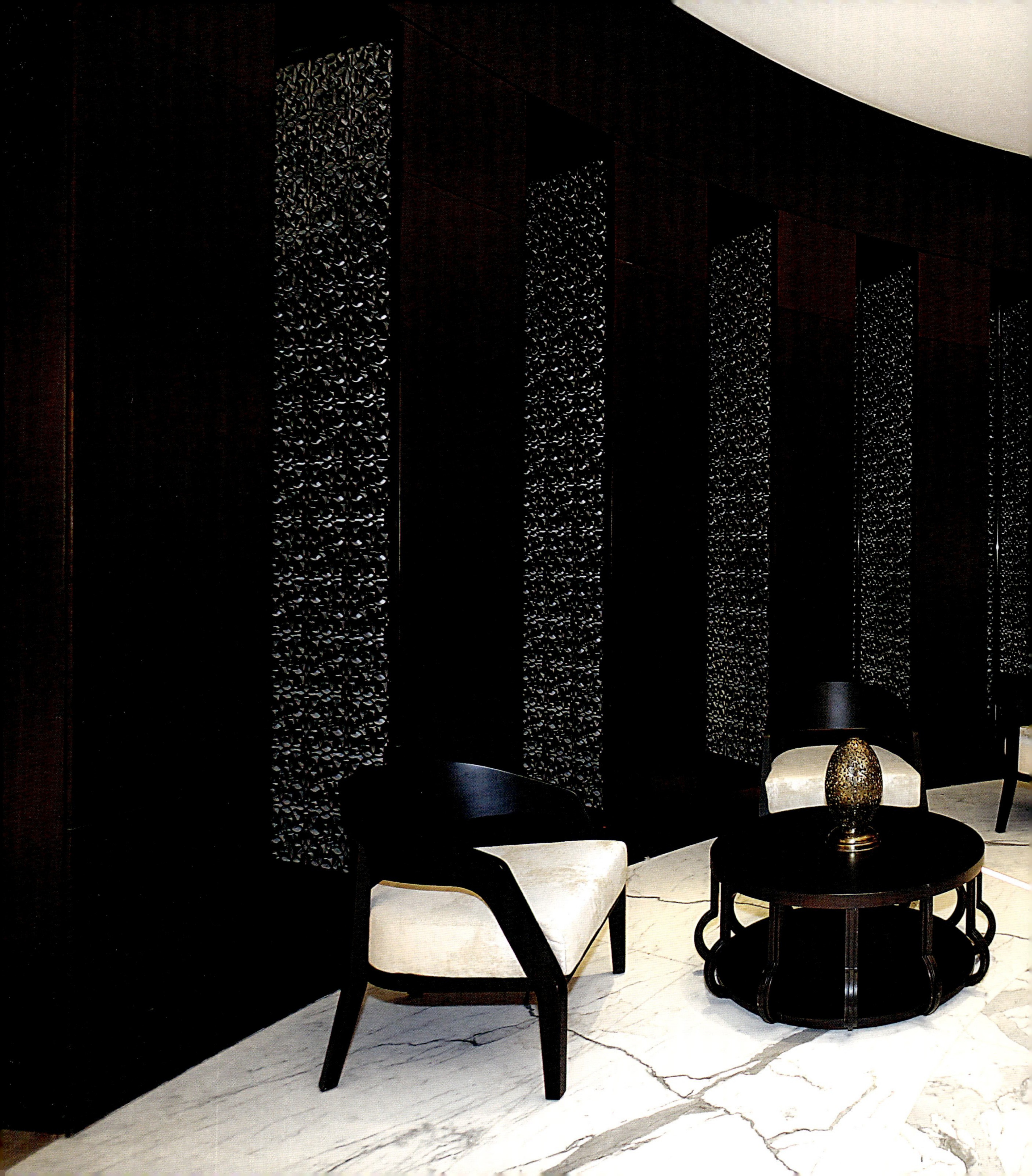

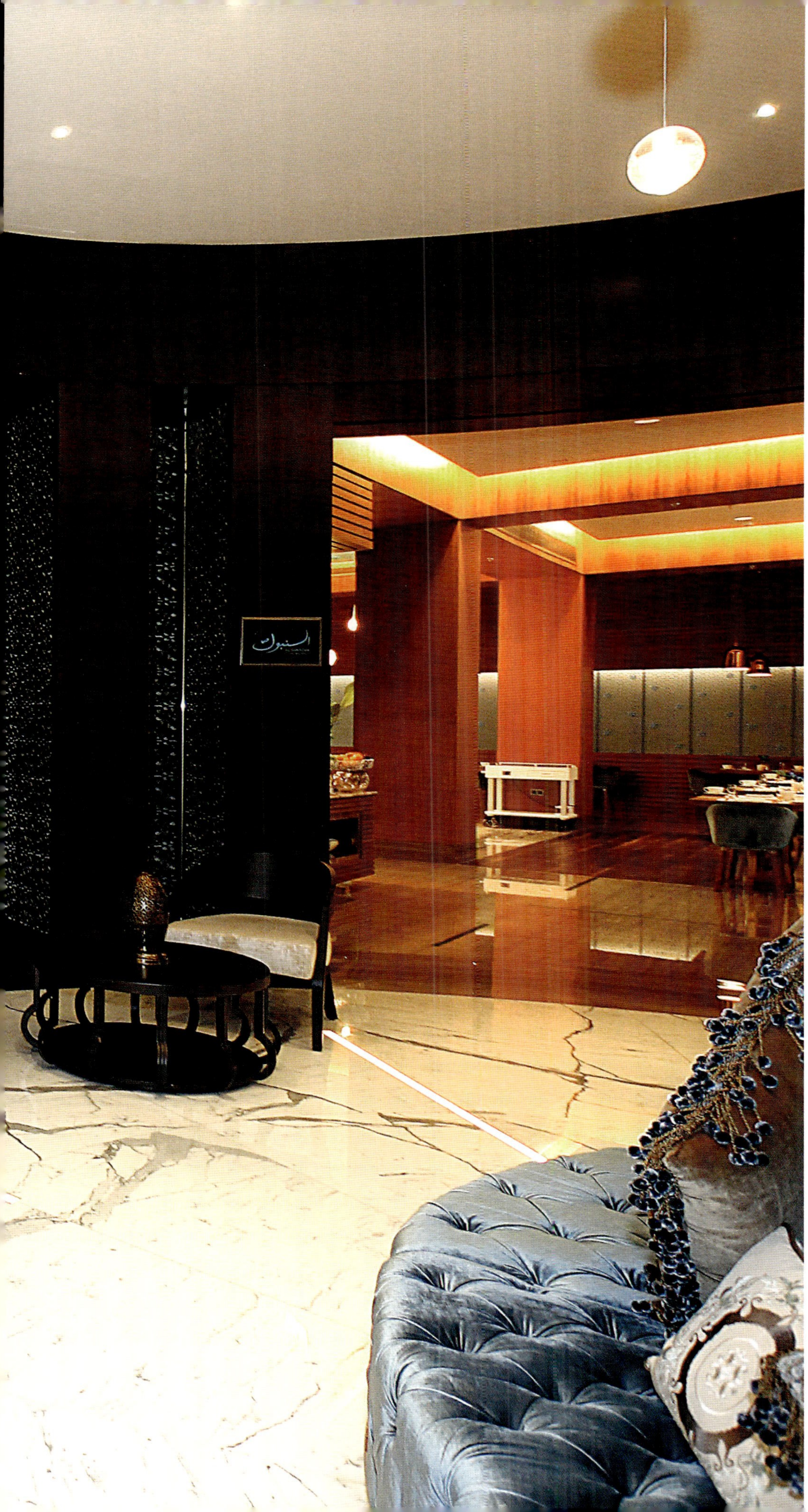

Dark wood is used to section off one area of the lobby, forming a semi-private space in a reference to the traditional *lūzīah*, which in this instance does not cover any windows but is rather used as a decorative element in the wall recesses.

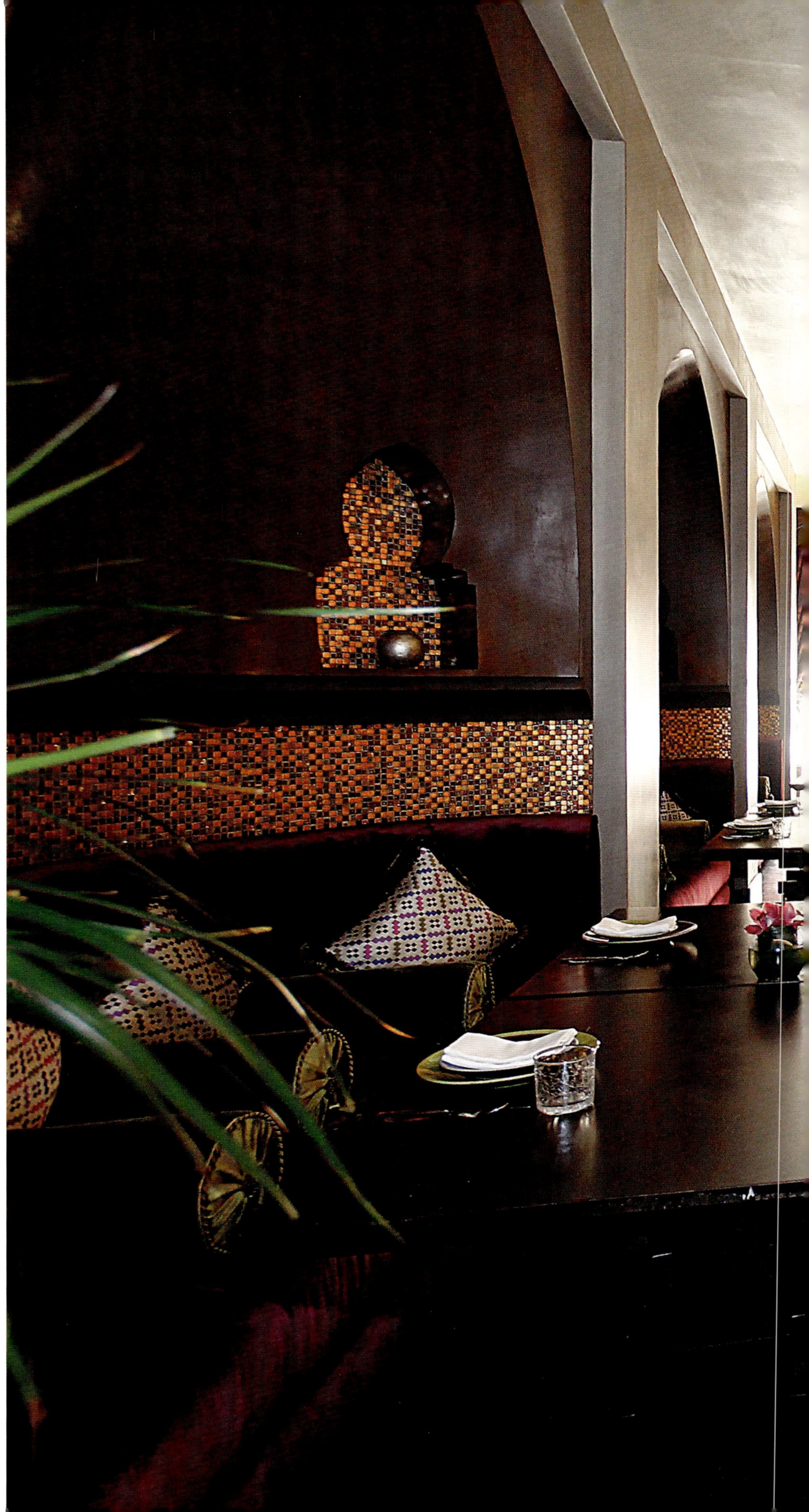

One of the restaurants in Al Jasra is designed in Moroccan style. Opulent fabrics of dark burgundy and golden tones are paired with colorful tiles and ornately decorated woodwork.

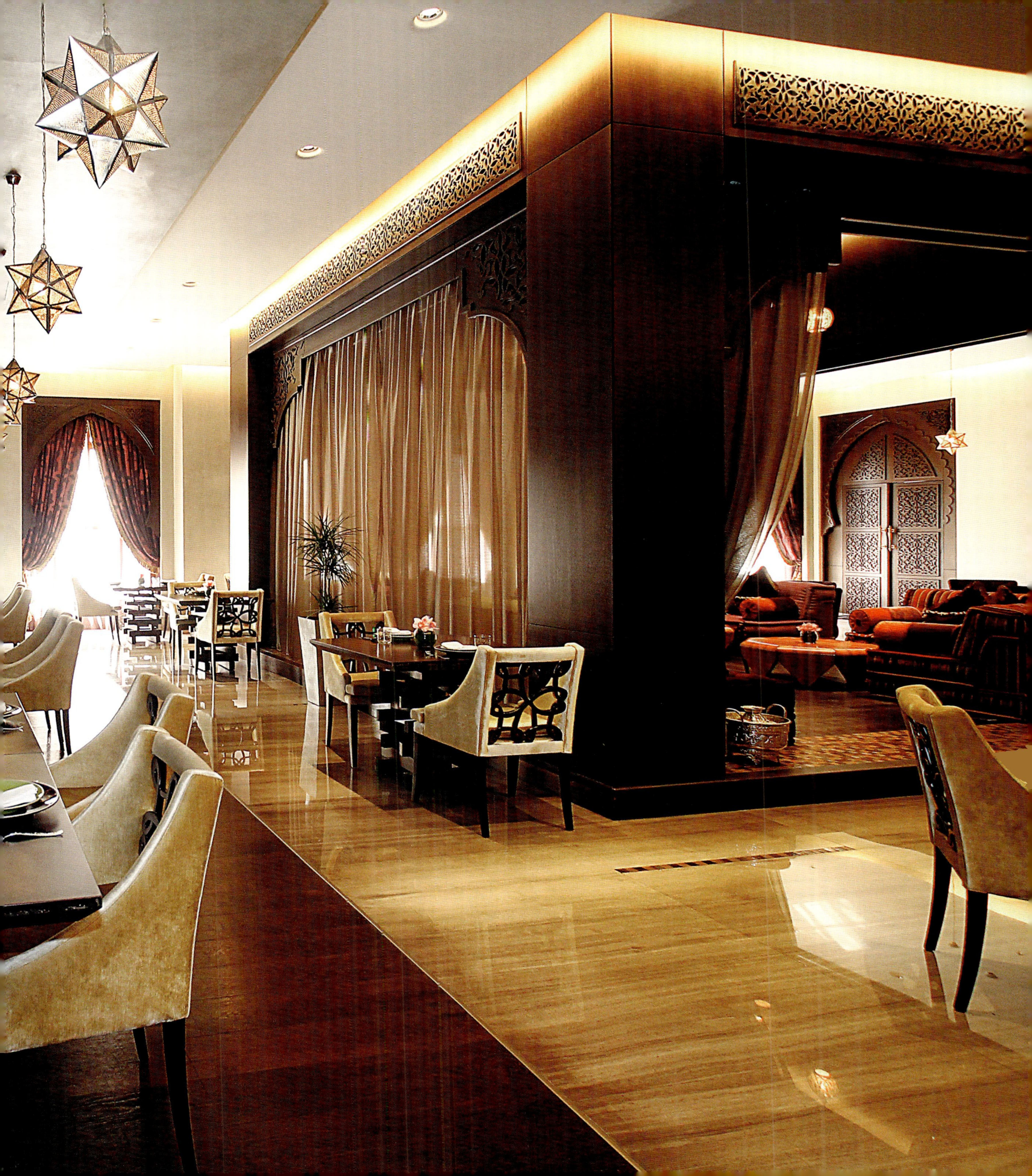

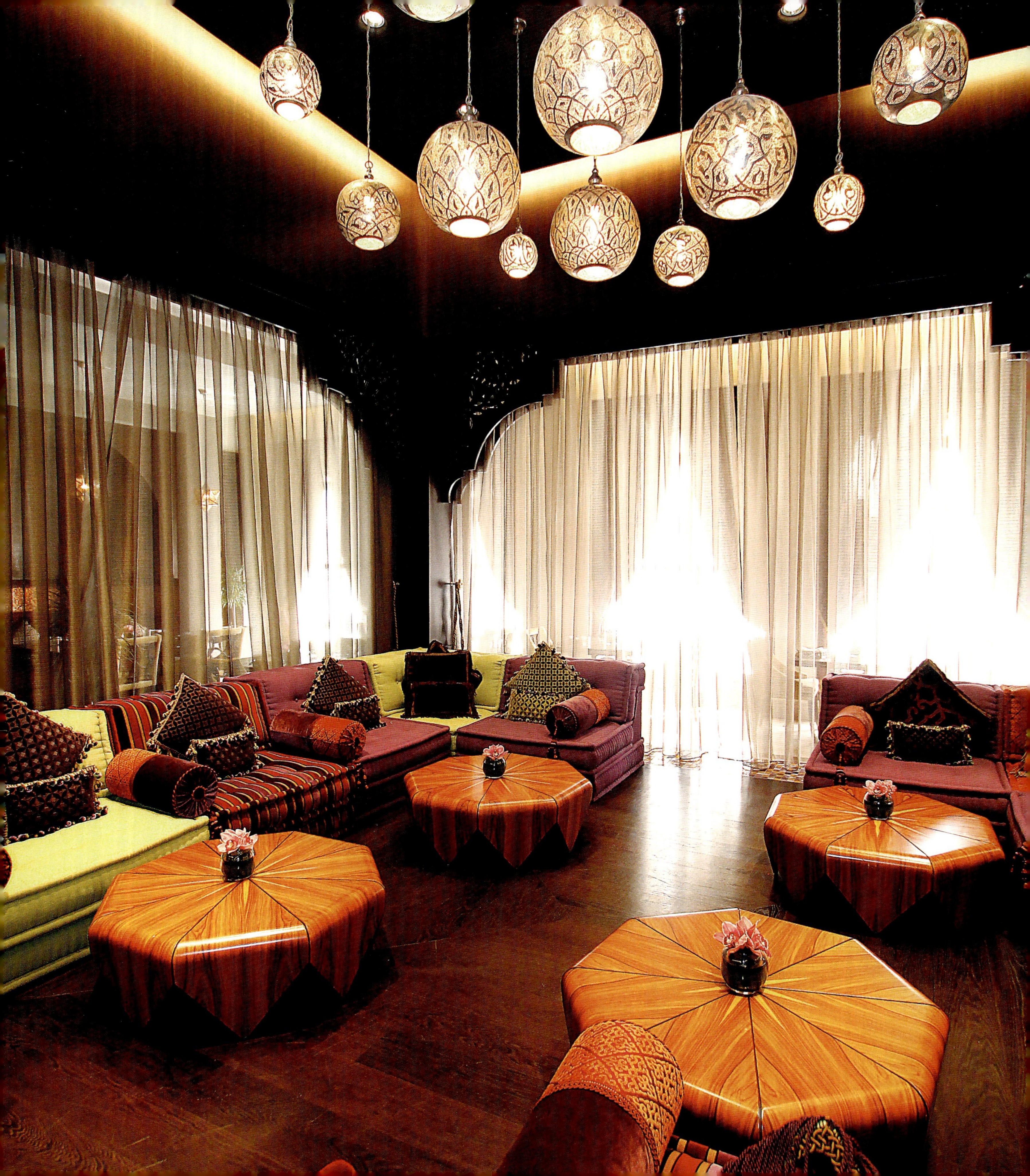

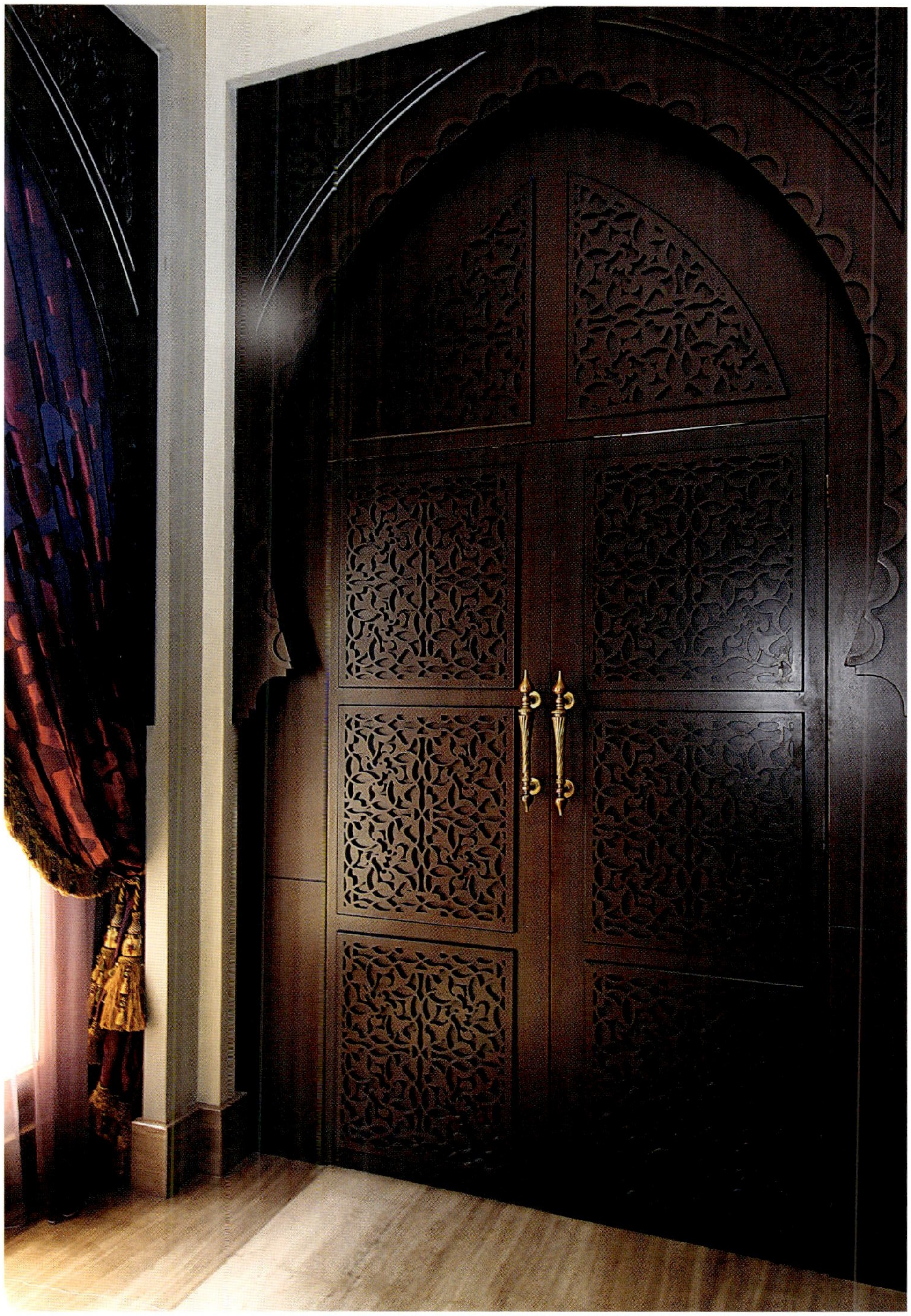

Above: An intricately carved wooden door.

Left-hand page: Modern furniture resonates with the style of the elevated *maylis* seating.

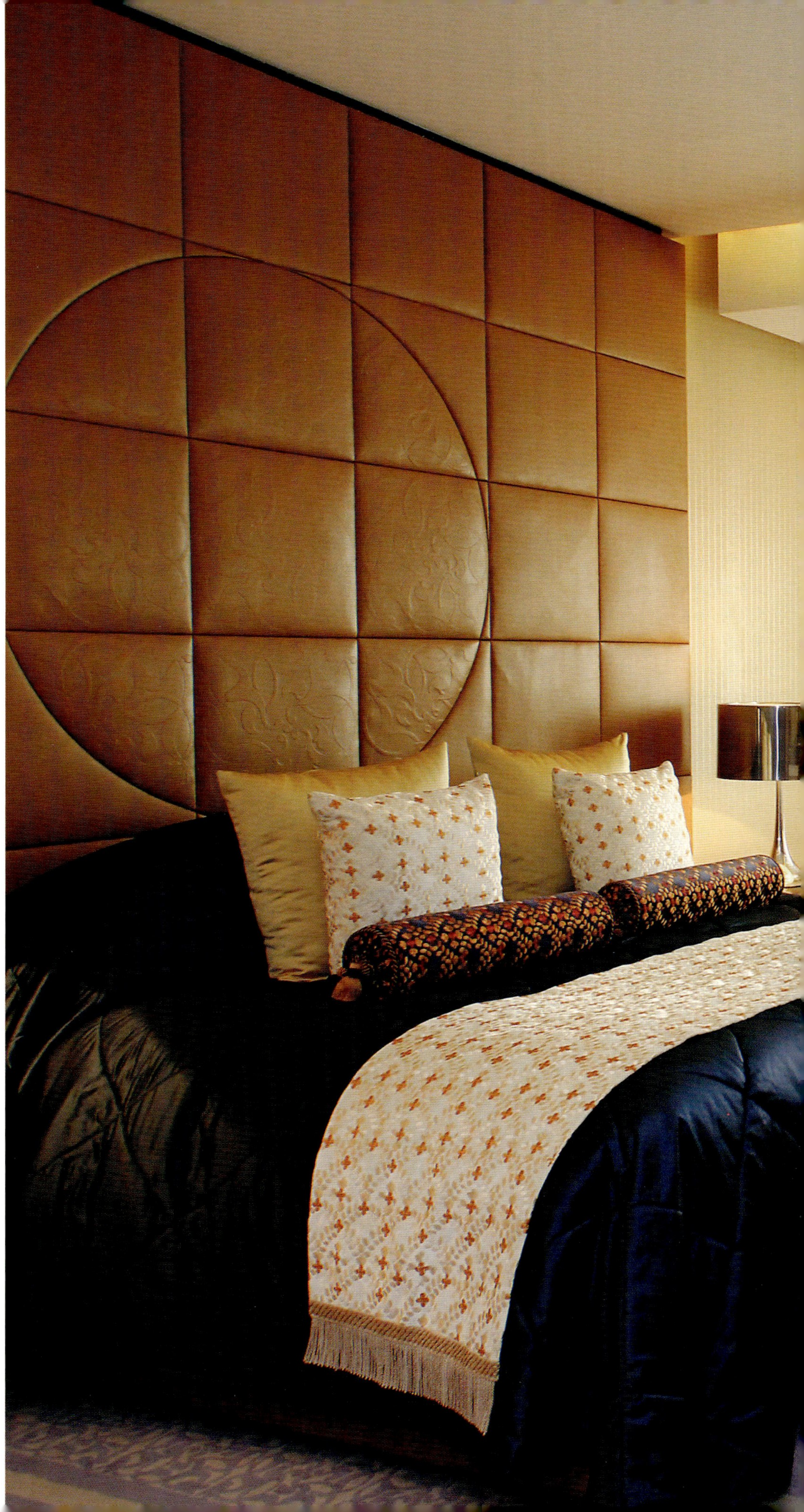

The use of patterns continues throughout the hotel. In the guest rooms, organic patterns are used in numerous instances on both textiles and furniture.

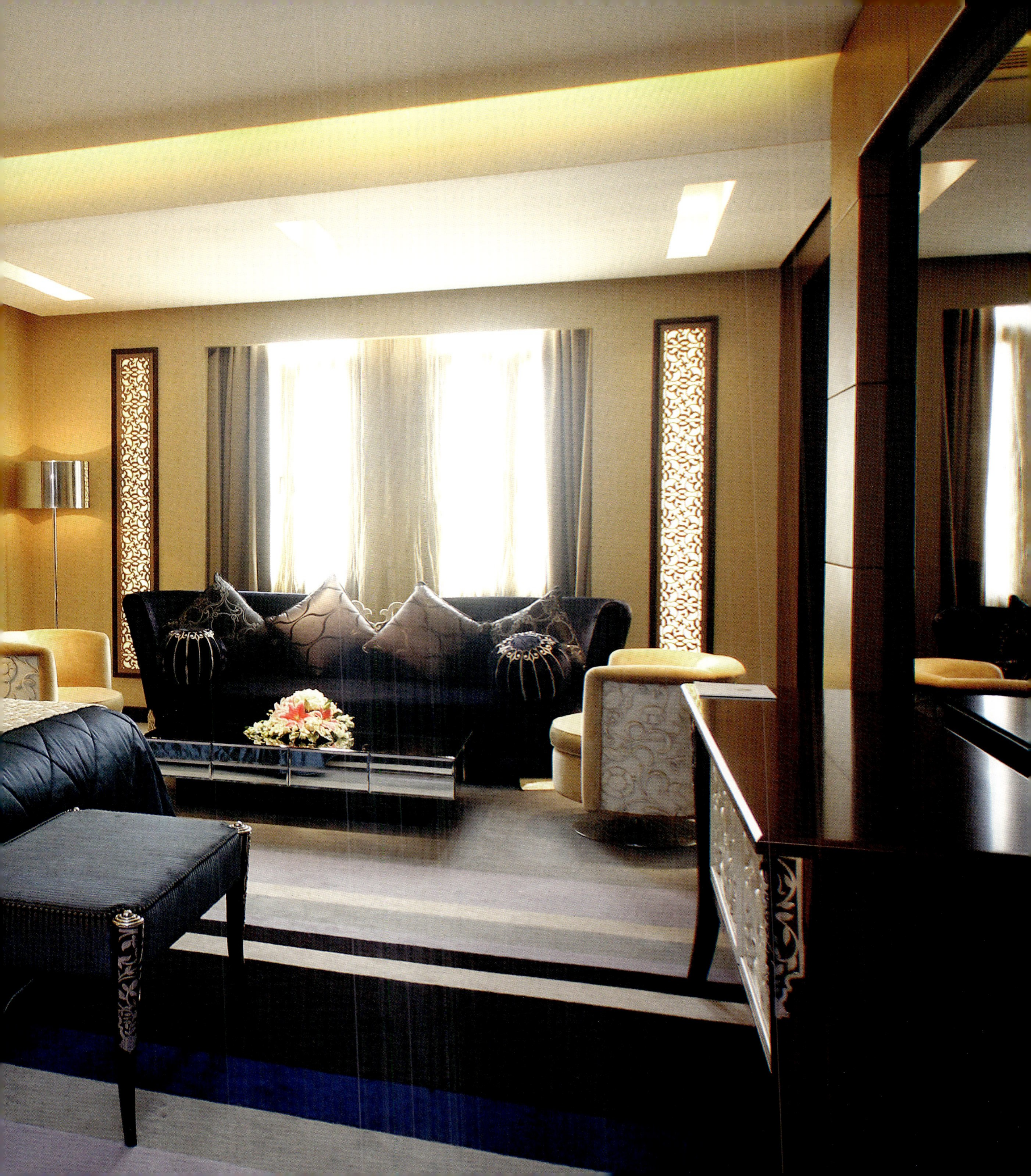

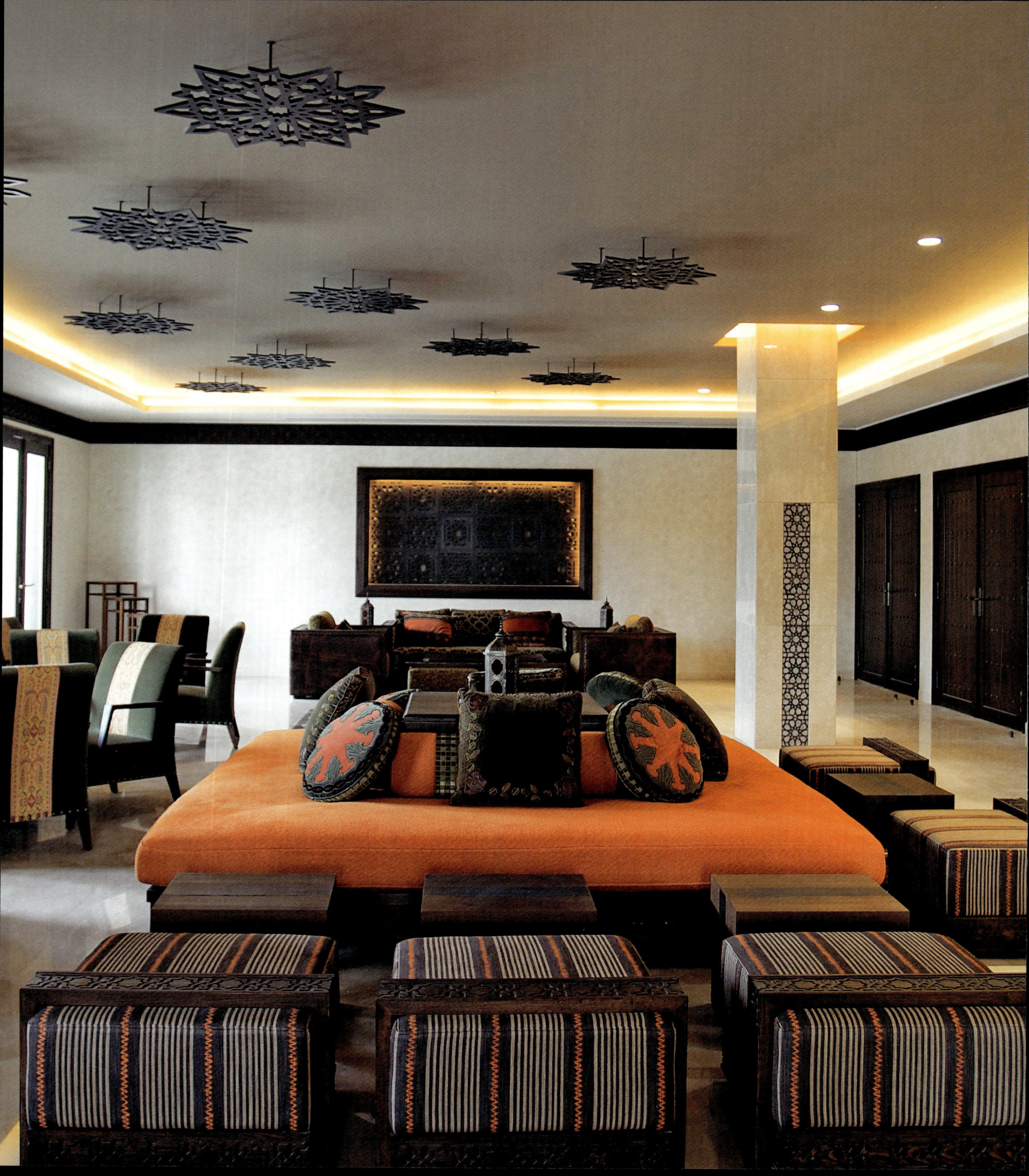

AL MIRQAB HOTEL AND THEATRE

Al Mirqab Hotel is located in Souq Waqif and reflects the inherent character of the site. The building itself creates a strong urban presence as it blends into the surrounding streetscape. The arcades encircling the hotel building create a shaded walkway for pedestrians and cast deep shadows which give expression to both surface and mass. The hotel also houses a 1,000-seat theatre used for a variety of cultural performances.

Arab Engineering Bureau's (AEB) intention here was for the design to match the atmosphere of Souq Waqif while borrowing from the different design schemes across the Middle East. The interior combines Arabic, Islamic, and Qatari visual vocabulary while subtly incorporating a contemporary approach marked by clean lines. The *rūshanāt*, traditional wall recesses located in the common areas, have been adapted to the overall design approach; all the recesses are backlit and incorporate a wooden base on which to display objects.

Also noticeable is the use of Islamic patterns which are evident in the wooden panels and flooring. The idea of the *lūzīah* was reintroduced as well and is evident in the lighting fixtures and decorative panels on the walls and ceilings of the lobby. In general, the design shows a creative repurposing of Arabic and Islamic patterns borrowed from mosques and citadels across North Africa and the Levant.

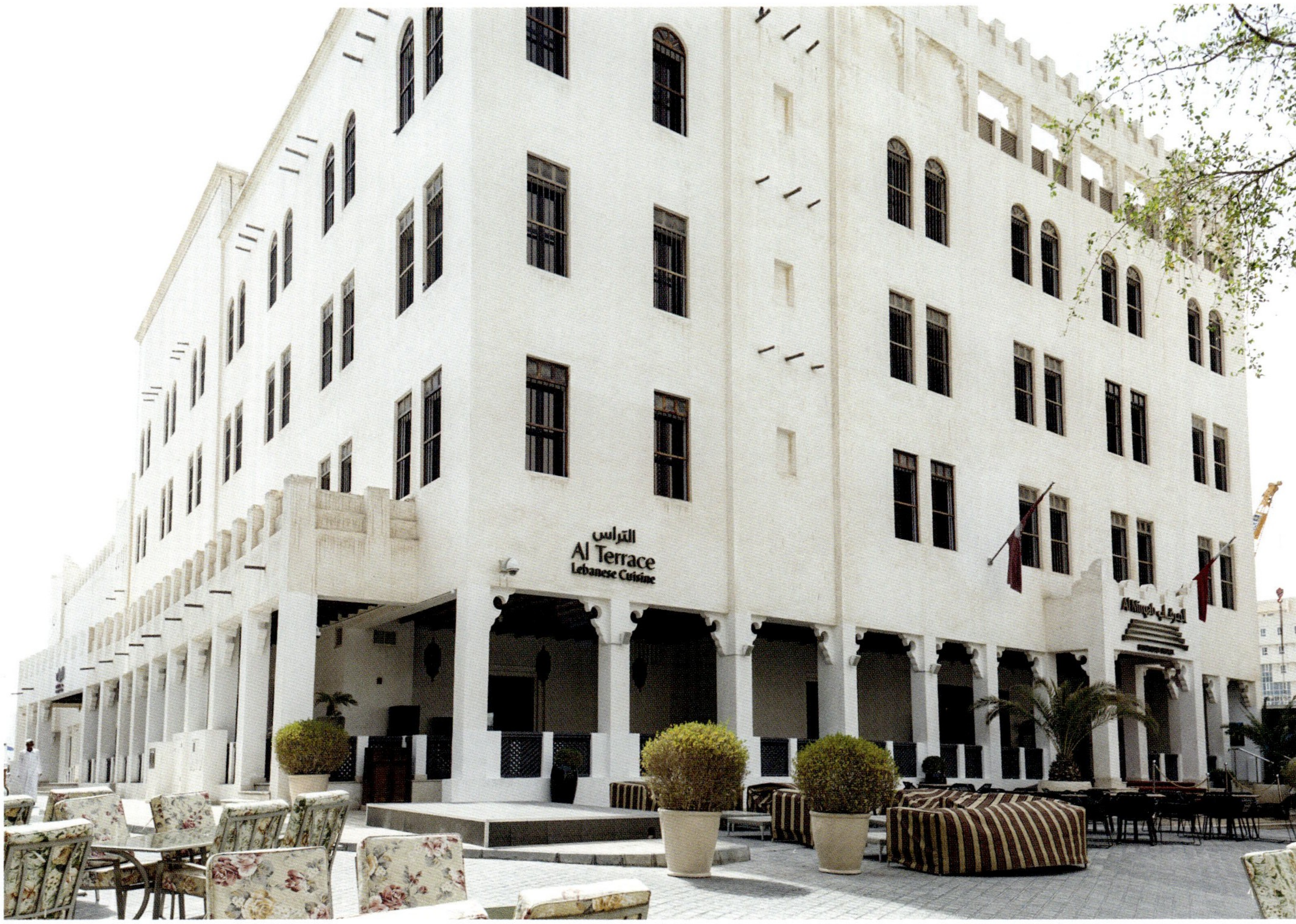

Above: The ground floor of the Al Mirqab hotel is completely enveloped by *līwān*. Unlike in the past where the *līwān* surrounded the central courtyard and provided the residents with shade, the *līwān* of the Al Mirqab hotel faces the busy streets of Souq Waqif and offers shade to the passers-by.

Right-hand page: Arched *rūshanāt* make up one of the feature walls in the hotel and are used as shelves to display various items as in the past.

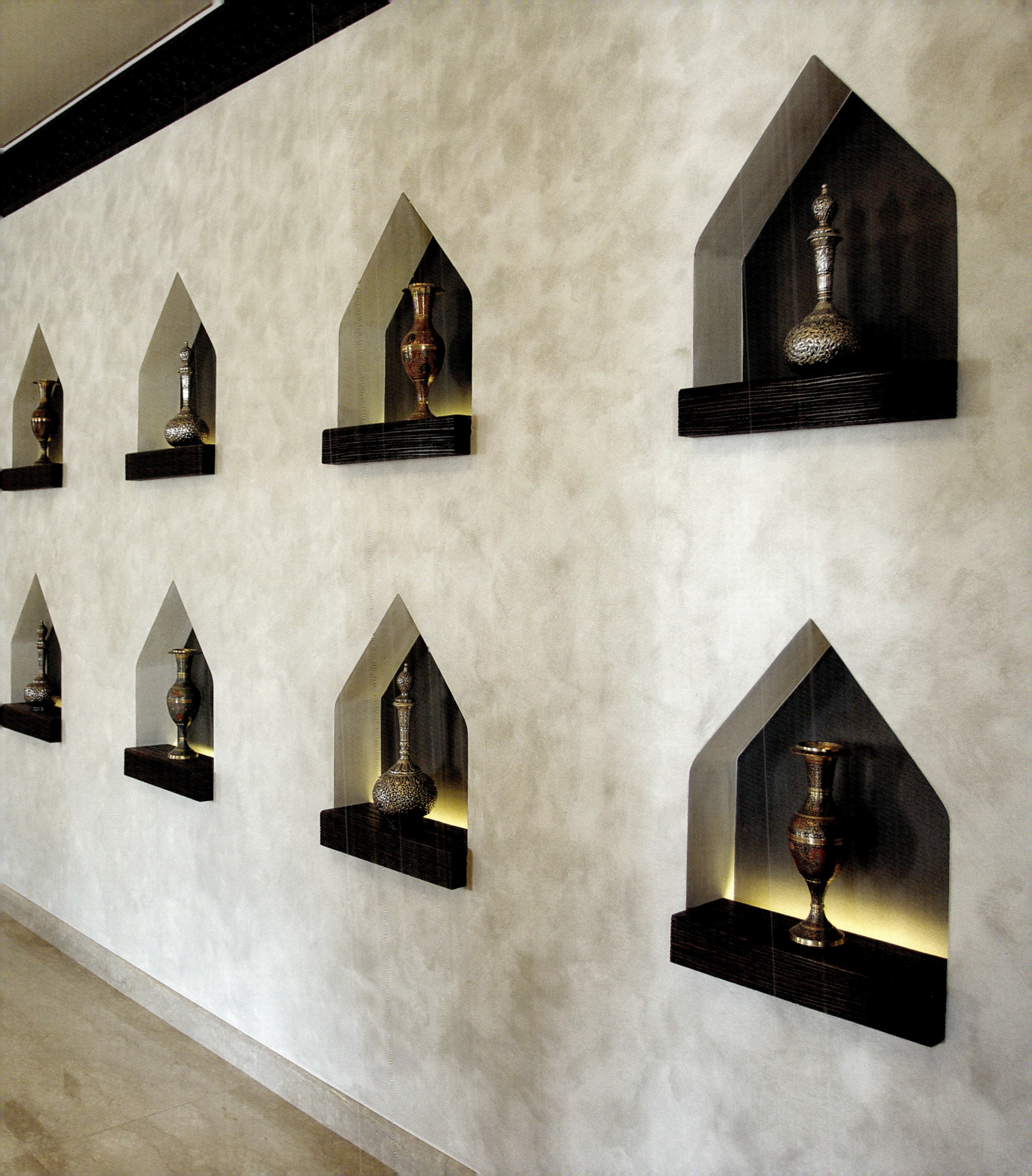

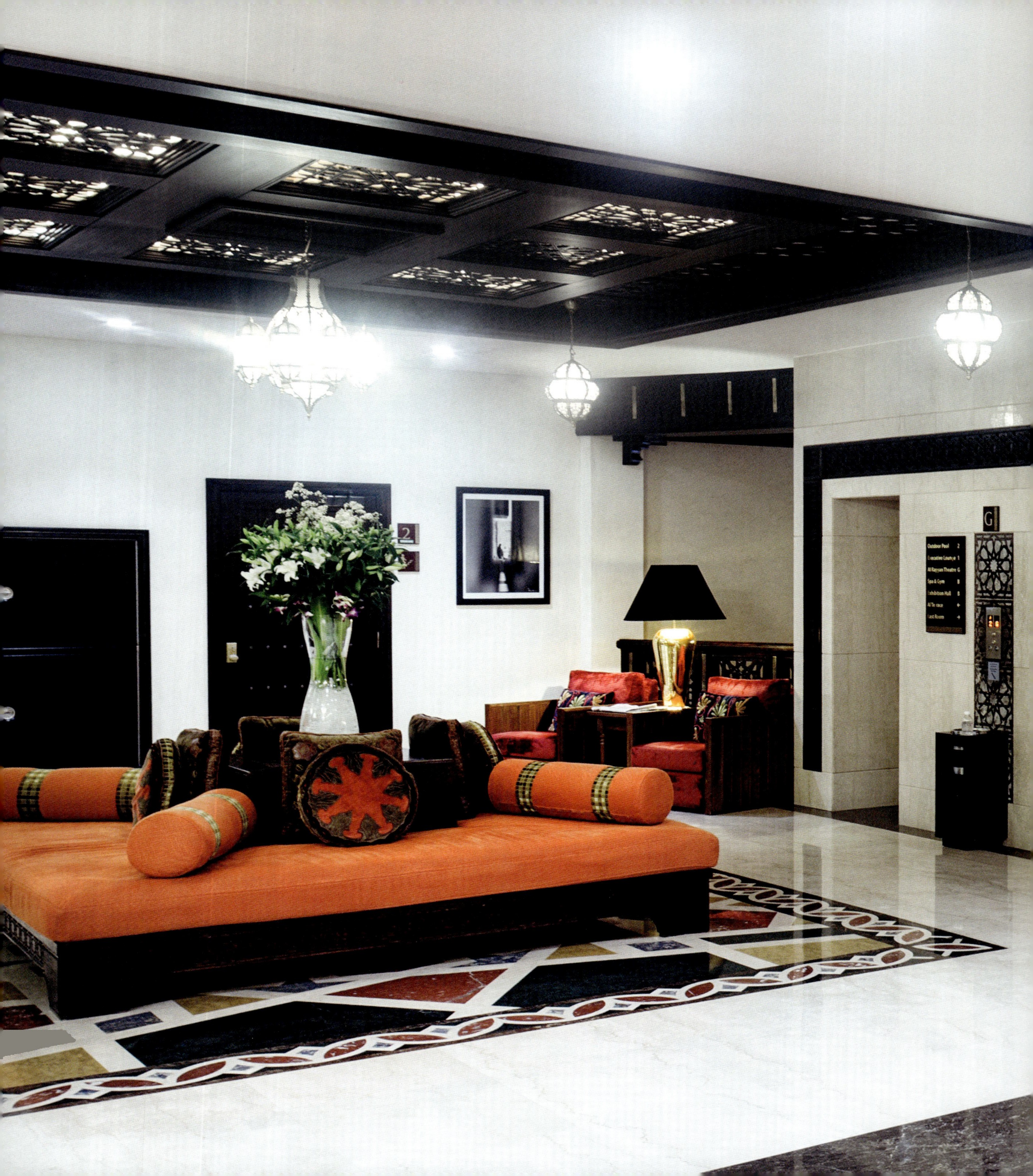
G
Outdoor Pool 2
Spa & Gym

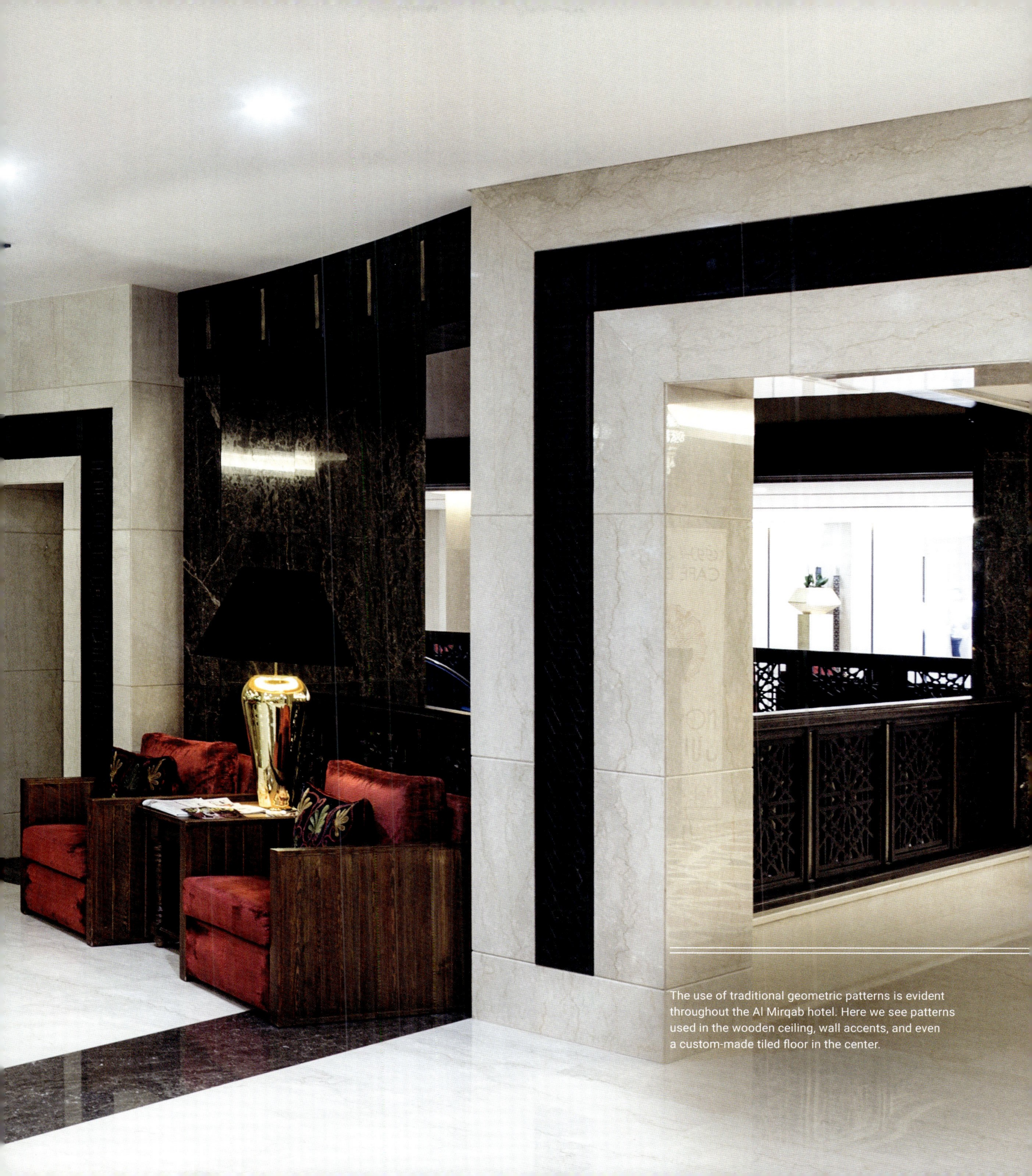

The use of traditional geometric patterns is evident throughout the Al Mirqab hotel. Here we see patterns used in the wooden ceiling, wall accents, and even a custom-made tiled floor in the center.

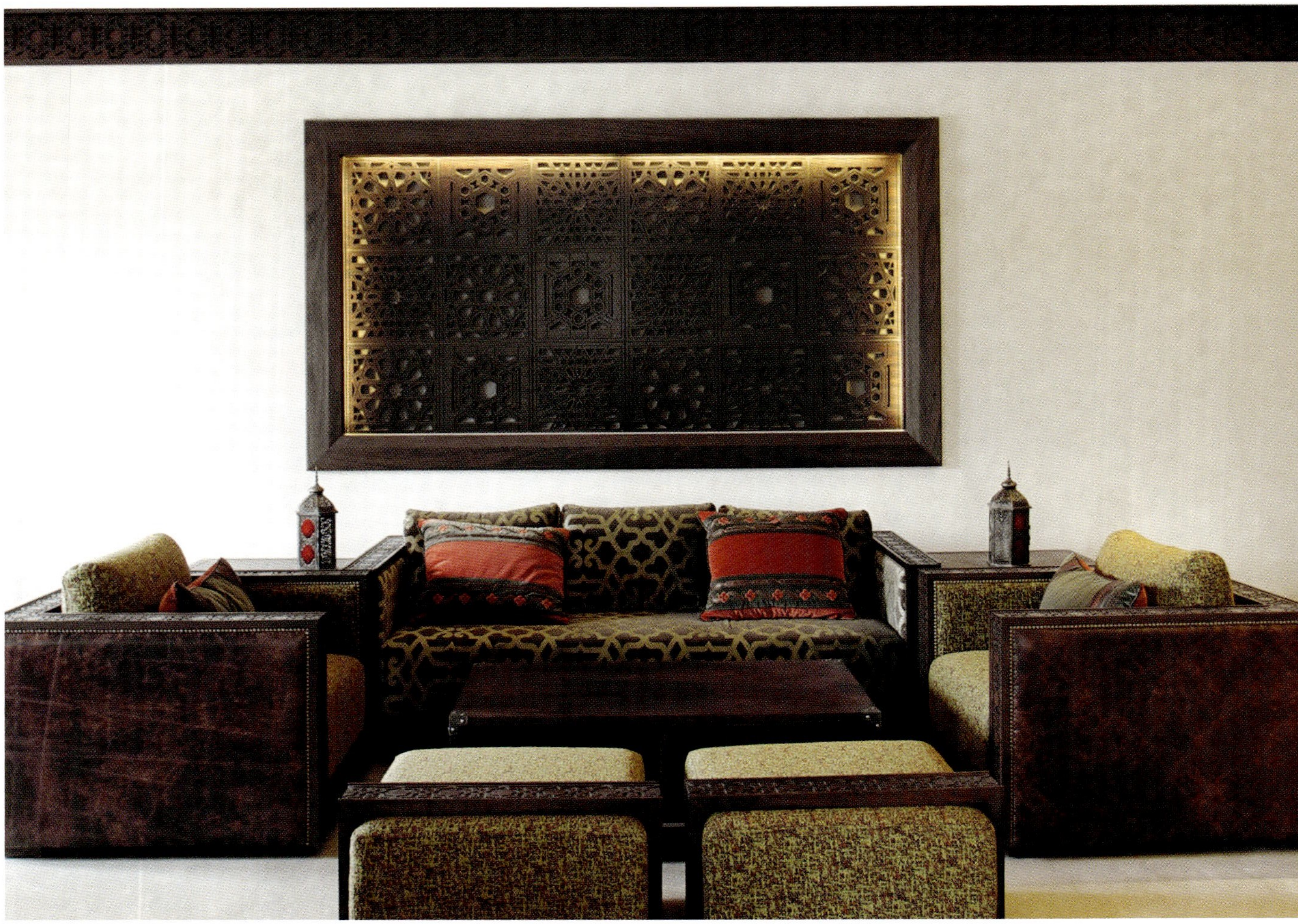

Above: Geometric patterns are used on the wall features and upholstery.

Right-hand page: *Maylis*-like elevated seating is evident in the hotel and is paired with elongated *rūshanāt*.

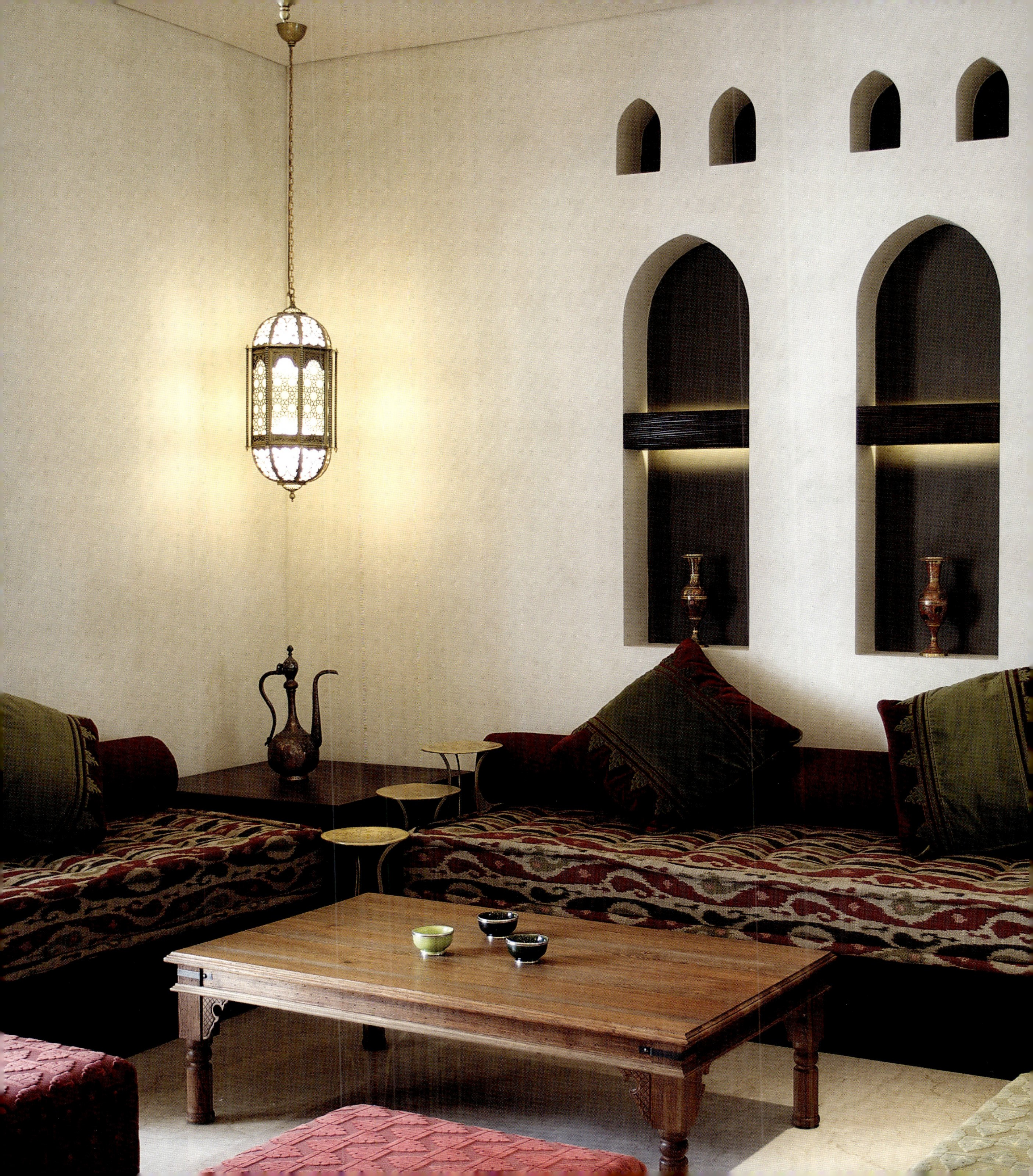

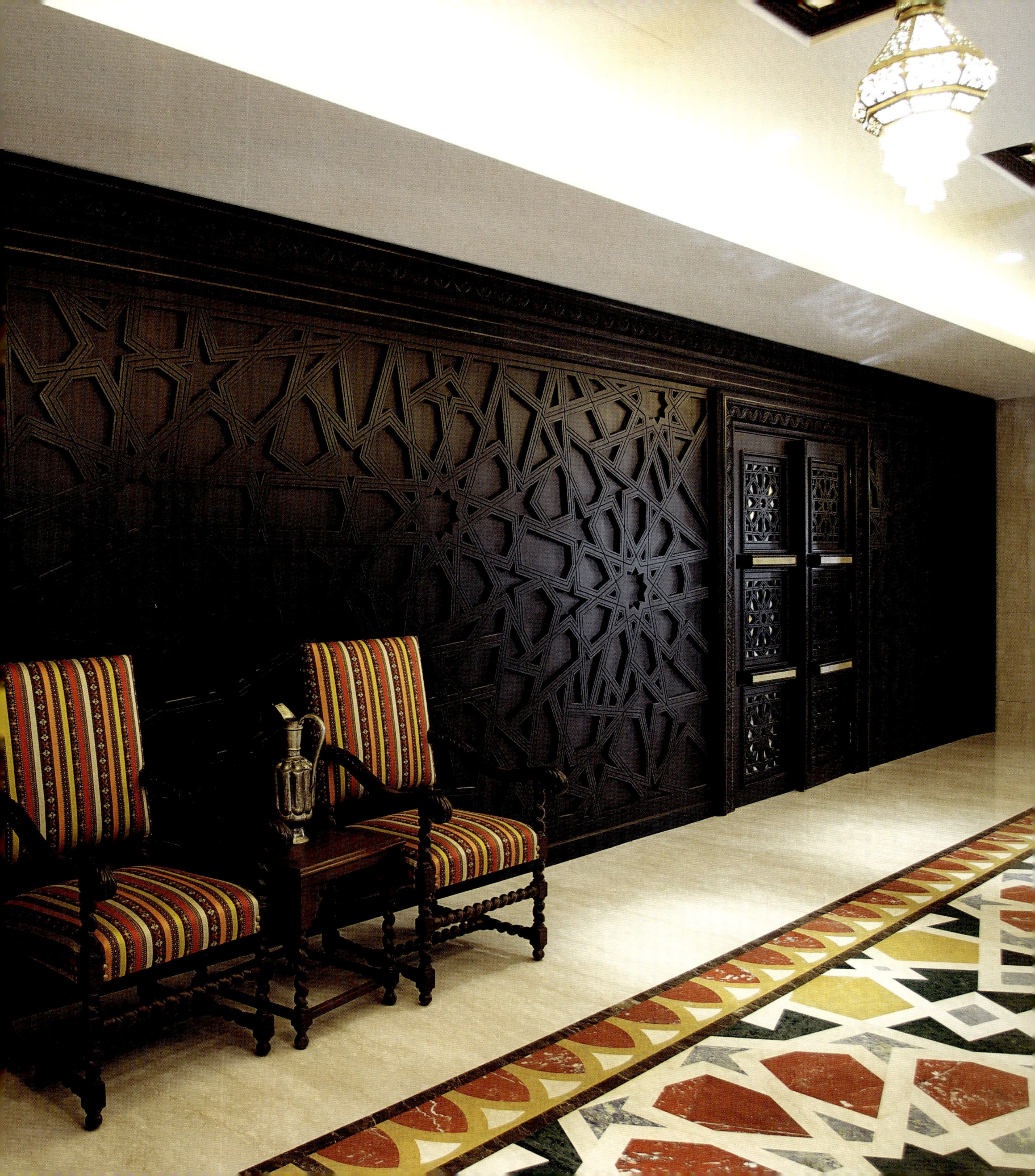

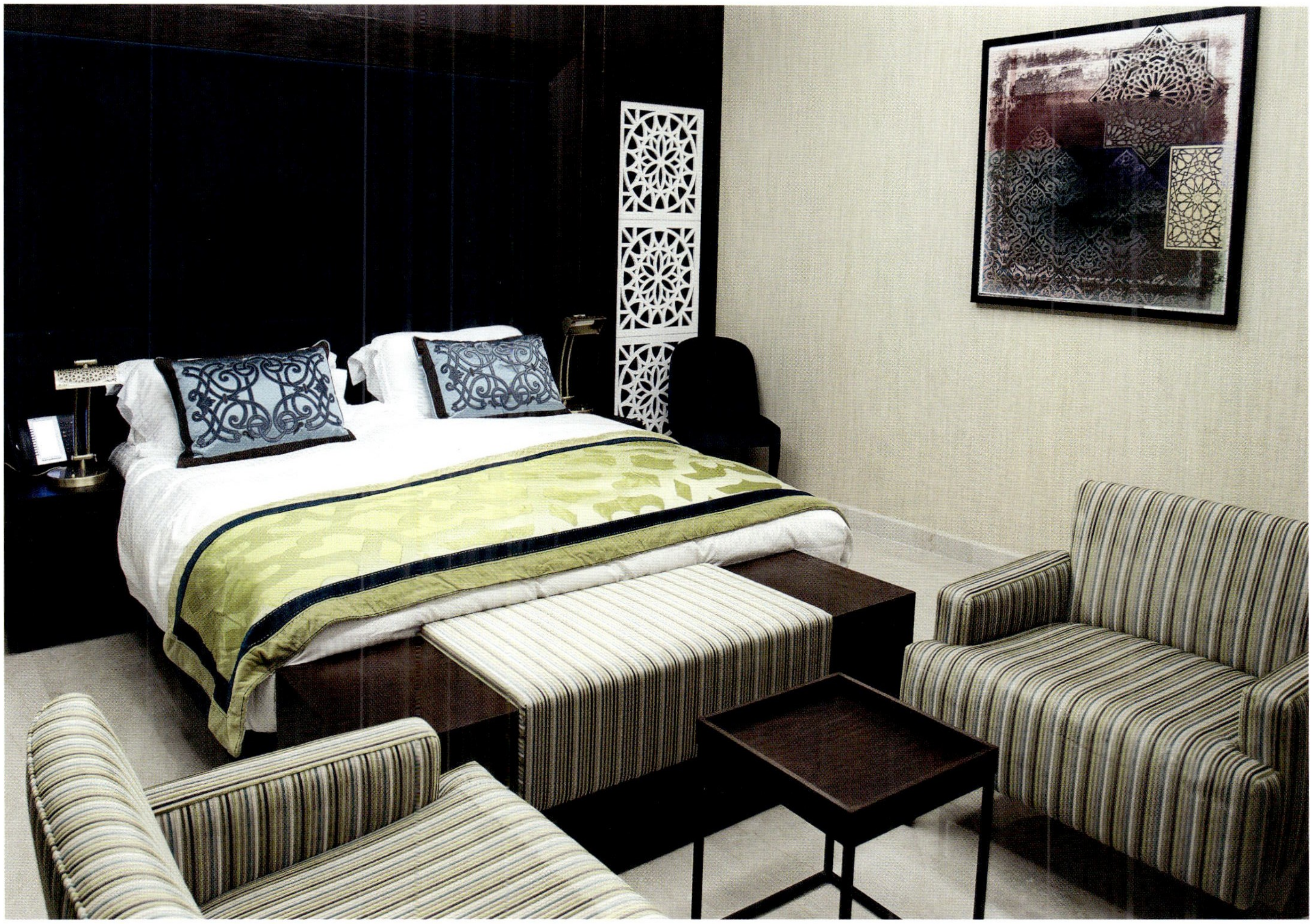

Above: The guest rooms are designed in a muted color scheme with geometric patterns carved to embellish the wood.

Left-hand page: In the hallways of the hotel, Qatari geometric patterns are used on the wooden wall features and the floor.

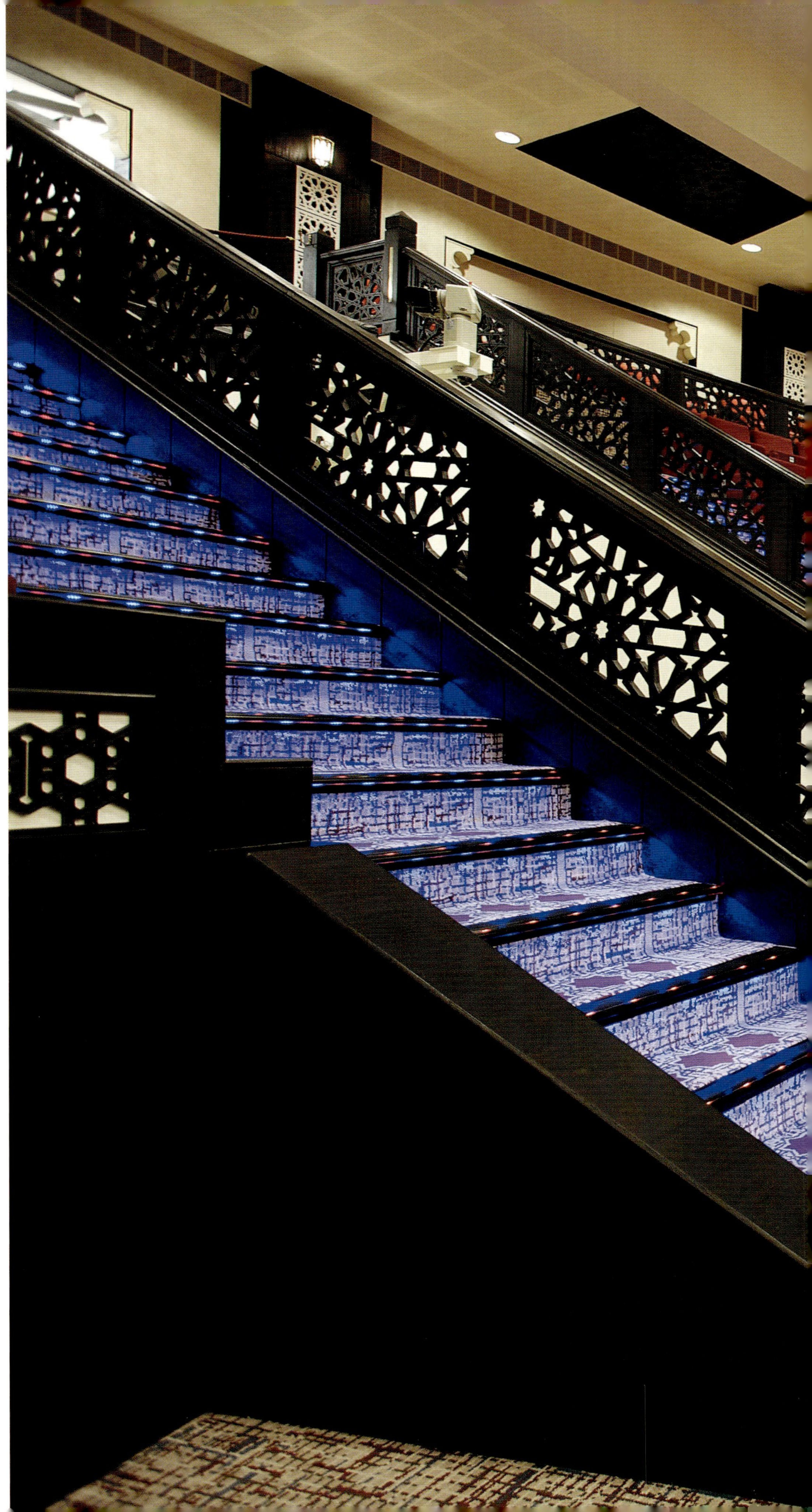

The amphitheater is in the vicinity of the hotel and geometric patterns are used here as in the rest of the hotel.

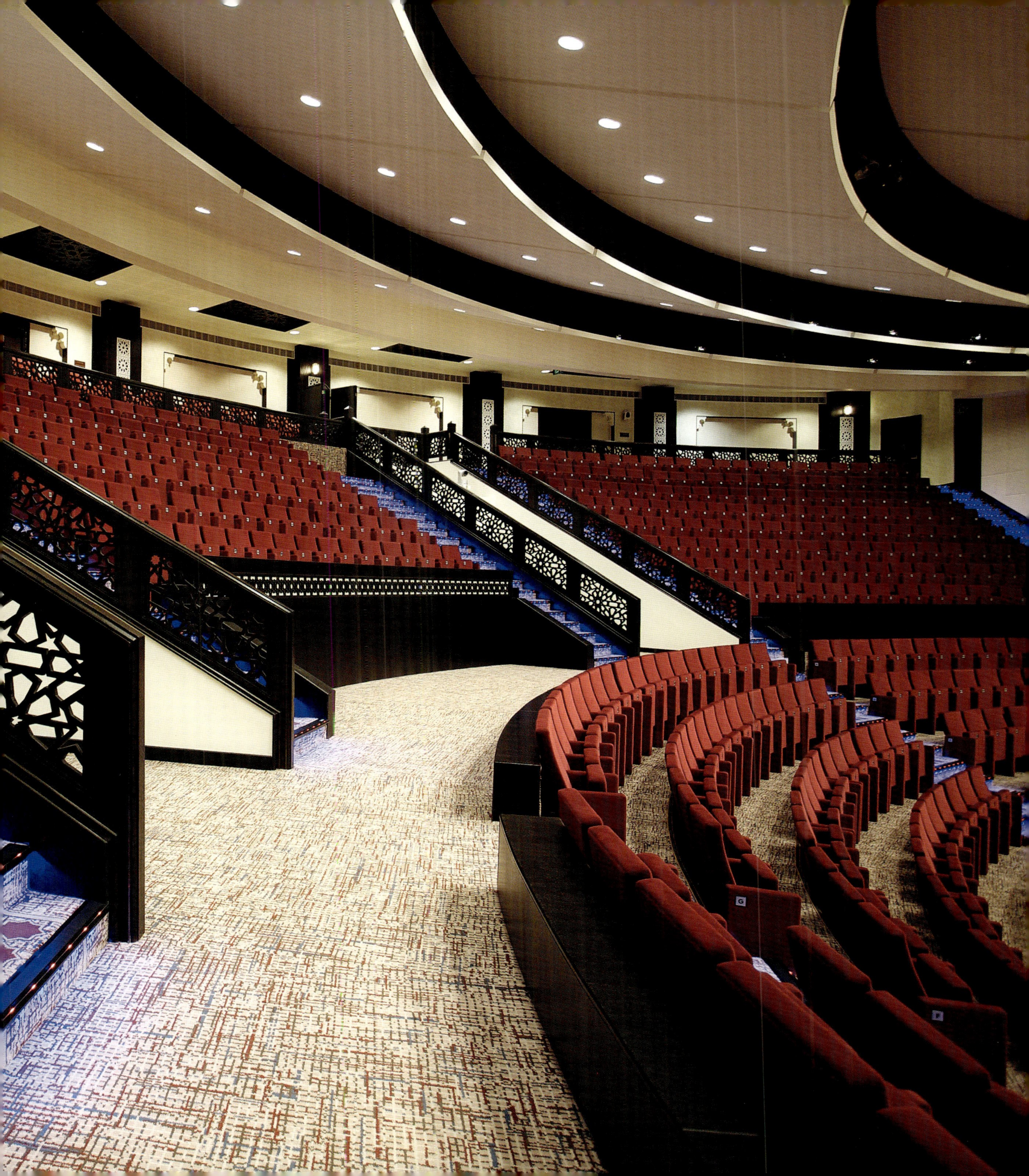

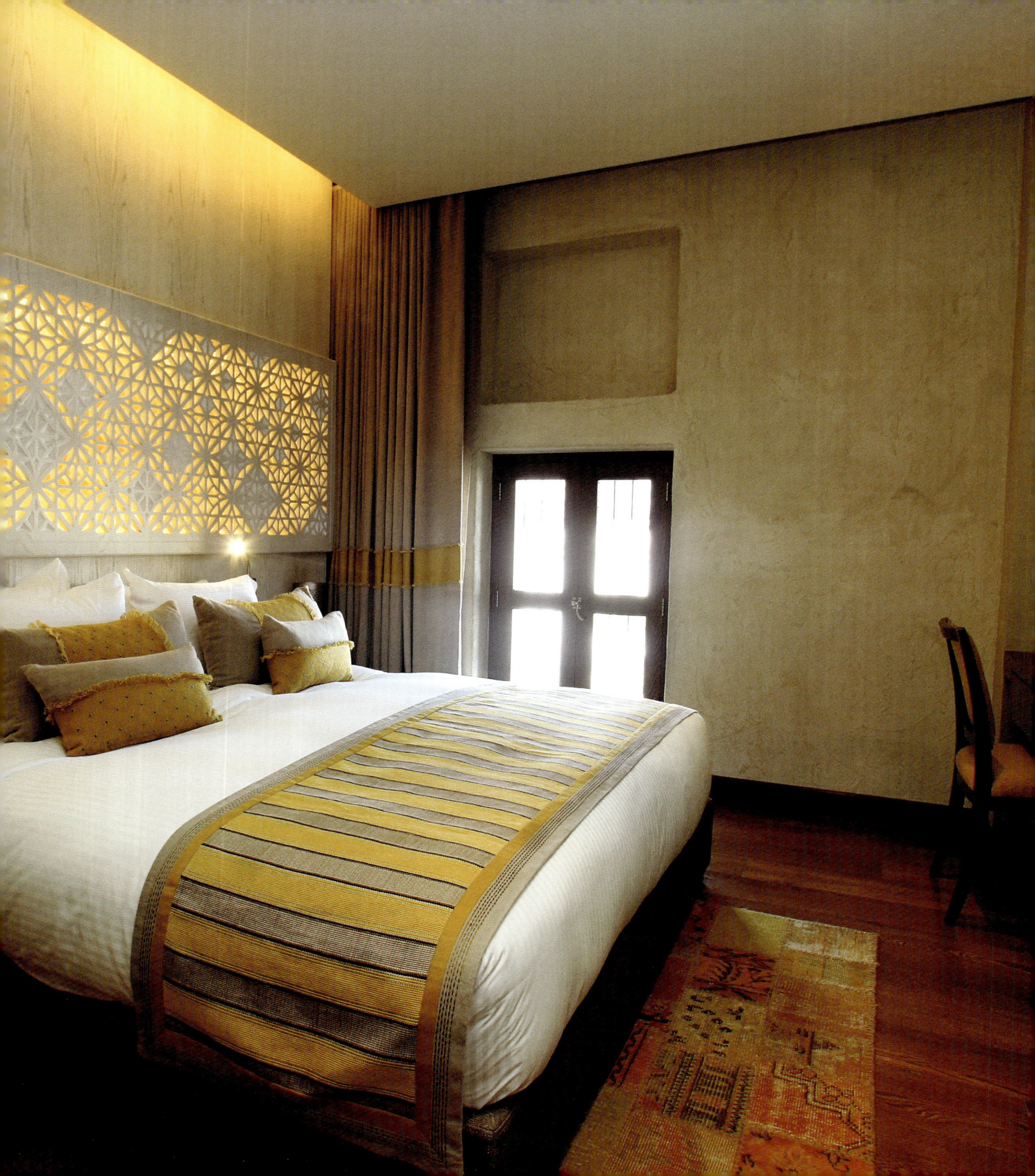

ARUMAILAH HOTEL

Arumailah Boutique Hotel, situated in Souq Waqif, was reconstructed and repurposed to maintain the traditional theme of the *sūq* itself. This five-story building responds to the architectural language of the surrounding buildings and the *sūq*'s open areas. The internal and external walls are rough and replicate the unfinished look of traditional walls in Qatar.

The interior design of the hotel further explores traditional Qatari interiors through the use of wood and wall gypsum patterns. Walls in the public areas such as the lobby and hallways are covered in wooden or gypsum panels with elegant geometric carvings and calligraphy. The wooden screening forms traditional *lūzīāt* creating interesting shadows inside the hotel while maintaining the privacy of the hotel's guests and its visitors. Across the hotel walls are black-and-white photographs of old Qatar, offering visitors a glimpse into the old ways of living.

Inside the private space of the guest rooms, a warm color scheme is used for the textiles; the walls are decorated with white gypsum patterns. The most prominent traditional features inside the rooms are the typical Qatari windows, *darāīsh*, which are situated close to the floor, as in the past. Unlike the past, when *darāīsh*, besides letting light inside the room, also allowed the cool breeze in and protected against animals and intruders accessing the private space, here *darāīsh* offer better views of the *sūq*.

Traditional Qatari *sufar* decorate the walls of the hotel's main restaurant, instilling the sense of nostalgia among the local community; *sufar* were used in the past both for serving food and for storage. The other restaurant at the top of the hotel continues the traditional theme manifested through the use of *lūzīah* across its railing and overhead canopies. In contrast to the colorful public areas of the hotel, and the warm tones in the guest rooms, the restaurants are furnished in cool-toned textiles contrasted against the natural dark wood.

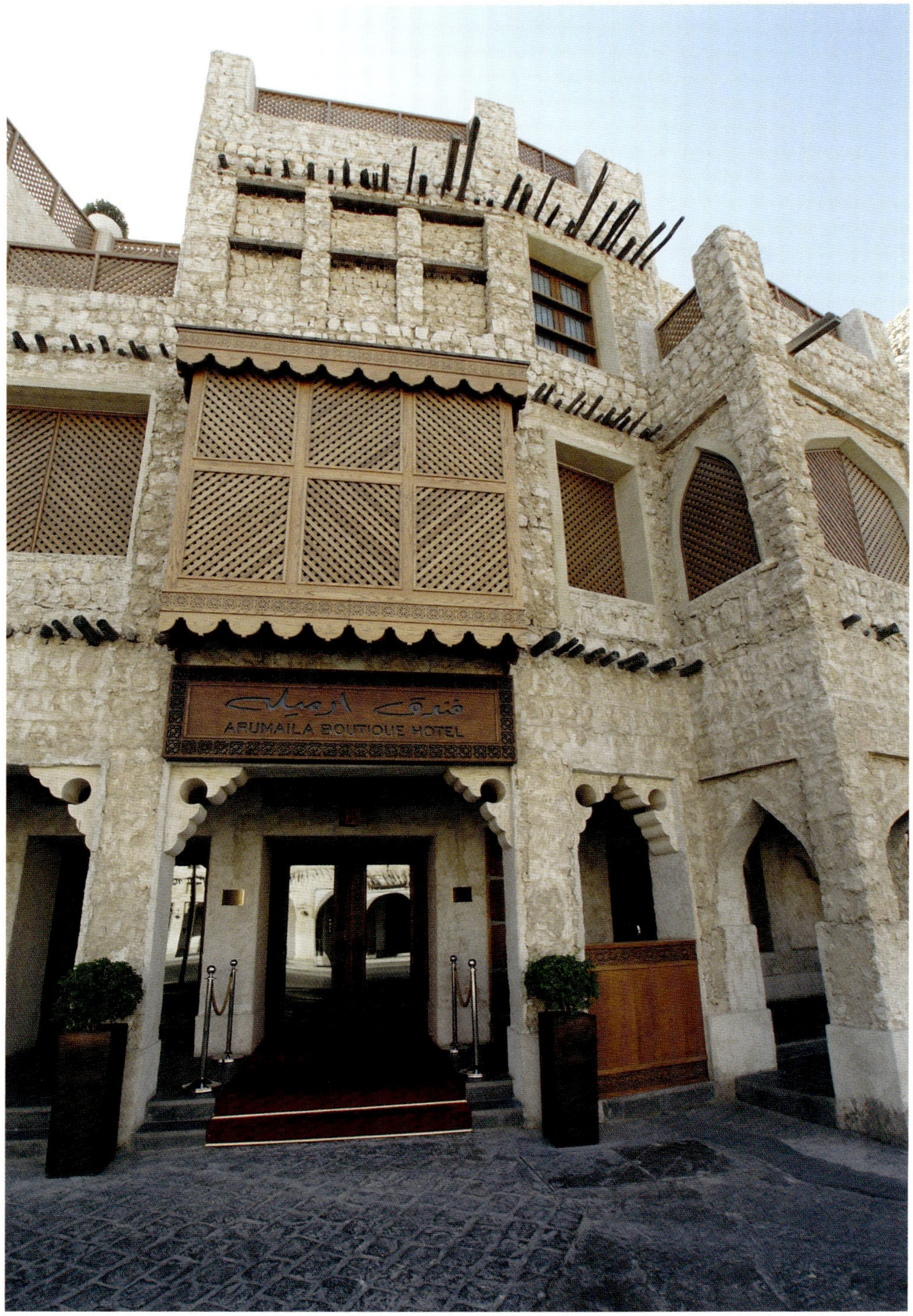

Above: As in Al Mirqab hotel, here a *līwān* envelops the entire ground floor of the building and offers shaded walkways for the hotel and *sūq* visitors.

Right-hand page: Here, traditional geometric patterns are modified and introduced in the design of the coffee table.

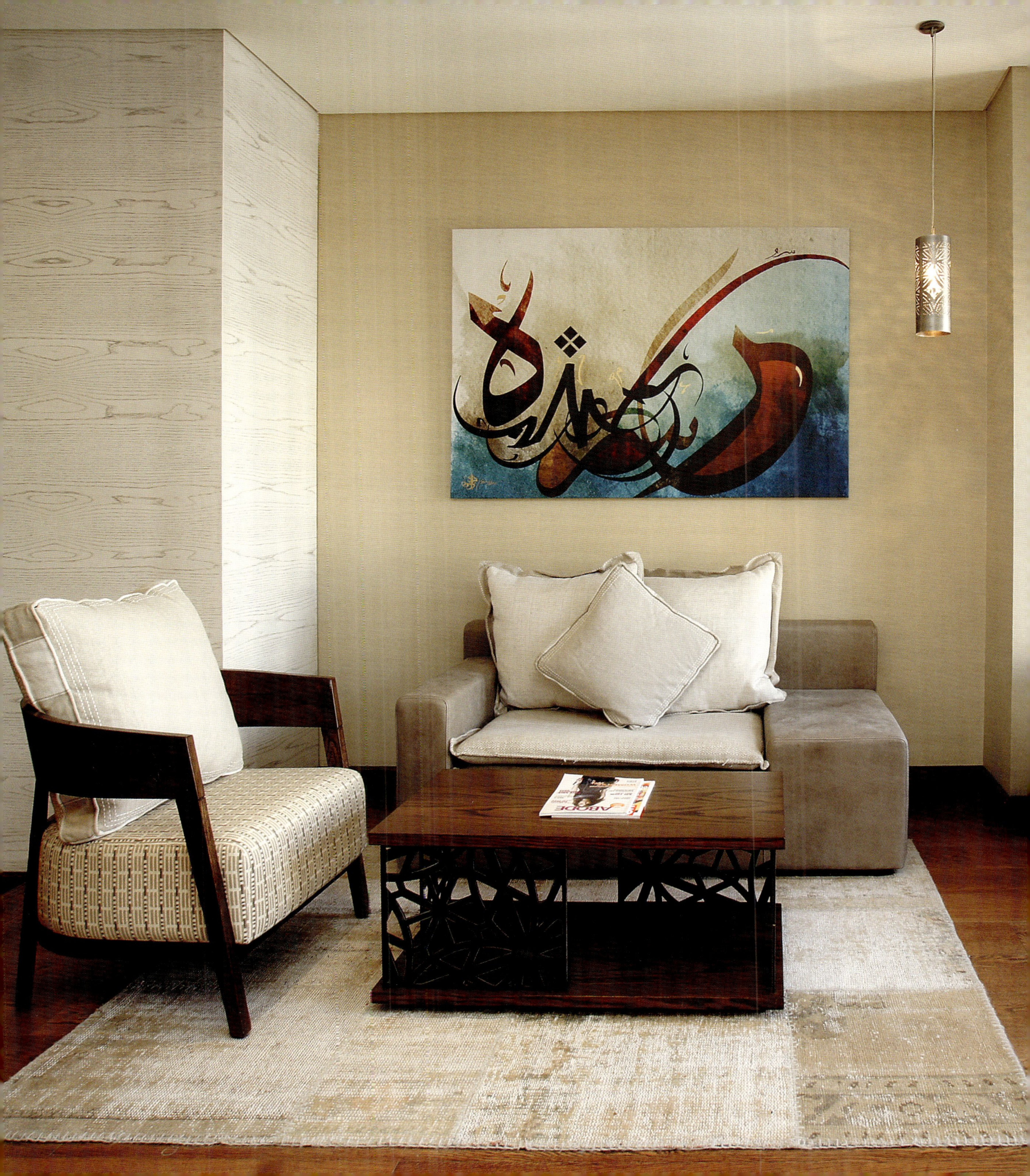

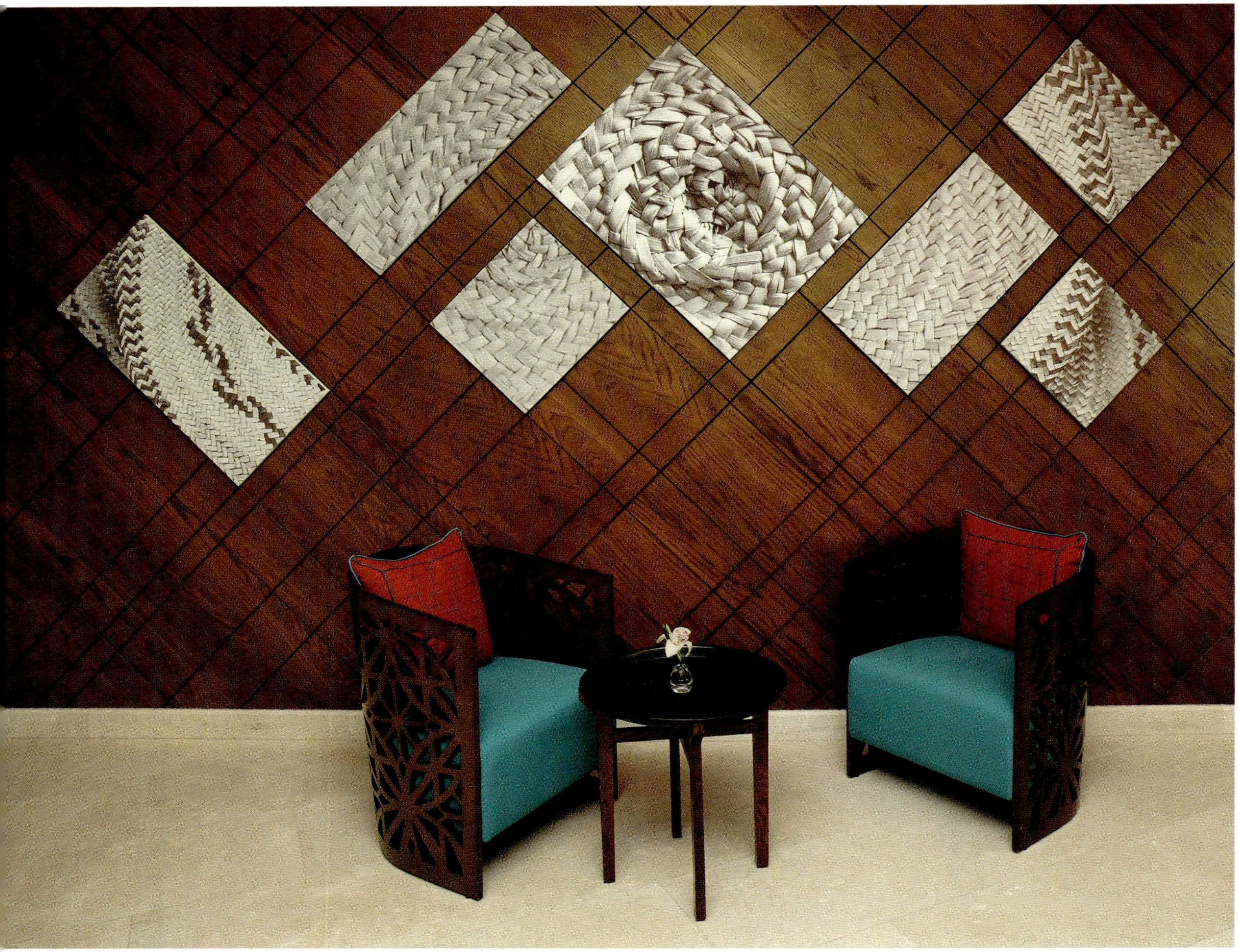

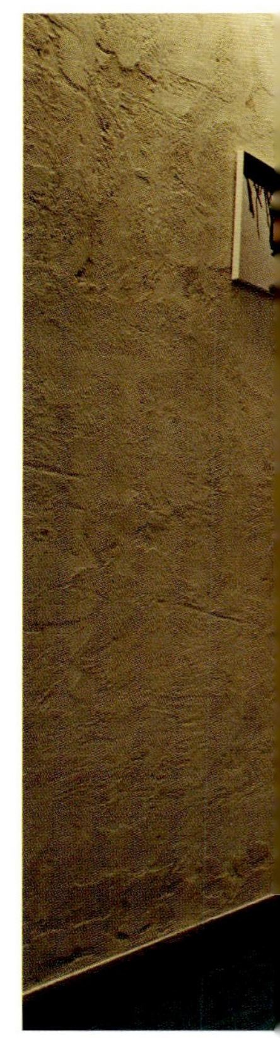

Above: The back of the furniture features traditional Qatari geometric patterns.

Right: Traditional geometric patterns are ubiquitous in Arumailah. Even the corridor carpet reveals the designer's interpretation of the traditional patterns.

Far right: The wall in the restaurant is decorated with numerous *sufar*, fitting for the intended use of the room.

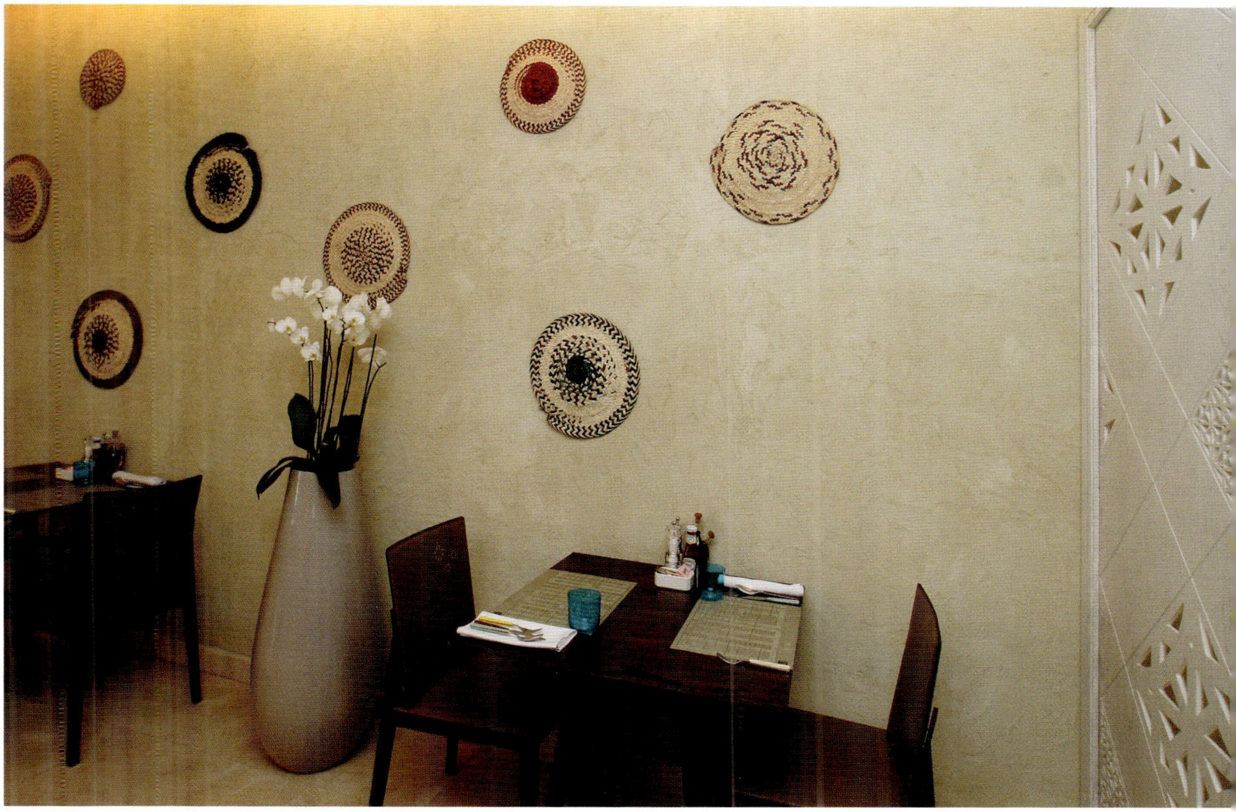

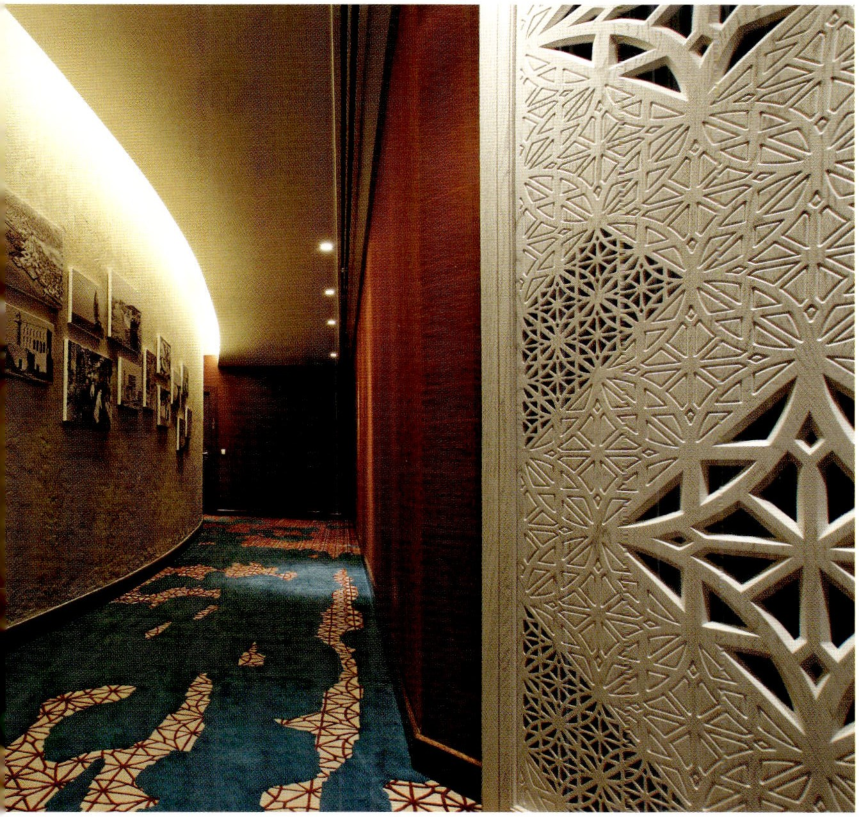

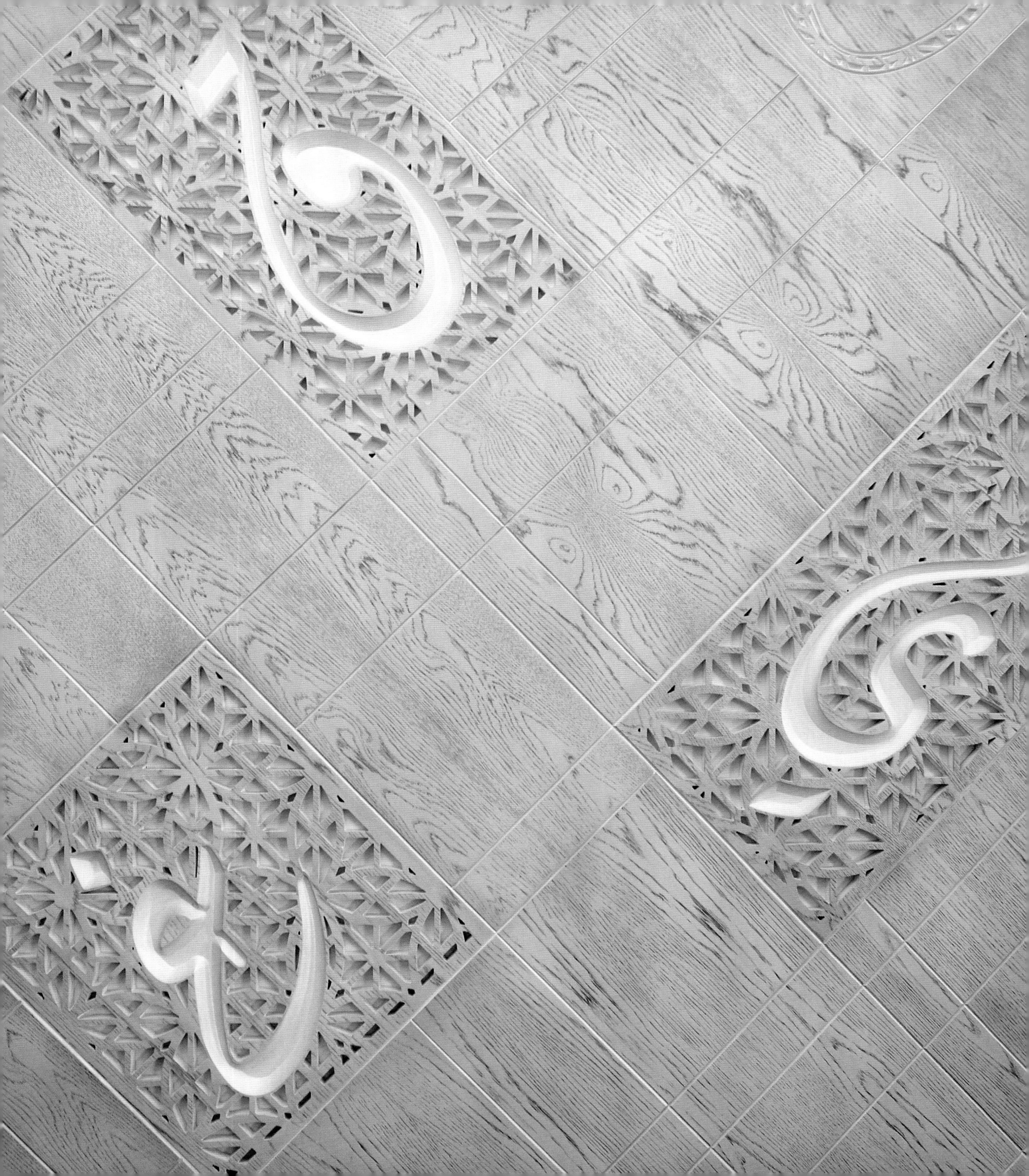

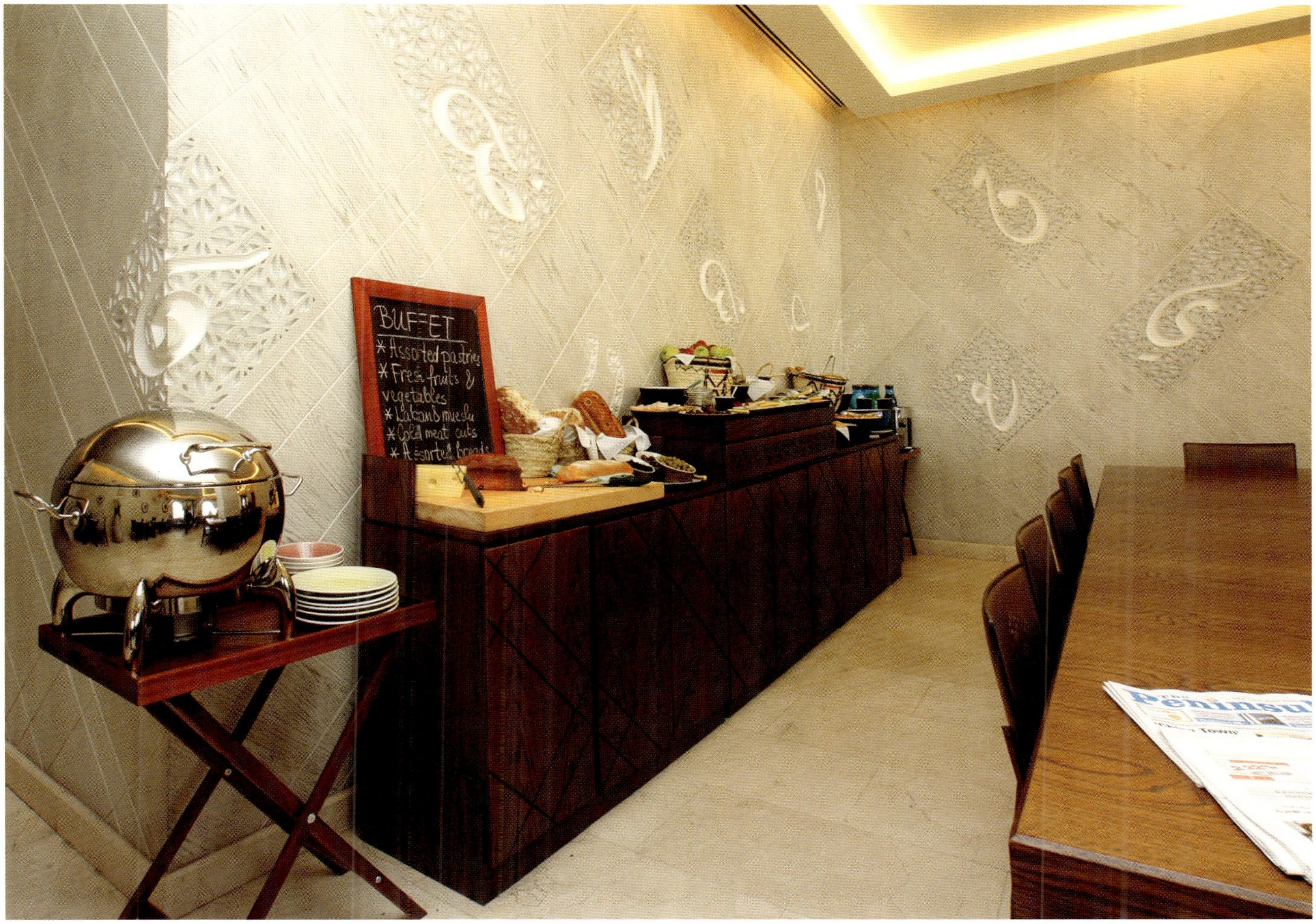

Above: Wall carvings of calligraphy and patterns are set in the irregular geometric grid of the wall tiles complemented by the contemporary geometry of the buffet fronts.

Left-hand page: Arabic calligraphy is combined with traditional Qatari patterns to create unique carving on the walls.

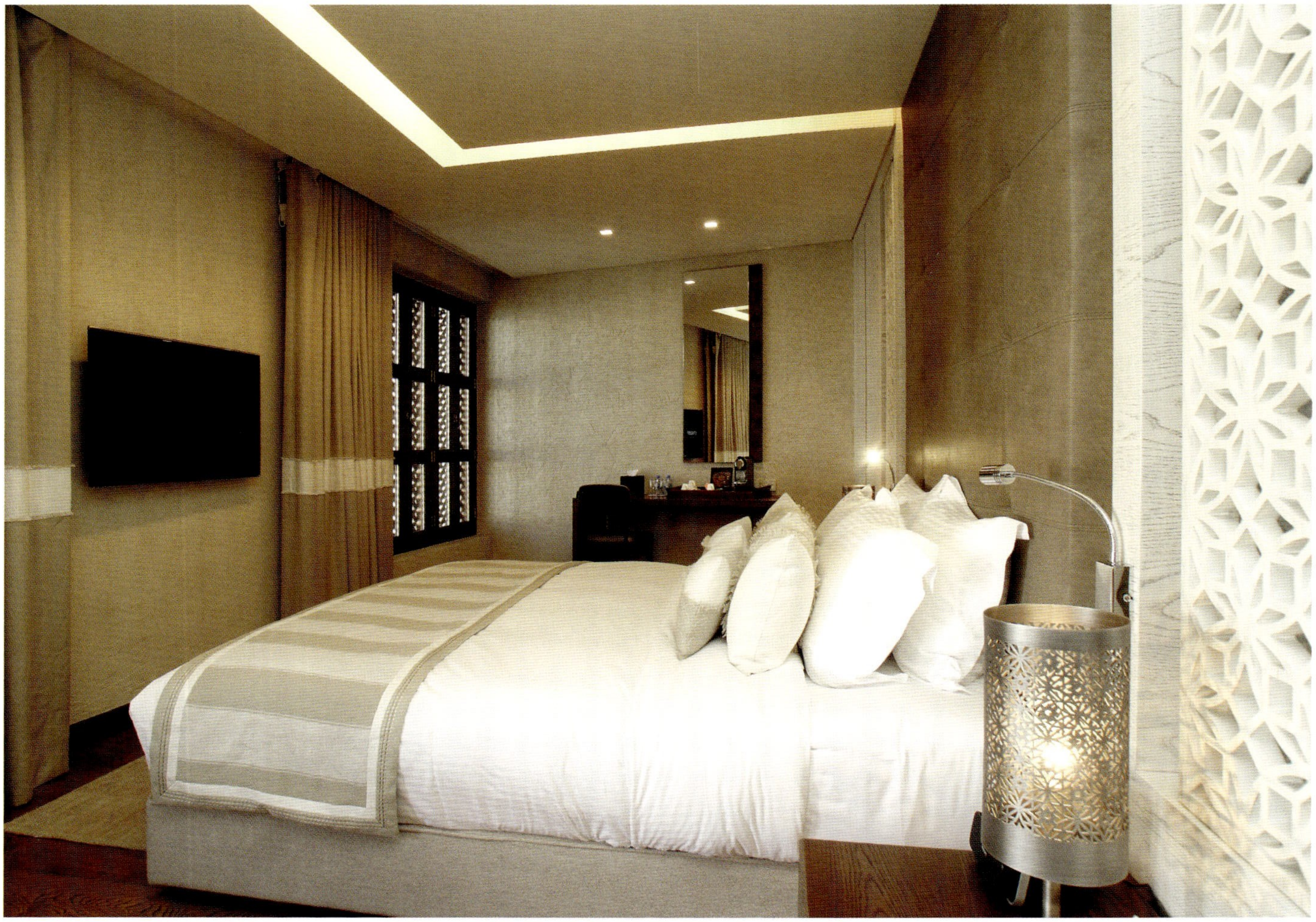

Above: The color scheme of the guest bedrooms is modern and muted, and is occasionally accentuated with tones of much warmer color such as yellow or orange.

Right-hand page: Wooden screens carved in traditional geometric patterns form the accent wall in the room and are also back-lit creating the ambient lighting.

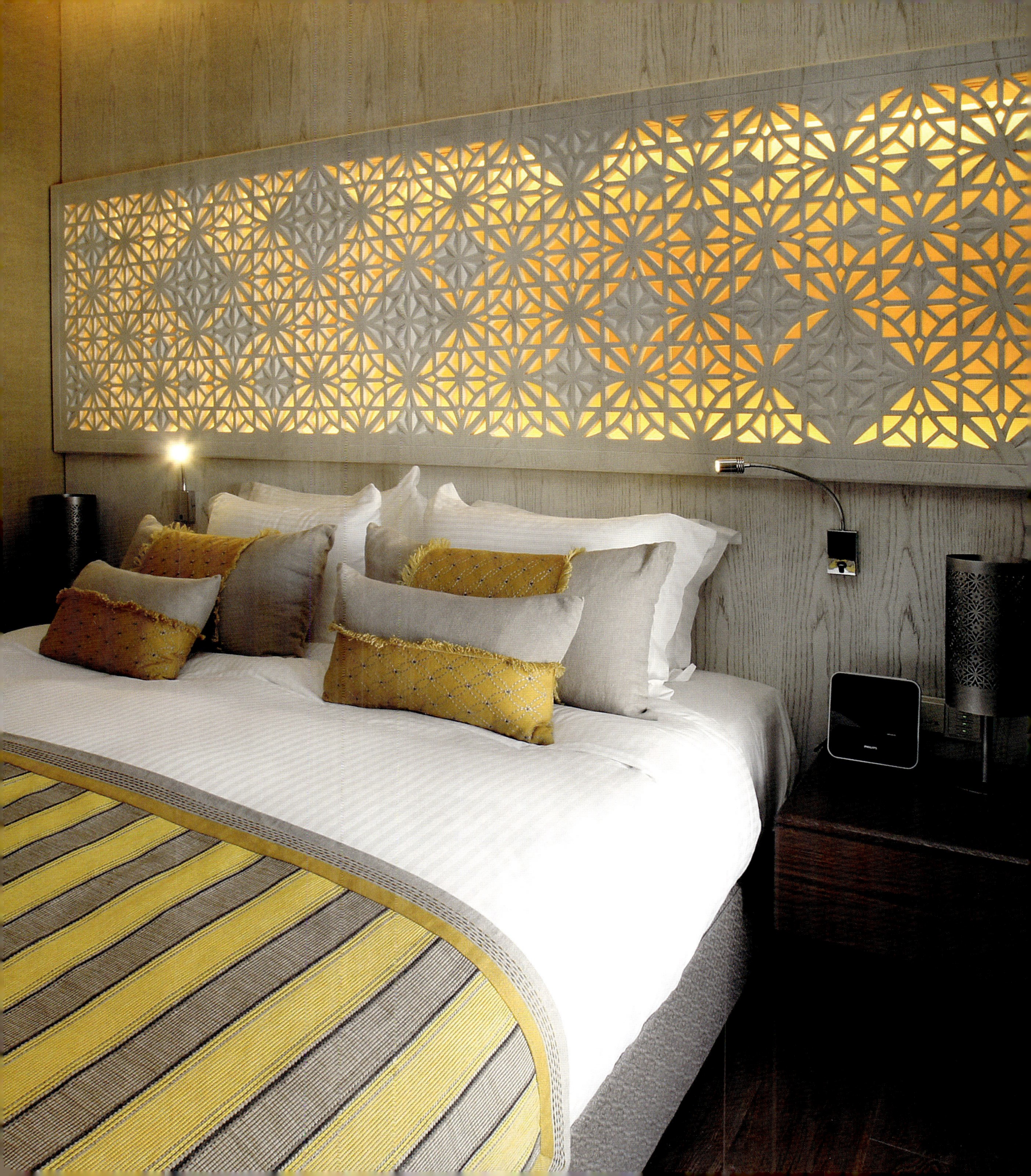

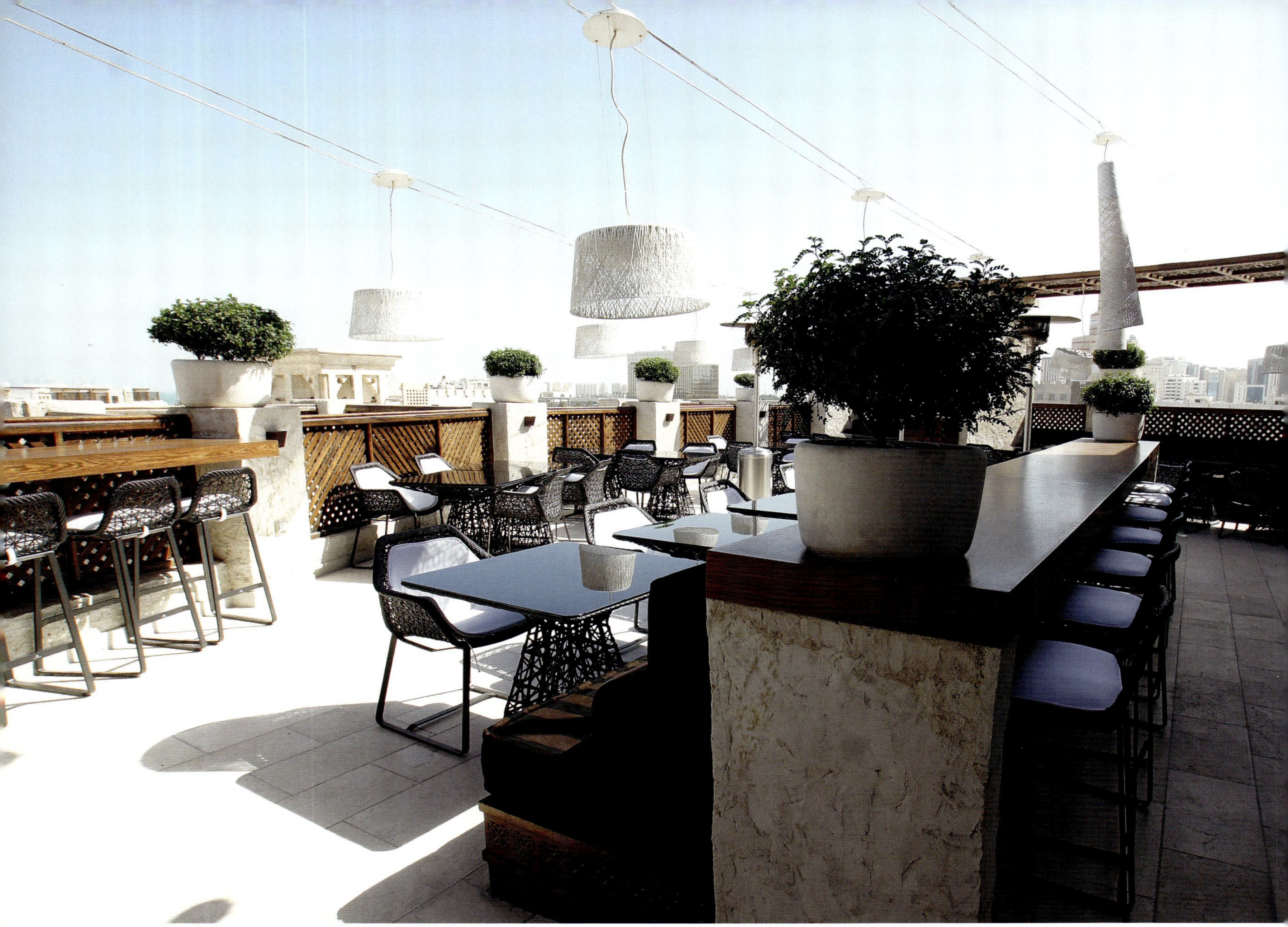

Above: The rooftop restaurant continues a contemporary approach to the traditional design. *Lūzīāt* are used as railings and to protect the privacy of the guests.

Right-hand page: *Dakkah*-type seating stretches alongside the walls of the restaurant. And *lūzīāt*-inspired wooden panels are used as shading devices.

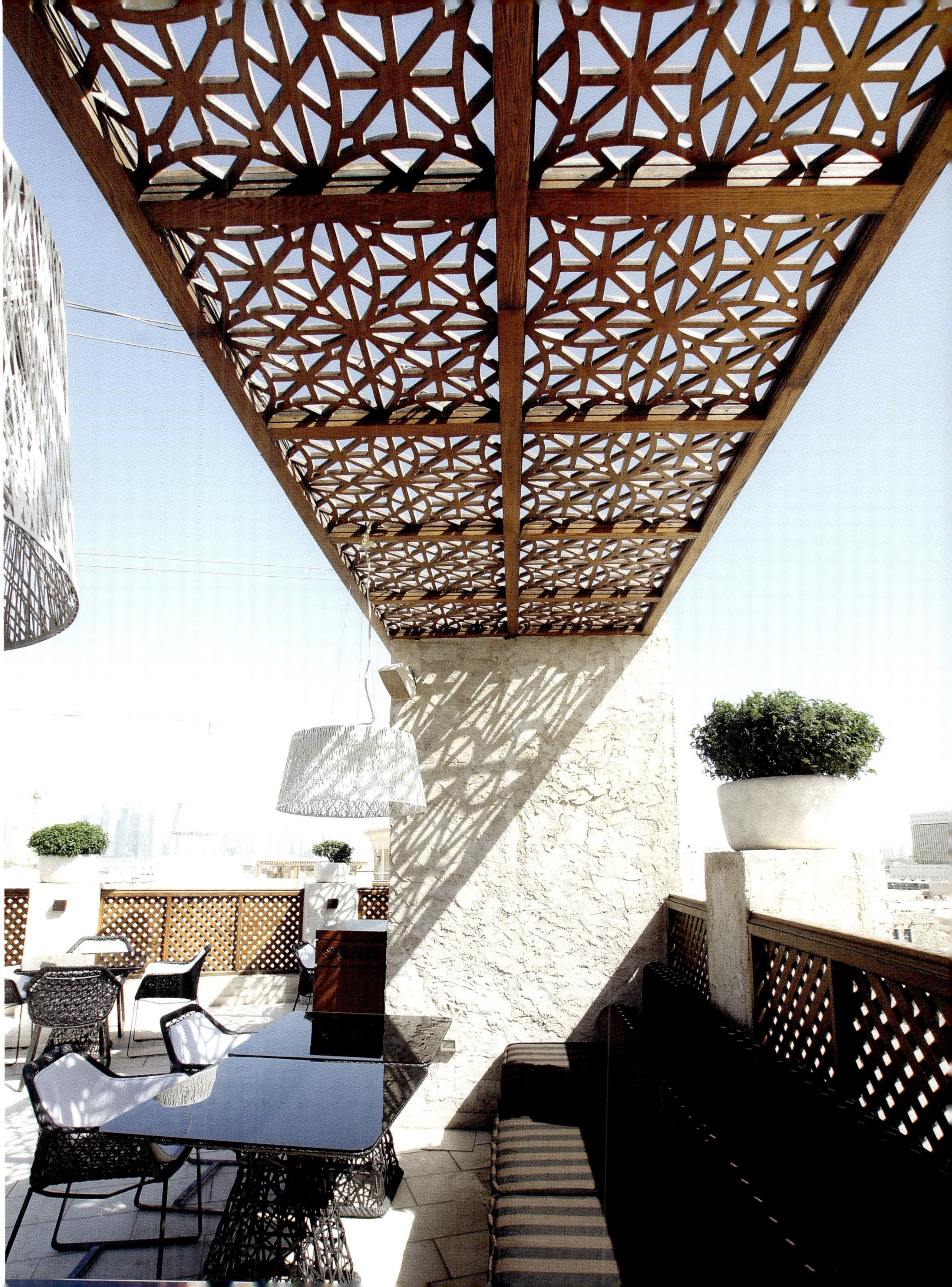

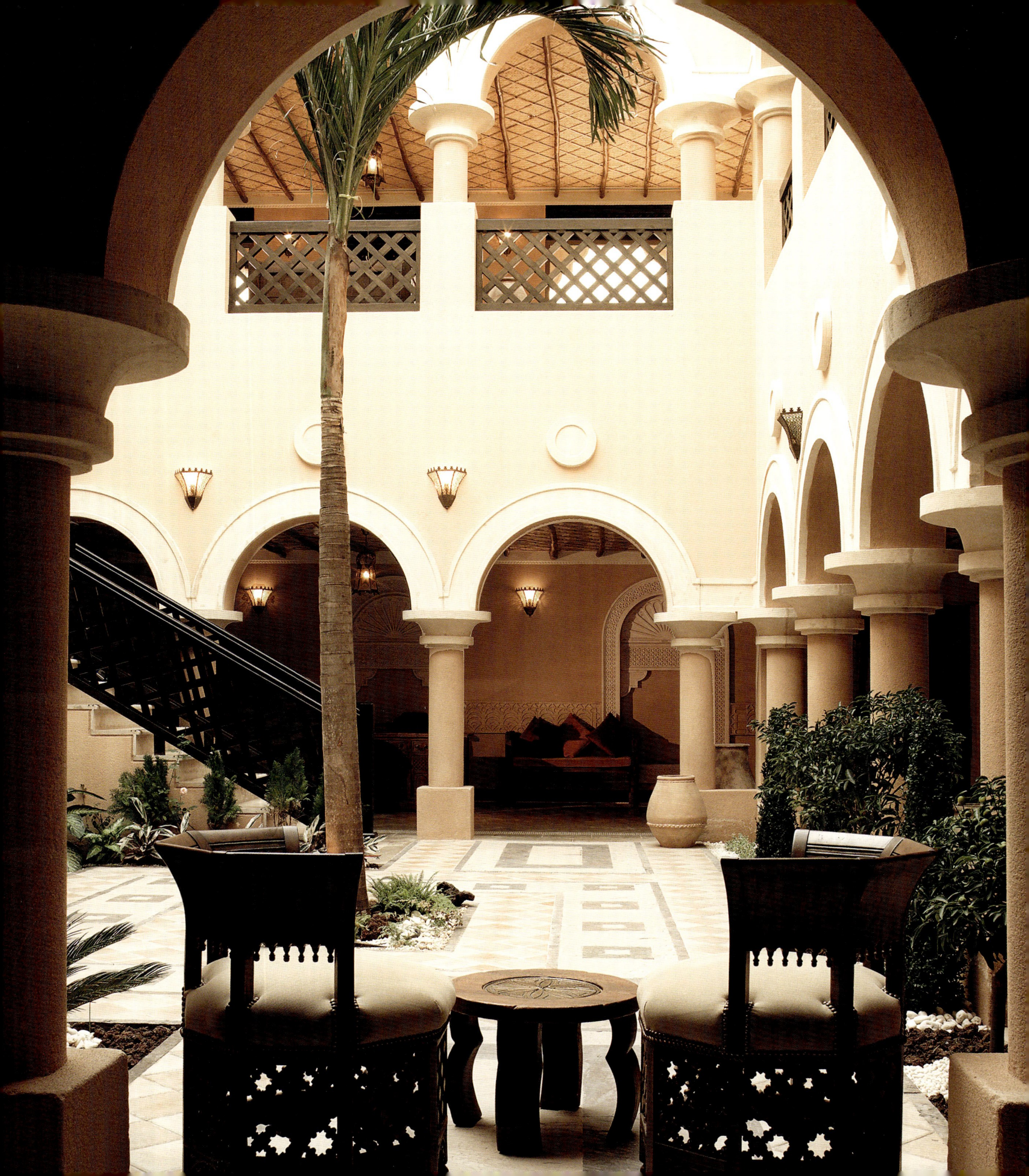

AL SHARQ VILLAGE & SPA

Al Sharq Village & Spa, designed by Arab Engineering Bureau (AEB), drew inspiration from the old architecture of the location, originally known as Alkulaifat. The resort extends across the site of over 95,000 m², and comprises the largest spa in the region, Six Senses Spa covering 5,200 m². The aerial photographs dating from the pre-oil era show the organic cluster of typical old houses forming a traditional *firīj*. AEB translated this historic architectural heritage into the present by designing a hotel and a spa where two-story buildings are clustered in a manner that resembles an old *firīj*. In broad strokes, through the hierarchy in size of the buildings the design utilizes the idea of different social classes in pre-oil Qatar living in the same *firīj*. The main lobby resembles the palace-like house of the sheikhs. The villas resemble the merchants' houses with their courtyards. The spa with its rustic touch reflects the fishermen's and pearl divers' houses. Connecting all these elements are the narrow alleyways known as *sakīk*. The vernacular architecture not only provided an aesthetic but also an environmental lesson which AEB took on as an opportunity to develop a more sustainable design. Learning from our ancestors, for example, the pathways were designed as *sakīk* to minimize exposure to the sun. The space dynamics stirs a nostalgic feeling of the simple past but in the comfort of the present facilities and technology.

The interior design relied on the vocabulary of the Qatari architectural elements. The aim was to emphasize the traditional elements with a contemporary twist. The interior design team from DiLeonardo, overseen by AEB, succeeded in finding the balance between traditional and contemporary interiors. Prominent architectural elements such as *danāshil*, *rūshanāt*, and *yīḥal* are evident across various buildings within the resort. The furniture is in dark colored wood juxtaposed against the earth tones of the walls and floors. Textiles are rich in color, pattern, and texture, and in certain areas of the hotel and spa, the fabrics reflect the colors of the *sadw* although the *sadw* pattern was not adopted literarily.

The rustic interior of the spa complements the rich interiors of the hotel. The spa stands out with the verticality of its design. Metal chains used as a fountain are suspended from the highest points in the spa lobby, while the rest of the hotel adopted a horizontal orientation. It is also evident that the spa has pared down all the visual stimulation to create a calming and relaxing environment where tranquil colors complement the wooden accents and furniture.

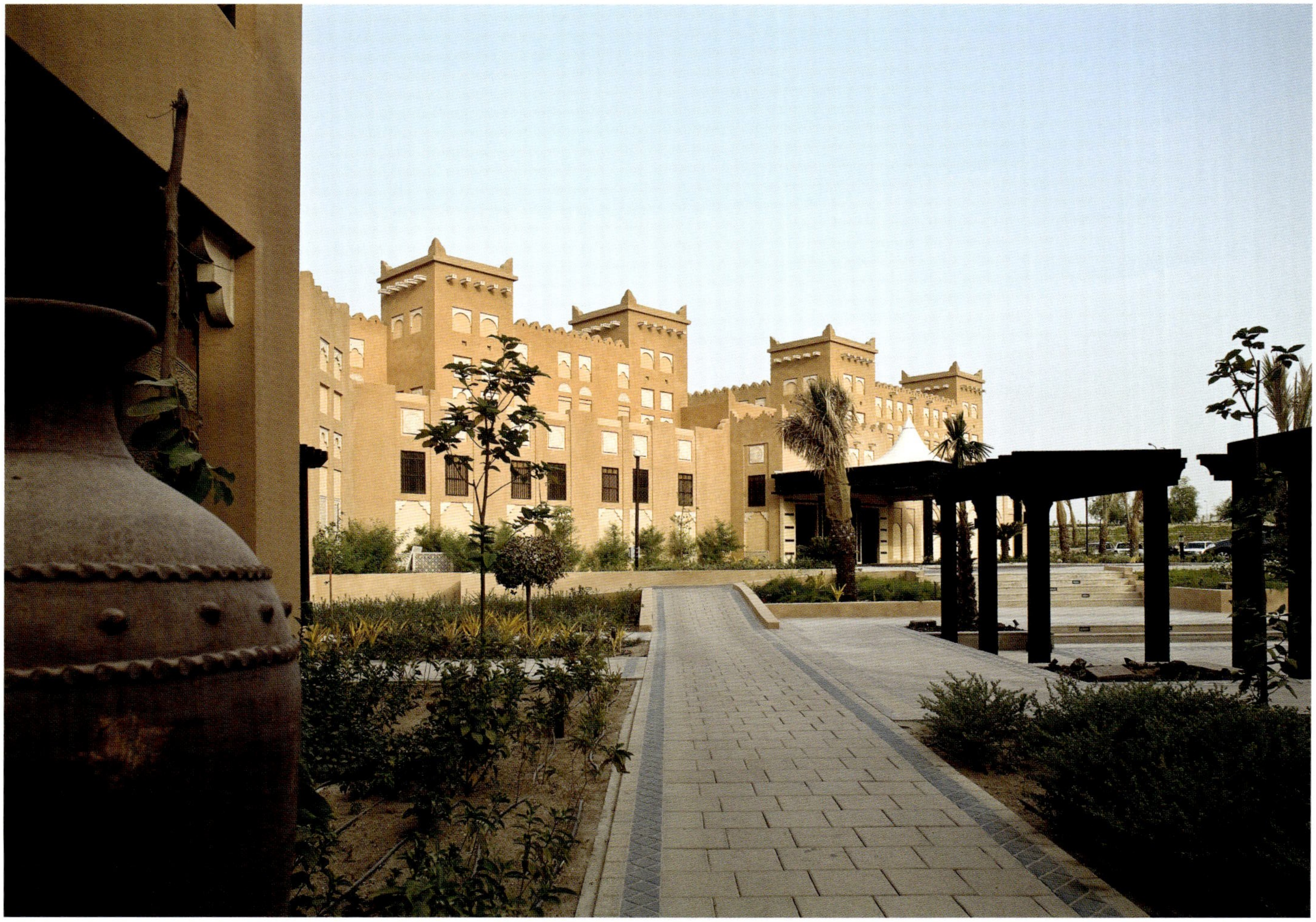

Above: The traditional architecture of Al Sharq Village and Spa has lent itself to a successful reinterpretation of a traditional Qatari neighborhood.

Right-hand page: Each unit within the resort features traditional *līwān* surrounding the central courtyard.

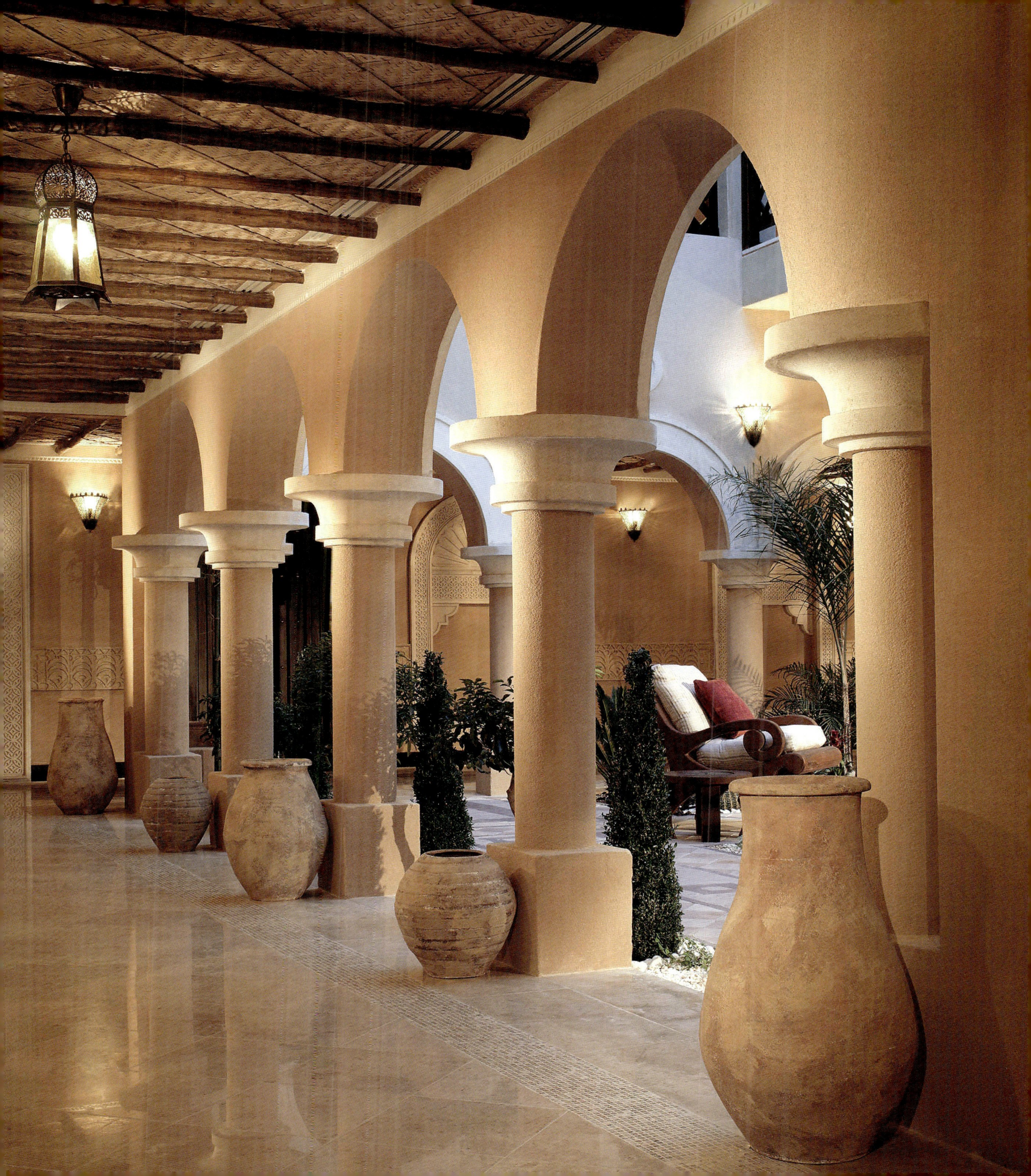

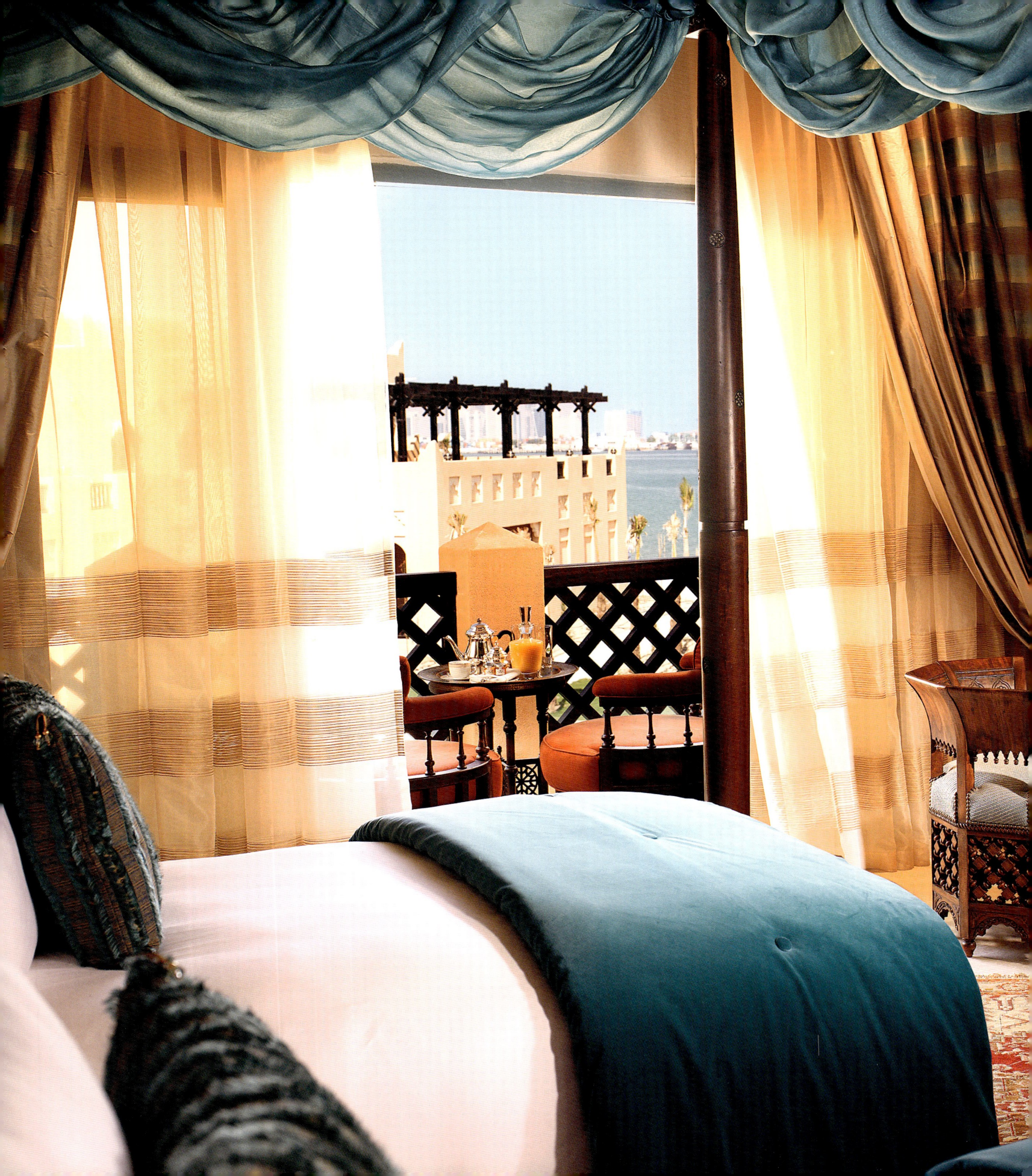

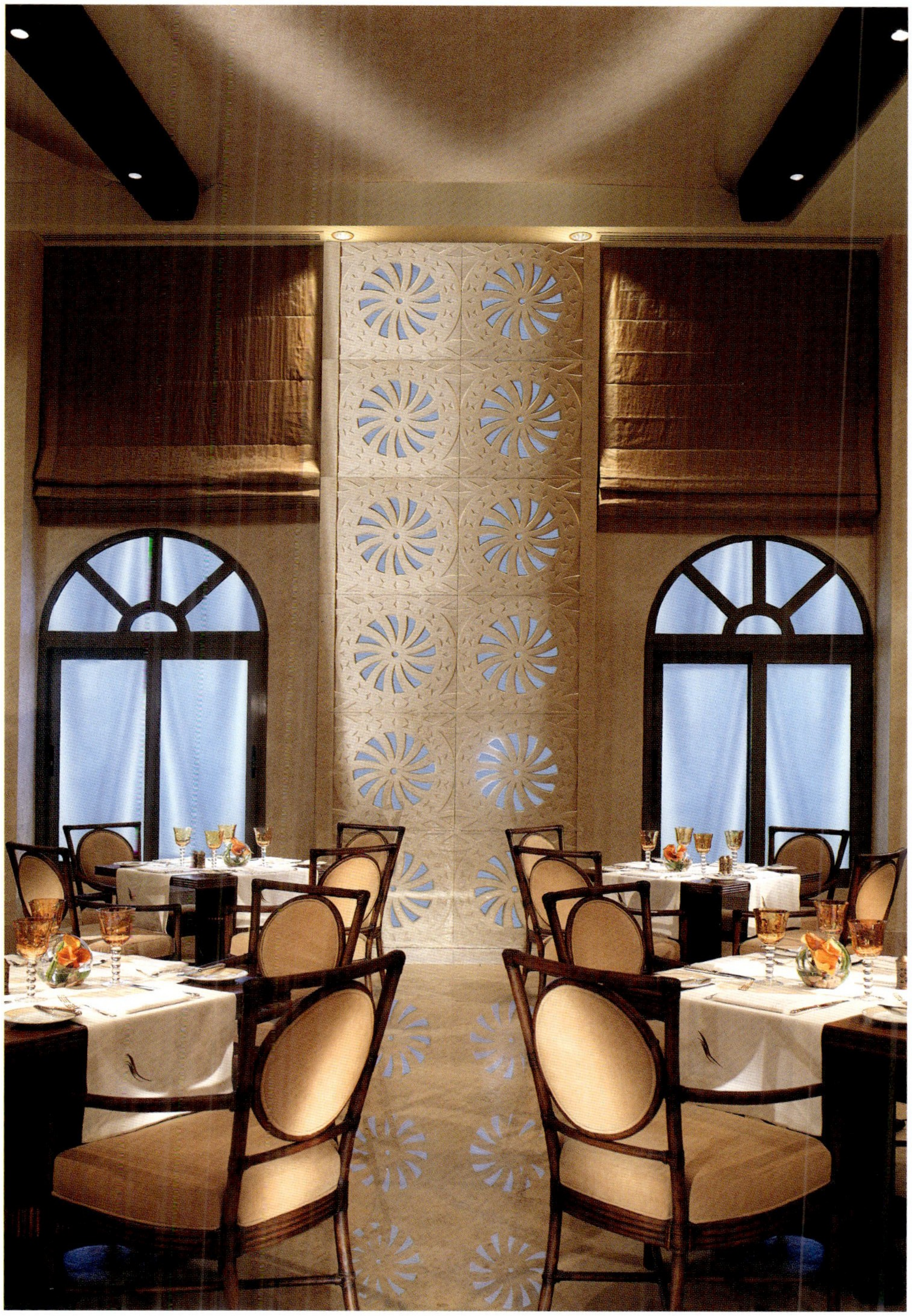

Above: A reinterpretation of the gypsum-carving tradition by rescaling the patterns and setting them individually along the wall.

Left-hand page: Natural wood was used extensively throughout the resort. Also evident is a contemporary interpretation of traditional *kurfāyah*, and certain furnishings were clearly inspired by Levant and Moorish styles.

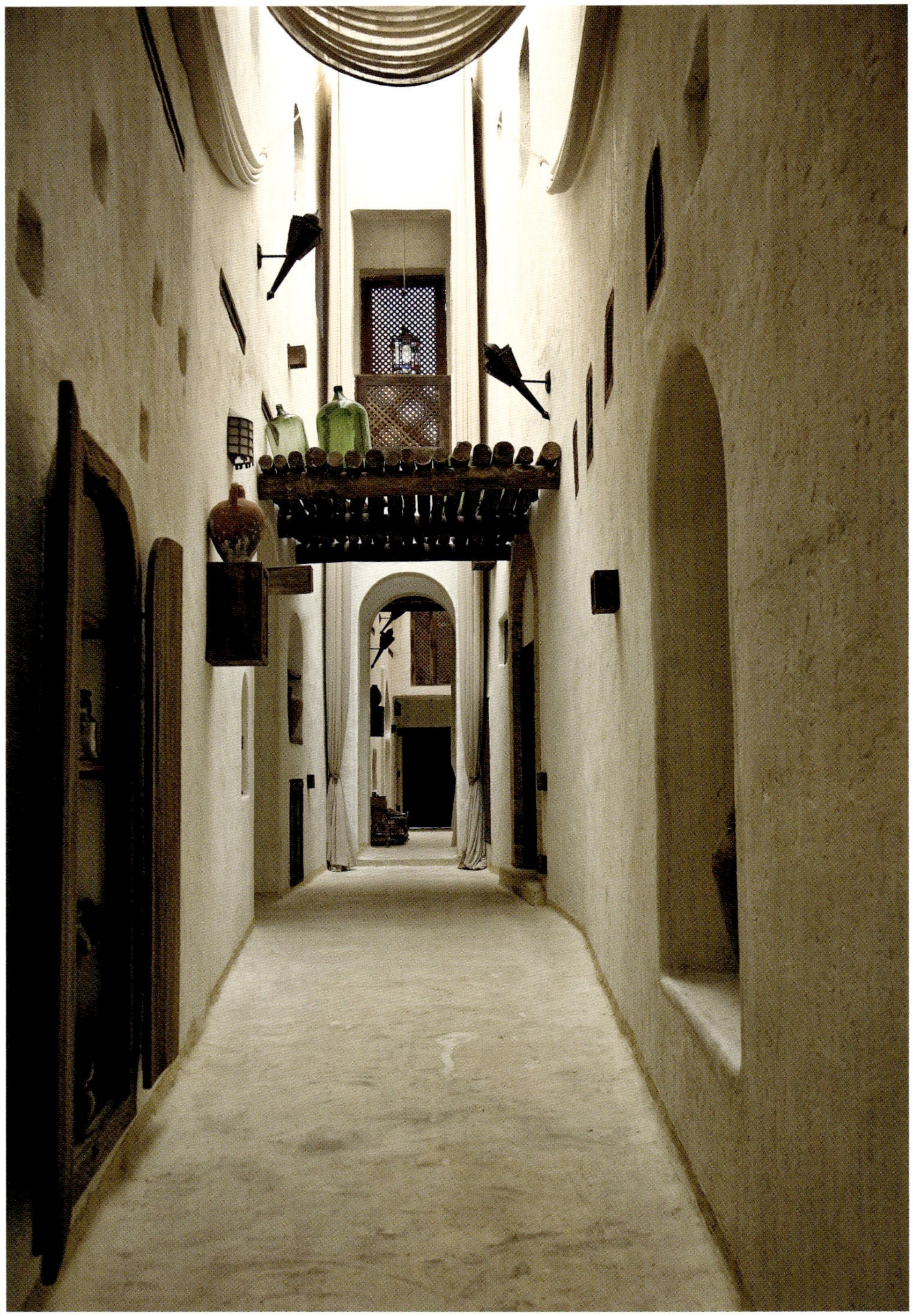

Above: Narrow and surrounded by tall walls, *sakīk* offered shaded walkways in the past. Here, although fully enclosed, the hallways resemble this traditional feature.

Right-hand page: The plunge pool of the spa is located in what traditionally would have been a courtyard of the house. Offering complete privacy, the pool is accessed from patios that are a modern interpretation of *lawāwīn*.

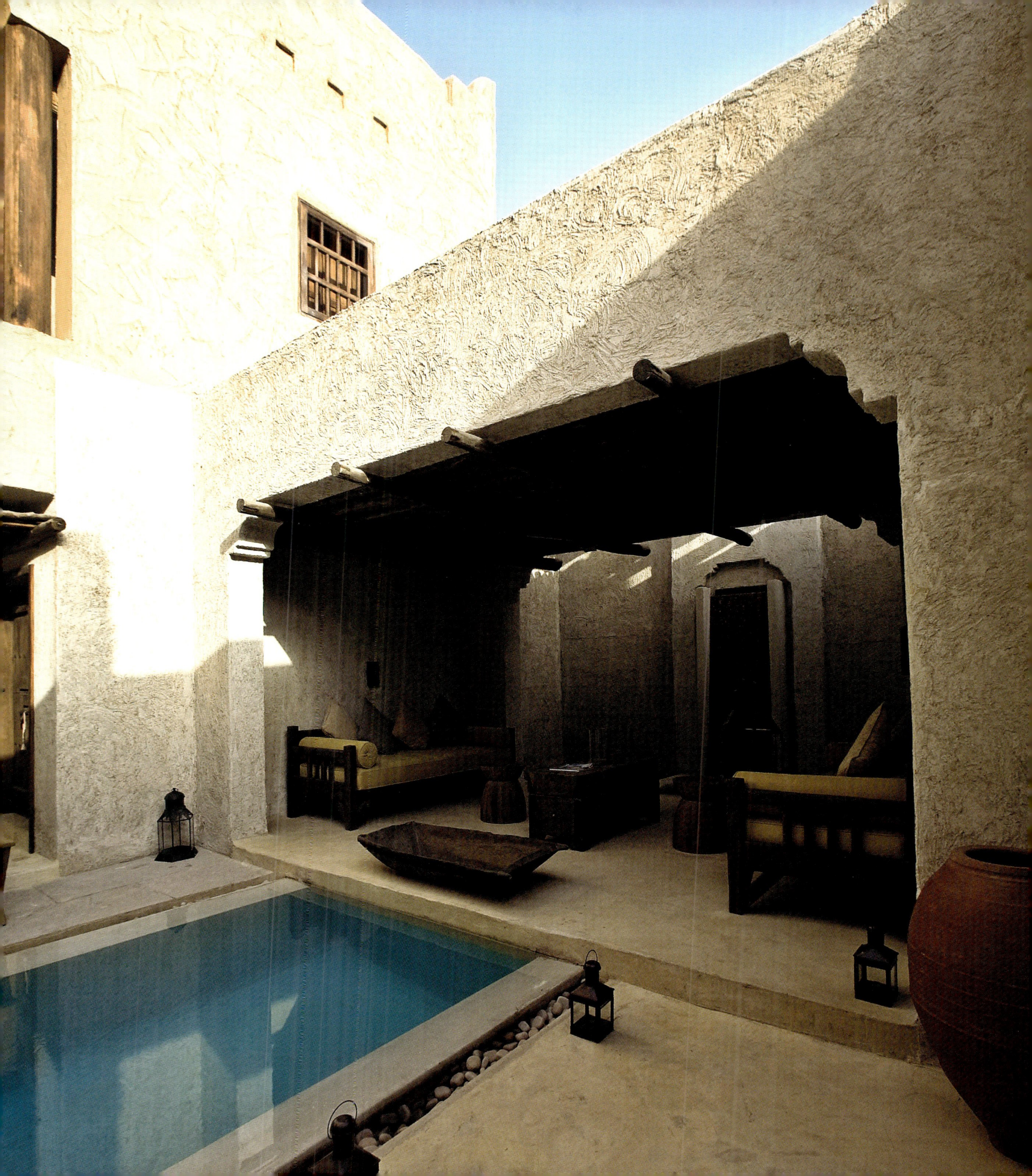

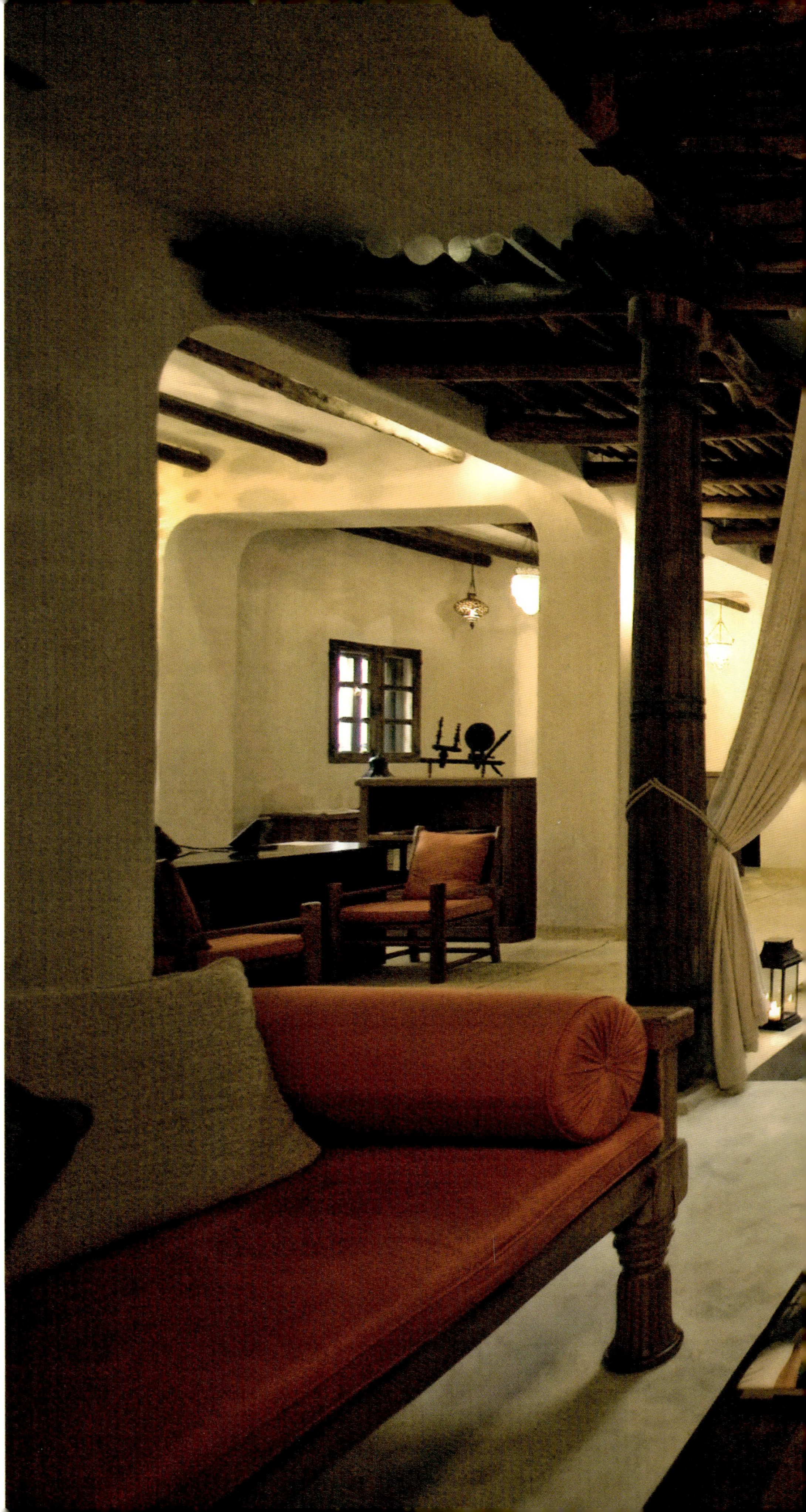

Visual tranquility in the spa reception is achieved by balancing out various materials such as warm wooden features and furnishings, white plastered walls, and a touch of harsh metal chains that are used in the water feature. In addition, wooden pillars support the wooden roof, creating a structure that resembles a traditional *līwān*.

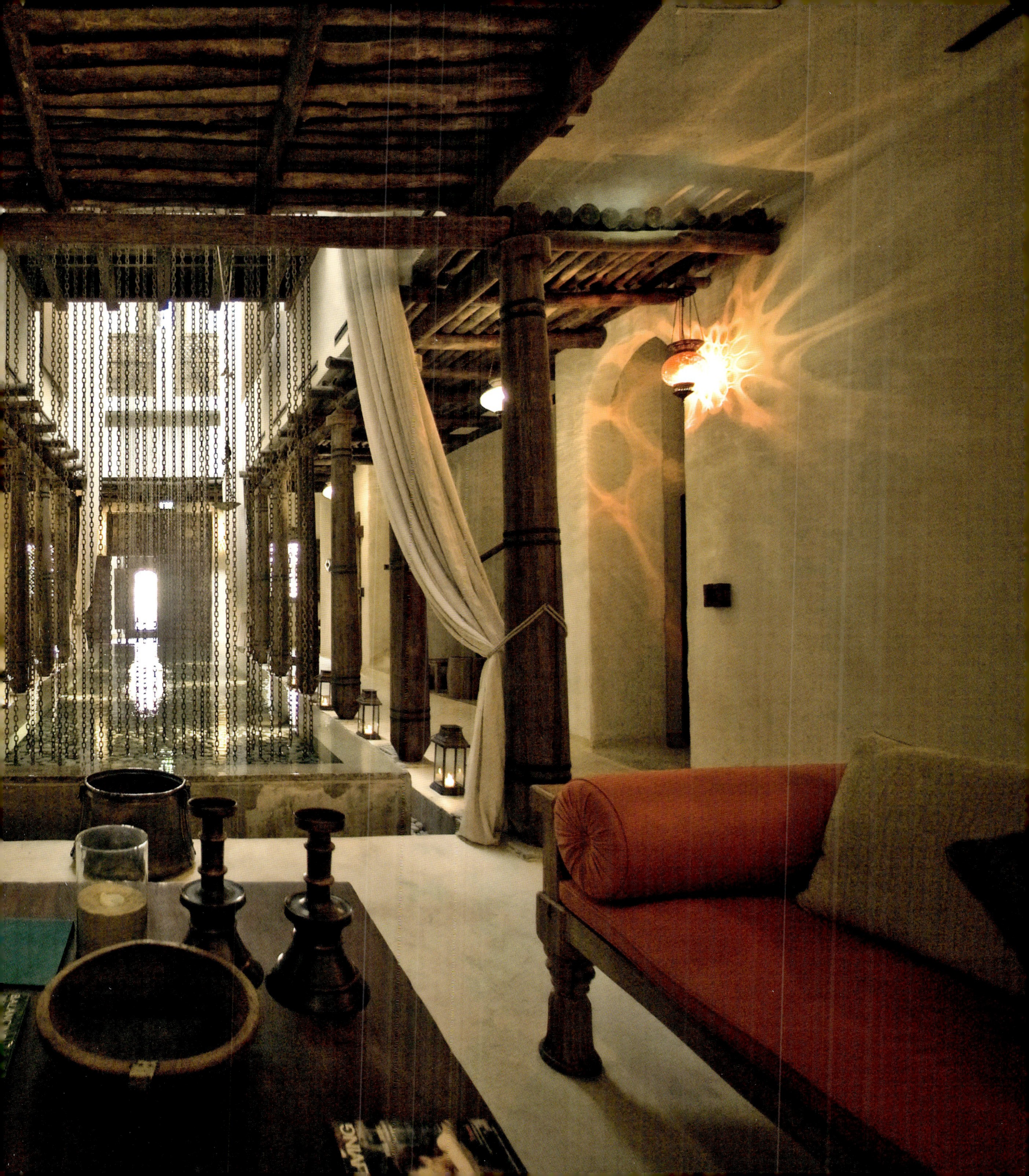

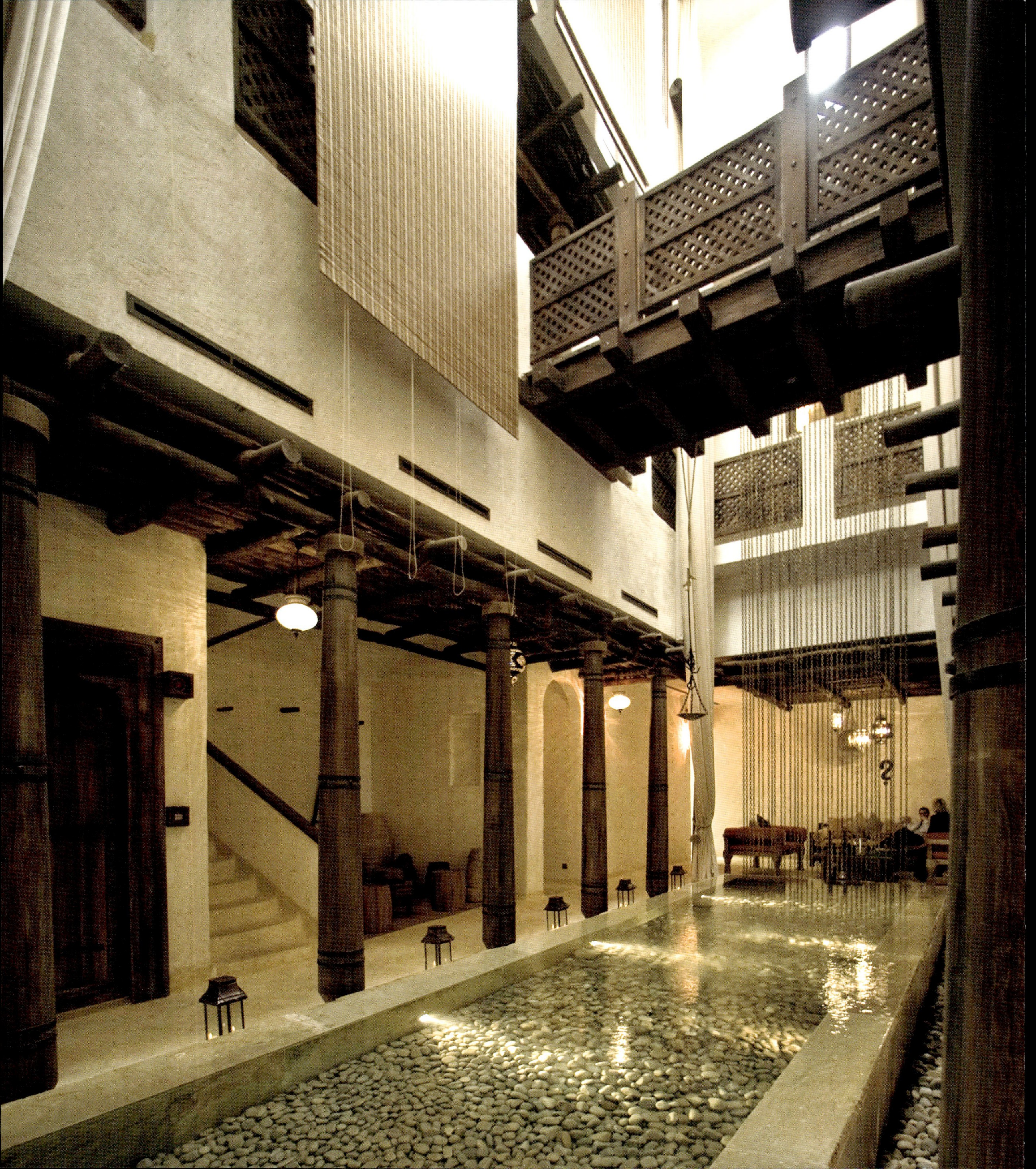

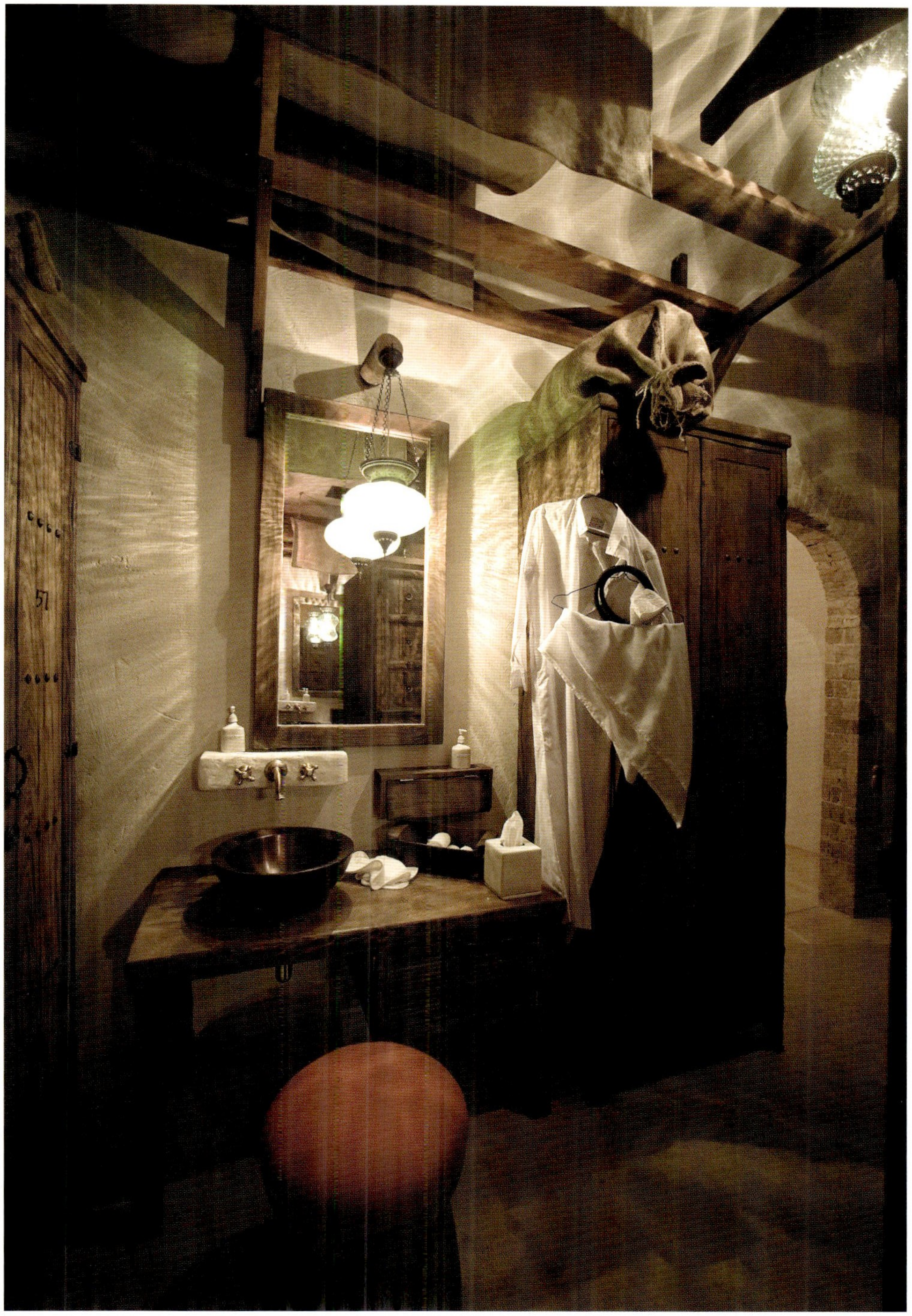

Above: The copper wash basin resembles the one that would have been used in the washing rooms in the past.

Left-hand page: Unlike the guest-room areas that sprawl horizontally in the resort, the architecture and design elements of the spa building emphasize the height of the building.

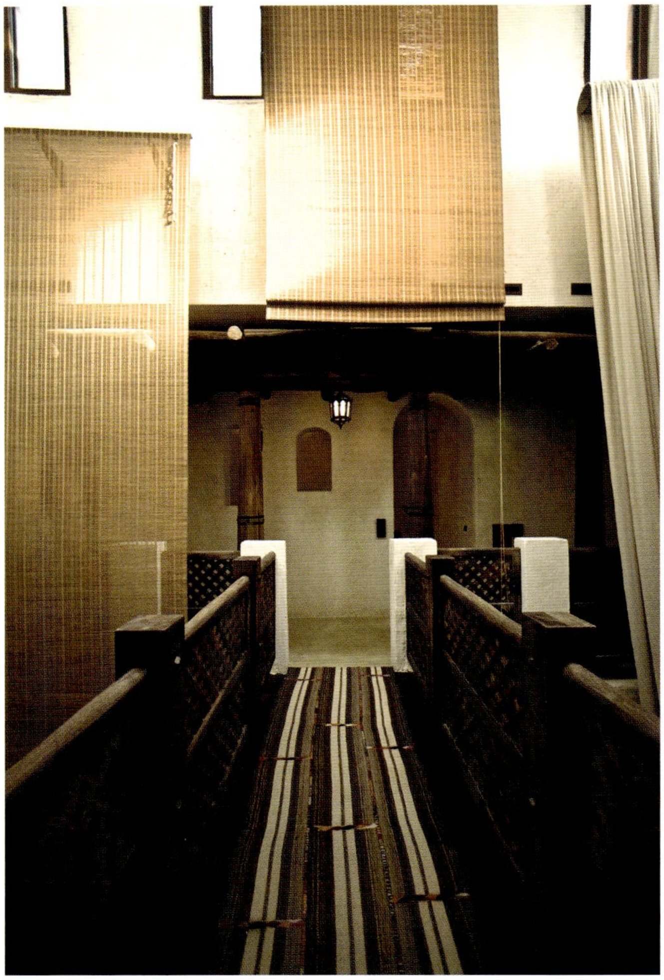

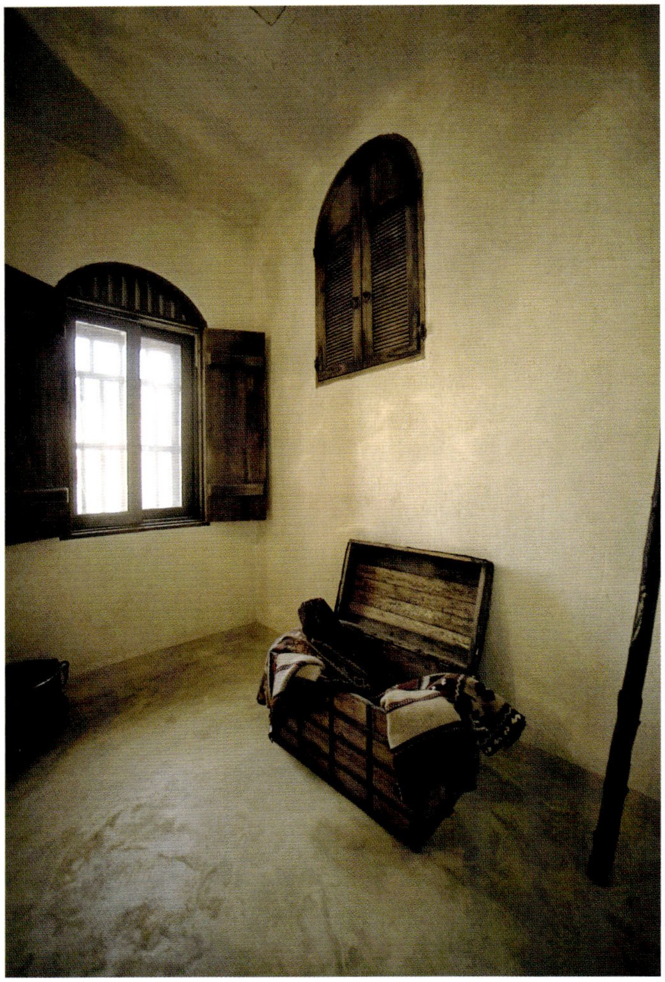

Above left: The bridge crossing on the upper floor of the spa features a *lūzīah*-like rail so that when crossing guests are hidden from the view of visitors in the spa reception.

Above right: *Sandūq imbaīyt*, which is traditionally used for storage, is used in this instance as part of a display of textiles and carpets.

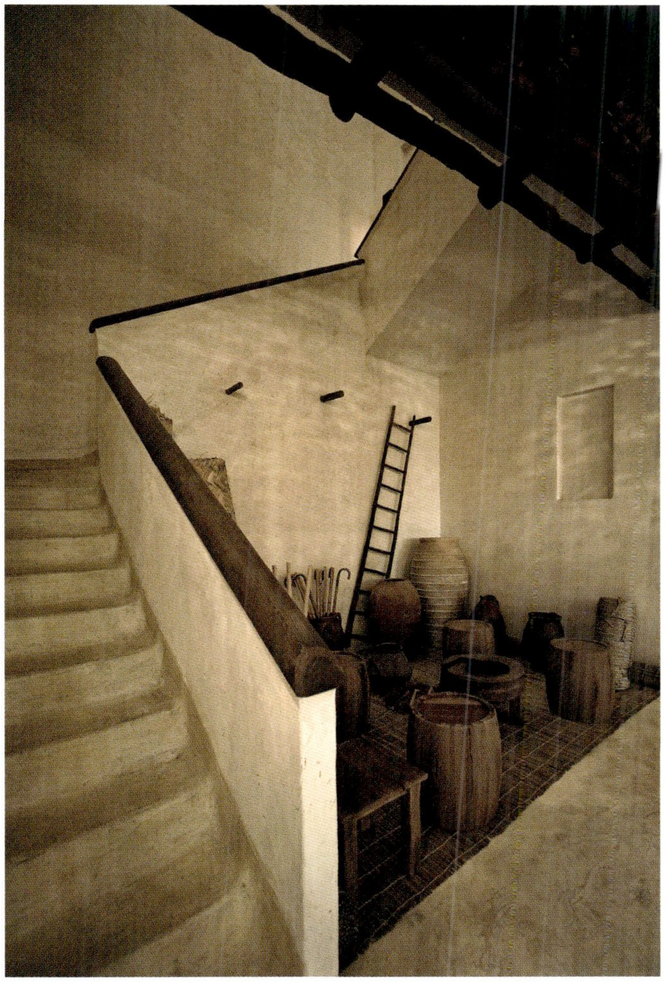 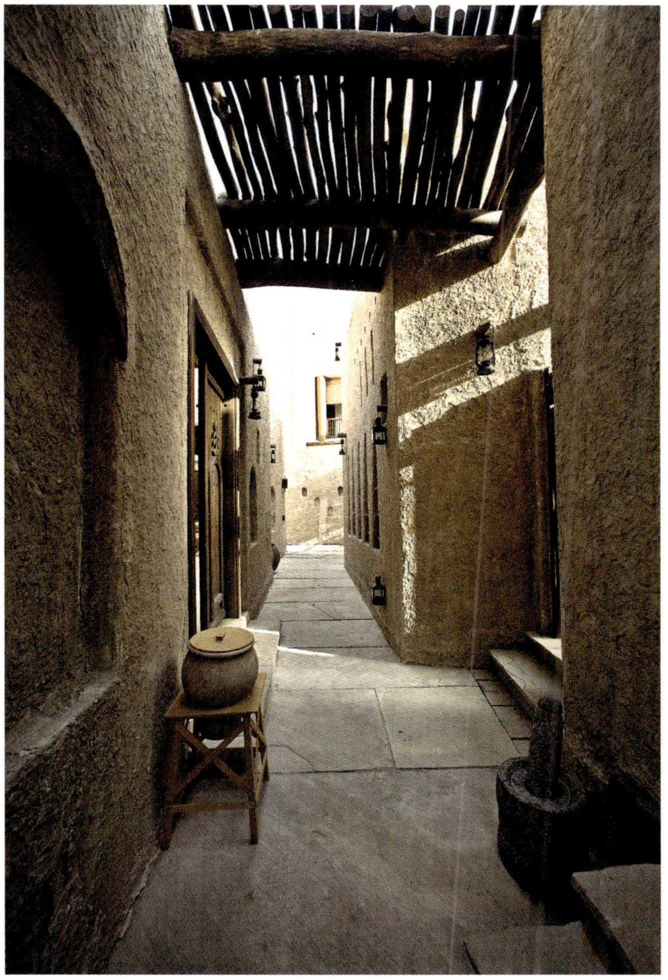

Above left: Here the designer has brought outdoor elements inside the spa with *danāshil* protruding from the wall. As *danāshil* are used to support traditional ceilings the ends of the beams would protrude outside of the house.

Above right: A *yīḥlah* and a *raḥá* decorating the shaded *sikkah*.

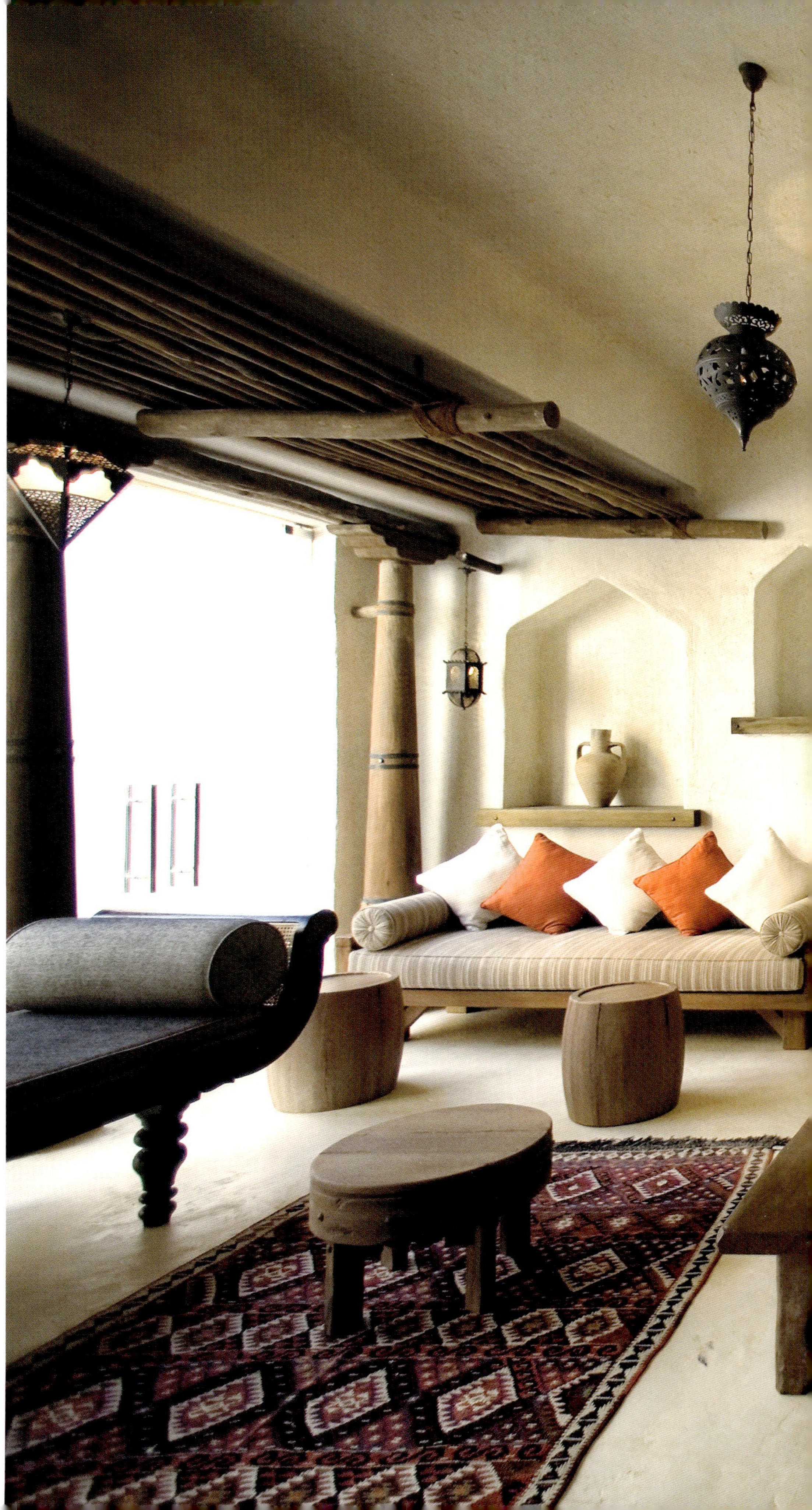

Evident here are *rūshanāt* of various shapes and sizes. Continuing with the theme of rustic Qatari authenticity, natural wood is coupled with woollen carpets and seating upholstered in more natural earth tones.

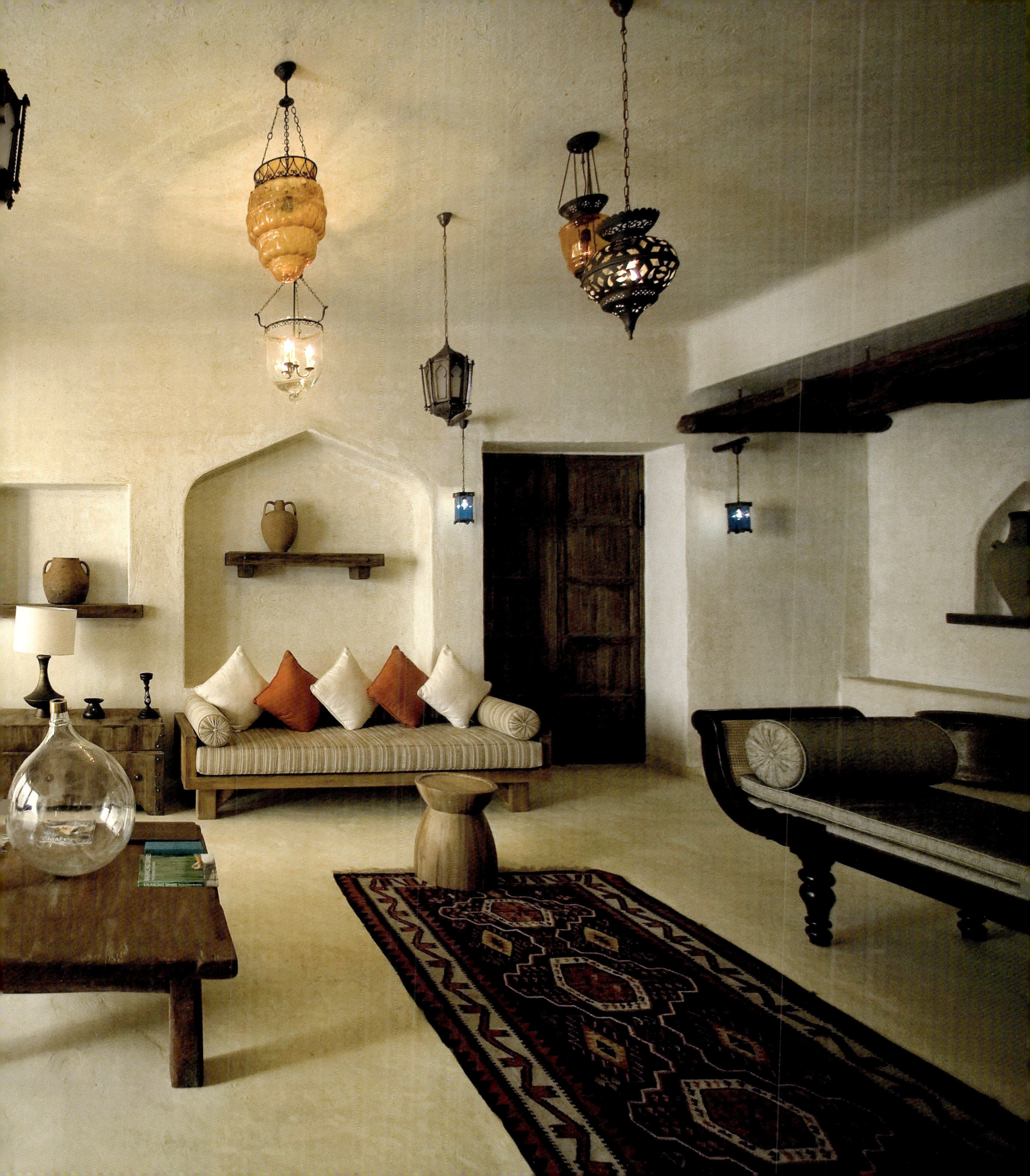

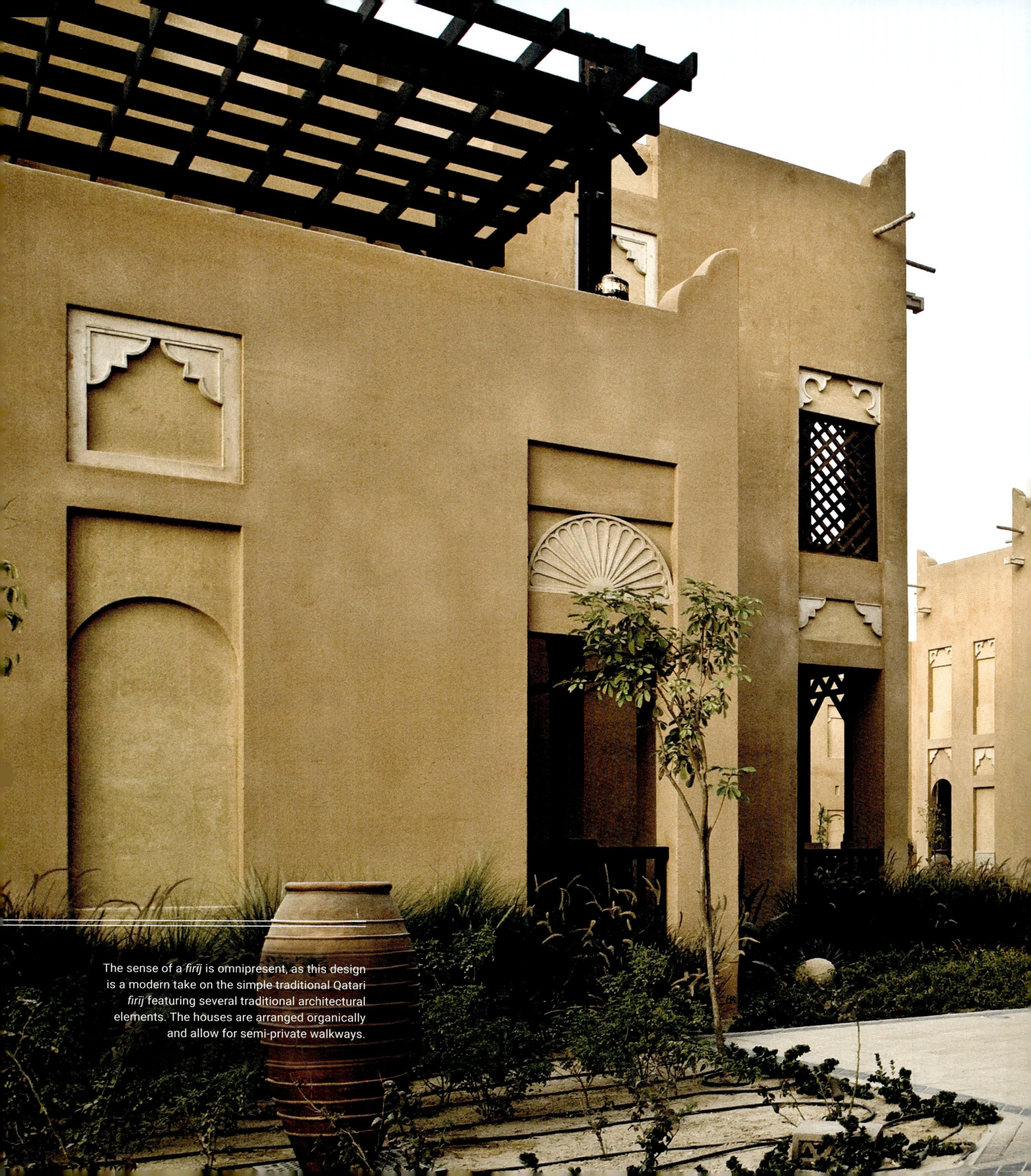

The sense of a *firīj* is omnipresent, as this design is a modern take on the simple traditional Qatari *firīj* featuring several traditional architectural elements. The houses are arranged organically and allow for semi-private walkways.

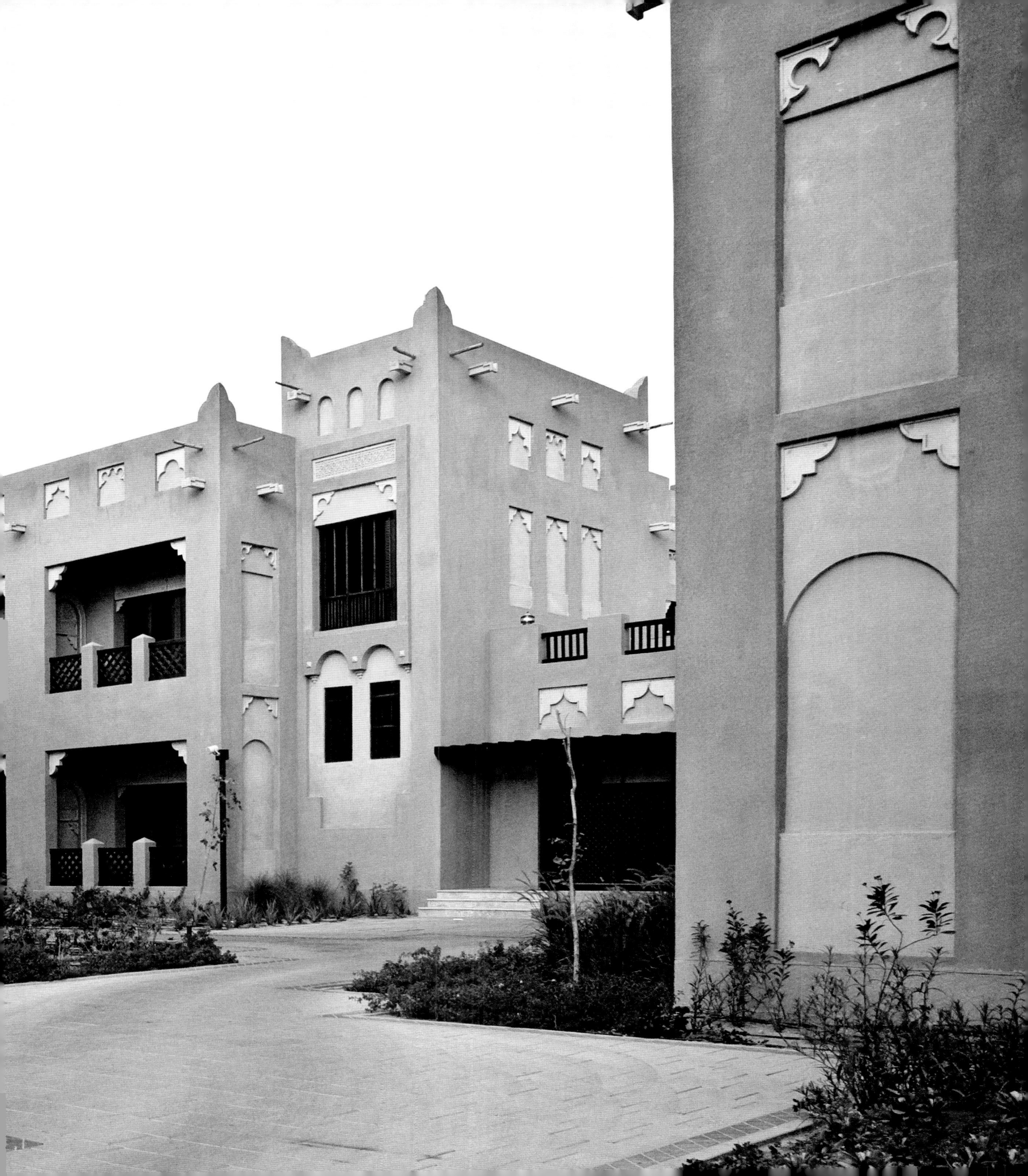

APPENDIX

GLOSSARY[1]

abāah (plural: *abāāt*) عَباءة
black long covering dress worn by Arab women

bāsjīl باسجيل
split bamboo from India decoratively painted and used on top of the wooden beams (*danshal*) to hold the *mangharūr*

baṭṭūlah بَطوله
mask worn by women in the Arabian Gulf region which signifies their maturity and varies in shape and color across the region

bayt al-sha'r بيت الشَعر
Bedouin tent made from sheep and camel hair

dakkah دكه
fixed outdoor seating that varies in shape and size

dalah (plural: *dilāl*) دله
traditional Arabic coffee pot

danshal (plural: *danāshil*) دنشل
beam that holds the roof; made of tree trunks imported from Zanzibar (now part of Tanzania) and India

dawshag[2] (plural: *dawāshig*) دوشق
multipurpose mattress filled with cotton and covered with fabric like *sadw*

dūwah دوه
tin bowl that contains coal; used to keep coffee and tea hot; also known as *al-mingalah*

dirīshah (plural: *darāīsh*) دريشه
traditional window, which consisted of a wooden frame divided horizontally in the middle, with vertical bars inserts for security

fanar (plural: *fnāra*) فنر
oil or gasoline lamp

firīj فريج
neighborhood

ghūrī (plural: *ghūārī*) غوري
teapot

gahwa[3], *tchāi* and *karak* قهوة، (شاي) وكرك
traditional coffee, tea and tea with milk and Indian spices

gidw قدو
similar to *shisha*; a tool used for smoking made out of clay

ḥaṣīr (plural: *ḥiṣrān*) حصير
mat made from straw and palm fronds

ḥawsh حوش
courtyard of a traditional Arabic house

jafīr (plural: *jīfrān*) جفير
woven basket from palm reed; it is a feature that originates from *Al-Hasa* and Oman

kurfāyah (plural: *kūrāfi*) كرفايه
ornate high bed inspired from Indian-style used in the past

līwān (plural: *lawāwīn*) ليوان
shaded space under an arcade that partially or fully surrounds the courtyard

lūzīah (plural: *lūzīāt*) لوزيه
artistically carved wood installed over windows for privacy and shade

mangharūr منغرور
woven cane branches

maylis (plural: *mayālis*)—*majlīs* in standard Arabic مجلس
formal room for receiving guests (also known as *diwaniyah*)

mibkharah مبخرة
object that holds the coal to burn incense *(bukhūr)*

midkhan (plural: *madākhin*) مدخن
wooden structure used to keep clothing at a safe distance from the mibkharah to allow the scent of the bukhūr to cling to the fabric without damaging it

mirash (plural: *mirāshīh*) مرش
perfume bottle with a long neck and prorated head for sprinkling perfume and rosewater

mirzām مرزام
wooden water spout

misnad (plural: *masānid*) مسند
rectangular thickly stuffed pillow used to support people while sitting on *dawshag*

nūkhizah (plural: *nawākhzah*) نوخذه
captain of the boat

raḥá (plural: *raḥāt*) رحى
manually operated grinder for legumes made from stone

rūshanah (plural: *rūshanāt*) روشنه
square or rectangular recess in the wall constructed for the purpose of making the walls lighter; it was used as a built-in shelf

sadw سدو
fabric woven from wool and used for rugs or upholstery; it was decorated with specific patterns that tell a story

ṣaḥārah (plural: *ṣaḥārāt*) صَحّارَة
wooden crates used to transport fruits and vegetables

ṣandūq imbaīyt (plural: *ṣanādyq imbaīyt*) صندوق مبيت
decorated chest mostly used to hold valuables and women's clothing; originates from Zanzibar

sidr—(Ziziphus Spina-Christi) سدر
tree that grows in Qatar around water wells

sikkah (plural: *sakīk*) سكه
alleyway

sufrah (plural: *sufar*) سُفره
round, woven mat made from palm fronds

sumbūk (plural: *sanābīk*) سمبوك
traditional boat commonly used in the Arabian Peninsula

sūq سوق
old Arabian market

tchoulah تشوله(شوله)
gasoline burner

ustādh[4] (plural: *asātidhah*) أستاذ
chief builder

yīḥlah (plural: *yīḥal*) يحله
clay pot used to keep water cold

1 ALA-LC 1997 was used to transliterate the local pronunciation of the words.
2 ق in the traditional dialect is pronounced as g, as in game.
3 Some of the transliteration of the Arabic words is of the dialectal pronunciation of the words, not in standard Arabic.
4 dh should read like 'z' in prize.

COLOPHON & IMAGE CREDITS

PUBLISHED BY
Hirmer Verlag GmbH
Bayerstrasse 57–59
80335 Munich
Germany

AUTHOR: Ibrahim Mohamed Jaidah
EDITOR: Lejla Nikšić
RESEARCH: Nada H. Fouad
CONTENT MANAGEMENT: Lejla Nikšić

PHOTOGRAPHY:
Al Sharq Village and Spa, Arab Engineering Bureau (AEB), Nada H. Fouad, Petros Grapsopoulos, Ruel Fulache

DESIGN, TYPESETTING AND PRODUCTION: Sabine Frohmader
PROJECT MANAGER HIRMER PUBLISHERS: Rainer Arnold
COPY-EDITING AND PROOF-READING: Jane Michael
PRE-PRESS: Reproline Mediateam, Munich
PRINTING & BINDING: Printer Trento, Trento
PAPER: Garda Premium Art 170 g/m^2
TYPEFACE: Beloved Sans, Roboto

PRINTED IN ITALY

BIBLIOGRAPHIC INFORMATION PUBLISHED BY THE DEUTSCHE NATIONALBIBLIOTHEK:
The Deutsche Nationalbibliothek lists this publication in the Deutsche Nationalbibliografie; detailed bibliographic data is available on the Internet at http://www.dnb.de.

WWW.HIRMERPUBLISHERS.COM

ISBN 978-3-7774-3097-3

IMAGE CAPTIONS FOR FULL-PAGE SPREADS:
PAGE 6/7: Al Sharq Village & Spa | PAGE 8: Bin Jelmood House | PAGE 10: Alfardan House
PAGE 12: Bin Jelmood House | PAGE 14: Al Sharq Village & Spa | PAGE 20: Radwani House